The death of the Irish language

Using a blend of statistical analysis with field surveys among native Irish speakers, Reg Hindley explores the reasons for the decline of the Irish language and investigates the relationships between geographical environment and language retention. He puts Irish into a broader European context as a European minority language, and assesses its present position and prospects.

Reg Hindley, who has been researching into minority languages for many years, is Senior Lecturer in Geography in the Departments of European Studies and Environmental Science at the University of Bradford.

Bradford Studies in European Politics

The death of the Irish language
A qualified obituary

Reg Hindley

London and New York

First published 1990
by Routledge
11 New Fetter Lane, London EC4P 4EE

Simultaneously published in the USA and Canada
by Routledge
a division of Routledge, Chapman and Hall, Inc.
29 West 35th Street, New York, NY 10001

New in paperback 1990

Laserprinted by Ruth Brandaro
Printed and bound in Great Britain by
Mackays of Chatham PLC, Chatham, Kent

British Library Cataloguing in Publication Data

Hindley, Reg, 1929–
    The death of the Irish language: a qualified obituary.
    1. Irish language
    I. Title
    491.6'2

    ISBN 0–415–04339–0
        0–415–06481–3 (Pbk)

Library of Congress Cataloguing in Publication Data

Hindley, Reg, 1929–
    The death of the Irish language: a qualified obituary/Reg Hindley.
        p.   cm. – (Bradford studies in European politics)
    Includes bibliographical references.
    ISBN   0–415–04339–5
        0–415–06481–3 (Pbk)
    1. Irish language – History. 2. Irish language – Revival. 3. Linguistic
    minorities – Europe. I. Title. II. Series.
PB1215.H5 1990   89–10933
491.6'2'09–dc20   CIP

To those who work to keep Irish a living language

'Oh the shame of Irish dying in a free Ireland . . .'
(unattributed)

Map 1 Ireland: provinces, counties, principal towns. The Gaeltacht as 1987

Contents

Contents

List of tables

List of maps

A note on place-names

The following guidelines have been applied to the presentation of place-names in the text:

The names of Irish-speaking Gaeltacht places are on first use given in Irish with an anglicized equivalent, but thereafter only in Irish unless far removed in the text. This also applies to Gaeltacht places with moderate Irish-speaking minorities. The use of the Irish forms is felt appropriate because (1) they alone represent the correct form (and often meaning) in the language to which the name belongs; (2) any further reading or research will demand acquaintance with the Irish forms, if any venture is made into Irish-language sources; (3) the language is dying and the correct forms of Gaeltacht names are often elusive, even to Irish speakers. They should therefore be recorded and used while they are still current. The anglicized equivalents of most names provide a rough but serviceable guide to the popular native Irish pronunciation. Where the anglicized equivalent is itself unpronounceable except to the initiated – e.g. Iveragh, which is pronounced *eev-raa* – I have attempted a passable approximation of my own, to assist the reader.

The names of nominally Gaeltacht places where little Irish is in everyday use are given in English, except in contexts where the Irish version is appropriate, as when using material from Irish-language sources.

County names are usually given in their English forms because they are internationally familiar and no county is mainly or substantially Irish-speaking; but in the regional survey and the tables they are given bilingually because the emphasis there is on Irish language survival in each county and it is therefore appropriate to indicate the Irish forms, which of course are the originals from which the English names derive.

Gaeltacht district names such as Corca Dhuibhne (Corkaguiny) and Dúiche Sheoigheach (Joyce's Country), Gaoth Dobhair (Gweedore), and Iorras (Erris) are used in their Irish forms, with the English equivalent provided on first use.

Directional indicators such as north or west are in English only, except where it is intended to indicate the full Irish-language name for a district.

In such cases the English version will also normally be given to maintain clarity of meaning.

Appendices three and four provide bilingual indices of the Irish and English names of current Gaeltacht national schools and district electoral divisions, arranged in county and Gaeltacht order more or less from north to south. These will usually be the forms employed in the text but in cases of conflict appendix three has precedence for greater accuracy in Irish orthography.

Appendix two provides a fuller outline of problems encountered in the rendering and identification of Gaeltacht place-names.

Preface

This book is written by a geographer with a central interest in language and the manifold factors which combine to determine and influence language distributions. He began work on the border-lands of the Welsh language in 1949 and extended this to Irish and Scottish Gaelic in 1956 when he conducted his first field survey in north-west Scotland. An exploratory field investigation of most of the surviving areas of native Irish speech followed in 1957, at much the same time that the official boundaries of the Gaeltacht (the legally defined Irish-speaking districts) were being redrawn. It was already clear that the new boundaries were generous in including within them many areas in which Irish was very little used, and the difficulties of boundary definition in conditions of language change and political sensitivity feature prominently in the work which follows.

Supervision of undergraduate field courses in later years involved detailed studies in north-west Donegal and in the Meath Gaeltacht colonies, and in 1987 the generous grant of study leave by the University of Bradford made possible a repetition and elaboration of the comprehensive survey undertaken thirty years earlier, before all the changes brought about in the wake of the advent in the Gaeltacht of universal secondary education, television, the near-universal private motor car, electricity in every home, piped water, and a revolutionary degree of access to employment in modern light industries. Given this list, a perceptible weakening of the Irish language over the intervening years is only to be expected and some surprise may be permitted that it still survives at all in normal everyday use.

Some Irish writers, including Desmond Fennell (1970, 1981), have already declared the native language moribund in the districts they know, and the author returned to the west in 1987 half expecting to report an obituary notice similar to his account of the final demise of Manx (1984). Fortunately this proved highly premature, but it was evident that close knowledge of the true extent of the survival of Irish in everyday use in the only places where it is or recently was a community language in natural use from the cradle and 'on the hearth' was uncommon. Hence this book, which sets out to show where Irish is still a normal means of daily intercourse in families and between groups of people who acquired it traditionally from their parents instead of learning it from school and college. This is not to disparage the second-language learner, who obviously has a much more difficult task in mastering Irish than the native speaker and merits credit for the fluency acquired. Support from second-language learners is important in encouraging the native speaking community to maintain its own 'natural' use of Irish, but it is very much this author's view that Irish as a *living* language will have expired once there are no longer mothers who speak it to their newborn infants, because it comes unconsciously and naturally to their lips, without measured thought of choice or national sentiment. Once that point has passed, reasons for learning Irish will remain, but only at an esoteric level and for select interest groups.

It has not yet come to this, but the threat is clear. Under ten thousand native Irish speakers are now living in communities with a sufficiently high level of attachment to the language to make probable its transmission to a substantial majority of their children as *a* language of the home (see below, p 251). They live in three separate territorial blocs, backing on to the sea and otherwise surrounded and separated by English speakers. They also speak distinctive Irish dialects and seem reluctant to listen to radio programmes in any but their own dialect. There are another seven or eight pockets of lesser, insecure survival where children can still speak Irish with native or near-native fluency at school-majority level, but these are so small and so shaky as to attract interest only for their marginality – at least to a geolinguist. The fact remains that the surviving pockets of Irish language survival include much of the most scenically spectacular and beautiful scenery in these islands, challenging the thinking visitor to ascertain the causal relationship between physical environment and language retention which this work, among other things, attempts.

One has inevitably mixed feelings in advising the reader to hasten to visit these last outposts of a dying language while they are still there and while there are plenty of old people still able to talk about the Irish-speaking life which is now being lost. It is sad, but talking to them in English will emphasize the inadequacy of their Irish and talking to them even in fluent 'school-Irish' (the synthesized standard language which is nowhere native) will do much the same, despite the best of intentions. Irish thrived on relative remoteness and lack of visitors, and it is symptomatic that one can now tour all the Gaeltacht districts in comfort by car in about a fortnight, omitting only a few of the offshore islands where ferries would add to the time. This could not be done thirty years ago, when cars were few in the west and roads much worse, and a hundred years ago such a tour would have occupied two months or more on foot or by wagonette. Travelling time has contracted immensely in a few short generations and most Gaeltachtaí (plural; see glossary, appendix 1) do now cater for visitors – another revolution since 1956 and, as usual, both excellent for the people and questionable for Irish survival. On reflection, the best advice must be to hasten. . . .

The thirty maps are designed to show the distributions of the Irish language as accurately as possible over the period since 1800, with emphasis (map 8 onwards) on the Gaeltachtaí in independent Ireland and still more on the present position, explored in maps 10–30. The last nineteen maps are devoted to the present official Gaeltacht, county by county. Six of these present the author's considered categorization of the different district subdivisions according to their real Irish strength or weakness. It is hoped that this precision will help to counter the prevailing tendency towards broad generalization about 'the state of the Gaeltacht' and avoidance of all local detail which might hurt people's feelings. Such imprecision leaves Gaeltacht studies all too often in a vague and foggy state. The language is dying at specific places among specific communities which the official Gaeltacht boundaries hardly help to pinpoint and which are hidden in the generalized and averaged data produced for the official Gaeltacht. There will no doubt be local disagreement as to the justice of my categorizations. Suffice it to say that my sources were sound, sometimes in disagreement, and that the judgements are my own, taken in the light of my own experience. They may be awry on nuances, i.e. on the margins of grades, for in the present state of the Irish language so much is transitional. Changes are most likely to be for the worse, as this is the historic trend.

The book is divided into three main sections. The first outlines the background to the development of the 'language problem' in Ireland. The second is the core of the book and shows what survives of Irish as a native language, indicating precise localities and stressing the tiny scale of the communities involved. It also examines critically the extent to which real gains have been made by revival efforts since 1893 and 1922, and devotes considerable attention to the value and severe limitations of the statistical data, which confuse anyone new to Irish language studies.

The third and final section abstracts the causative factors which have a bearing on Irish language survival, and goes on to place Irish in the context of the many other European minority languages as a preliminary to a final assessment of its present position and prospects. The title of the book anticipates its guarded conclusions.

Acknowledgements and sources

This is not meant to be a book-bound work, for the main source is the author's questions to and answers from people living and working in the various Gaeltachtaí or otherwise concerned with their administration from more distant places such as Dublin. The bibliography provides the literary underlay. Teachers, school inspectors, parish priests and curates, and officials of various ministries, semi-state bodies and local government authorities have all been extremely helpful over the years, their frankness to me usually helped by assurances of confidentiality which I assume are valid until death, unless bilaterally rescinded. The subject is sensitive in nationalistic terms and extremely complex psychologically, in that probably most Irish speakers and most advocates of language 'revival' are constantly torn between what they would wish the future of the language to be and what on the other hand they feel obliged to speak themselves in the normal course of everyday exigencies, even if they are fluently bilingual (see pp. 177–8). People therefore often feel deeply ashamed of their considered views of language prospects, sensing them to be disloyal or defeatist, even when they are thoroughly objective in terms of everyday realities; and if they do not feel disloyal, etc., they know this is what their political or social enemies will say if such views are openly broadcast.

Acknowledgements

A book which has germinated over thirty years or more owes many debts, far too many for full acknowledgement. The first inspiration came from Welsh scholars, including most notably Professors G. R. J. Jones, Emrys Bowen, and Estyn Evans, and the detailed practicalities were spelled out with his usual precision by (later) Professor T. W. Freeman. In Ireland itself early direction and impetus were supplied by Professor B. Ó Cuív and S. Ó Súilleabháin of the Irish Folklore Commission, whose local 'folklore collectors', usually retired schoolteachers, proved a mine of information.
   Donncha Ó Laoire, secretary of Comdháil Náisiúnta na Gaeilge,

pointed me towards the real as against the spurious Gaeltachtaí, the distinction being more obscure in 1955 than it may appear now, and Muiris Ó Cinnsealaigh, Deputy Chief Inspector of National Schools, shared a lifetime's wisdom and experience with me, as well as opening numerous doors to my searching enquiries. He introduced me to the three regional Gaeltacht inspectors of national schools who were the main data providers for the 1956 redefinition of the Gaeltacht borders, and to whom I remain deeply indebted for their realistic and sympathetic explanations of the problems of the language in both school and community. Officials of the Gaeltacht Department were then more Dublin-based and had no responsibility for *deontas* awards, but did give valued assistance on the generalities of language policy. Officers of the Land Commission introduced me to the Gaeltacht colonies in Co. Meath and the general field of Gaeltacht 'decongestion' policies.

R. de Valéra, Donn Sigerson Piatt, and Heinrich Wagner also gave advice and guidance.

My work in the Gaeltachtaí has relied heavily on local teachers, priests, folklore collectors, and a miscellany of officials concerned with language work. Assurances of confidentiality for their frank expression of opinions and assessment of local conditions and problems deter me from naming my most recent local informants, lest my own expressed conclusions be attributed to them. This would be doubly unjust, as I have often had to discount a particular view when it was countered by other evidence, and the conclusions here are always my own. However, the quality of my local helpers may be judged by the following list of notable contributors to my groundwork in 1955–7:

Pádraig Breathnach NT, Caisleach, Kerry; John Casey NT, Kilmakerin, Kerry; Annraoi Ó Corrduibh (Henry Corduff) NT, Rosdoagh, Mayo; Seán Costigan NT, Rathcarn, Meath; Tomás mac Cúileannain (Hollywood), Blackrock, Dundalk; Patrick Joyce NT, Derreens, Achill, Mayo; Pádraig Mac Conmidhe, secretary of Comhaltas Uladh; Micheál Mac Enrí (Henry), retired NT and folklore collector (gave evidence to Gaeltacht Commission 1925 –6), Bangor Erris, Mayo; Michael J. Murphy, folklore collector and writer (sometimes as M. Ó Murchadha), Warrenpoint, Down; Mairead Nic Dhonnchadha, Tourmakeady, Mayo; Caomhín Ó Cinnéide NT, Baile na nGall, Kerry; Joseph O'Driscoll NT, Clear Island, Cork; Peadar Ó Dubhda, Dundalk; Séumas Ó hEocha (James Hough: 'An Fear Mór': on the Gaeltacht Commission 1925–6) Ring, Waterford; Sean Ó Heochaidh, folklore collector, etc., Gortahork, Donegal; Rev. J. O'Reilly PP, Clonbur, Galway; Mrs Sheridan, Doolough, Mayo; 'An Suibhneach Meann', Coolea, Cork. Spelling and accentuation are as in their correspondence or as otherwise communicated.

There was little need for expert assistance in locating and studying the Conamara and north-west Donegal Gaeltachtaí in the 1950s, for their presence and authenticity were indisputable except on the outer margins.

Many librarians contributed greatly to the basic research which under-lies the historical sections of the book. Most notable were staff of the (then) British Museum, the Manchester Central Reference Library, the National Library of Ireland, and the Royal Irish Academy. Assistance from the librarians of the University of Bradford has been sustained and unstinting over many years.

More recent and/or long-term help which must be acknowledged has come from Pádraig Ó Durcáin and Séumas Ó Raghallaigh of the Gaeltacht Department, and the regional officers at Letterkenny (now Gweedore), Furbogh, and Tralee. Valuable updating was provided by Professor Máirtín Ó Murchú and Nollaig Ó Gadhra, and in their special fields Art Ó Maolfábhail and Nollaig Ó Muraíle of the Place-names Branch of the Ordnance Survey have saved me from countless errors. Pádraig Ó Riagáin was of direct personal assistance at An Foras Forbartha in 1969–70 and his prolific publications on language matters have continued to guide if not to direct me.

Invaluable assistance was given by officers of the Departments of Education in Dublin and at Bangor, Co. Down, and Údarás na Gaeltachta, Gael-Linn, Raidió na Gaeltachta, and Comhaltas Uladh put me deeply in their debt.

The innumerable Gaeltacht residents who over thirty and more years have welcomed me to their homes, even when I arrived as an unannounced stranger and simply knocked on their doors soliciting guidance, deserve my special thanks. Whatever their views of my conclusions I hope that they will find ample and fair echoes of their own and, if I have sometimes mentioned the unmentionable, will accept that my paramount aim has been to clarify the cloudy issues and to be frank wherever lack of frankness has befogged them.

I must thank Stewart Davidson, cartographer of Bradford University, for his work on the maps. European Studies departmental secretaries under Mrs Jean Davison have struggled nobly with the manuscript and especially with the unfamiliar Irish names and terms.

To my wife I am indebted for her careful and constructive criticism of the draft, the invaluable sorting out of wood from trees, and the provision of much-needed impetus when the depth of material seemed over-whelming. Completion of the book is due mainly to her.

I am indebted to the following for their permission to quote extensively from their own publications and works:

The Controller, Stationery Office, Dublin, for permission to reproduce the substance of pp. 53–8 of *Tuarascáil an Chomhchoiste um Oideachas sa Ghaeltacht* and table 9 (pp. 39–44) of vol. 8 of the Census of Population of Ireland, 1981; and also for general permission to quote from the Census of Population of Ireland for 1936, 1946, 1961, and 1971.

Acknowledgements

Pádraig C. Ó Durcáin, Priomhoifigeach Cúnta, Roinn na Gaeltachta, Na Forbacha, Gaillimh, for permission to quote with warning of the dangers of too literal an interpretation the provisional 1985 –6 figures of *deontas* awards for the Gaeltacht national schools.

Colin H. Williams, Department of Geography and Recreation Studies, Staffordshire Polytechnic, for permission to reproduce maps 8, 9, and 10 from my chapter in his edited volume *Linguistic Minorities, Society and Territory* (forthcoming, 1989).

Printed sources

Background reading has constantly intruded to pose its own questions and challenges, and while the bibliography which concludes the book attempts full coverage of the relevant works which have influenced the findings it is appropriate to mention here the more useful and stimulating printed sources.

When the author began work on Irish in the 1950s there was only one current publication which purported to describe the location of the Irish-speaking districts and to discuss their problems. This was a twenty-three page pamphlet entitled *A Board for the Gaeltacht* (1953), prepared as a memorandum for the Taoiseach (Prime Minister) by the state-sponsored language body Comhdháil Náisiúnta na Gaeilge (see appendix 1, glossary), with five useful maps. These showed the contraction of the various Gaeltachtaí since 1925, but only partially, as they still exaggerated their real extent in a few key areas. The map of the Gaeltacht borders (*Límistéirí Gaeltachta 1956*) published to help define the responsibilities of the newly created Roinn na Gaeltachta (Gaeltacht Ministry/Department) improved on them somewhat, but bibliographic searching failed to find anything useful in print by way of commentary on the language and its problems apart from a splendid but misleadingly titled little work, *Irish Dialects and Irish-speaking Districts* (1951), by Brian Ó Cuív, over half of which consists of a history of the vicissitudes of the language and a very detailed appendix abstracting many of the major sources on the distribution of Irish in (especially) the early nineteenth century. This is still a useful *aide-mémoire* .

Official statistics on language distributions were available in the *Report of the Census of Population of 1946*, unpublished until 1953, but that contained a discouraging introductory warning against placing any reliance upon the figures (p. viii). For any comprehensive account of the Gaeltachtaí and their problems it was necessary to go back to the 1926 *Report of the Gaeltacht Commission* , its excellent maps, and its elusive *Minutes of Evidence* , which were published on a daily basis as evidence was gathered between April and October 1925. The statistics were again unreliable but the work as a whole forms the essential basis of any thorough study of the fate of the living language in the twentieth century. Almost all the ideas currently being debated on language policy were already aired in it, including the need for and dangers of industrial development in the impoverished heartlands of Irish residual survival.

The detailed local evidence on the basis of which the official Gaeltacht boundaries were drastically contracted in 1956 –7 was never published, but the author's own surveys of that period were greatly assisted by the Gaeltacht inspectors of schools, whose findings and experience were paramount in the redefinition. Many of the local folklore collectors of the Irish Folklore Commission were equally helpful, and as old Gaeltacht residents, commonly retired teachers, they were very well placed as guides.

The nearest thing to a fully objective survey of language survival was published in 1958 as an incidental and subsidiary part of the introductory volume of H. Wagner's *Linguistic Atlas and Survey of Irish Dialects*. The purpose of the survey was to describe the characteristics of the surviving Irish dialects, and these were ascertained by interviewing elderly (average age 70) people at eighty-seven localities between 1949 and 1956. The summary description of these localities, many of which were outside what could still be regarded as Irish-speaking districts, included a pithy assessment of the current state of the language there (vol. I: ix –xvii, including map), and the map classified the survey areas into six categories of Irish usage, three of which rated English the true vernacular. These latter grades were shown to embrace all south-west Donegal and all the present official Gaeltachtaí of Munster except western Corca Dhuibhne/ Corkaguiny: a point which should be noted by all who think decline there is recent. The survey was not meant to be comprehensive in terms of area coverage and did not seek to establish the language boundary, but the use of specifically Irish linguistic criteria to ascertain the extent to which people were truly at ease in the language was unprecedented and, so far as is known, has not been repeated. Adverse comment at the time held Wagner over-meticulous in finding evidence of English dominance in the many anglicisms which characterized the spoken Irish of many districts which it was insisted were otherwise sound in their habitual use of Irish, but my own independent enquiries in 1957 in all cases confirmed Wagner's prognosis.

The bibliography at the end of this book lists all the main sources which have provided background material for it, but the following may be picked out for their special value.

De Fréine's *The Great Silence* (1965) is an idiosyncratic work which nevertheless explores in some depth the causes and consequences of language change in Ireland. It is in marked contrast to the Final Report of the Commission on the Restoration of the Irish Language (An *Coimisiún um Athbheochan na Gaeilge*), published in a 143 page English summary in 1963 and in full (486 pages) in Irish early in 1964. Both are valuable on the history of efforts at revival but the Irish version is essential for anyone able to make a reasonable attempt at reading it. It is symptomatic of the cost problems of publication in Irish and of the perceived lack of interest that no full translation was ever thought necessary.

The Commission report was quickly followed by a government White Paper, *Restoration of the Irish language* (1965), which in turn engendered brief progress reports in 1966 and 1968. Far more impressive from the point of view of detailed practical proposals to maintain the Irish-speaking population in their home areas were the *Gaeltacht Planning Reports* published by An Foras Forbartha (for the state) in 1971 and the rival Galway Gaeltacht Survey, which though originally intended to be an integral part of the series was published independently by its director, B. S. Mac Aodha, in 1969 (Hanly, 1971; Ó Riagáin, 1971; Mac Aodha, 1969). Despite brief caveats, none of these studies dealt frankly and fully with the basic fact that much of the area they were concerned to develop and maintain had ceased to speak Irish for normal everyday purposes some time earlier. This weakness has been a major stimulus to the present author's work, for it has long seemed obvious to him that an attempt to extend effective state aid to 'the Gaeltacht' must be directed precisely and with careful discrimination to just those places where Irish is either in full daily use *or* understood at levels of traditional fluency sufficiently high to make its restoration to daily use a realistic and practicable proposition for the immediate future. This point was made in the Gaeltarra/SFADCO report *Gníomh don Ghaeltacht: Action Programme for the Gaeltacht* (1971), but again the sensitivity of the issue prevented any pinpointing of areas in question. These reports, taken together, do nevertheless form a firm bedrock for objective study of the Gaeltacht areas and their problems.

The state's creation in 1969 of a council, Comhairle na Gaeilge, to advise on Irish-language matters generally, resulted rapidly in the publication of five substantial papers on language policy and Gaeltacht local government. No. 1, *Language and Community* (1970), by Máirtín Ó Murchú, made a notable start, followed up by practical proposals. The most authoritative work on national language policy to be produced in the 1970s was the 1975 *Report* of the Committee on Irish Language Attitudes Research (CILAR), the result of a thorough sample survey conducted throughout the Republic but with detailed attention to twenty-three district electoral divisions within the official Gaeltacht. This forms essential reading, but involves the terrible frustration for a geographer or anyone else with a sense of place that its valuable data were published for DEDs which were coded by number so as to retain their anonymity (p. 231). Hence although 'some kind of bias in the Donegal 11 report' is indeed suspected (p. 253) it is not possible to make the normal local assessments and adjustments which knowledge of any particular Gaeltacht setting makes possible when attempting to understand apparently anomalous linguistic evidence from a specified place. Anonymity for individual informants should be distinguished from anonymity for areas and districts, though it must be admitted that attitude surveys on a district basis may be expected to be distorted by considerations of the possible loss of language-related grants which might be expected to follow from publication (as distinct from confidential communication) of objective local linguistic attitudes and performance.

Ó Riagáin and Ó Gliasáin (1984) repeated much of the CILAR survey a decade later, with several refinements, and largely confirmed its findings in their *Preliminary Report* – which has remained their final one so far (1989). Ó Riagáin (1988b) has yet more recently exposed some dangers of more narrowly drawn Irish language attitude surveys, especially in relation to compulsory Irish in the schools.

The flow of substantial official and semi-official reports and papers temporarily dried up in the mid-1970s, when real progress was being made in Gaeltacht secondary education and economic development and the new (1975) Bord na Gaeilge, founded by the state to oversee the general promotion of Irish, was pondering how to undertake its task. It eventually produced its *Action Plan for Irish 1983–86* and three annual progress reports thereafter. They are all realistically depressing and overly bureaucratic in their approach and record, attempting to push language maintenance and revival out of the narrow bounds of token respect and symbolic usage. Public bodies were required to report annually on progress with Irish in their own offices and work, and their reports were summarized in Irish or in English, presumably as submitted. The nadir of these is probably the fourth item of 'implementation' reported by the Geological Survey Office in 1986: 'A table was set aside in the tea room each Wednesday for those who wish to speak Irish' (Bord na Gaeilge 1986: 72).

Much more has been achieved by Údarás na Gaeltachta, the elective Gaeltacht Authority set up in 1979 as a successor to the Gaeltacht Industries Board, Gaeltarra Éireann, but with wider powers and responsibilities in the fields of education and cultural activities. Weighty and broad-ranging publication on language matters has not yet featured in its strictly practical programme. Its annual reports are businesslike in every sense and signify little unless one knows a mass of essential background, a reasonable amount of which is given in *Rural Development in the West of Ireland* , ed. P. Breathnach (Maynooth 1983), and more thinly in *Change and Development in Rural Ireland*, ed. P. Breathnach and M. E. Cawley (Maynooth 1986).

Polemical comment on the school-based attempt to revive Irish as the first language of Ireland has been plentiful for many years and is neatly summarized in J. R. Edwards's *Language, Society and Identity* (Oxford

1985: 56–62). The Irish National Teachers' Organization 1941 *Report
. . . on the Use of Irish as a Teaching Medium to Children whose Home
Language is English* is a classic critique, ignored by the state until well
after J. Macnamara had published his analytically critical *Bilingualism
and Primary Education* in 1966, in Edinburgh. The abandonment of fixed
dogmas has led to much more objective consideration of schools' policies,
represented by E. A. Hilliard's *Changes in the Usage of Irish among
Gaeltacht Children at School Entry 1970–1980* (ITÉ 1981) and Bord na
Gaeilge's own Advisory Planning Committee report *Irish and the
Education System* (1986), neither of which allows revivalist sentiments to
cloud its judgement.

The same cannot be said of Bord na Gaeilge's most recent (1988)
Advisory Committee report on *The Irish Language in a Changing
Society*, which denounces current state policies as tending towards
'benign assimilation ' and 'anglicization by stealth'. It recognizes the
innumerable obstacles posed to successful language policies by prevailing
socio-economic trends and ambivalent public opinion, but demands that
'the state' assert firm leadership to restore supportive motivations and
incentives by a return to the public-sector compulsion which was dis-
credited by the 1960s and recommends as essential its extension into the
private sector as well. This reads very much as a counsel of despair, a
'coded' way of saying that the prospect is hopeless without extreme
measures which the report's own evidence demonstrates are unlikely to be
attempted, let alone successfully implemented. Responsibility for this is
placed on the people and the state, with appropriate socio-economic
excuses for both; but the overt recommendations are unrealistically
utopian at this terminal stage in Irish decline and would need enforcement
by an elite class of Platonist 'guardians' which it is difficult to envisage
finding acceptance in modern Ireland.

ITÉ, i.e. Institiúid Teangeolaíochta Éireann (Linguistics Institute of
Ireland), has been publishing on language matters, initially under the aegis
of the Department of Education, since about 1976, and the twenty-five
issues of its journal *Teangeolas* (up to early 1989) contain much essential
material – occasionally in Irish only and frequently about languages other
than Irish. The title means *Linguistics*.

General works on the language which may be commended are now
quite numerous but some established classics still deserve mention,
starting with Douglas Hyde's *Literary History of Ireland from Earliest
Times to the Present Day* (London 1899) and T. F. O'Rahilly's *Irish
Dialects Past and Present* (Dublin 1932). D. Corkery's *The Fortunes of
the Irish Language* (Dublin 1954) was too tendentious for comfort and the
best early history of the language is in numerous references to it in the
works of E. Curtis, especially his *History of Medieval Ireland from 1086
to 1513* (London 1938 edn) – this is now slowly being replaced by the

multi-volume *New History of Ireland* (T.W. Moody *et al.*, 1976 ff.). On the modern revival of Irish and its struggle for survival S. Ó Tuama's *The Gaelic League Idea* (Cork 1972) is a small but sound symposium volume, and the same applies to the same publisher's *The English Language in Ireland*, edited by D. Ó Muirithe (1977) and presenting some of the other side of the Irish language's historical problems.

A View of the Irish Language, ed. B. Ó Cuív (Dublin 1969) is a well balanced symposium by eleven leading authors, originally prepared for a lecture series on Radio Éireann and covering most aspects of the language's history and literature. T. P. Coogan's *Ireland since the Rising* (London 1966) has hardly dated and provides a cogent account of the history of the state, distilling that of the Gaelic movement into a useful twenty-two pages (183–205), roughly four of which are about the Gaeltacht. Quite different in character but very well illustrated, readable, and entirely reliable is Máirtín Ó Murchú's seventy-seven page booklet *The Irish Language*, published by the Department of Foreign Affairs (and in this case Bord na Gaeilge) in its 'Aspects of Ireland ' series. Final reference must be made to volume 70 of the *International Journal of the Sociology of Language*, 1988, edited by Pádraig Ó Riagáin and entirely devoted to language planning in Ireland. Ó Riagáin's name is a recommendation in itself – he was a leading figure in the Gaeltacht Development Studies of 1971 – and he has here contrived to bring together almost all the leading Irish authorities on the language in education and socio-economic life except Ó Murchú himself.

I am sorry to have relegated to the bibliography many other helpful sources and all non-Irish writers except Edwards, who has so greatly broadened my horizons at the psychological end of sociolinguistics and to whom I feel indebted for introducing me to G. F. Streib's *exposé* (1974) of the concept and practice of 'patterned evasion', i.e. the regularized evasion or violation of utopian or 'heroic' standards or norms otherwise notionally expected to control actual behaviour. This provides the key to understanding why it is so normal for large majorities of Irish people both to favour the revival of the language and to be prepared to do nothing inconvenient towards that end.

Part 1

Background

Chapter one

Irish before 1800

The Irish language is one of the Celtic sub-group of the Indo-european language family and is closely related to Scottish Gaelic, which only slowly broke away from it in the thousand years after *Irish* Gaelic speakers had set out to colonize south-west Scotland from around the fifth century A.D. Before that Gaelic seems to have been confined to Ireland, save for a few colonies in western mainland Britain, which was otherwise dominated by people speaking Brittonic languages from which modern Welsh and continental Breton are descended. In northern Britain the enigmatic Picts appear to have included Celts with Brittonic linguistic affinities and an older, more northerly group of different but pre-Indo-european speech, about which little is known and a great deal speculated.

Irish was thus a militantly expanding language until around A.D. 1000 and did succeed in displacing its Brittonic rivals (including Strathclyde or Cumbrian Welsh) and Pictish in Scotland, even subduing Northumbrian English in the Lothians, though impermanently. The first recorded external attacks on its supremacy in Ireland were those of the Norsemen from the early ninth century onwards. The Norsemen or Vikings are usually credited with the introduction of urbanism to Ireland, and especially the foundation of the historic port-cities, including Dublin, Cork, Galway, Waterford, Wexford, and Limerick, the last three of which still bear Norse-derived names. The areal extent of their displacement of the Irish language was none the less extremely limited and within two centuries they were almost entirely assimilated, very much as happened in Normandy, Rus (Russia), and the English Danelaw. Lack of numbers and lack of women settlers must have played a part here. The only significant areas in which the Norse language may have been established sufficiently well to lay the groundwork of future anglicization after the Anglo-Norman conquest which began in 1170 were Fingall in the north of present Co. Dublin and the so-called 'English baronies' of Forth and Bargy in the extreme south-east of Co. Wexford. There are obvious parallels here with the Norse settlements in Gower and the peninsula of southern Pembrokeshire in Wales, and with north-east Caithness in Scotland, all of which afforded later footholds for English in otherwise Celtic hinterlands. Fingall and south-east Wexford seem never completely to have reverted to Irish speech again.

The Anglo-Norman conquest rapidly enveloped the whole island and established the juridical supremacy of Norman French, relatively soon displaced by English for all but narrowly legal purposes. Yet in most parts of Ireland the conquest proved a veneer and the new landowners intermarried with native families, becoming themselves Irish speakers and indistinguishable from the native Irish to English officials and visitors. Laws enjoining the use of English and prohibiting the use of Irish in the courts and the corporate boroughs recur throughout medieval Irish history, the most comprehensive embodied in the Statutes of Kilkenny of 1366. The salient point is that they were felt necessary – again and again – because they were ineffective and Irish was always insidiously asserting itself despite its lack of legal status. The term 'Old English' had to be invented to distinguish great families which were conscious of their historic rights and status as conquerors for the Crown but who otherwise spoke and behaved like Irishmen and were just as inclined to revolt against royal authority.

Lack of numbers was again crucial. The Anglo-Normans were an elite group with relatively few plebeian settlers, almost everywhere enormously outnumbered by the native Irish, with whom intermarriage was inevitably attractive after initial antipathies. Inadequate medieval transport links could not maintain close relations with the home country, except again in a handful of coastal ports, and the only indigenous linguistic allies were the Norsemen of the tiny territorial pockets already referred to. Fingall with adjacent Dublin formed the core of the 'English Pale', a constricted area covering no more than Co. Dublin with parts of Meath, Louth, Kildare, and Wicklow. Even here the evidence points more closely to subjection to English law than to any consistent or exclusive use of the English language by the people at large. It must always be remembered that in pre-modern times government impinged little on everyday life, so unless there were other pressing reasons to learn English, e.g. for trade, there would be no cause to do so; nor would the government itself be concerned with the language of ordinary people.

It is remarkable that throughout medieval Irish history the province exhibiting least English influence was Ulster, from which Scottish missionaries and conquerors had earlier transferred their Gaelic language and their very name to Scotland. The latter had been known under various names, including Caledonia, Pictavia/Pictland, and Albania/Albany, but these applied only to the parts north of the Forth–Clyde isthmus and it was the Scots from Ireland who united as their kingdom the territories now known as Scotland. Linkages across the North Channel of course worked both ways and were even reinforced by the seafaring Norsemen. This meant that whenever the Anglo-Normans attempted to conquer or settle Ulster the northern Irish could always seek help or refuge in and from Scotland, and Scotland in turn valued Irish friends who could divert the attentions of the English when, as under Edward I, they threatened the survival of the Scottish state. The Donegal name Gallagher (in Irish *Ó Gallchobhair*) means 'foreign help' and is an ethnic marker similar to Walsh (Irish *Breathnach*), which is widespread in the South, signifies Welsh origin, and is often spelled and/or pronounced *Welsh* in Munster and Connacht. (See Mac Lysaght 1973.) The Welsh, however, came only as auxiliaries of the Anglo-Normans, whereas the Scots represented a balancing political and cultural force which despite the progressive linguistic anglicization of the medieval Scottish monarchy and the Lowlands continued to share the Gaelic heritage in the islands and peninsulas closest to Ireland.

The Tudors under Henry VIII and his successors undertook to pacify their turbulent Irish subjects by enforcing English law and imposing the English language. The Reformation is commonly credited with consolidating the attachment of the semi-hibernicized Old English to Irish customs and usages but it should also be remembered that the first modern-style attempt at English colonization outside the diminutive Pale was the carving out of King's and Queen's Counties (Offaly and Leix) from Irish lands under the Counter-Reformation Mary I and her consort Philip II of Spain in 1556. This met with violent resistance and experienced the usual shortage of ordinary English settlers much below gentleman-adventurer level. Ireland had never attracted the English peasant class, for it combined a hostile population with a cooler and damper climate for agriculture. France had always been far more attractive to the English gentry too and it is scarcely coincidental that the effective end of English aspirations there with the loss of Calais (1558) was followed by their transfer to North America – not swiftly but after less than a century of struggles which confirmed that Ireland was no safe or profitable field for colonization.

The Marian plantation was a failure that disrupted traditional Irish proprietorship but left a solidly Irish under-tenantry, as no one else wanted their place and new landlords had no use for land without tenants to work it. Much the same applied to Elizabeth's plantation of Munster in 1586 but the Ulster plantation of 1609 onwards was a different matter, for the Union of the Crowns of England and Scotland under James VI and I for the first time united British interests in the joint exploitation of Irish resources.

The agricultural potential of Ireland may have been uninviting to most English countrymen but was an attractive prospect viewed southerly from much of Scotland. Hence the prominent part played by Scots in providing the basic numbers on which the partial success of the 'Great Plantation' was founded. The plantation excluded three of the nine Ulster counties, and it is remarkable in terms of subsequent linguistic history that both Antrim and Down were excluded whereas Donegal was not. Again the geography of soils and accessibility by sea provide a readier explanation of the regionally varied progress of colonization than mere changes in land ownership, for new grantees found it very difficult to secure British tenants for poorer land or for land far removed from one of the new defended towns. Private initiative was also used by settlers keen to secure tenancies in the eastern coastal counties. In general the better land fell to immigrant Protestant settlers, and the hills and lowland bogs (as around Lough Neagh) were left to the native Irish Catholic tenantry. The latter can also be shown to have fared better in areas granted to the (Anglican) Church of Ireland, and some interesting anomalies in later denominational distributions relate to this. See for example the land ownership map of the Londonderry plantation in Moody (1939) and the religious map of Ireland for 1911, here map 2. The lowland 'Catholic triangle' marked on the latter at the mouth of Lough Foyle became Church land from 1609. The linguistic result of this was for about two centuries a quiltwork pattern of English- and Irish-speaking districts.

This pattern was not established at one blow, for colonization was severely disrupted by native revolts and concomitant wars which were at their most bloody in the Cromwellian and early Williamite periods. The net result was the almost total exclusion of Catholic landowners from Ulster but a major survival of native people in all but a few small and rich lowland areas. Map 2, compiled from the census reports of 1911, gives a good indication of the extent to which the English-speaking incomers were able to impress themselves on the province. The Protestant element represents the incomers, the Catholic group the native Irish, and although modifications of the pattern have undoubtedly occurred since the last wave of colonization which accompanied the Williamite settlement they consisted principally of the migration of native Irish people into the towns. The religious pattern and with it the pattern of British and Irish settlement was effectively fossilized in the early years of the eighteenth century, and it is most significant that almost everywhere where Catholics formed more than about 30–40 per cent of the population in 1911 there is evidence that Irish was still spoken by all or most of the indigenous inhabitants around 1800.

The Cromwellian settlement scheme of 1653 was grandiosely conceived to clear Leinster and Munster of Irish gentry and landowners and to plant all the corporate towns with 'new English'. It did little to shake the hold of the Irish language among ordinary working people anywhere in the country but did greatly advance that alienation of the gentry from the people which was finally consummated at the end of the century. Without doubt many native Irish landowners changed their religion to save their

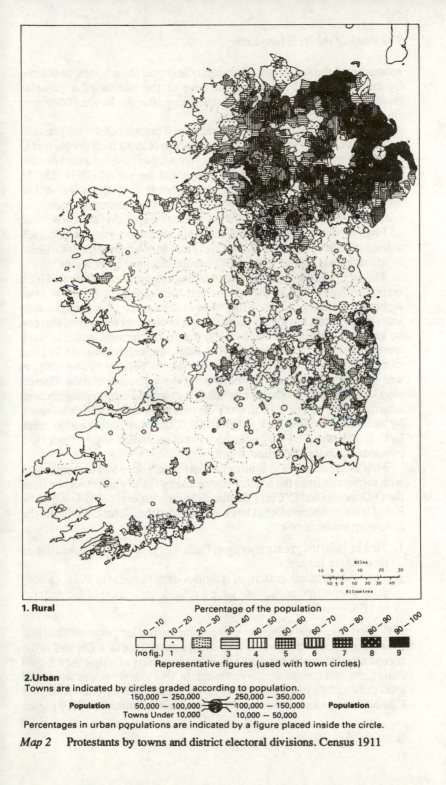

1. Rural

Percentage of the population

0 – 10	10 – 20	20 – 30	30 – 40	40 – 50	50 – 60	60 – 70	70 – 80	80 – 90	90 – 100
(no fig.)	1	2	3	4	5	6	7	8	9

Representative figures (used with town circles)

2. Urban

Towns are indicated by circles graded according to population.

	150,000 – 250,000	250,000 – 350,000	
Population	50,000 – 100,000	100,000 – 150,000	**Population**
	Towns Under 10,000	10,000 – 50,000	

Percentages in urban populations are indicated by a figure placed inside the circle.

Map 2   Protestants by towns and district electoral divisions. Census 1911

estates but at the same time they usually accepted the advantages offered by cultivation of the English language in the pursuit of a peaceful civilized life which became a real possibility after the Boyne (1690) and final military pacification.

The political instability and recurrent civil disorder of the seventeenth century made sheer survival the main concern of most Irish people and Ó Cuív's review of contemporary sources shows that Irish remained current (if not dominant) in Dublin itself throughout the period (1951: 18). In many country districts outside the planted North its position was still so secure that descendants of Cromwellian settlers were commonly monoglot Irish by 1700. Thereafter it is fairly clear that the spread of the knowledge of English which radiated from the main cities and towns made such assimilation infrequent, but it is unlikely that Irish began to fall into disuse in native homes before about 1750, except in a handful of towns.

The onset and extent of the spread of English and abandonment of Irish among ordinary folk in eastern Ireland received scant attention from eighteenth-century writers, a few of whom remarked on language use at individual places; but there was no comprehensive survey and all that can be said with certainty is that by 1800 the gentry throughout the country were entirely anglicized in their first-language preferences and in most eastern and central Ireland spoke no Irish at all. Yet in very few districts was the language entirely extinct among the native population. Garrett FitzGerald (1984) has shown how the age-grouped Irish-language census returns of 1881 can be used to establish minimum levels of Irish speaking by baronies extending back to before 1800, thus developing earlier work by G. B. Adams (1964–79), who made use of the census returns from 1851 onwards and noted their limitations.

Map 3 here attempts to synthesize their conclusions and to merge them with inferences from the sources abstracted by Ó Cuív and evidence from the O'Donovan and O'Curry Ordnance Survey papers (*c*. 1834–40) in the Royal Irish Academy. Detail has been added in the Ulster counties on the following assumptions:

1. That in 1800 the great majority of Catholics in the North spoke Irish as their native language.
2. That the detailed pattern of religious distributions in 1911 (when details were first published) gave a reliable indication of the patterns in 1800).

In the first case, local ministers who commented on language usage at that time considered it remarkable if Catholics did not speak Irish, and in the second all reliable observers note the relative stability of religious strengths during the nineteenth century, except in the towns, where industrial growth brought a marked Catholic influx. In the country districts higher Catholic birth rates were countered by job discrimination plus higher

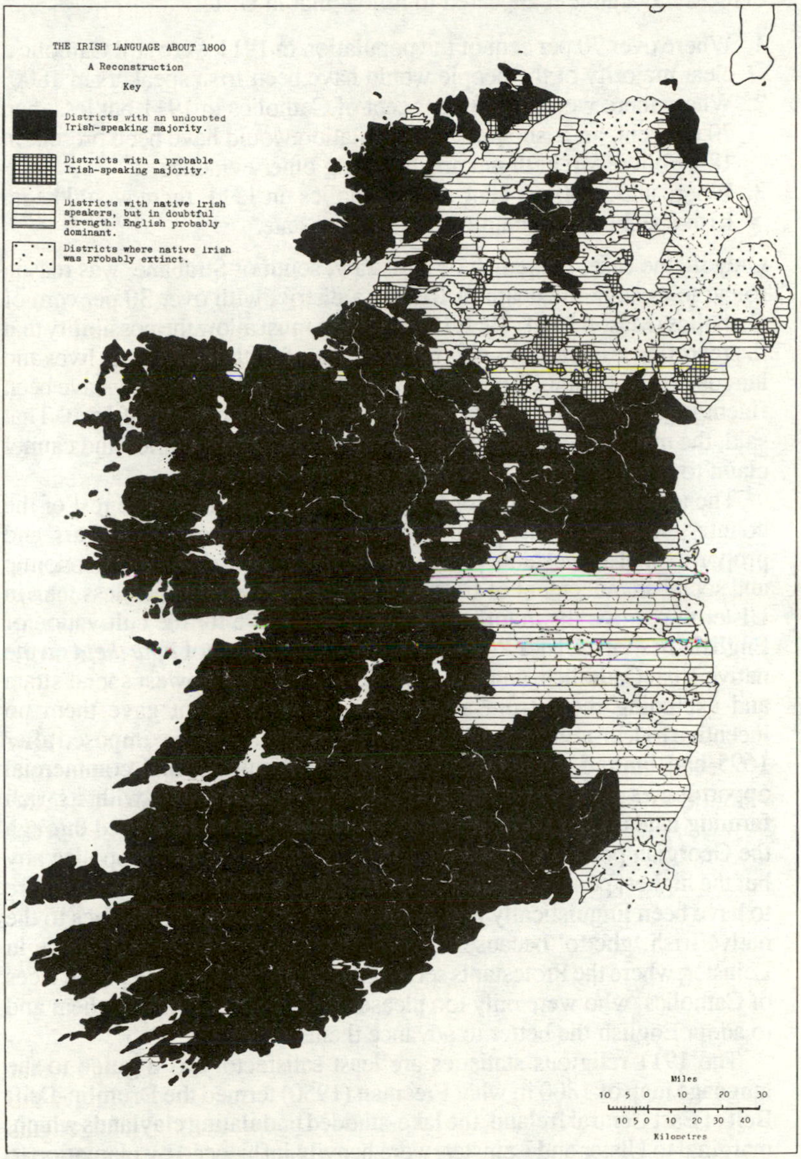
THE IRISH LANGUAGE ABOUT 1800
A Reconstruction
Key
Districts with an undoubted Irish-speaking majority.
Districts with a probable Irish-speaking majority.
Districts with native Irish speakers, but in doubtful strength: English probably dominant.
Districts where native Irish was probably extinct.
Miles
10 5 0 10 20 30
10 5 0 10 20 30 40
Kilometres

Map 3 The Irish language about 1800. A reconstruction based on literary sources and censuses 1851, 1881, 1911

mortality and emigration.

From these two basic assumptions and a study of the contemporary evidence available it appeared to follow that in Ulster:

1. Where over 70 per cent of the population in 1911 were still Catholic a clear majority of the people would have been Irish speakers in 1800.
2. Where there were over 30 per cent of Catholics in 1911 but less than 70 per cent, an Irish-speaking population would have been present in 1800, but of strength unknown, failing other evidence.
3. Where under 30 per cent were Catholics in 1911 there would be no Irish-speaking community at the earlier date.

Only in one case, the parish of Ardstraw, south of Strabane, was reason found to assume the death of Irish in a district with over 30 per cent of Catholics (Mason 1814–19: I, 123), and one must allow the possibility that the reporting minister was not fully acquainted with the intimate lives and language of his Catholic parishioners, who would undoubtedly have been fluent in English but not necessarily to the total exclusion of Irish. That said, the map is merely an assessment of broad probabilities and cannot claim to be more.

The assumptions made for Ulster cannot be applied in the rest of the country, where in general the presence of much lower numbers and proportions of Protestants posed much less of a barrier to the economic and social advancement of Catholics and therefore did much less than in Ulster to remove the main reason they could have for the cultivation of English. In short, Ulster Protestantism imposed a sort of *apartheid* on the native Irish Catholics and by confining them to the lowest social strata and excluding them from all but menial employment gave them no incentive to learn English. The anti-Catholic 'Penal Laws' imposed after 1695 had limited effect on the ordinary agricultural and commercial opportunities available to Catholics in Leinster, which, with its rich farming lands and the capital city of Dublin, steadily developed through the Georgian period and had insufficient Protestants to monopolize any but the highest positions. The influence of Protestantism seems therefore to have been linguistically negative in Ulster, confining Catholics to the native Irish 'ghetto' because of a denial of opportunity, but positive in Leinster, where the Protestants set a lead in which they needed the services of Catholics, who were only too pleased to profit by providing them and to adopt English the better to advance themselves.

The 1911 religious statistics are least satisfactory as a guide to the language map of 1800 in what Freeman (1950) termed the Drumlin-Drift Belt of East Central Ireland, the lake-studded undulating claylands which, marginal to Ulster and Leinster, were heavily influenced by plantation to the north and were prevented by their physical geography from fully sharing the economic advance of Leinster. The area undoubtedly stayed

Irish-speaking late in reaction to Northern Protestantism, just as now it provides most of the securer refuges of the IRA. Location midway between Belfast and Dublin must also have played a part in helping the survival of Irish, for this was the farthest from both on the east coast and therefore less subject to their influence; but the presence within it of planted Newry and the port of Dundalk suggests that the negative reactive factor must have been important.

It is impossible to point to any particular event in eighteenth-century Ireland as the one prime cause which initiated the long slow death of Irish among the people. Rather one must look at the general setting, which favoured the adoption of English as a second language and only later led on to the abandonment of bilingualism as Irish came to be felt super-fluous. Political and legal factors are often overemphasized by popular Irish historians but it is obvious that the essential basis for the promotion of English was indeed the Williamite settlement and the imposition of authority exercised entirely through English at all higher levels. That some Anglo-Irish landlords found it expedient to remain or become bilingual in Irish even in parts of inner Leinster until towards 1800 is not contested, but for any real advancement for Irish people a command of English became a necessity.

The successful pacification of Ireland and the long Georgian peace to 1798 led to increased prosperity, reflected in the building of fine country houses throughout the land as well as in Dublin, whose finest buildings generally date from this period. These generated employment and opportunities access to which was made easier by much improved communications by road and canal. Although the living standards of ordinary people remained appalling by modern standards they were evidently a great improvement on what had gone before and all estimates show a considerable increase in population and a healthy growth in the numerous country towns. This resulted from increased productivity and increased trade and again could only involve more constant daily links with bigger towns and the outside world, for which English would be either a necessity or at least very useful. The best markets (and most obviously the British one) outside Ireland would be those where Irish was least likely to be understood, and it is impossible to find any tradition of surviving use of Irish for commercial purposes so late as this.

The beginnings of modern factory industry in Ulster came late in the century but were to prove revolutionary in creating major demands for the labour of the Catholic underclass. Increased opportunities of (relatively) remunerative employment eroded patterns of discrimination and although residential segregation was replicated in the growing towns rural Catholics were thereby drawn into the linguistically English-centred urban economic systems from which they had usually been excluded, at least in Ulster. By 1800 much of eastern Ireland was affected by this drawing of the native

Irish into a peaceful, stable socio-economic system offering possibilities on a wide scale for self-improvement, using English as a helpful medium and allowing sufficient capital accumulation to make migration and even emigration attractive and practical possibilities for many ordinary people.

That the popular and technically illegal 'hedge-schools' of the Catholic rural population were already by then instructing their ragged and unshod scholars in the rudiments of English was not a cause but a consequence of mass attitudes. The people wanted English as a useful tool for any child with minimal ambition. In much of the country there can have been few opportunities to transform school-English into real fluency, for Irish remained the language of everyday life and schooling was brief, seasonal, and haphazardly available. Nevertheless a fundamental psychological change had come over the nation. The Union of 1800 was probably irrelevant to language, for it made no difference to the role of English in the state, but it nevertheless broadly coincided in date with the time when the majority decided that collectively it needed English for its own utilitarian purposes. The maintenance of linguistic separation from English-speaking Britain and its colonies was no longer practicable and found no significant support.

The suddenness of Irish language collapse around and after 1800 may be understood in terms of the Marxian model of quantitative changes slowly building up to major qualitative change. The desire for English built up slowly because opportunities for the masses through English built up only slowly. The steady increase in bilingualism was the quantitative change which led around 1800 to qualitative change represented by the mass abandonment of Irish. This is hardly surprising, for a necessary precondition of adjudging Irish unnecessary or 'useless' would be the achievement of very widespread near-universal fluency in English. That is to say, universal bilingualism was the essential transitional stage on the way from an Irish-speaking Ireland to an English-speaking Ireland. By 1800 bilingualism was well advanced and the ultimate fate of the native language was near to a final decision.

Chapter two

Irish in the nineteenth century: from collapse to the dawn of revival

It is impossible to say why or when exactly the majority of Irish-speaking people in eastern Ireland collectively decided that the English language would be more useful to them than Irish, but it plainly happened in much of Leinster first, and between 1800 and 1850 spread to most of the planted North, missing only the strongest pockets of Catholic survival in the Antrim Glens, Rathlin Island, the Sperrin Mountains, the Farney of Monaghan, the Omeath district of Louth, and below Slieve Gullion in south Armagh, in all of which it lingered until the 1940s or later. West Donegal is of course excluded from this generalization and still has its living Gaeltacht. Causation is often attributed to English schooling, to the influence of the Catholic Church, which accepted English as its language of mission once expelled from Douai by Revolutionary France and given finance for its Maynooth seminary by George III, and above all to the Great Famine which devastated Ireland from 1845 to 1849, killed around a million, and initiated mass emigration which halved the population by 1900.

As has been seen, the onset of major decline came too early for such 'explanations', for although there were Irish speakers nearly everywhere in 1800 monoglottism was becoming unusual in the eastern half of the country and in almost all the Leinster and Ulster counties the language was no longer in use among the children of the great majority of families. This marked the beginning of a statistical phenomenon which became more and more common as language decline intensified: ability to speak Irish and having it as mother tongue ceased to correlate with normal habitual use, for parents came to see it as a hindrance to the prospects of their children and deliberately excluded it from their homes, likewise wherever possible seeking to ensure exclusively English-language education.

It cannot be overemphasized that there was in effect no language question in Ireland in either the late eighteenth or the early nineteenth century. What interest was taken in Irish was chiefly scholarly, or by foreign visitors and the occasional Protestant activist hoping to use it as a medium for conversions. Hardly any use was made of it in the 1798 rebellion of the United Irishmen, the long and successful agitation for Catholic emancipation (to 1829), or the longer and unsuccessful movement for the repeal of the Act of Union of Great Britain and Ireland which had been engineered in 1800. All Irish political leaders had come to accept that the future of Ireland and its people lay through the English language, and O'Connell, himself a native speaker from west Kerry, was explicit in commending it as a liberator for his people. The 'Young Irelanders' of the 1840s tried to draw inspiration from the Gaelic past but did little in practice to promote or use Irish. The Famine and its consequences helped to snuff out their meagre support and little wonder that the energies of the nationalist movement for the ensuring decades turned to focus on tenants' rights and land reform, rather than on anything to do with saving the language. The Fenian revolt of 1867 had minimal impact and no linguistic significance.

The national education system created in 1831 left the management of the schools of Catholic Ireland entirely to the Church and with general support it provided the children whose parents could afford it with instruction which was only ever through English. Education universal, compulsory, and free did not arrive until the final decade of the century, another reason for not exaggerating its influence in promoting a decline which it accompanied and encouraged but hardly had the strength to cause.

The 1851 Census was the first attempt to record the numbers of Irish speakers in Ireland. Table 1 includes the most notable estimates of numbers in the preceding half-century. The total population figures are abstracted from Freeman (1957) and are based on official census calculations and returns and do by their constant increase to 1841 suggest why the numbers of Irish speakers may also have been increasing. The other estimates are derived from Anderson, who gathered a number of them together in the second edition of his *Native Irish* book (1846), from Hyde (1899), and from Ó Cuív's invaluable summary (1951). The latter notes (p. 19) the over-optimism of the Education Commissioners, who as early as 1810 proclaimed the diffusion of English throughout Ireland as near to completion, but it would be excusable for the reader to consider their estimates of 1835 as far more soundly based than most others quoted, given the figures which the people themselves returned in 1851. The latter figures were in fact a serious understatement caused by defective methods of enumeration, as was admitted in the Census Report of 1881 (Part II, General Report: 74), which had to explain an apparent 13.9 per cent increase in the numbers of Irish speakers since 1871, whereas every other decade from 1851 to 1891 recorded a decline of between 26 and 28·4 per cent.

Table 1   Irish-speaking population 1799–1851

Date	Source	Total Irish-speaking	Irish only	Bilingual	Total population
1799	Stokes	2,400,000	800,000	1,600,000	5,400,000
1812	Wakefield	3,000,000[1]			5,937,856
1812	Dewar	2,000,000	1,500,000	500,000	
1814	Anderson	2,000,000			
c.1821	Anderson/Graves	3,740,000			6,801,827
1835	Education Commission	1,500,000	500,000	1,000,000	
1835	Lappenberg	4,000,000			7,767,401
1841	Anderson	4,100,000			8,175,124
1842	MacComber	3,000,000	2,700,000[2]		
1851	Census	1,524,286	319,602		6,552,365

Notes

[1] Mostly monoglot.

[2] Virtually monoglot.

Before 1881 the census queries about Irish had been confined to a footnote which was evidently often overlooked by heads of households and enumerators, but from 1881 it received a section to itself. It may be assumed that, as no boost for Irish occurred in the 1870s, the reality of language trends was continued decline on a scale between the 26 per cent of 1861–71 and the 28·4 per cent of 1881–91. In other words, better enumeration transformed a real decline of around 27 per cent to an apparent increase of 14 per cent, which strongly suggests that the earlier figures understated the numbers of Irish speakers by some 40 per cent. In round figures this would have made the 1851 total 2,134,000. It is not easy to relate this to Anderson's estimate of over 4 million for 1841, but the grave losses of the Famine decade could account for the disappearance of a million and it is generally held that the figures were further depressed by a widespread reluctance to admit to a knowledge of Irish because it was associated with illiteracy and low social status. This cannot be proved but is extremely likely, and any reversal of this socio-psychological tendency to understate proficiency in Irish was to await the propaganda efforts of the Gaelic League, founded in 1893. (See Ó Tuama, 1972.)

Adams (1975, 1979) has written most cogently on the difficulties of the language censuses from 1851 to 1911 and should be read for further details. Whatever the doubts about their accuracy, their age-group tables allowed no room for doubt about the increasing disuse of Irish among the children, for in 1891 they showed only 3·5 per cent of all children under 10 as able to speak it. Ó Cuív (1951: 25–6) did well to draw attention to the census proportions of those who were returned as unable to speak

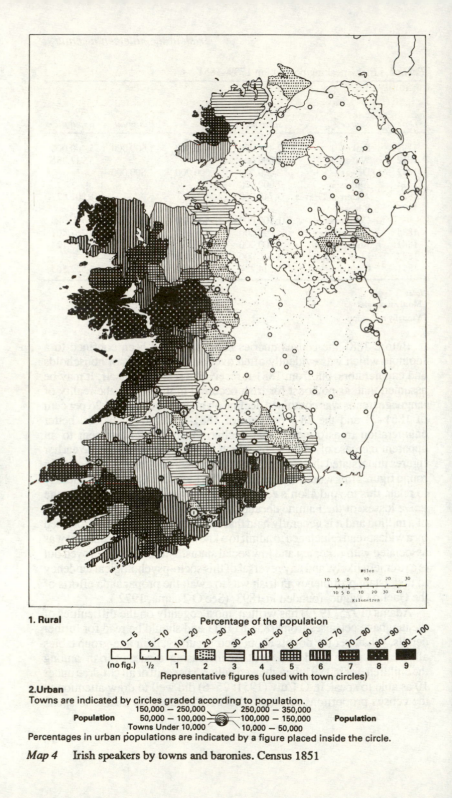

1. Rural

Percentage of the population

0 – 5	5 – 10	10 – 20	20 – 30	30 – 40	40 – 50	50 – 60	60 – 70	70 – 80	80 – 90	90 – 100
(no fig.)	½	1	2	3	4	5	6	7	8	9

Representative figures (used with town circles)

2. Urban

Towns are indicated by circles graded according to population.

Population — 150,000 – 250,000 / 250,000 – 350,000 — Population
50,000 – 100,000 / 100,000 – 150,000
Towns Under 10,000 / 10,000 – 50,000

Percentages in urban populations are indicated by a figure placed inside the circle.

Map 4   Irish speakers by towns and baronies. Census 1851

English, i.e. the monoglot Irish, as an indicator of the relative strength and durability of the language. There were only eleven baronies of the 333 in Ireland (baronies averaged near ten in each county and were the basic unit for which language statistics were provided up to 1851) with monoglot majorities among their Irish speakers in 1851. All the present surviving Irish-speaking districts were in them except for the marginal pockets in Achill, Clear Island, and at Coolea (west Cork), which can certainly not be accounted primarily Irish-speaking today. The only other barony in which generous assessment might allow some persisting use of native Irish was Erris (Mayo), with 49 per cent of its Irish speakers returned as monoglots in 1851. Conversely Kilmaine (Mayo) was the sole barony with a monoglot majority in 1851 to have lost all claim to any Gaeltacht status by 1956. (See FitzGerald, 1984: 151.)

Necessary perspective here is that in 1851 scarcely 5 per cent of the total population were returned as monoglot Irish and over the next thirty years this already tiny proportion fell by three-quarters to 1·25 per cent. The admission of complete inability to speak English must, however, have been much more difficult than confessing to bilingualism, and it is this author's strong suspicion that the 'Literacy' tables in the census reports from 1851 to 1871 may well give a better indication of the true scale of Irish survival (including monoglottism) than those specifically devoted to language: i.e. high illiteracy was usually correlated with strong survival of Irish. However, there can be little doubt that by the closing years of the century Irish monoglottism was becoming relatively rare, at least in terms of complete inability to speak or understand English. The trouble with the monoglot figures is that any simple answer (yes or no) to the question 'Do you speak Irish only?' was bound to be difficult in the complex circumstances of the onset of Irish decline, and different degrees of knowledge of English might be thought to fall short of ability to speak it or to justify a claim to be able to do so. At least in the nineteenth century the Irish monoglot figures provide a solid minimum, for any nationalistic tendency to deny knowledge of English was again deferred until the Gaelic League had had time to reinvigorate Irish pride.

Maps 4 and 5 show the proportions of Irish speakers by baronies in 1851 and more reliably in 1891. In each case the large size of many baronies, especially in the impoverished western counties, where Irish survived best, concealed marked Irish strength in many districts which shared a barony with anglicized neighbours. This was particularly the case in Donegal and it is necessary to consult map 6, based on the much smaller district electoral divisions for which statistics were first published in 1911, to appreciate the complexity which must have characterized the language map throughout the nineteenth century, wherever language decline was taking place. In all cases it is clear that the more fertile eastern lowlands fell to English first, followed by the western towns and their more

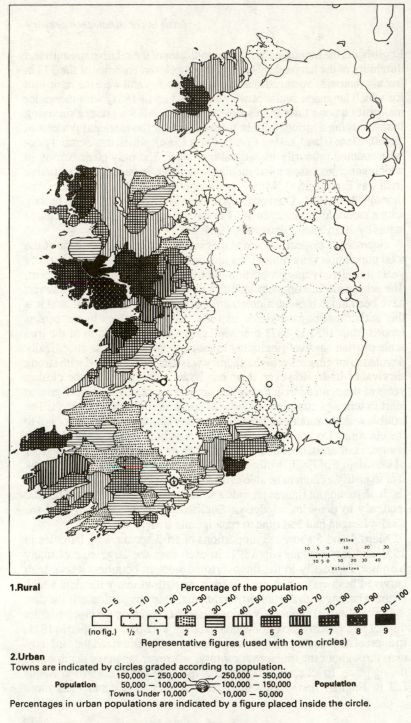

1.Rural   Percentage of the population

0 – 5   5 – 10   10 – 20   20 – 30   30 – 40   40 – 50   50 – 60   60 – 70   70 – 80   80 – 90   90 – 100

(no fig.)   ½   1   2   3   4   5   6   7   8   9

Representative figures (used with town circles)

2.Urban
Towns are indicated by circles graded according to population.

	150,000 – 250,000		250,000 – 350,000	
Population	50,000 – 100,000		100,000 – 150,000	Population
	Towns Under 10,000		10,000 – 50,000	

Percentages in urban populations are indicated by a figure placed inside the circle.

Map 5: Irish speakers by towns and baronies. Census 1891.

prosperous hinterlands. By 1891 barony majorities for Irish were already dispersed in ten geographically separated blocs, isolated from each other by anglicized districts which usually included their principal market centres. The sole substantial bloc with more than a single barony with 70 per cent or more of Irish speakers was that around Galway Bay, where there were eight. Here was where the language found its last strongholds, but the majority in Galway city had already been lost, depopulation was rife, and nowhere was there any expectation of imminent efforts to reverse the trends of a century and more by restoring Irish to popular favour and use.

National figures are rarely helpful as an index of the geographical range of a language, for again they 'average out' important regional and local variations. They do nevertheless show the general context within which a language operates and which influences public assessments of its communicative value. Table 2 gives some basic statistics from the censuses from 1851 to 1901, with the total population for 1841 (no language figures) as the starting point for general demographic collapse and the figures for 1901 as an early pointer to a radical change of trends.

The collapse in the numbers of reported monoglot Irish speakers from 319,602 in 1851 to 20,953 in 1901 was probably most significant as showing that by the close of the period everyone felt able to claim a command of English and hardly anyone chose to deny it. Even so, it is remarkable that when in 1881 the census authorities took care to check on supposed monoglots living in otherwise overwhelmingly English-speaking districts they eliminated many on finding that they were in fact bilingual (Census 1881, Part II, General Report: 73–4).

Table 2   Irish-speaking population 1851–1901

Census date	Total population	Speakers of Irish only		Total Irish speakers[1]	
		No.	%	No.	%
1841	8,175,124	Not enumerated		Not enumerated	
1851	6,552,365	319,602	4·9	1,524,286	23·3
1861	5,798,564	163,275	2·8	1,105,536	19·1
1871	5,412,377	103,562	1·9	817,875	15·1
1881	5,174,836	64,167	1·2	949,932[2]	18·2
1891	4,704,750	38,121	0·8	680,174	14·5
1901	4,458,775	20,953	0·5	641,142	14·4

Notes
[1] Including Irish only.
[2] Increase in totals of Irish speakers because of improved method of enumeration. See above, pp. 14–15. The numbers of speakers of Irish only were corrected *downwards* before publication – after scrutiny.

Source: Census Reports.

The general and overwhelmingly downward trend of the statistics of the Irish language was manifest and unquestionable. Any idea of a major revival in its fortunes can have seemed only a little more fanciful than a suggestion that it might outlive the coming century. The writer of the 1871 census report (part 3: 190) was sure about this:

> The disappearance of this ancient member of the Celtic family of tongues from living speech may be somewhat delayed or somewhat accelerated by circumstances beyond calculation or conjecture, but there can be no error in the belief that within relatively a few years [*sic*] Irish will have taken its place among the languages that have ceased to exist. . . .

The caveat was wise and allowed for the advent of the Gaelic League as a major retarding and reviving force.

Chapter three

The twentieth century: survival, revival, and metamorphosis

Since the foundation of the Gaelic League in 1893 the position of Irish in Ireland has been transformed, but in ways not wholly to its advantage. The dying language of a rural peasantry has continued to die as the language of a rural peasantry living in geographically well-defined territories, but respect for Irish has become the norm for almost all the people of the twenty-six Counties which became the Irish Free State in 1922, and all their children study it lengthily at school. The census figures which made such depressing reading in the nineteenth century summarize the achievement. (See table 3.) Thus the proportion of the population returned as able to speak Irish was by 1981 almost a third of the total and despite massive emigration losses was in absolute numbers close to the totals returned for 1861. Compare table 2 and remember that the latter refers to thirty-two counties, whereas the figures since 1926 are for twenty-six only. Unfortunately the census language returns have become increasingly misleading as the century has advanced, and the statistics represent very largely the replacement of dwindling numbers of native speakers by primary English speakers who in the large majority lack fluency in Irish and hardly ever have occasion to speak it.

The census of 1926 did attempt to distinguish native speakers of Irish from learners but was defeated by the utter incredibility of the returns and ended by counting both as simply Irish speakers. Native speakers were returned as 50 per cent more numerous at ages 10–14 than at 5–9 and there were too many obvious discrepancies in other respects (Census 1926, vol. 8: v–vi) for them to be fit to publish. The numbers of the enumerated monoglot Irish fell from the 20,953 of all Ireland in 1901 to 12,460 (Free State only) in 1926 but ceased to be published after an unbelievable increase to 18,283 in 1936. The censuses have continued to ask for details of speakers of Irish only but have never seen fit to publish them, for in each and every case the returns have 'lacked verisimilitude and . . . having regard to the places of residence and the ages of the persons concerned, could only have been due to a considerable degree of misinterpretation of the question' (Census 1936, vol. 8: xi).

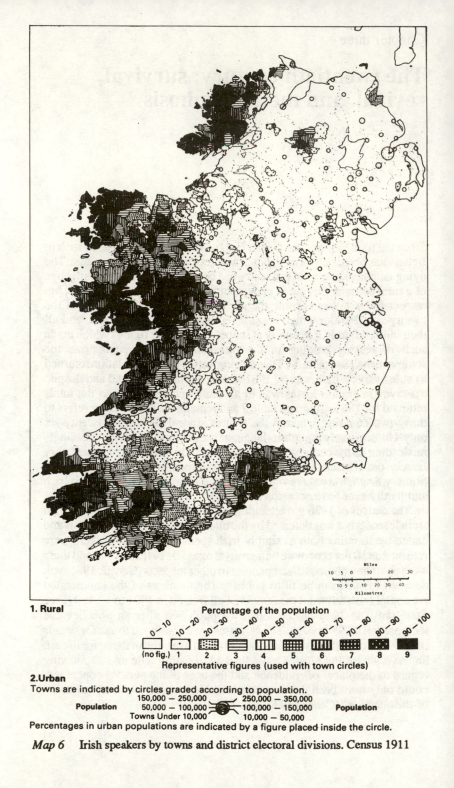

1. Rural

Percentage of the population

0 – 10	10 – 20	20 – 30	30 – 40	40 – 50	50 – 60	60 – 70	70 – 80	80 – 90	90 – 100
(no fig.)	1	2	3	4	5	6	7	8	9

Representative figures (used with town circles)

2.Urban

Towns are indicated by circles graded according to population.

	150,000 – 250,000	250,000 – 350,000	
Population	50,000 – 100,000	100,000 – 150,000	**Population**
	Towns Under 10,000	10,000 – 50,000	

Percentages in urban populations are indicated by a figure placed inside the circle.

Map 6   Irish speakers by towns and district electoral divisions. Census 1911

Table 3   Irish-speaking population 1901–81

Year	No. of counties	Total population	Irish Speakers	
			No.	%
1901	32	4,458,775	641,142	14·4
	26	3,221,823	619,710	19·2
1911	32	4,390,319	582,446	13·3
	26	3,139,688	553,717	17·6
1926	26	2,971,992	453,511	18·3
Age 3 years and upwards				
1926	26	2,802,452	540,802	19·3
1936	26	2,806,925	666,601	23·7
1946	26	2,771,657	588,725	21·2
1961	26	2,635,818	716,420	27·2
1971	26	2,787,448	789,429	28·3
1981	26	3,226,467	1,018,413	31·6

Source: Census Reports.

After 1946 there was a general suspicion that publication of all language statistics was to be discontinued, because of their generally accepted unreliability, and no language data were published in the census report for 1956. Coogan (1966: 186) thought the 1961 figures were not being published either but was proved wrong, probably because he drew attention to the issue. It is nevertheless indicative of state priorities that each census language volume is always published late. The dates of publication (bracketed) were as follows: 1926 (1934), 1936 (1940), 1946 (1953), 1961 (1966), 1971 (1976), 1981 (1985). This is not as deplorable as it might seem, for no state or other planning agency awaits these figures as a guide to its actions or strategy. The inflation of the language figures is a tribute to the work of the Gaelic League and the entire language revival movement but their lack of diagnostic value is also a damning indication of the severe limitations of the League's achievements.

The Gaelic League was not the first organization to demand recognition for Irish and although the Society for the Preservation of the Irish Language (1876) and its rather more militant offshoot the Gaelic Union are usually mentioned it is still more remarkable that the Irish National Teachers' Organization (INTO) from as early as 1870 officially favoured the use of Irish for instruction in the schools of Irish-speaking districts (INTO 1941: 66). The first state concessions were the inclusion of Irish in the syllabus for the schools' Intermediate Examination in 1878, and the following year primary schools were allowed to teach it outside school hours; but not until 1900 was this permitted inside hours – with attendance optional and permission conditional on the inspectors' approval of the standards in the required subjects. Only 51 per cent of all national schools were approved as efficient in 1902 (*Gaeltacht Commission Report 1926*: 13) and the schools of the Irish-speaking districts were usually the worst equipped and staffed, so this permission had little immediate effect.

The declared aims of the Gaelic League (*Connradh na Gaedhilge* in the old spelling) were the preservation of Irish as the national language of Ireland and the extension of its use as a spoken tongue, together with the promotion of historic Gaelic literature and the cultivation of a modern literature in Irish. This was so contrary to existing trends that support at first was low and confined to small numbers of the urban populations, which did not include many native speakers. The advent of the League nevertheless coincided with the great flowering in Anglo-Irish culture associated with the names of Yeats, Lady Gregory, Synge, and others who brought about a belated 'Romantic Revival' of public interest in traditional Irish myth and legend. At a time when parliamentary nationalism was at a low ebb they helped stimulate a revival of national pride in which, because it was overtly non-political, both Catholics and Protestants could share.

It was an easy step for many from pride in the Irish past to recognition of the role of the language in that past, and so on to a desire to recreate the Celtic 'Golden Age' (of early Christian and pre-Christian times) by the restoration of Irish throughout Ireland. For most this meant relearning the language which their parents and grandparents had denied them and there was little appreciation of the difficulties of transforming class learning into fluency, or fluency into a general reversion to Irish as native language. Nevertheless by 1904 the League was attracting around 50,000 members to its almost 600 branches. These not only organized language classes and cultural activities themselves but also put pressure on the state, the Churches, and the schools to defend and promote Irish. They were not unresponsive and for instance in 1904 the use of Irish as a medium of instruction was at last permitted in Gaeltacht schools.

Support for Irish wrung from the British authorities was always permissive but did reflect real public sentiment, as almost all educational matters were devolved to Dublin. Thus by 1915–16 roughly half the schools of the Fíor-Ghaeltacht – the 'truly' Irish-speaking districts as defined in 1925 – were using Irish as a medium of instruction and their teachers receiving extra grants accordingly. A quarter of primary pupils nationally were learning Irish at school in 1921 at the close of the British period and in secondary schools the proportion was as high as two-thirds (*Gaeltacht Commission 1926*: 13–14) as a result of the imposition in 1913 of a pass in Irish as a matriculation requirement for entry to the National (Catholic) University which had been established in 1908. The Church hierarchy had bitterly opposed this insistence on Irish but it was to be of prime importance in encouraging middle-class Catholic study of the

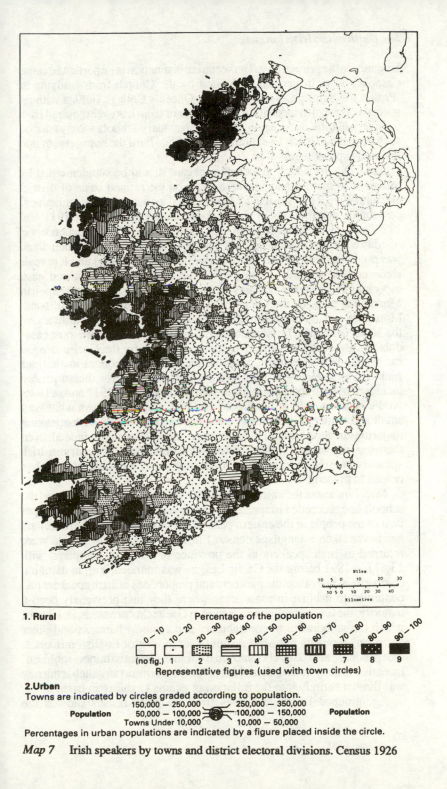

1. Rural   Percentage of the population

0 – 10   10 – 20   20 – 30   30 – 40   40 – 50   50 – 60   60 – 70   70 – 80   80 – 90   90 – 100

(no fig.)   1   2   3   4   5   6   7   8   9

Representative figures (used with town circles)

2. Urban

Towns are indicated by circles graded according to population.

	150,000 – 250,000	250,000 – 350,000	
Population	50,000 – 100,000	100,000 – 150,000	**Population**
	Towns Under 10,000	10,000 – 50,000	

Percentages in urban populations are indicated by a figure placed inside the circle.

Map 7   Irish speakers by towns and district electoral divisions. Census 1926

language to the present day. The sectarian distinction is important because Catholics were in general prohibited by the Church from studying at 'Protestant' Trinity College Dublin or Queen's College Belfast without special episcopal dispensation, and neither of them has ever required Irish for matriculation. Hence non-Catholic secondary schools were under no such pressure to teach Irish until the Free State built the requirement into its grant support regulations.

Table 3, with which this chapter began, should be supplemented by reference to maps 6 and 7, which show on the refined basis of district electoral divisions (similar to British civil parishes) the geographical percentage distributions of the Irish-speaking population in 1911 and 1926. A census was impossible in 1921 because of the War of Independence.

Map 6 is striking because 1911 was the first time for which such detail was published (large rural districts were the base in 1901) and it reveals some notable pockets of survival in the heart of the anglicized east, especially in or on the margins of Protestant Ulster, where the Sperrin Mountains, parts of the Glens of Antrim (with Rathlin Island), south Monaghan and the Omeath district of Louth showed concentrations above the 30 per cent level. Lesser concentrations in the east were in most cases dubious, the result of second-language teaching by the Gaelic League rather than native survival, or of the presence of important institutions such as the seminary at Maynooth, which accounts for the surprising incidence of Irish speakers in north-east Kildare both in 1911 and in 1926. At the opposite pole of language trends the map also shows what very small and scattered enclaves in the west now maintained Irish-speaking majorities in the reasonably secure range above 70 per cent: indeed, even there security was only apparent, for all too often the 30 per cent non-Irish speakers were the children of the 70 per cent who could speak Irish but had ceased to transmit it.

Map 7 indicates the extent to which by 1926 the Gaelic League and the schools had succeeded in spreading a knowledge of Irish to around 10 per cent of the people in the eastern parts of the new state. (Northern Ireland has never taken a language census.) In that year 101,474 people were returned as Irish speakers in the province of Leinster, compared with 13,677 in 1891 before the Gaelic League was founded. Yet, in damning comparison, both absolute numbers and proportions of Irish speakers had continued to decline in most areas where they had previously been a majority, the few exceptions occurring in Gaeltacht core areas, in a few of which the withdrawal of constabulary and customs barracks and other 'garrison' elements removed a significant monoglot English influence. Independence also no doubt removed from such districts a minor 'snobbish' incentive to deny knowledge of Irish, for from now on any such tendency was thrown entirely into the inflation of claims to ability in Irish.

Age-grouped language figures from the 1926 census showed the numbers of Irish speakers in the school ages (up to 14) had almost doubled since 1911; yet whereas those aged under 20 had increased by 103,680, those over 20 had decreased by 113,886. The real decline of the language was represented in the latter figure, and the scholastic revival in the former. The 'school-age bulge' which has distorted all subsequent Irish language statistics was visible as presented here in table 4, but of course had less effect in the older age groups, which had not yet been as totally exposed to instruction in Irish as the new school regulations required. Once children had been taught Irish at school there was inevitably a tendency, sometimes warranted, to claim in the census returns they were able to speak it, but already the 1926 report (vol. 10: 136–7) had noted a clear lapse rate of loss of Irish-speaking ability between one census and another, exemplified by comparing the 12,608 Irish speakers aged 12 in the 1911 census with the 6,030 aged 27 (the same age cohort) in 1926. Allowing for losses by emigration and death, the estimate was made that 23·1 per cent of persons aged 12 in 1911 had lost Irish by disuse by 1926. Figures were for the twenty-six Counties in each case.

The point is usually made that census figures represent *self*-estimates of language ability, as the enumerator collects the returns from heads of households. Obviously this never in fact represents self-assessment for schoolchildren, for their language abilities are assessed by their parents, and over-generous estimation is therefore particularly likely compared with the normal level of optimism about command of language which might be expected from the children themselves once adult and in charge of their own returns.

Table 4   Irish speakers, classified by age group, census 1926

	Irish Speakers	
Age group	No.	As % in age group
0–4	8,170	2·8
5–9	56,273	19·8
10–14	115,579	39·1
15–19	79,004	27·6
20–44	131,409	13·4
45–64	85,149	15·1
65 and over	67,927	25·0

The proportions in the upper three age groups had been approximately halved since 1881 and represent true decline. The increase in the school years is given perspective by the 2·8 per cent for infants under 5, itself inflated slightly by school attendance, which quite often in Ireland began (and begins) at 4. What revivalist credit there is in the figures nevertheless belongs clearly to the Gaelic League, for the short years since 1922 had been torn by civil war and there had been no time to restructure Irish education in any way different from that inherited from the British period, in which the League had been the sole major moving force for the teaching of Irish both inside and outside schools.

Doubts about what these figures signified for Irish survival as a community language were expressed early by some of its leading advocates. Earnán de Blaghd (Ernest Blythe) declared as early as 1914 that a year's residence in the Gaeltacht had convinced him that the League had been totally ineffective there: 'there was not . . . as much as one ordinary Gaeltacht farmer or fisherman speaking Irish to his children who would not have done so if there had never been a language movement' (1949: 4). He went on to assert that the few Gaeltacht houses in which Irish was habitually spoken because of the movement were those of teachers and others who used Irish in their profession, and assessed as around 200 the total numbers of all those who had attended League classes before independence and emerged able to speak it with reasonable fluency. He was making a political point, as a leading Fine Gael politician and government minister, in giving the credit for all the other non-native speakers who learnt Irish reasonably well to schools and colleges conducted at the expense of the British Exchequer. This is also a useful reminder of the other main strand of language maintenance work which, begun under British rule before the League was established, undoubtedly did far more to preserve Irish where it was in everyday use and yet had no such objective.

The Congested Districts Board was set up in 1891 to bring special economic assistance to those areas where the rateable valuation was less than £1 10s per head and where problems of rural poverty were at their most intense. This territorial definition coincided uncannily with the Fíor-Ghaeltacht identified by the Commission of 1926, and the coincidence was increased by the addition of areas of east Galway and Clare in 1909. (See map in Freeman 1950: 127, and cf. map 7.) Assistance was given in numerous ways, including building harbours and piers, new roads, sub-sidies for steamer services, improvements to housing, water supply, fisheries, and local industries, the provision of agricultural and fishery instructors, and the purchase and redistribution of large grazing farms. Arrangements were also made to transplant better-off tenants to still better holdings farther east, so that their vacated land could be used to enlarge neighbouring uneconomic holdings. (See Micks 1925, *passim.*) Freeman credits the Board with a major diminution in the emigrant drain from the west from 1891 onwards and relates it otherwise to the Land Acts of (especially) 1885, 1891, and 1903, which almost abolished traditional landlordism in Ireland. The work of the CDB ran in parallel with a spate of Light Railway Acts which between 1891 and 1903 at last joined the present-day Gaeltacht cores to the national rail network as lines were opened to Dingle (1891), Achill (1895), Clifden (1895), Glenties (1895), and Burtonport (1903), among others.

It was nevertheless symptomatic of future planning problems that both the CDB and a Royal Commission in 1908 considered congestion (i.e. the excess of population over resources) to be so severe in the heartlands of west Donegal, Erris (north-west Mayo), and Connemara that no amount of migration or resettlement would make the bulk of the holdings economic. All the major efforts at improvement were therefore concentrated elsewhere, where there was some hope that returns might be commensurate (*Gaeltacht Commission 1926*: 39, 45). The intractable problem areas were largely those in which 80 per cent or more of the people were Irish speakers in 1926. The Gaeltacht Commission and the other Free State authorities which took over the responsibilities of the CDB all assumed that the decline of the language was bound up with the impoverished state of the Gaeltacht cores and did what they could with their limited resources to enhance their economic and social development. They did not choose to consider the possibility that Irish survival might occur *because of* the lack of modern development and economic opportunities in those areas. True as subsequent history has proved this to be, it is impossible to blame the proponents of language survival and revival for refusing to countenance a Gaeltacht economic policy of benign neglect – except as, by default, was largely imposed on the state by its own inability before the 1960s to afford much for the Gaeltacht out of the relatively low tax revenues of the rest of the country.

Irish language activists today often criticize their government because it does less for Irish in various ways such as support for the language on television than the British government does in supporting Welsh. This is true and represents another area of conflict between policies of national independence designed (among many other things) to sustain the language and the logical consequences of independence in the economic sphere, which left Ireland worse placed after 1922 to finance language-support programmes which would pose few difficulties for British governments as a normal part of regional aid in the cultural sector. Since 1922 the Irish economy has almost always been weak, and when this author began visiting the Gaeltacht districts over thirty years ago it seemed littered with the remains of picturesque harbours and piers left by the Congested Districts Board and since neglected. The economic proposals of the Gaeltacht Commission of 1926 came to little because the Great Depression intervened.

The functions of the Congested Districts Board were dispersed between the Land Commission and the Ministries of Industry and Commerce and of Fisheries, for whom the backward western districts were of marginal concern. The rural industries (chiefly tweed, knitwear, lace, and embroidery) became the responsibility of the new Gaeltacht Services

Division of the Department of Lands in 1930 and contracted badly during the Depression. The survivors, plus a few new additions, including the manufacture of toys and utility goods, passed in 1957 to an independent board, Gaeltarra Eireann, and finally in 1969 to Údarás na Gaeltachta (the Gaeltacht Authority), with a much wider remit and with industries greatly expanded after 1960.

No one department has ever been made responsible for the general oversight of language policy nationally *and* in the Gaeltacht, and it was 1951 before the state set up a junior Office of the Gaeltacht and the Congested Districts, which functioned only through other departments and was responsible mainly for non-Gaeltacht people. This was quickly superseded in 1956 by a full Ministry (or Department) of the Gaeltacht – always known as Roinn na Gaeltachta – which also has broad co-ordinative functions but has considerable 'teeth' in its control over the disbursement of a wide range of educational, housing, and other language-support grants, both directly and through subordinate agencies, including Údarás.

I have told elsewhere how the official boundaries of the Gaeltachtaí were benevolently inflated in 1926 in the hope of encouraging a swift return of the whole wide area to Irish first-language usage, led by an almost immediate imposition of Irish as the first language of the schools and all public administration in the defined Fíor-Ghaeltacht districts (Hindley 1989). Map 8 shows the general exaggeration of the extent of the Fíor-Ghaeltacht, using mainly the criteria adopted by the Gaeltacht Commission itself. Map 9 shows the contraction of the Gaeltacht approved in 1956, the parts retained in it for mainly administrative convenience, and the questionable areas which were said to be predominantly Irish in speech but which the author's own survey found were not. Map 10 attempts to categorize degrees of Irish usage in the Gaeltachtaí, using data from the 1981 census and the 1985–6 primary-school *deontas* returns. The final general map 11 refines this analysis in the light of a field survey in 1987, and its components are represented in greater cartographic detail in the Gaeltacht-by-Gaeltacht county surveys in chapters 5–8 (maps 14, 17, 20, 23, 26, 29, 30). Suffice it to say that the attempts to arrest the decline of the Gaeltacht since 1893 and since 1922 have clearly failed, though the fact that Irish is still alive at all as a community language is an unquestionable achievement, given the rate of decline at the end of the nineteenth century.

The Census Report of 1926 (vol. 10: 135) was demonstrably true for now in what it said then:

> From the regularity of the decline . . . it could be deduced that, were it not for the efforts which were made to save the language very few persons attaining the age of sixty in 1951 would be able to speak it.

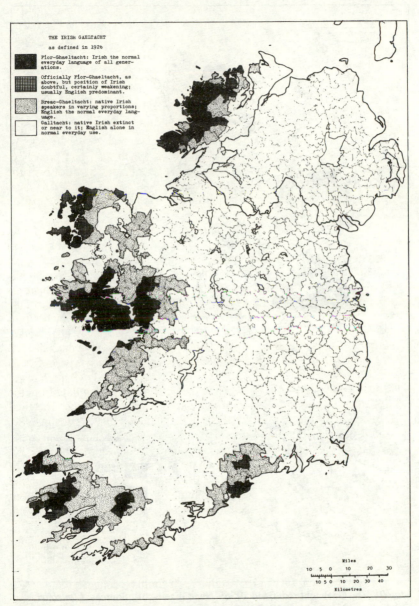

THE IRISH GAELTACHT

as defined in 1926

Fíor-Ghaeltacht: Irish the normal everyday language of all generations.

Officially Fíor-Ghaeltacht, as above, but position of Irish doubtful, certainly weakening; usually English predominant.

Breac-Ghaeltacht: native Irish speakers in varying proportions; English the normal everyday language.

Galltacht: native Irish extinct or near to it; English alone in normal everyday use.

Miles
10 5 0   10   20   30
10 5 0 10 20 30 40
Kilometres

Map 8   The Gaeltacht 1926. Source: Gaeltacht Commission Report

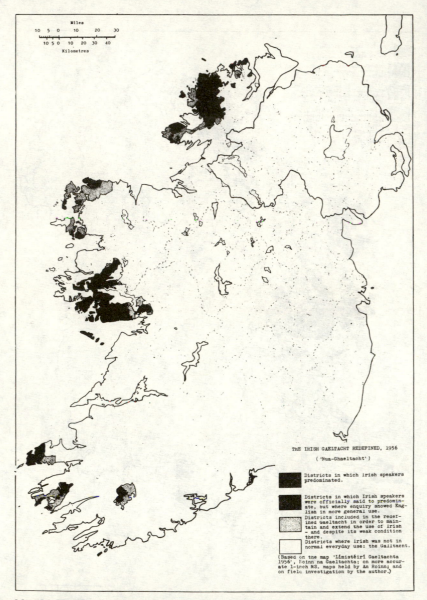

The scale shown on the map:

Miles
10 5 0   10   20   30
Kilometres
10 5 0 10 20 30 40

THE IRISH GAELTACHT REDEFINED, 1956

('Nua-Ghaeltacht')

Districts in which Irish speakers predominated.

Districts in which Irish speakers were officially said to predominate, but where enquiry showed English in more general use.

Districts included in the redefined Gaeltacht in order to maintain and extend the use of Irish – and despite its weak condition there.

Districts where Irish was not in normal everyday use: the Galltacht.

(Based on the map 'Límistéirí Gaeltachta 1956', Roinn na Gaeltachta; on more accurate 1-inch MS. maps held by An Roinn; and on field investigation by the author.)

Map 9   The Gaeltacht redefined 1956: 'Nua-Ghaeltacht'. Sources: *Límistéirí Gaeltachta 1956*; author's 1957 survey

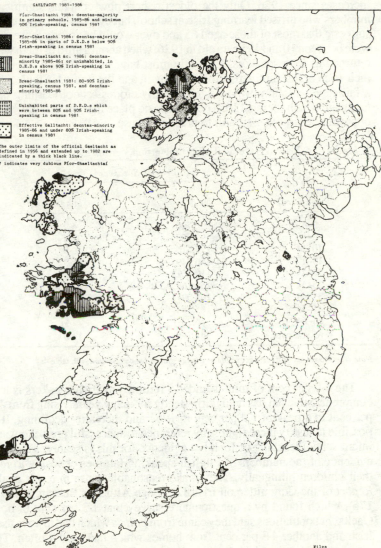

GAELTACHT 1981-1986

Fíor-Ghaeltachtaí 1986: deontas-majority
in primary schools, 1985-86 and minimum
90% Irish-speaking, census 1981

Fíor-Ghaeltacht 1986: deontas-majority
1985-86 in parts of D.E.D.s below 90%
Irish-speaking in census 1981

Breac-Ghaeltacht &c. 1986: deontas-
minority 1985-86; or uninhabited, in
D.E.D.s above 90% Irish-speaking in
census 1981

Breac-Ghaeltacht 1981: 80-90% Irish-
speaking, census 1981, and deontas-
minority 1985-86

Uninhabited parts of D.E.D.s which
were between 80% and 90% Irish-
speaking in census 1981

Effective Galltacht: deontas-minority
1985-86 and under 80% Irish-speaking
in census 1981

The outer limits of the official Gaeltacht as
defined in 1956 and extended up to 1982 are
indicated by a thick black line.

? indicates very dubious Fíor-Ghaeltachtaí

Miles
10 5 0   10   20   30

10 5 0   10   20   30   40
Kilometres

Map 10   The Gaeltacht 1981–6: a tentative categorization of the real state of the
language. Sources: Census 1981; *deontas* returns 1981–2, 1985–6

For 1981 the age-grouped language figures for the Republic were as presented in table 5. All age groups except the oldest show substantial increases since 1926. Only the oldest cohort now contains significant numbers who missed learning Irish at school, but even so life expectation suggests that most of those aged 65 and over would be among those who were between 10 and 19 years old in 1926, when about a third of them were returned as Irish speakers. Evidently most have subsequently forgotten their Irish or lost motivation for claiming it, and the figures in table 5 are a fair representation of how age normally erodes school learning of a language which for most Irish people has no place in everyday life, so no opportunities or other stimuli to practice its use.

Table 5   Irish speakers, classified by age group, census 1981

Age Group	Irish Speakers No.	As % in age group
3–4	6,700	4·9
5–9	97,058	27·8
10–14	173,516	50·8
15–19	166,549	51·0
20–24	110,561 ⎱	40·0 ⎱
25–34	156,760 ⎰ 375,412	32·8 ⎰ 33·7
35–44	108,091 ⎰	30·0 ⎰
45–54	85,184 ⎱	28·3 ⎱
55–64	66,209 ⎰ 151,393	22·9 ⎰ 25·6
65 and over	47,785	13·0

Note: The second set of figures consolidates the age groups for comparison with table 4.

The 4·9 per cent of infants under 5 returned as Irish speakers is less comprehensible but has held fairly steady for many years, rising from 4·1 per cent to a peak of 5·9 per cent in 1961 and thereafter declining. It is possible to justify these figures by reference to successful pre-school and infant school teaching of Irish but evidence for this is scanty, as is firm evidence of the numbers of English-speaking families choosing to rear their children bilingually. They make reasonable sense in terms of the *Report* of the Committee on Irish Language Attitudes Research (1975: 176), which found by a questionnaire survey that 1·3 per cent of non-Gaeltacht populations said they came from homes which had always used Irish and another 4·3 per cent from homes which had used it often. The proportions were much higher in the homes of teachers and civil servants.

Ó Riagáin (1988a: 33), himself centrally active in language work, says guardedly that the census 5 per cent at ages 3 to 4 '. . . is generally taken as a measure of the incidence of Irish-speaking homes' and that '. . . some regard this as evidence of language maintenance'. It seems, regrettably, rather more a measure of wishful thinking in the community, and more probably of the acceptance of the use of occasional Irish words and phrases encouragingly injected into otherwise English conversation as 'use of Irish in the home' and a measure of children's ability to speak it. The true national figures for use of Irish as the *first* language of pre-school children can hardly be above 1 per cent and numbers in the Gaeltachtaí are now so low as to make little difference to this estimate.

Given the persistence of the roughly 5 per cent of Irish people who have returned their 3 or 4 year old infants as Irish speakers in every census from 1926 and given that the language has been declining in everyday use throughout the period, it would not be inappropriate or facetious to suggest that some research might be advisable into the proportions of people who might always be *expected* to give perverse or manifestly over-optimistic answers to questions about their linguistic attitudes and abilities, or those of their children. It might fairly be argued that such perverseness would operate both for and against Irish, as there are undoubtedly many in Ireland who are against it: but the CILAR *Report* (1975: 28) found only 20·5 per cent of its national sample willing to express negative attitudes towards public efforts to transmit Irish, plus a further 15·7 per cent whose neutral stance sometimes verged upon negative, so it is obvious that pro-Irish sentiments will have weighed more heavily in any distortion of reported realities. Only 7 per cent of the Gaeltacht sample expressed any sort of negative or neutral attitude to Irish (ibid.), which in itself is a striking illustration of conflict between purported attitudes and behaviour, as the abandonment of the language in Gaeltacht homes was continuing and far more than 7 per cent must have been doing nothing to sustain it in their everyday lives. What is implied here is not deliberate deception but in essence self-delusion. Mac Aodha (1972: 26) estimated that only between 5 and 10 per cent of census Irish speakers had attained fluency and this may be accepted, with depressing qualifications:

> These new recruits to the Irish language networks are typically persons who learned Irish at school rather than in the home; they are scattered through English-speaking communities; they do not command any domains of language use, except in some homes and schools; and they do not, by and large, reproduce bilinguals for the next generation.
>
> (Ó Riagáin 1988a: 48)

Of course people who have spent years studying a language at school and college like to think they can speak it and when asked to say yes or no to a question about it might with some legitimacy give the answers recorded in the censuses. CILAR's more detailed questions (1975: 118) evinced more meaningful responses, and only 2·7 per cent in the national survey claimed 'native speaker' ability and 10·8 per cent ability to understand 'most conversations'. This is much nearer to reality and not far out of line with the claim of 6·8 per cent of the non-Gaeltacht sample to have spoken Irish often in normal conversation after leaving school, though one must weigh more lightly the 9·1 per cent who said they had done so 'several times' (ibid.: 182). Ó Riagáin and Ó Gliasáin (1984) repeated the CILAR survey a decade later, adding a few refinements, but their summary of findings shows no significant changes in Irish-language ability or use at the higher and crucial levels.

The value and limitations of the original CILAR survey were discussed by J. R. Edwards (1977). The greater dangers of simpler tests of supposed public opinion have been exposed more recently by Ó Riagáin (1988b). He queries conclusions derived from a single-question survey conducted by the Market Research Bureau of Ireland and published in April 1988, purporting to show that 77 per cent of respondents felt that Irish should become a 'subject of choice' for the (schools') Leaving Certificate and that only 17 per cent wished it to remain compulsory. A subsequent survey (in August) on behalf of Bord na Gaeilge showed that 42 per cent did not know what the present policy was; and after having had it spelled out to them an overall 64 per cent favoured the compulsory *teaching* of Irish without compulsion to *pass* the exam in it (i.e. the present policy), whilst a further 7 per cent favoured compulsion in both. Ó Riagáin sees the April survey as having tapped 'residual public antagonisms' towards the severe pre-1973 'compulsory Irish' policies, but it is surely as important to note the level of indifference to language policies indicated by such widespread ignorance of changes which occurred as long ago as 1973. Favourable replies induced by a surveyor's correction of an initial misconceived basis for a negative answer can certainly not be taken as removing a generally adverse attitude among the public as a whole, for it is self-evident that the correction can have been made only to the people sampled (approximately 1,400) and *not* to the much greater number whose opinions they were representing. The latter presumably remain at least suspicious of state language policies, unhelpfully neutral or unconcerned, if not positively hostile. 'Attitude' surveys, like census declarations of language abilities, must be treated with extreme caution, for in general both reflect aspirations rather than performance, and it is the latter on which the future of the language depends. Hence the emphasis on locating the residual Irish-speaking communities which is the basis of this book.

It would be premature to attempt to explain in this chapter where revival efforts went wrong, but the methods employed to promote the language merit summary. In essence they concentrated on political, legal, and educational action designed to make Irish generally known and respected but falling short of more drastic action which might have made it *used* outside the limited fields of state employment. Even there the normal interplay of government and governed, the great majority of whom could not speak Irish in 1922, left English dominant in virtually all fields of state activity except education. Except for a small minority of mal-contents who always disapproved of Irish, almost all vocal opinion took the view that the best way to revive Irish was to make the teaching of it compulsory for all children, on the reasonable argument that loss of transmission to children was what had killed it, so giving it to them in school would best restore it to use.

Irish was proudly proclaimed the national language in the new constitution of 1922 (article 4) but it was accepted that this was more an aspiration or a historic assertion than reality, so equal recognition was accorded to English for official purposes and a further article which provided for the publication of all parliamentary Acts in both languages gave precedence to the English version in the event of conflict. On entry to the EEC in 1973 Ireland became the only member which did *not* require translation of all Community papers and documentation into what since 1937 had been constitutionally its first official language. Irish has never achieved more than ceremonial status in the Oireachtas (Parliament) and although the new state was quick to require Irish-language qualifications from new entrants to the general grades of the civil service there was never any suggestion that eligibility for election to the legislature should be made dependent on a command of Irish.

The priority given to the promotion of Irish qualifications in the civil service and among teachers was nevertheless warranted, as for instance in 1925 only 10 per cent of all public officials serving in the Gaeltacht areas could speak Irish and a mere 4 per cent were native speakers (*Gaeltacht Commission 1926*: 29). Among teachers there, 32 per cent were entirely unqualified in Irish and only 41 per cent had the bilingual certificate or better. It might have been thought logical to concentrate on a crash programme for civil servants and teachers in the Gaeltachtaí, but the latter were already regarded as the equivalent of Siberia in the respective professions and in addition it was rightly felt that ignorance of Irish *everywhere else* was a major driving force impelling Gaeltacht people towards English. So the logic was to encourage Irish throughout the state by using the power of the state as paymaster to provide incentives for learning.

As early as February 1922 all national schools were instructed to teach Irish or to use it as a medium of instruction for at least an hour a day wherever competent teachers were available. Official policy thenceforth was for the extension of the use of Irish as a medium of instruction to infants throughout the country, on the old anti-Irish logic that only by using the (English) language from the earliest years could a full and fluent command of the idiom be attained. The Irish National Teachers' Organization had patriotically accepted this but developed doubts by 1926 and got written into the education code the proviso that such instruction should be mandatory only where the children were able to follow the lessons profitably and easily. The acquisition of language qualifications by existing and intending teachers was nevertheless expedited by tying their salaries to them and Department of Education circulars in 1931 and 1934 related efficiency gradings to the degree of use of Irish as the teaching medium. Strong teacher resistance was expressed by INTO in 1936 after a national survey, but the economic state of the country was so bad then and the ultra-nationalist Fianna Fáil government so well entrenched that this was ignored. In most of eastern Ireland by 1937 roughly 40 per cent to 60 per cent of national schools were employing Irish as the medium of instruction in part of their work and 12 per cent were using Irish only.

The aims and policies of extending Irish-medium instruction were restated by the Minister of Education in 1955, but already by that time the complaints of ordinary parents, who believed their children's prospects were being blighted by education in a language they could not understand and which offered them no prospects of employment unless they were in the select minority that could afford secondary education (not free until 1967), were becoming strident and retreat was in progress. Macnamara (1966) finally initiated fundamental scrutiny of the results and justification of the 'all-Irish' policy and it steadily withered as an effectively compulsory element in the school system, re-emerging by 1980 in state-supported voluntary schools for children whose parents choose it and who also seem to be disproportionately urban and middle-class. The teaching of Irish as a subject in all state-supported schools remains compulsory.

One is inclined to ignore secondary education as a pillar of state encouragement for Irish since 1922 because until 1967 there was hardly any secondary schooling available for the children of the Irish-speaking districts and it was everywhere subject to fees. It was nevertheless the secondary schools, largely run by religious Orders, that produced most of the present elite of fluent but second-language Irish speakers who dominate Irish-language political, economic, educational, cultural, literary, and social life outside and very often inside the Gaeltacht. Their influence has thus been enormous and in marked contrast to the reluctance shown by the Church hierarchy when the Gaelic League first began to make demands on its schools and colleges (see Ó Dubhda 1943).

One major influence in favour of Irish in secondary schools has already been mentioned – the requirement of matriculation in Irish for entry to the National University in 1913. The new state followed this up in 1924 by giving increased grants to secondary schools in which all or part of the work was done through Irish, and by the early 1960s about half of secondary school pupils were receiving instruction through Irish in at least one subject other than Irish itself. A fair impression of the comparative scales of educational provision before 1967 will be gathered from the Department of Education figures of pupils for the session 1954–5:

National (all-age primary) schools 495,163
Secondary schools 56,411
Vocational (technical etc.) schools:
    Full-time 20,895
    Part-time 69,882

The vocational schools (*gairm-scoileanna*), which resemble the old English secondary technical schools, were introduced by the state to circumvent the heavily academic bias of the secondaries and did not have an Irish requirement in their examinations; but they lacked prestige to attract the more ambitious upwardly-mobile and were generally regarded as an irrelevance necessary mainly to serve the lower strata of society, which were notorious for their incapacity for mastery of the language. This particular chicken came home to roost when from 1967 free secondary education was at last made compulsory for all and the lower-ability and lower-income groups which had hitherto been confined to the all-age national schools began to flood in and eventually to enter for the Leaving Certificate. The numbers in recognized secondary schools trebled between 1960 and 1980 and brought about the collapse of the core of the 'compulsory Irish' system.

In 1973–4 the requirement of a pass in Irish to gain the Intermediate or Leaving Certificates at all (they were 'packaged', like the old English School Certificate and Matriculation, with required passes or credits in specified subjects) was abolished and so was the Irish requirement for entry to most public-sector appointments (Ó Gliasáin 1988: 91, 100). It was at last accepted that compulsion had failed to convert the vast majority to any practical desire to speak the Irish they were taught at school. The retention of the Irish-language qualification for entry to the National University is the chief remaining protection for Irish in the secondary schools, for the Department of Education's requirement that it must be studied but need not be passed almost invites a 'tokenist' response and the grant-discrimination system of encouragement for Irish-medium teaching has lost most of its effectiveness as a result of the economic and social changes which Ó Gliasáin discusses.

It should be clear from this brief consideration of the manifold work for Irish through the schools since 1922 and even earlier that its almost total failure to make Irish speakers of the children is a measure of the strength of external environmental pressures towards English, and further shows how foolish it would be to attribute the decline of the Irish language in the nineteenth century exclusively to the schools. Education is indeed usually a means which facilitates changes which are wanted for other important reasons. The Irish people adopted English and had their children taught it not because they liked it but because it opened boundless opportunities to them. Attitude surveys continue to show that substantial majorities of

39

Irish people would like Irish to be revived as the language of Ireland, but they also show them averse to compulsion and generally pessimistic about its utilitarian value and its future. Almost 80 per cent think Irish less useful than a continental language ... (Ó Riagáin and Ó Gliasáin 1984: *passim*).

The question of why the Gaelic League failed to maintain its early impetus must be answered in terms of the relatively low level of political activity in Ireland in the 1890s, after the Parnellite debacle. This enabled an abnormally wide spectrum of national interest to focus on language and related cultural activities, in part as a diversion from political despair. De Blaghd (1972: 35–6) has shown how already by 1913–14 the apparent imminence of Home Rule and an Irish government had made language work 'seem a less urgent obligation on the individual citizen' and how this in turn led to demands for more aggressive policies from the activist residue. Personal and political differences divided the League in 1916 but much worse after December 1921, when the Treaty establishing the Free State was signed. The League president Eoin Mac Neill became Minister of Education in the new government but large sections of the membership supported De Valéra's anti-Treaty forces in the ensuing civil war and it is hardly surprising that the number of League branches fell from 819 in 1922 to 139 in 1924 (Mac Aodha 1972: 29).

Another major factor was of course the institutionalization of the language in the new constitution and especially the new regulations enshrining a greatly enhanced role for it in the schools and civil service. These made voluntary activity and effort seem far less necessary, in addition to which the promotion of Irish became something for which substantial sectional interests could now expect to be remunerated by the state. It is no criticism but a matter of inevitability that the revival movement, once established as a national institution, became bureaucratized, i.e. most practical (as distinct from propagandist) measures were made the responsibility of paid officials acting on behalf of government departments and committees.

It would be extremely naive to suppose that sustained public enthusiasm without such formal state support could either have been sustained or have achieved better results. The example of Northern Ireland ('the Six Counties'), where state support has been minimal and voluntary activity paramount since 1922, suggests the reverse, and the death of native Irish in its last refuges in Rathlin, the Glens of Antrim, and the Sperrin Mountains has not been balanced by any substantial accretions of effective second-language learners who have proved their ability to transmit Irish naturally or semi-naturally to their own offspring. (See below, pp. 150–59.) As in the Free State, inherited economic and social structures virtually predetermined that the Gaelic League leadership should derive primarily from the urban and predominantly middle-class learners instead of from the remote and depressed Gaeltachtaí.

The Free State Gaeltachtaí too often had little reason to see any relevance for themselves in the urban revival or to see much difference between officials who had hitherto ignored their Irish and new officials who, learners of the 'artificial', standardized, and orthographically 'reformed' Irish which a modern state inevitably had to try to introduce, for the next forty years or so too often succeeded in projecting to Gaeltacht people the idea that Gaeltacht Irish was 'wrong', i.e. grammatically and in other ways incorrect. This did no more good to Gaeltacht self-confidence than overt anti-Irish attitudes had done and the fact that the effort to modernize Irish came from Dublin, the prime source of earlier anti-Irish influences and in Gaeltacht eyes a centre of 'privilege', tended wholly in the same direction. It cannot be overemphasized that Gaeltacht people resent the expropriation of *their* language by wealthy townspeople who are not native speakers. (See p. 212–3.) With great utilitarian misgivings they love it as a central part of their heritage, and if they abandon it for their children they do so with profound regret and psychological turmoil, and greet with hostility priggish criticisms of their alleged dereliction of national duty which emanate from 'well-off people who have done well out of the language'.

It is to the credit of the League and of the revival efforts of the state that plenty of Gaeltacht native speakers have themselves done well out of the language since 1922, and since around 1960 they have done disproportionately well out of state investment in economic development. But the starting base was so low that this has not made sufficient difference to the balance of the utilitarian argument on the language question to alter fundamental Gaeltacht attitudes of linguistic despondency, founded on the continued expectation of emigration to Britain, America, or Australia, or at best migration to English-speaking Galway, Dublin, etc. Idealism stimulated by the League and its successors persists and slows the course of Irish decline; but idealism thrives best where people are prosperous enough to be able to afford to give priority to their ideals instead of thinking above all about elementary needs. The surviving Gaeltachtaí are beautiful places where the visitor is constantly reminded that 'you can't eat the scenery' (untrue of modern tourism) and where elementary needs still obtrude in any serious discussion about the choice of language for the children.

A number of relatively detailed examples of revival policies will be dealt with in the later parts of this book. They include the Irish summer colleges which were started by the League as early as 1904 and intended to inspire young learners with a love of the Gaeltacht as well as giving them experience of the living language; the preparatory colleges which gave many Gaeltacht children preferential entry to teacher training and helped produce many, perhaps most, of the most dedicated and effective Irish teachers in the atrophied Gaeltacht of today; and not least the much maligned *deontas*, an annual £2 grant (later increased) which from 1933 was paid to encourage the continued fostering of fluent native Irish speech in Gaeltacht homes. These and the Gaeltacht housing grants and the 'Gaeltacht colonies' are more central to the story of the Gaeltacht which follows, itself centring on the now difficult question of where precisely living Gaeltachtaí may still be found and what numbers of habitual native Irish speakers still reside in them ready to transmit the language to their posterity.

The metamorphosis of Irish from the disparaged and unwritten dialects of an impoverished and remotely located peasantry into the modern literary but second language of a privileged urban elite is indeed a great achievement and one without international parallels except for the still more remarkable revival of Hebrew in the unique circumstances of modern Israel. Comparisons with other European minority languages will be considered in chapter 12.

Part 2

Locating the living language

Chapter four

The uses and snares of official language statistics

It is at first sight odd but nevertheless understandable that locating the last outposts of native and habitual use of Irish as the first language of area-defined communities is exceedingly difficult. This results in part from the degree of success achieved by the teaching and use of Irish in the schools, which have spread a moderate knowledge of the language to far more than are ever inclined to make use of it and which therefore confuse all data concerning the speaking of Irish. It also results from benevolent state policies in support of the language, for a wide range of grants now make it financially rewarding to exaggerate the degree of use of Irish both individually within families and in whole communities where un-announced observation shows it to be disused or very little used.

The newcomer naturally and with justification turns to the officially defined Gaeltacht in seeking the living language, but soon recoils perplexed. The Gaeltacht is legally the Irish-speaking districts and the term is used either collectively for all such districts or in reference to any single 'Gaeltacht district' in the designated Gaeltacht counties. As has been seen, the first inflated definition of 1926 was modified by drastic contraction in 1956, but the redefinition included its own deliberate inflation 'for administrative reasons', plus more by presumed inadvertence and/or bestowal of the benefit of the doubt in marginal districts. (See map 9.) Subsequent minor expansions of the boundaries in Kerry, Cork, Waterford, and by the inclusion of the 'Gaeltacht colonies' in Meath, bear no relationship to any true resurgence of the sort once hoped for.

It is normal when seeking precision on language distributions to expect to find it in official statistics from census and similar sources. Enough has been said to show that the Irish language census figures have become for the most part superficially worthless as an indicator of the incidence of Irish survival and use. This is, however, true only at the superficial level, and if used with circumspection they can be very helpful. They are especially so if studied together with Roinn na Gaeltacht's own statistics of schoolchildren who qualify for the *deontas*, or grant for native Irish speakers. These latter figures pose further problems in interpretation, and it is now proposed to consider current census and *deontas* evidence in sequence, with emphasis on the latter because of its relative unfamiliarity and high potential value – if used with sensitivity.

Interpreting Irish Language census figures

The official census language enumeration as long ago as 1926 abandoned any attempt to ascertain degrees of fluency or of native and habitual use of Irish and records only 'ability' to speak Irish as returned by the householder who completes the schedule (Census 1926, vol. 8: vi). The teaching of Irish has now been compulsory in schools for over sixty years, so regardless of the (normal) ineffectiveness of second-language teaching in English-speaking countries, large proportions of the population who cannot speak Irish with any ease think they know enough to claim they can and know no genuine native Irish speakers to serve for comparison. Parents who may be frank about themselves commonly class their children's scholastic attainments as amounting to fluency, no doubt in hopes of progress.

A normal 'age pyramid' for a declining language is broad at the top, with strength in the upper age groups, and pointed at the bottom, with weakness in numbers and proportions among the young. In the Irish census it is broad at the bottom, in the school attendance years, and tapers sharply upwards as 'school-Irish' is forgotten. The significant exception is among children aged 3–4 years, most of whom have not yet got to school and who therefore in most age-grouped figures to 1981 tend to reveal the true depths of decline, admittedly allowing for a margin of fond parental over-optimism when completing their infants' returns. The diagnostic value of the 3–4 age group may well be diminished by 1991 as a result of the successes of the *naíonraí* (Irish-language pre-school playgroups) since around 1980, for whether or not they achieve their aims they will certainly result in many more parents of young children recording their offspring as Irish speakers: that is, assuming the *naíonraí* survive in their present form until 1991 and that present hopes are maintained.

Perhaps the most disconcerting thing for the fledgling user of Irish language census statistics is that they show majorities in all the little Gaeltacht centres – such as Dungloe (Donegal), Belmullet (Mayo), and Dingle (Kerry) – which are so audibly anglicized and which are notoriously the radiating centres of anglicization in their districts. This seems nonsensical unless it is realized that knowledge of a language is relative and bears little relationship to actual use.

The census language figures do have a certain diagnostic value and W. S. H. Evans's (1977) work on the 1971 census returns for Munster confirmed the present author's suspicions that all Gaeltacht language figures in recent years could be interpreted as follows:

1. Where 90 per cent or more of the people are returned as Irish speakers, Irish may be expected to be the main language, i.e. the one habitually and normally used among them and their language of 'first resort' – including usually (but not universally or exclusively) with their children.

2. Where between 80 and 90 per cent are returned as Irish speakers it may be expected that the language is still to some extent in everyday use as a normal medium of communication, but English will in most cases predominate and it is unlikely that Irish will be the first language in use with or between the children. It will probably still predominate as the normal medium of familiar conversation among the elderly and some of the middle-aged but it will be secondary to English among parents with young children and children of school age.

3. Where less than 80 per cent are returned as Irish speakers it may still be the mother tongue of the older generation, at least in the upper percentiles, but English will be the common everyday medium of communication outside a very few homes, and very few children will have Irish as their first and native language. They may be quite fluent in 'school-Irish' but they will generally lack a native idiom on extra-curricular matters or any inclination to speak it outside school and a few related organized activities. This also tends to apply to the children in category 2.

The census figures for the pre-school age group 3–4 are much nearer to objective linguistic reality, so that, for instance, whereas in 1981 59·3 per cent of children aged 10–14 years in the Meath Gaeltacht colonies were returned as Irish speakers, the proportion aged 3–4 was 9·1 per cent (Census 1981, vol. 6: 36). However, even this low figure is a gross exaggeration of Irish fluency appropriate to the age and it must be emphasized that all the census language figures are inflated by patriotic and nationalistic sentiment, 'wishful thinking' by persons who would like to speak Irish but whose other priorities leave them with only a token amount, and parental over-optimism about the language attainments of their children at school. This makes the figures little better than a public opinion poll on what the status of the language *ought* to be, that opinion being evidently weighted by official classification of a district as Gaeltacht and by awareness of the grants, subsidies, and other benefits deriving from it.

A general point which may be made about statistics for declining languages is that, because they usually occupy districts with a declining population and little immigration, and because their native speakers will almost all be fluently bilingual in another language, any minority which does not speak the 'local' language will be disproportionately influential in driving it from public use. Where, as is so often the case, that minority is in fact the children of the majority who have thereby demonstrated that they do not wish to pass on the language, the significance of what might seem a 'mere' 10 or 20 per cent minority is vastly greater, for it indicates a wider loss of the will for the language to survive and necessarily means that Irish-speaking parents and (where present) grandparents are acquiescing in abandoning Irish as the language of the family in future, even if they retain it for their own private purposes, as when they do not want the children to understand them. Until the industrial expansion of the 1970s brought major immigration to some of the Gaeltacht core areas the non-Irish-speaking minorities were indeed usually the children of the majority.

The 1970s expansion was mainly successful in attracting former emigrants to return with their skills to the new opportunities in the Gaeltacht, where they were able to resume the use of their native language at work, but they also brought with them wives and children born outside the Gaeltacht and ignorant of Irish, the wives injecting an adult element to the non-Irish-speaking population which was further augmented by managerial staff and skilled workers brought in by the same industries. Most of these people undertook some commitment to learn Irish, the wives usually in connection with support for their children's Irish-language education at school and qualification for the *deontas*, housing grants, etc., but their degrees of success have been very variable and introduce yet another complication into interpretation of the census language figures for the districts most affected.

Scéim Labhairt na Gaeilge: the *deontas* figures as a guide to Irish language maintenance

The official Irish title means 'the Irish-speaking scheme' and implies its support for the continuance and expansion of Irish as an everyday native language. It was introduced in the school year 1933–4 with the payment of a £2 bounty or grant (*deontas*) for every schoolchild aged 6 to 12 years where it could be certified by the parent, local school manager, and principal teacher, and verified on inspection, that Irish was the language of the child's home. Each child that has been entered for the award is required to demonstrate this by fluent natural speech (*an chaint líofa nadurtha*) in a short interview with a departmental officer. Initially this was a school inspector of the Department of Education and the inspection (as it was always regarded) took place in the school. The results were not unnaturally seen as reflecting on the language-teaching efficiency of the school, especially as teachers are paid bonuses for teaching in the Gaeltacht and through the medium of Irish. This was bitterly resented, as teachers saw no reason to take the blame for failures which resulted from parental neglect of Irish in the home, but it was generally understood that holding the inspection on or after the sixth birthday rather than at the normal school entry age (which could be as low as 4$^1/_2$ and was usually 5) was deliberately intended to enable the schools to get the children up to 'pass' level, which many did.

The outcome of prolonged debate was that responsibility was eventually (1975–6) transferred to the officers of Roinn na Gaeltachta, the Gaeltacht Department, which has no authority over the schools and is in no way required to judge teachers in this or most other respects – though it does in relation to appointments to a number of extra-curricular remunerated posts involving language promotion, especially in summer. The examination should officially be conducted in the home of the child but because of weight of numbers this is impracticable in the Gaeltacht heartlands in north-west Donegal and south Conamara and is common only in the smaller Gaeltacht 'pockets' in Munster, where decline is so advanced and so notorious that many parents do not submit an application form. Many apply once and do not do so again, once they feel the position is clear. The inspection by the Gaeltacht Department officer is therefore normally conducted in the school, as before, but as a matter of pure convenience and with a clear understanding that it is not the school which is being assessed.

Unfortunately, because the language is now so very weak among the majority of Gaeltacht children, it is utterly impossible for an examination which takes place after a year or more of schooling to avoid giving credit for effective language teaching, unless the inspectors are to insist strictly that the degree of fluency attained by the child (appropriate to its age) shall be clearly *native and natural* and exhibit few signs that it derives mainly from the classroom. The converse of this is inevitably that low proportions of *deontas* awards in a school suggest ineffective language teaching, but to minimize adverse publicity the results are not distributed collectively to schools and are sent individually to the parents concerned. They are not secret and are collated by the department, which makes them available to interested parties. Most schools I visited did not know 'their' figures for recent years and only a few had read the 1981–2 ones published in the 1985 Chomhchoiste report. The old fear of the annual *deontas* inspection has evidently died and there is abundant evidence that it is conducted with sympathy and understanding of the difficulties faced by parents, teachers, and children struggling to maintain a place for Irish. This virtue creates the critical difficulty in interpreting the *deontas* figures and makes detailed individual consideration of many of them essential.

The published *deontas* figures for the Gaeltacht primary schools for 1981–2 and the provisional (hitherto unpublished) figures for 1985–6 are included in appendix 3 together with some basic notes. The data provided by Roinn na Gaeltachta never include percentage renderings, though these were used as the basis of the bar graphs (*Céatadan de na daltaí a thuill an deontas £10* /Percentage of pupils qualifying for the £10 grant) published in Tuarascáil an Comhchoiste (1986). The central reason for hesitation in reducing the numbers of awards to percentages of the numbers of pupils on the school rolls is that in almost all cases some of the pupils on the rolls will be ineligible for consideration for the award because they have not reached the qualifying age. Children below that age are included in the rolls – partly to help small rural schools that might otherwise be threatened with closure or loss of staff because of pupil–teacher ratios, and despite the fact that attendance is not compulsory until age 6; but no figures for under-age pupils are published to enable the necessary adjustment to any percentage calculations to be made. In addition, the proportions of such children attending school vary considerably from place to place according to local custom, and for example the 100 per cent *deontas* return for the Galway island school of Máinis in 1981–2 necessarily means that no child under 6 was attending there then, a quite exceptional case.

There is also sometimes a proportion of parents who refuse on principle to apply for the grant for their children who may otherwise be good Irish speakers and are thus omitted from the qualified numbers. Usually these are professional people who 'do not believe you should expect to be paid for speaking your own language' and/or otherwise feel the £10 sum disdainful. I met more than one teacher's family which had taken this view until it needed one of the much more valuable Gaeltacht housing grants (up to £3,000), a condition of which is that any schoolchild in the family must qualify for the *deontas*. Such failure to apply on the part of well qualified families is nevertheless exceptional and in most of the cases quoted to me I noted that one parent, although professionally qualified in Irish, was not a native speaker, and it is obvious that for a child of a newly arrived teacher (especially the head) to fail the *deontas* exam would be ignominious and best not risked until some longer residence in the district and subjection to (the usual) Irish-medium instruction. High-principled objection to the test would provide an acceptable explanation or possibly a subconscious rationalization of avoidance of the test.

There is a much larger proportion of the school population which is not entered for the *deontas* because the parents know they are not qualified for it, as they speak no Irish at home and/or may have been entered and failed badly before, and/or may have older siblings who have had that experience. In such cases, which include most official Gaeltacht schools with low *deontas* figures, there is no distortion. Irish is bound to be dead as a native language where even the pretence of speaking it to the children is abandoned.

A further complication, usually marginal but important in one or two schools (especially Dún Chaoin, west Kerry), is the presence of children sent on scholarships from the Galltacht (the anglicized rest of Ireland) for three months of Irish-medium instruction plus life in an habitually Irish-speaking family. These are popularly known as 'Gael-Linn children', after the organization which sends them under its *Scéim na Scoláireachtaí*

Trí Mhí (three-month scholarships scheme) with careful selection to ensure that they already have enough Irish to benefit and after similar checks on the recipient schools and homes in the Gaeltacht to see that they do have the required Irish-language dominance. In 1986 forty-five Gaeltacht primary schools were classed as eligible to receive Gael-Linn children (out of a total of 132 schools) and twenty-six did so in the course of the year, receiving 129 in all. Twenty of them received one to five, three received seven to nine, and three received thirteen to nineteen. The upper limit set was five at a time in any one school, to avoid risks of linguistic 'dilution', and similarly only one child was placed in each Gaeltacht home. Appendix 3 lists the schools affected but there is no indication of how many children were present for each three-month period nor whether any were in fact present at the time of the *deontas* inspector's visit. This is therefore a 'joker' to be borne in mind when the school figures are otherwise puzzling. Gael-Linn children do not qualify for the *deontas* but do count on the rolls.

It is an obvious temptation to regard the Gael-Linn list of eligible schools as the hard core of the Gaeltacht, the schools judged by an efficient language organization to be the best fitted to absorb keen young learners. In general this would be justified, and only five of the forty-five eligible schools are asterisked in appendix 3 to indicate Irish virtually dead, though a further eight show serious weakness. Gael-Linn emphasizes that lack of accommodation either in classrooms or in suitable families may cause the exclusion of some schools from the list and the sending of low numbers to others where Irish is strong. It also admits to helping certain smaller schools by sending larger numbers to boost their rolls, as these extra children count for staffing purposes. The figures suggest that this can have been a major factor only at Dún Chaoin/Dunquin and An Mhuiríoch/ Murreagh, both in west Kerry. The presence in 1986 of four scholarship children in Máinis/Mynish school (Conamara), where there were twenty-four pupils on the role in 1981–2 and thirty in 1985–6, should explain most of its concomitant decline from 100 per cent *deontas* awards to 80 per cent – also assuming a rise of two in infants under 6 years of age in the normal entry from the catchment area.

Careful scrutiny of Gael-Linn's list of eligible schools suggests that it includes all that still enjoy a predominantly Irish-language home background. Even those with asterisked doubts in appendix 3 were all commended for the quality of their Irish teaching, which spills out beneficially into a number of homes – especially those authorized to receive scholarship children and the income so derived. In such marginal areas and homes threatened by anglicizing pressures all around the Gael-Linn money provides an extra incentive–defence for the continued use of the language, at least in some of the community. It therefore gives an extra depth of meaning to the *deontas* figures in terms of everyday use of Irish, even though the visitors do not qualify.

A variable which affects the school statistics in unusually large Gaeltacht centres which have two national schools caused the author to concoct plausible but unnecessary hypotheses on noting that the girls' schools at An Spidéal/Spiddal and An Daingean/Dingle were both much larger than the boys' and also less successful in 'the *deontas*' in the 1981–2 returns. There are other factors, but the main one is that despite the names of the schools all the infants in each case go to the girls' school, run by nuns, and it therefore has all the ineligible younger children, who usually depress the percentages for all other schools. To avoid such complications the two national schools in any one place are treated as one in the tables here.

A final but diminishing variable which may distort some schools' *deontas* proportions lies in the fact that although free secondary education was introduced as from the session 1967–8 some parents were slow to send their children on from the national school. Because of their seniority and longer exposure to Irish-medium instruction such pupils could be expected to inflate the *deontas* percentages to some extent; but I have not met an example of this and am assured by the Department of Education that it brings pressure to bear whenever such 'over-age' children are detected on a school's roll. This should in fact never arise except in the specifically 'special' schools which are classed as primaries but deal with children of all ages who have special learning difficulties.

These many variations in the composition of the schools' populations help to explain many puzzling discrepancies between the *deontas* figures for schools in districts which an impartial observer who has done careful research might find indistinguishable or even more or less Irish in directions opposite to those suggested by the statistics. However, whilst they must be taken into account when using the data it is unusual for them to cause major distortions on such a scale as to make an Irish-speaking school appear anglicized. The few cases where this does happen will be specified in the regional survey (chapters 5–9).

At least as important in generating apparent discrepancies are variations in the application of the criteria for the award by the Roinn na Gaeltachta officers in their annual inspection and adjudication. There are six responsible officers, i.e. two for each province, and a chief officer. All are fluent Irish speakers and well able to detect a child who is a mere school 'learner', however fluent, in a minute or two. Long discussions with four of them and direct enquiry by visits to thirty-three schools made it clear that there are good reasons why they may not always feel able to discriminate meticulously between the learner and the native speaker but quite often award *deontas* to the former as well as to the latter – especially in schools where true native speakers from habitually Irish-speaking homes are few, yet excellent progress is made by the school (with some parental back-up) by the age of 6.

One fundamental reason for 'flexibility' is that the basic aim of the Scéim Labhairt na Gaeilge is to support, sustain, and if possible extend the speaking of Irish as a home language. The key criterion for the *deontas* award is that the child should demonstrate by its fluency at 6 years of age (and annually thereafter) that Irish is its normal family language. This has to be interpreted in a context in which, on the evidence of numerous teachers throughout the erstwhile core areas of the different Gaeltachtaí, often confirmed by direct questions to their classes in my presence, the great majority of children in Gaeltacht schools now arrive at ages $4^1/_2$ or 5 either with little Irish or with English clearly their first language as the one in which they are most fluent and to which they resort at play. In the core areas, which are almost exclusively Gaoth Dobhair/Gweedore in north-west Donegal, central south Conamara, and western Corca Dhuibhne/Corkaguiny in Kerry, the great majority of parents are native Irish speakers and make *some* use of Irish in the home. This is usually between themselves rather than to the children, but the latter are used to hearing it spoken and have 'an ear' and 'a feel' for it when it comes to learning it and learning through it at school.

Many teachers assured me and indeed demonstrated that the children 'lap up Irish' at the age of 5 and further assured me that now that parents are no longer afraid of school neglect of English blighting their children's career prospects most are susceptible to persuasion to help their school work by, for example, speaking Irish to the children for one meal per day or at some other regular time. Where, as is usually the case, this results in reasonable fluency by the age of 6, this relative merit is usually rewarded with the grant, for the obvious reason that the interests of the language are thereby advanced and child, family, and teachers alike are encouraged.

There is also ample anecdotal evidence to show that in marginal cases where there is some Irish ability but in obvious subordination to English refusal of the grant commonly leads to a total exclusion of the language from the home. There are innumerable gradations between Irish being *the* language of the home (as is strictly required) and Irish as *a* language of the home, which it may be to very differing degrees. The regulation has to be interpreted constructively to achieve the purposes of the scheme, and the interpretation varies with the linguistic and related circumstances of each school. There is therefore no apparent consistency in the degrees of 'liberality' manifested in the *deontas* figures for different schools, for the circumstances of different schools vary from year to year, not least as heads and teachers come and go, some of them better language teachers than others.

Individual character and ability are conspicuous in Gaeltacht school staffs because they are so small. Sixty-six (44 per cent) of 150 Gaeltacht national schools listed in the 1985 Comhchoiste report had only one or two teachers in 1981–2 and a further sixty-eight (45·3 per cent) had three to five teachers, i.e. 89 per cent had five teachers or fewer, and non-teaching heads are unheard-of. A change of head or of the teacher in charge of the reception class can make fundamental differences to the position of the language in a smaller school in a linguistically marginal area. All permanent appointments require fluency in Irish and ability to teach 'through the medium', but some have that extra ability to fill the school, children, and sometimes even the parents with enthusiasm for Irish and with willingness to work for it.

Such teachers change the atmosphere both of a school and of its small, close-knit community, and their departure after a lifetime's dedicated work is rapidly signalled in loss of impetus and a lapse into relative apathy, as attentions turn to other priorities which the *deontas* inspector cannot but perceive in the language attitudes of the children and their parents. The successor may be wonderful at something else which many would regard as more vital, so there is no criticism of teachers or inspectors in stating bluntly that staff changes are often very significantly mirrored in changes in the *deontas* percentages in districts where the language position is shaky. A fine but extreme example was that of Caisleán na Mine Airde/ Minard Castle in Corca Dhuibhne, which had 79 per cent of *deontas* awards in 1981–2 (the published figure of 90·9 per cent in Tuarascáil an Chomhchoiste: 57 was later corrected) but fell to 48 per cent in 1985–6 after the retirement of an immensely respected head renowned for his language work. A young Gaeltacht inspector (several are young) would need to be brave or foolhardy to reject a *deontas* application supported by such a man and might be expected to suppress residual doubts of the sort articulated by this author when he first saw that high figure for what is indisputably an English-speaking area with a modest degree of Irish survival.

Where the position of the language is weak and good work is being done for it against all the odds it is hardly the job of Roinn na Gaeltachta to point out that the work is shallowly rooted, does not attain true native fluency, and is not supported by wholehearted endeavour by native-speaker parents who continue to give priority to English in talking to their children in the home. It seeks to build on whatever limited success is attained and to encourage work for more. Strict adherence to the regulations would defeat their objects. Against this it must be said that a child with the level of command of Irish which would qualify it for the *deontas* in eastern Corca Dhuibhne would probably be refused it in Gaoth Dobhair or in those parts of Cois Fharraige (south Conamara) where there are still plenty of children at school with good Irish from the home and where generous awards to backsliding neighbours would be resented by true Gaeilgeoirí (Irish speakers). Circumstances do alter cases and withholding grant may here be the best way to encourage the maintenance of

Irish in homes which have it naturally, are just beginning to neglect it, yet still want access to the full panoply of Gaeltacht grants to which the *deontas* award provides an essential key. Here it is not a matter of encouraging environmentally exotic efforts to bring the language back into use and prominence after the lapse of a generation, but of discouraging an ill-considered lapse into anglicization by a sharp shock sufficient to induce reflection and appropriate action in the home.

It is quite usual for refusal of the *deontas* to be accompanied by advice as to the action necessary to convince the inspector next time and the much bigger housing grants are graded according to how long it takes an applicant to attain the required language standard. This combines both 'stick' and 'carrot', but because of the weakness of the language 'sticks' are not much in evidence in the *deontas* statistics, which almost always reflect a sympathetic view of the anglicizing pressures to which the people of the Gaeltacht are subject.

The general impression is that semi-successful efforts to cultivate Irish in already anglicized districts receive rather more sympathetic treatment than semi-successful efforts by children from homes where it is known the parents are native speakers and doing little to transmit it to their offspring. Hence for anyone new to the study of the Gaeltacht the *deontas* figures for the wide expanses of Munster, Mid Galway, Mayo, south-west Donegal, the Rosses, and other districts which were already almost lost to Irish by 1956 will seem often too high, whereas those for the Gaeltacht 'cores' will seem reasonably accurate and even rather low, the lowness being due to the statistical complications outlined earlier. In the really weak areas such complications are compensated by liberality in making the award: except, that is, in the numerous cases where parents do not bother to apply for it.

It must not be supposed that the granting of the *deontas* as an encouragement is open-ended. If in a given year a number of applications are received on behalf of children in a school area that has made none for some time and if, as is usually the case, this upsurge of interest and enthusiasm results from the advent of a new head or other local language activist, Roinn na Gaeltachta will always respond with encouragement which, if the children's attainments in the language are fair, may extend to the *deontas* award, in anticipation of more substantial progress later. If such substantial progress fails to materialize and encouragement thus proves ineffectual this form of it will cease. Such is often the explanation of a sharp decline in several schools' *deontas* percentages since 1981–2, and several sharp increases result from the onset of encouragement in response to an increase in applications. It would be invidious to specify examples in either direction but the figures usually speak for themselves if taken together with my asterisked assessment (appendix 3) of the objective state of the language in the school area.

It is not the purpose of Roinn na Gaeltachta to be dispassionately objective but to encourage all subjective efforts to promote the language. The *deontas* figures must always be studied with this in mind, as it is only incidental to their purpose that they do happen to give a broadly sound indication of the main relativities of language distributions, with a few striking and superficially grotesque exceptions and many more minor ones which make perfect sense if attention is focused on the purpose of the Irish-speaking Scheme rather than on a strict interpretation (anyway not very easy) of the criteria laid down for the *deontas* award.

Permission to award the *deontas* in closely adjacent districts outside the Gaeltacht reflects the death of the language within its bounds and recognizes that good (or better) school work for Irish is to be found outside. Given that the basic purpose of the scheme is to extend the use of Irish and to expand the Gaeltacht (as has officially been done on several occasions), not just to preserve it, this is logical enough, though there is little evidence to correlate scholastic successes with any real advance in everyday use of Irish as an ordinary medium of daily intercourse in a normal rural community.

It is a pity to have to record that some apparent upsurges of renewed enthusiasm for Irish have a direct and crude material base which offers few prospects of sustained enthusiasm or real recovery to regular everyday use. The attraction of individual housing grants has already been mentioned but as these are widely diffused and not all people are likely to want them at once their impact on the *deontas* figures is likewise diffuse. Not so the grants for the building of community halls, for which major grants have been available for some years, conditional on evidence of active use of the language in the locality. If the language is plainly weak there the condition may be met by adult demand for Irish in evening classes, support for local *feiseanna* (Irish cultural festivals) and similar activities, and by evidence that real efforts are being made for Irish among children in the home. A close-knit community intelligently led and guided can quite quickly move itself to produce such evidence; but the few examples which the *deontas* figures led me to investigate suggested that such enthusiasm is ephemeral and disappears once the grant has been secured, or at least after a decent interval of no more than a year or two.

This is one of many reasons why many language workers deplore attempts to 'buy support' by 'paying people to speak Irish': not just because it demeans the nation but also because it does not work. On the other hand it may be argued that a small financial incentive may give the initial impetus to parents to introduce their children to a language which they go on to cultivate and love. Unless the children remain free from the environmental influences which led to parental neglect in the first place, it is likely that such cultivation and love will remain minority charac-teristics; but, again, the creation or preservation of an Irish-cultivating minority can only be regarded as a desirable gain when the alternative is uninterrupted progress towards extinction.

New in recent years but likely to become a permanent influence tending to increase the *deontas* figures in many schools is the establishment in their vicinity of Irish-language pre-school playgroups, or *naíonraí*, generously supported and sometimes even initiated by Údarás na Gaeltachta, the Gaeltacht Authority, which works in parallel with Roinn na Gaeltachta and has hitherto been most noted for its support for Gaeltacht industry. Fifty-three *naíonraí* were in operation in 1986–7 and where they can be associated clearly with a Gaeltacht national school the latter has been annotated in appendix 3 with an N after its figures. It is not clear that the presence of a *naíonra* has made a radical difference to the *deontas* achievements in a school, but several heads and teachers commended the *naíonraí* as a great help to the rapid achievement of fluency in the reception class, speeding considerably progress towards full Irish-medium instruction, which of course signals a degree of fluency likely to qualify for the *deontas*. The groups are, nevertheless, voluntary and run by parents, and attendance is not compulsory. Only two of the fifty-three had more than ten children in April 1986.

The distribution of *naíonraí* covers a wide range of local language situations, from very weak to quite strong, with a natural tendency towards the better populated parts of the latter, where numbers are more likely to be 'economic' and interested parents cannot but be aware of the threat to the language from the dominance of English-language television in the pre-school home of the strongest Gaeltacht areas. Údarás would like *naíonraí* in every primary school area but it is not always possible to assemble sufficient interested parents willing to pay their own contributions, nor to find a suitable director or an available and properly equipped building.

Parallel to the *naíonraí* as a generally lesser influence on the strength of Irish is the distribution of *coláistí samhraidh* (summer colleges), to which children from the Galltacht come on scholarships to improve their Irish by several weeks' residence in the Gaeltacht. Forty-two were scheduled for summer 1987. Another twelve were to be held outside the Gaeltacht in centres which in this case usually have their own residential accommodation and miss the benefits of placing the children in Gaeltacht homes as happens at most of the rest, with considerable financial benefit to the host families. The latter, who are subject to the same commitment if they board 'Gael-Linn children', must promise to speak Irish all the time the college child is present, and this is commonly declared to be a very good local influence for Irish in some homes that might otherwise not be so attentive. However, each college is organized independently under the auspices of the Dublin-based Comhdháil Náisiúnta na Gaeilge (lit. National Convention of the Irish Language), arrangements for boarding differ widely, and abuses of the scheme as a 'money-spinner' in the Gaeltacht and a cheap holiday by the sender families, both neglectful of Irish, have necessitated a recent tightening up, with more rigid selection of the beneficiaries at both ends. Even so, one college is notorious for allowing the boarding of over ten children at a time in some of its homes, plainly defeating the purpose of their sharing a natural Irish family atmosphere; and examples elsewhere showed by the small number of homes which they used that not many in their vicinity were linguistically or otherwise suitable.

Ideally a summer college encourages local people (including children) to feel greater pride in their Irish because of strangers actually paying to come to learn it, and encourages them to make more use of it themselves – which should show in the *deontas* figures. I have identified no example where high *deontas* figures seemed wholly or largely due to this cause and it should be noted that the college students are between 10 and 18 years old, so only just touch the top of the primary range. Also, if selection of the Gaeltacht homes is done properly, their children should qualify for the *deontas* without this extra impetus. Schools with a college near them are nevertheless identified by a C after their figures in appendix 3 to draw attention to this evidence of additional language promotion as part of their setting. As some are at places where Irish is almost dead among the children – e.g. Teileann/Teelin (south-west Donegal), Minaird/Minard (west Kerry) and Baile an Sceilg/Ballinskelligs (south-west Kerry) – they cannot be expected to be an influence other than on the margin.

Most of the officers responsible for awarding the grant confess to occasional doubts about their own decisions in particular cases, because they have to make a clear decision for or against an award in linguistic circumstances which are normally very complex in Gaeltacht homes. There is a natural tendency to feel more generous towards a home in which one parent is 'married in' with no Irish and yet has a child with a modest command of Irish, compared with a home with two fluent native-speaker parents whose child has only a similar modest command. And where neither parent is a native speaker but both are using their own school-Irish to help the child towards fluency by speaking in (admittedly stilted and imperfect) Irish for parts of the day at home the merits of the case easily incline the inspector away from the requirement that Irish should be *the* language of the home, narrowly interpreted. Introduction of a standardized oral test to produce a consistent and uniform pattern of awards would be possible but subject to evasion by drilled preparation and in any case would remove the flexibility which does allow the inspectors to adjust their application of the scheme to the wide range of circumstances encountered.

A final possibility to be taken into account when using the *deontas* figures is that of sheer error of judgement by the inspector, apart from the normal hazards of errors in summation or transcription, as occurred with the Trian Lár/Trean Middle and Caisleán na Mine Airde/Minard Castle figures for 1981–2. There were in 1987 six officers sharing the burden of the scheme, with other jobs to do as well. Just over 4,000 primary children received the award in 1985–6, i.e. on average 670 per officer. All had to have the award validated by an officer. In addition of course each officer was responsible for an unstated number of rejected awards, which presumably needed even more attention, as a parental right to appeal against rejection is respected if not written into the regulations. Where a family has established itself as soundly Irish-speaking it is unlikely that all its children in school (five is still not unusual) will be examined annually, and if the inspection takes place in the home (unusual outside Munster: see p. 51) the extra travel by the inspector will be balanced by the economies of seeing the entire family at once. Nevertheless it is obvious that the burden of numbers is immense, given that at least each family should be dealt with individually, and if the school manager and head support poorly justified applications which they leave the inspector to detect it is inevitable that he will sometimes remain hoodwinked, simply because of lack of time plus willingness to believe and trust the local authorities who are in a position to know, but who also are subject to parental and wider social pressures within the Gaeltacht community.

Here again the problem is not usually one of downright mendacity, much as it feels it when being assured by respectable people in positions of considerable trust that the children in their area all speak Irish excellently and are devoted to it, whereas the infants in the playground are playing loudly in English and the teenagers of whom one enquired directions were chatting in English when interrupted. The assurance is not untrue, but it is only part of the truth and very creditable to the school, given the rest of the truth, which is that English has often become the first language of the children of such districts. Heads and teachers are then very pleased to have achieved Irish fluency in the children and are usually unwilling to discourage them (and their parents) by objecting that the fluency falls short of a native ease and idiom, is not reflected in habitual use outside school, and shows very little sign of everyday use in the home. They may warn the parents of this privately or even in a local public meeting, but they will not usually tell a visiting inspector, let alone a casual visitor such as myself. Some will, and I found on visiting schools that teachers who were defensive or evasive if asked directly about the state of Irish in the district would give considerable detail if I made it clear that my main concern was to ascertain the problems met by the school in bringing the younger children up to the necessary standard of fluency for the lessons (except English) to be conducted entirely in Irish, as is the case in all the Gaeltacht core area.

In a minority of cases I was assured by heads on enquiry that a significant fall in the *deontas* proportions for their school between 1981–2 and 1985–6 was caused by their having explained to the inspector that the scale of awards was too high in terms of native Irish and that some families who were receiving it gave no support at home. Another, larger minority assured me that was so but asked me not to tell the inspector, as they wished to maintain good relations with the parents! Elsewhere a head confronted by high awards for his school in an area now plainly primarily English-speaking and known as such throughout the wider district believed that a high rate of awards was given because the school had a tradition of a high rate of awards! The inspectors either had not noticed the change or for a variety of reasons did not choose to record it.

Pressure on the officers is increased by illness in their ranks; during my last tour one of the six was on sick leave and another had retired without replacement. An inspector from the Munster office was examining for the *deontas* in Gaoth Dobhair (Donegal) schools, to help out a hard-pressed colleague. Because Munster Irish is very different from Donegal or Connacht Irish, this sort of eventuality leads to a popular but ill-founded 'explanation' of low *deontas* figures in some areas and by some parents, namely that the inspector spoke to the child or children in the 'wrong' dialect, so confused it into silence, and failed a good Irish-speaking child because it allegedly could not answer a simple Irish question. This is highly improbable. The inspectors are fully sensitive to the dialect differences, enjoy and respect them, and would be far more likely to give credit for proficiency in good dialectal Irish than to mark it down. Good dialect is clear evidence of native Irish, which is what the scheme seeks to promote. The inspectors are also well able to recognize a child that has 'frozen' in interview and are pleasant enough to help it unfreeze: except just possibly on a 'bad day', in a great hurry at the end of a day, or in other human circumstances of the sort which inevitably cause the occasional lapse of judgement and lead to the multiplication of apocryphal stories which are mainly elaborate parental excuses for the failure of children whose weak Irish did not merit their passing.

Parallel with the 'wrong dialect' excuse for *deontas* failure is the wider one that the inspector in a particular case spoke stilted 'Gaeilge B'l'Áth' ('Dublin Irish'), the artificial synthetic norm created by the state for official publications and taught in all schools outside the Gaeltachtaí as well as in most schools in the parts of the latter where Irish is no longer the vernacular. This is sometimes called Nua-Ghaeilge (new Irish) and may indeed cause a few problems in very marginal cases. Even so, almost all the Gaeltacht inspectors are native speakers with responsibilities in their own province of birth, so are inspecting schools with whose dialect they are fully conversant, however much their own prolonged education in and through the medium of Irish may have modified their usual speech towards the standard.

Standard Irish has a vastly greater vocabulary of modern terms than the dialects, but of course in fields utterly irrelevant to the *deontas* inspection. It is almost inconceivable that any child should fail the *deontas* exam for anything to do with this. If, as is sometimes alleged, this used to happen when the Department of Education school inspectors were responsible for the award, the author would retort that he interviewed all of them in 1956–7, plus their Chief Inspector in Dublin, and they too were as fully aware of the nuances of the language situation as are their successors under Roinn na Gaeltachta and showed every ability to recognize and deal with the difficulties which they are alleged to have ignored. Their sense of power and authority was, however, much greater than could be felt by any state officials at the present day, and if they made a mistake it would have been less likely to be challenged by teachers whose bonus payments they directly influenced. Even so, I met no examples where more than an isolated individual injustice was alleged, and the same is true today.

The broad statistical validity of the *deontas* figures is not affected by this factor, and there is greater danger of their objectivity being destroyed by the inspectors' own direct personal and professional involvement in local revival work in state-financed community language projects which they quite properly wish to see succeed and, as they are personally involved, cannot readily view with complete impartiality. The tendency to see profound sustained success where the experienced outsider sees commendable but shallowly rooted progress is natural, not least when the inspector's own ideas are being put to the test by friends and co-workers in the language movement who share them. The author had only a single case of this sort drawn to his attention by the highly unusual circumstance of its current *deontas* figures appearing to show a major improvement in the strength of Irish since 1957. This will be examined in the regional section but to identify it here would be to exaggerate its significance.

Nevertheless similar cases are liable to arise and there have been several in the past, the results of which have never included sustained recovery. It is impossible to prove the success or failure of such a local revival effort except with time and it would also be unfair to blame Roinn na Gaeltachta for too readily accepting the first enthusiastic steps as evidence of merit at *deontas* level, given that widespread refusal might well trigger the onset of disillusionment and abandonment of an effort which above all needs faith and confidence to sustain it.

Thanks to the economic advances of the last thirty-odd years one major distorting influence on the *deontas* figures, mentioned in 1957 by the most senior Department of Education officer who advised me, has become almost wholly redundant. It was sheer human sympathy for abject poverty. This wise, experienced, and utterly responsible man described the squalor he had met in many Gaeltacht homes in his inspecting days, and confessed that while he applied the regulations meticulously, if there were doubts in his mind because the children's fluency did not seem quite

61

good enough for it to be *the* language of the home, he sometimes flinched in the face of abject poverty and felt tempted to 'give the poor devils the money...' The needs may now be better met by other means, but marginal cases are undoubtedly plentiful and it would be difficult to believe that the benefit of the doubt did not still prevail, if with less burning urgency than in the 1930s or 1940s.

After all these warnings the reader may well conclude that the *deontas* figures are as unreliable as the census as a guide to Irish-language maintenance and survival. This is not so, for cases demanding special attention are relatively few and gross exaggerations which are typical in the census returns are no more than a handful and do have special local justifications which are real even if not always entirely convincing. Attention is here drawn to special cases because they *are* special and disturb the normal pattern, which combines reliability in rank order with mild benevolence in the grant of the award. Thirty-nine of the 152 school areas in appendix 3 are double-asterisked to warn that the work of the school has taken the *deontas* figures much higher than my own evidence suggests is its first-language status among the children; but as well over half these returned between 20 and 50 per cent, well inside the range in which serious weakness is self-evident, the distortion is not as dangerous as above 50 per cent, where one ought to be able to expect genuine majorities of habitual native speakers. The single asterisks in appendix 3 which denote school areas in which Irish is effectively dead for the vast majority of children are confirmed by percentages between zero and 20, representing odd exceptional families maintaining native Irish or cultivating the acquired language.

Gross understatement of the strength of Irish occurs in the *deontas* figures for Toraigh/Tory Island (Donegal) and Dún Chaoin/Dunquin (Kerry) for special local reasons which will be dealt with in the regional survey which follows (pp. 68, 112 and 114).

There has been no upper age limit to the award of the *deontas* since about 1964. Suffice it to say that potential distorting influences manifestly increase with length of schooling, so it is not considered appropriate to attempt a Gaeltacht-wide assessment based on secondary school statistics – the more so as Gaeltacht children so frequently receive secondary education outside the Gaeltacht in schools whose catchment areas would make analysis on an area basis extremely hazardous.

Approaches to the regional survey

It has been conventional for many years to publish census Gaeltacht figures aggregated into county units, the counties themselves arranged under provinces. The latter is convenient, as the surviving language subdivides into three distinct Ulster, Connacht, and Munster provincial dialect groups which are sufficiently different to cause many native speakers to switch off when Raidió na Gaeltachta broadcasts in other than their own, discrimination being most common against Donegal (Ulster) Irish, which is very distinctive and often closer to Scottish Gaelic. (See p. 173.) Otherwise arrangement by county gives a false impression that there is a unified and territorially contiguous Gaeltacht in each county, which is not the case even in terms of the official Gaeltacht boundaries of 1956–82. The 1956 redefinition seriously overstated the territorial extent of Irish prevalence from the beginning, and subsequent decline has reinforced a pattern of fragmentation which is fundamental to the linguistic geography of every Gaeltacht county except Waterford, which has only a single tiny Gaeltacht.

The survey which follows will maintain a county order under provinces arranged geographically from north to south, but with the exceptional 'Gaeltacht colonies' in Co. Meath (Leinster) left until last. Each separate Gaeltacht 'pocket' within each county will be discussed separately and the Dúiche Sheoigheach/Joyce's Country Gaeltacht, which overlaps Galway and Mayo, will be treated as one instead of being divided (as in the censuses) between its two counties. The appendices follow the same order.

For each Gaeltacht county except Meath there are three accompanying maps. One shows the district electoral divisions of the Gaeltacht and renders their names in Irish as spelt in the 1981 census volumes. It serves as a map 'key' to appendix 4. The second maps the Gaeltacht national schools which feature in appendix 3 and renders their names almost invariably in the Irish orthography approved by the Place-names Branch of the Ordnance Survey. A few other names are featured because they occur in the text, as also are several important Galltacht places which help to fix location. The third map for each county synthesizes the findings of my 1987 survey and the deductions made by comparisons with the statistical analysis in appendices 3–5. It divides the Gaeltachtaí into four grades of strength and weakness and should enable the interested visitor to proceed with accuracy to communities which fall into the respective categories – unless sudden and recent change has taken place. An exception is made for Co. Meath, which because of the small size of its two 'Gaeltacht colonies' is given only one general location map, which also incorporates the language categorization of the two school areas.

The regional survey concludes with a review of the state of the language in the Galltacht, i.e. the rest of Ireland, and attempts to assess the extent to which new Irish-speaking communities may be seen to be emerging there, whether north or south of the Border.

State of the Gaeltacht 1987: National
- 1. Fíor-Ghaeltacht: primarily Irish-speaking in all age-groups
- 2. Breac-Ghaeltacht: partly Irish-speaking:
    - (a) Upper Transitional Zone: more Irish than English
    - (b) Lower Transitional Zone: more English than Irish
- 3. Effective Galltacht: primarily English speaking
- 4. Mainly uninhabited parts of Gaeltacht DEDs: 'buffer zone'
- 5. Points of doubt, possibly ranked too highly

Base boundary lines are those of DEDs within or partly within the Gaeltacht: solid if 80% (or more) Irish speaking, Census 1981, hatched for rest including parts outside official Gaeltacht.

Map 11 Final analysis 1987: the state of Irish within the official Gaeltacht. Gaeltacht district names in English. Sources: census 1981; *deontas* returns 1981–2, 1985–6; field survey 1987

Chapter five

Gaeltachtaí of Ulster

Co. Dhún na nGall/Donegal

The sole surviving Gaeltachtaí of Ulster are in west Donegal.

Cloch Chionnaola, Gaoth Dobhair, agus Na Rosa/Cloghaneely, Gweedore and the Rosses: north-west Donegal

Since the death of the language in the Glens of Antrim around 1940, its passing in the Sperrins and on Rathlin in the 1960s and its steady abandonment in the rest of the official Donegal Gaeltacht this district has become the last stronghold of Ulster Irish. 'Foothold' might be the more appropriate word, as strength is everywhere lacking. Some native Irish survives in the villages of An Fál Carrach/Falcarragh and Anagaire/Annagary, which mark the edges of its inner core, but as long ago as 1957 young mothers in Gort an Choirce/Gortahork who could not speak Irish excused themselves because they came from Falcarragh.

In the Lower Rosses around Dungloe and Burtonport (an Clochán Líath and Ailt na Chorráin: but the Irish names are seen only on signposts) Irish has been disused for many years. The area is often called 'Pa's Gaeltacht', after P. A. O'Donnell, who was the local TD (Member of the Dáil) and a government minister at the time the boundary was drawn. When the author in 1957 remarked on the unusual quality of the road to Burtonport – Gaeltacht roads were (and some still are) notoriously bad – he was told it was 'Pa O'Donnell's road' and the minister lived at the end of it. 'Patronism and clientelism' are characteristic features of Irish politics, more visible than in major urban industrial countries where numbers help concealment and anonymity. In short, the Lower Rosses (excluding Árainn Mhór/Aranmore) should not have been 'Gaeltacht' in 1956. It is regrettable but typical of most Gaeltachtaí that all these named places were major village centres for the real Gaeltacht core, which here lay in the district around Cnoc Fola/Bloody Foreland ('the Foreland', normally) including Gort an Choirce to the east and more especially the

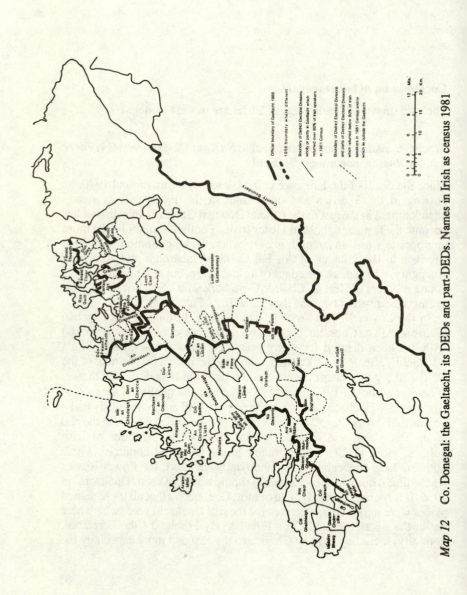

Map 12 Co. Donegal: the Gaeltacht, its DEDs and part-DEDs. Names in Irish as census 1981

Official boundary of Gaeltacht 1956

1956 boundary where different

Boundary of District Electoral Divisions
wholly or partly in Gaeltacht which
returned over 80% of Irish speakers
in 1981 Census

Boundary of District Electoral Divisions
and parts of District Electoral Divisions
which returned below 80% of Irish
speakers in 1981 Census and/or
which lie outside the Gaeltacht

County Boundary

0 1 2 3 6 9 12 Mls.
0 5 10 15 20 Km.

well-populated Doirí Beaga-An Bun Beag (Derrybeg/Bunbeg) district of Gaoth Dobhair to the south, where major industrial developments since around 1965 have created a 'rural town' in the true Gaeltacht, attracting banks and other facilities which have broken the dominance of the peripheral anglicized villages but combined with the new factories to set up powerful anglicizing influences of their own.

All schools from just west of Gort an Choirce (excluded) west and south to Dobhar/Dore (also excluded) had 1985–6 *deontas* majorities which reflected a persistence of native Irish in the district, but most heads and teachers to whom I spoke confessed that three-quarters of the children now arrived speaking English as their first language, though they quickly picked up Irish, as they heard it often in the home. The medium of instruction was Irish but it took some months getting them up to the standard to benefit from it. Local naíonraí helped but not all children attended, so reception classes were linguistically very mixed. Most schools enforced a rule that no English must be spoken in school or playground and it appeared to be obeyed; but no one believed it extended further. The main cause of the manifest collapse since I last conducted studies in the area in 1970 was the success of the Gaoth Dobhair industrial estate, which drew back large numbers of emigrants with skills now at last valued at home and with wives and children married and born when abroad, usually in Britain.

Helpful teachers asked the children in their class who had been born or lived in 'England' (which covered Scotland) to put up their hands for me. It looked a majority but in any case was ample to show the difficulty of maintaining native Irish. The native-speaking children were mostly impressed by their fellows from the exotic English-speaking world of the 'big city', which they knew only from the 'telly', and as they themselves were permeated with television-English absorbed through most of their leisure hours they were only too pleased to practise their own on the newcomers. One little girl who was making fair progress with Irish was thrilled to hear I was from Bradford, for so was she. Teaching such children successfully through Irish is a splendid achievement – few are first-language Irish, if they know it at all on arrival – but one can have no confidence that they will transmit it as mother tongue to the next generation. For children who arrive after the reception class the plunge into the Irish medium can induce culture shock, with strong adverse reactions, but all the local children now speak English by the time they arrive at school, so no child is utterly isolated, and sensible sympathetic teachers bend the all-Irish rule or feign deafness to avoid this.

It was instructive to have a Cloch Chionnaola class asked in my presence what its favorite television programmes were. I did not expect the answer to be an Irish-language programme, for few exist; but the answer was 'Dallas' (American), 'Coronation Street', and 'Emmerdale

Farm' (British). They were thrilled that I lived in a Yorkshire dale.

The residual Irish-speaking core of Cloch Chionnaola and Gaoth Dobhair measures thirteen miles in length along the inhabited coastal road route from Gort an Choirce to Dobhar and nine by the largely uninhabited direct main road. It includes a strong little outlier in Rinn na Feirsde/Rannafast in its broad peninsula south of An Bun Beag and a weaker and more isolated one at Mín na Manrach/Meenamara around its fourteen-pupil school in the depopulated upland south of Loch an Iúir/Loughanure. The main inhabited coastal strip is never more than two miles wide and is usually narrower.

Appendix 4 gives statistical estimates of the residual effective Irish-speaking population of this north-west Donegal Gaeltacht, based on the 1981 census returns and the application to them of calculations based on the strength of the *deontas* returns for 1985–6 (as in appendix 3). The tables should be studied together with the distribution map 14. There is considerable mismatch between school catchment areas and DED boundaries but not sufficient to make estimation difficult. In compiling data for the minimum Irish-speaking population three sets of school *deontas* percentages have exceptionally been raised to put them in the 70 per cent class. Mín an Chladaigh/Meenaclady and An Luinneach/Lunniagh schools serve Mín an Chladaigh DED, and their proportion of infants is held to justify lifting their *deontas* percentages from 68 and 69·4 respectively to above 70 for this purpose.

Toraigh/Tory Island (63·6 per cent) is in the same DED and is accepted by all authorities as the most solidly Irish community in Donegal. This seemed odd but enquiry revealed that eight of the twenty-two pupils were aged under 6 years on 1 January 1986, so its 63·6 per cent was 100 per cent of those eligible. The initially shattering 47·2 per cent of 1981–2 (see appendix 3) is utterly misleading, for very good reasons: the thirty-six numbered on the rolls related to 30 September 1981, but only twenty-one remained by summer 1982, when seventeen received the *deontas* (80·95 per cent) – again all those eligible, because four were under-age. Fifteen pupils had meanwhile left with their families in March or April for resettlement on the mainland at An Fál Carrach/Falcarragh, after a long dispute which split the community over the question of total evacuation but was not concerned with language matters. There has been some drift back since 1982. Only one Toraigh home had a non-Gaeltacht parent 'married in' in 1987 and the one child spoke Irish fluently, having picked it up at school at play with friends, who were pleased to use their blossoming English to help her Irish.

The general points to be made here are the exaggerated statistical significance of small variations in the numbers of children under 6 when total numbers in a school are already small, and the vast significance of quite a small outward movement when it constitutes a high proportion of an island's population. Árainn Mhór, a much larger, more populous, and inshore island has been worried about evacuation as long as I remember it, and Gabhla/Gola was evacuated in the 1960s.

Small islands suffer the extremes of Gaeltacht 'deprivation', i.e. lack of ready access to urban amenities as well as doctors and hospitals, and are inclined to panic when emigration leaves them with too few men to man a boat. Two-way radios and emergency helicopters have allayed the worst fears. Now that secondary schooling is expected it usually involves boarding on the mainland and leads to skills which bar ultimate return to the island. The television, now in every home, wildly inflates the islanders' ideas of what they are missing. Partial evacuation to (for them) expensive council properties at An Fál Carrach has dampened such ideas on Toraigh, where Irish is as safe as anywhere, even allowing for growing fluency in English and the death of the old monoglot Irish speakers whose presence made the use of Irish essential until a generation ago.

Árainn Mhór's Irish was dying among the young of its eastern half, round the quay, over thirty years ago, but this was only just beginning to spread to the Aphort school area in the south-west. Emigration was blamed and the island population continued to decline, from 1,131 in 1956 to 773 in 1971, recovering to 803 in 1981. It was 1,461 in 1926. All external links are through long-anglicized Burtonport, till 1940 the terminus of the railway to Derry. The abandonment of Irish has continued and English is now the first language of all but a small proportion of the children in all districts. There are two small Údarás-assisted enterprises, compared with six, mostly larger, at Burtonport and nine at Dungloe (Dunglow), which as the anglicized centre of the Lower Rosses also has a major factory (Údarás Report 1985: 1986c).

Dobhar/Dore school was fairly represented with 47 per cent *deontas* awards but is really on the language boundary, its percentage representing the aggregation of children drawn from the more anglicized interior districts of Dún Lúiche/Dunlewy, Torr, and Croithlí/Crolly, with others from a stronger district around and north-west of it. Anglicization arrived early here, with 'planter' influence in the beautiful glen at Dún Lúiche and much improved access via the diminutive Londonderry and Lough Swilly Railway at the start of this century. School closures and amalgamation resulting from rural depopulation and changing ideas about minimum numbers and educational requirements in schools here created a linguistically mixed school catchment area for Dobhar, with the usual consequences for the Irish language despite the school's efforts in Irish-medium instruction; but here as elsewhere in Gaoth Dobhair the main threat no longer comes from across a language boundary round the edge of the Gaeltacht but from the television in every home and the family car outside, giving access in an hour or two to metropolitan Letterkenny and even Derry city – both of them to the older generation places men visited

69

twice a year on the way to or from seasonal work in Scotland, or which both sexes passed through once only, when emigrating.

Rinn na Feirsde's strong Irish is in part sustained by the fame of its early Irish college (*c*. 1907), but it must be noted that although Machaire Robhairtaigh/Magheraroarty shares the same benefit it has not saved Loch an Iúir, which has been struggling to avoid subsiding into English for at least thirty years but is now far gone. It is on the main road and was near the railway too.

All north-west Donegal teachers complained about a lack of good Irish school textbooks for most subjects, a complaint common in all the living Gaeltachtaí. All agreed that most Irish texts were written for learners and unsuitable for native speakers. (See p. 185.) Matters are made worse in Donegal by the individuality of Donegal Irish. Only 1,209 primary children qualified for the *deontas* in the entire county in 1985–6 and only 935 were in or close to this north-western heartland where alone the native dialect persists fairly strongly. A group of teachers was meeting in 1987 to prepare its own texts but with such numbers the chances of achieving quality of content or production to compete with the attractions of mass-marketed English texts for bilingual Gaeltacht children are small, even with state financial backing.

A related factor less powerful as an influence towards English in primary schools here than in any other Gaeltacht except south Conamara is the influence of the secondary schools. Many Gaeltacht children nationally attend secondary schools in traditional centres outside the truly Irish-speaking districts and in which Irish is not the normal medium of instruction. (See pages 166, 204.) The Gaoth Dobhair district now has its own *pobalscoil*/community school (similar to a comprehensive) in which Irish does have the major role, but its numbers of pupils (380 in September 1985) reflect a 'leakage' to its rival at An Fál Carrach (761 pupils), which makes little use of Irish as a teaching medium. Southerly districts tend to prefer to attend Dungloe, in a long anglicized setting.

Gaoth Dobhair and Cloch Chionnaola are hardly big enough to sustain a self-sufficient Irish-speaking community even if there are the 5,656 habitual native speakers that the larger estimate (appendix 4) allows. If the lower 1,944 is near to correct there is cause for alarm. There were by 1985–6 only ten primary schools with a majority of pupils in receipt of the *deontas*, the recipients totalling 697. If Toraigh and Mín an Chladaigh were added (for reasons already stated) to the three schools with 70 per cent or more of *deontas* recipients they made a total of five, with 226 such pupils. 'Mixed marriages' by returned emigrants while abroad have been adduced as a major adverse influence against Irish in connection with the Gaoth Dobhair industrial estate. With such school numbers and so few high concentrations of Irish speakers in the schools it is difficult to envisage linguistically mixed marriages being other than the norm for present-day Irish-speaking children here.

Thirty years ago most adult able-bodied males of normal working age were absent from north-west Donegal for much of the year on seasonal work in Britain, from which they sent (or brought) back earnings which kept the Irish language alive, secure with the mothers. Gang work helped the men preserve their own Irish and the community survived because unlike the emigrants they did come home. Emigration was nevertheless high and ran in parallel and all intelligent local people could see that the Gaeltacht was dying of attrition. Séamus Ó Raghallaigh, an inspiring regional officer for Roinn an Gaeltachta, himself an Irish 'learner' from Belfast with a long experience of Irish College work before he joined An Roinn, initiated the idea of an industrial estate in Gaoth Dobhair and organized the entrepreneurs to get it underway. The danger that success might 'bring in English' and kill the Gaeltacht was fully appreciated; but it was already dying of emigration and slow depopulation. No DED in 1971 had more than 77 per cent of its 1926 population, Anagaire falling as low as 50 per cent and the rest in between, except interior Cró Beithe/ Crovehy, which was down to 42 per cent and a mere 226 people. To halt depopulation by offering Irish speakers jobs at home in modern industries of the sort common throughout the Western world, including high technology as well as advanced developments of indigenous textiles, seemed the best hope of preserving this exceptionally densely populated Irish-speaking community. This would also convince it that a normal working life with normal modern career prospects – not just one for the small elite with pretensions in education, the Church, or the bureaucracy – could be pursued and reach fulfilment through the medium of Irish.

It was appreciated that managers and skilled men would need to be brought in for the new industries, but plenty of potential leaders and recruits were known among Irish-speaking emigrants who were readily persuaded to return. Large grants were given to foreign and native firms willing to invest here, always tied to conditions which sought to assure the supremacy of Irish on the shop floor and wherever possible in management and the offices. Cynics not only questioned the sanity of locating modern industry in an area like this, lacking in most resources except people, devoid of infrastructure (bad roads, an atrocious telephone service, no piped water, electricity just arrived), but also predicted the disruption of the language community as an inevitable consequence. 'O Raghallaigh and his collaborators and backers took the robust view that the state owed modern employment opportunities to the people of the Gaeltacht, that the haemorrhage of emigration had to be stopped if there was to be any hope of language survival, and that if the language could not survive such manifest social and economic benefits it hardly deserved to survive. The language, after all, exists for the people, not vice-versa.

Successful industrial growth brought population increases, usually

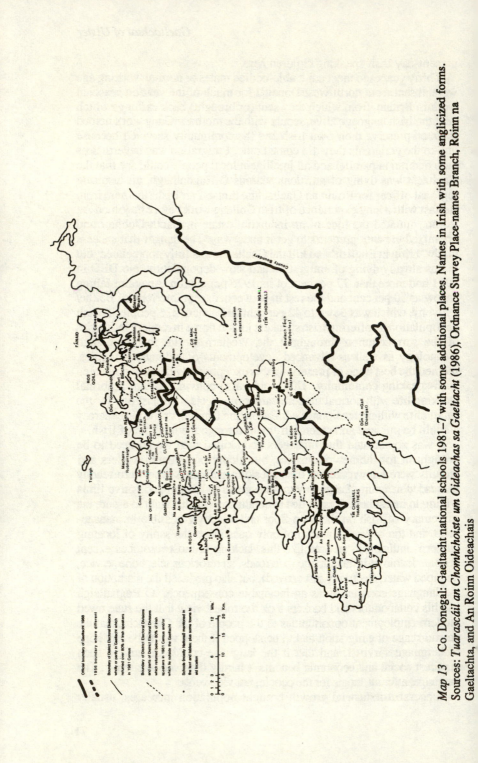

Map 13 Co. Donegal: Gaeltacht national schools 1981–7 with some additional places. Names in Irish with some anglicized forms.
Sources: *Tuarascáil an Chomhchoiste um Oideachas sa Gaeltacht* (1986), Ordnance Survey Place-names Branch, Roinn na Gaeltachta, and An Roinn Oideachais

substantial, to all the heartland DEDs in the decade 1971–81 while the interior glens continued to empty. The impact on the schools has been seen but despite resumed emigration since 1981 the numbers employed in Údarás-supported industry here have held remarkably steady. Yet it is a frequently stated fact of Gaeltacht life that all returned emigrants and seasonal migrants, however much they love Irish, are determined that their children will never feel as they did when they arrived in London, Glasgow, etc., with only broken English, 'poor Paddies' fit only for navvy work. All see English as of paramount importance for a career for the young and most put it first, before Irish.

When I first visited Cloch Chionnaola and Gaoth Dobhair in 1957 poverty made 'marrying in' exceptional. In a (then) mainly agricultural country girls never 'married up the hill' or on to a poorer farm. This potent defence against the entry of English-speaking mothers has now happily gone as the 'wealth gap' has been closed or even reversed. There used to be disproportionate numbers of elderly single people as well as women with husbands absent abroad.

It is pleasant to note that the boundaries of the extensive parish of Gaoth Dobhair are now marked with signs, in Irish only, saying 'Welcome to Gweedore'. Adjacent Cloch Chionnaola has no such signs, and it is typical that neither offers any formal welcome to the Gaeltacht as such (see p. 208), as well as disagreeing on whether to signal their presence at all.

Despite the serious weakening of Irish noted among the children, this is the second strongest of the Gaeltachtaí, i.e. one of the only three which most observers think may survive. The total population of the DEDs with 80 per cent or more of enumerated Irish speakers in the 1981 census was 12,008, the Irish speakers themselves 10,276. This was more than in Conamara and indeed in 1957 I had considered this at least as secure. Now, however, only 5,656 of the 1981 population can be counted as living in areas which maintained *deontas* majorities in 1985–6 and a mere 1,944 where those majorities exceeded 70 per cent. This latter is 20·8 per cent of the national total and amounts to 346 primary school children in six schools, three of which are included because they were very close to 70 per cent and local circumstances warrant it. There are altogether ten schools with a simple majority of *deontas* earners, but that says little about native habitual Irish, as has been seen.

The statistical base of the community which still speaks some Irish to its children as a normal part of home life is thus fundamentally defective and insufficient for the maintenance of a substantial socio-economic network at much above family level. The most elementary shopping requirements have to be met 'outside' and almost all paid employment is at places which fail the 70 per cent *deontas* test. Most local people consider the decline of the language to be terminal, and unless one is speaking of Irish as a second language all evidence supports that view.

Fánaid, Ros Goill, Gleann Bhairr, An Tearmann, etc./Fanad, Rosguill, Glenvar, Termon and the north-eastern outliers

These are for the most part examples of industrial inertia on the part of the Irish-language planning authorities. None of them had significant native Irish strength among the children in 1956 and neither H. Wagner's (1958a) dialect survey nor my own geolinguistic investigations found other than residual survival of Irish among the elderly or middle-aged. The fragmentary pattern of the new (1956) Gaeltacht boundaries represented a genuine attempt to include only those townlands (subdivisions of the DEDs) where there was some living Irish but English was the dominant vernacular in all of them and the limited Irish strength was mainly the artificial one of a decent fluency acquired by many children at school but scarcely at all reflected in their life outside. Irish summer colleges at Na Dúnaibh/Downings and Gleann Bhairr/Glenvar promoted some above-average interest in Irish but they depended on a handful of local and imported enthusiasts for survival and their wider impact on local use of the language was generally at 'token' level.

Deontas figures were strictly confidential in those days but I was reliably informed that although about 60 per cent of the children in north Fánaid received the *deontas* only 10 per cent made habitual use of Irish and the proportion was fast declining. This was the most strongly Irish district, and Ros Goill to the west was worse-off, though the peninsula at least had some native Irish among the children. The interior pockets seemed mainly to represent areas in which the school was doing exceptionally good work through the medium of Irish, and which the inspectors did not wish to discourage by deleting them from the Nua-Ghaeltacht. Even the Fánaid pocket amounted to only about twelve square miles and the rest were smaller, down to one or two, and all surrounded by totally anglicized districts which included all the villages.

Little wonder that they have now all died, the recent *deontas* figures denoting extinction thinly concealed by a certain generosity in continuing to recognize good school work in Irish in districts so English that this is very hard to achieve. Fluctuations such as the drop from 66 per cent *deontas* awards at An Caiseal/Cashel (in Fánaid) to 35 per cent in a mere four years must not be taken literally, as such falls are likely to represent a tailing off of 'encouragement' awards which have not proved efficacious and which therefore do not merit continuation. An Caiseal was the only school of twelve in the area to exceed 20 per cent of awards in 1985–6 and eight achieved 3 per cent or less. None of this meant anything for the survival of Irish as a community language. Gleann Bhairr's 27 per cent *deontas* return for 1981–2 was partly sustained by the Irish college, which died around 1984 of lack of interest and of genuinely Irish-speaking homes in which to accommodate the students. Hence the nil return for

1985–6. The retirement of old teachers who have dedicated their lives to the language always hit these residual pockets most severely – and of course made it more humanely possible for the inspectors to cease to pretend via the *deontas* figures that real success had been attained in maintaining the language in the homes as well as in the classroom.

Not all the schools listed in this area in appendix 3 are even in the official Gaeltacht, Dún Fionnachaidh/Dunfanaghy and Maigh Ráithe/Murroe being obvious examples, the latter with a better *deontas* score in 1985–6 than all but the Caiseal school. (See p. 56 above.) None of this area is true living Gaeltacht and it would be wrong to pretend anything to the contrary. Elderly native speakers still survive in the northern peninsulas, but it was their generation which began the failure to transmit Irish to the children by ceasing to use Irish in the home, where in nearly all cases it is now a foreign language to be learnt at school.

Tír Chonaill Láir/Mid Donegal

On general maps of the Donegal Gaeltacht this looks as if it belongs to a big homogeneous Gaeltacht bloc which includes the north-western core already discussed above. In fact it has always been isolated geographically from the north-west by wide expanses of uninhabited moorland and itself subdivided by broken ribbons of settlement in narrow upland valleys. I noted in 1957 the weakening of Irish around An Dúchoraidh/Doocharry in the Abhainn Ghaoth/Owenwee valley and this has now collapsed, as is hardly surprising with population figures by 1981 down to 37 per cent of 1926. This breaks any direct contact between the Irish majority area around Baile na Finne/Fintown and the Gaoth Dobhair district. All other directions have been into anglicized districts for all or most of this century and the roads all lead down-valley into anglicized service centres such as Na Gleannta/Glenties and Ballybofey (Bealach Féich, but entirely un-Irish in speech).

Applying the *deontas* criteria as in appendix 4 here produces a Gaeltacht core amounting only to Baile na Finne DED and a fragment of An Clochán/Cloghan, with a maximum habitually Irish-speaking community (all in Baile na Finne) of 248. Higher estimates were first arrived at but were abandoned because local enquiry showed the schools' *deontas* scores to be unusually out of line with local language habits. There are only two '*deontas*-majority' schools, anyway, but 78·6 per cent at Baile na Finne looked solid enough and 58·8 per cent (74·6 per cent in 1981–2) at An Coimín/Commeen was also in the usually 'real' range. It therefore came as a surprise to discover that at both places the language was nearly dead as a normal medium of daily intercourse and that only a minority of families sent children to school as native speakers with Irish as their first language. An tÉadan Anfach/Edeninfagh, west over the watershed from

Coimín, was in a similar state. All three schools maintained the Irish medium but co-operation and help from parents were slight except when a Gaeltacht grant was being sought. It seems clear that there would be few *deontas* awards anywhere in the district if the requirement of *native* Irish was strictly applied.

For most children Irish 'finishes with the national school', as almost all secondary education is in all-English schools at Glenties or Ballybofey, both of them places where no Irish is normally to be heard. A new all-Irish *gairmscoil* (vocational school) was set up at Béal an Átha Móir/Bellanamore about 1982–3, centrally placed to remedy this, but it has had extreme difficulty securing more than provisional (one year at a time) recognition from the Department of Education and there were only thirty-seven pupils on the roll in September 1985. There were about fifty-five in May 1987, with seven teachers. Enquiries showed that many pro-Irish people in the district were unwilling to risk their children's prospects by sending them to a school which might disappear before their courses ended and others were worried about the lack of subject choice with such numbers; but the wider reason attributed to the mass of the potential clientele was lack of respect for Irish and rejection of its value at secondary level. Given that Irish is no longer the preferred language in most homes, this seems very likely.

Parents and children prefer secondary education in a bigger school in a bigger place with the attraction of (some) urban amenities; and in English. Hostility to Irish was entirely denied by parents, but there was simply no interest in it, and young people were all thinking of careers outside the Gaeltacht and often outside Ireland. There was nothing new about this, even though the actual language collapse is commonly dated to the past decade or so. Baile na Finne's 1981 population was down to 45·5 per cent of 1926 and the adjacent DEDs of Gleann Léithín/Glenleheen and An Grafadh/Graffy were worse at 37 per cent and 40 per cent respectively. There have been few industrial developments, though Údarás (1985) supports two 'major' companies at Baile na Finne and three minor ones. None seems to deviate widely from the district's language norm. Nor does the local *comharchumann* (co-operative).

Mid Donegal may therefore be disregarded as an area with an active Irish-speaking community making collective efforts to maintain the language for future generations. Total depopulation is perhaps less of a major threat than before 1970 as the universal private car gives wider access to work. It has also made 'marrying in' more common and knocked another nail into the coffin of the language. As one teacher said to me, it is getting very difficult for a young native speaker to find another one to marry. Most do not try, for in such matters, as in so many things, language is not a centrally relevant consideration, if it features at all.

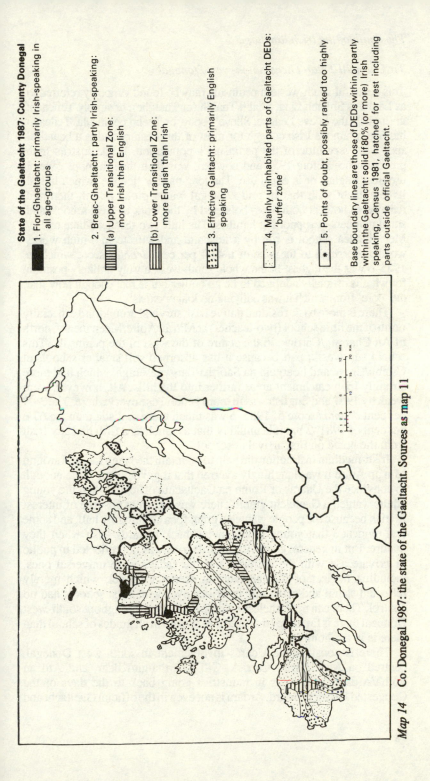

State of the Gaeltacht 1987: County Donegal

1. Fíor-Ghaeltacht: primarily Irish-speaking in all age-groups

2. Breac-Ghaeltacht: partly Irish-speaking:

   (a) Upper Transitional Zone: more Irish than English

   (b) Lower Transitional Zone: more English than Irish

3. Effective Galltacht: primarily English speaking

4. Mainly uninhabited parts of Gaeltacht DEDs: 'buffer zone'

5. Points of doubt, possibly ranked too highly

Base boundary lines are those of DEDs within or partly within the Gaeltacht: solid if 80% (or more) Irish speaking, Census 1981, hatched for rest including parts outside official Gaeltacht.

Map 14   Co. Donegal 1987: the state of the Gaeltacht. Sources as map 11

Tír Chonaill Thiar-Theas/South-west Donegal

This beautiful south-western peninsula may be found variously referred to as Leithinis Shliabh Liag, Sliabh Tuaidh (or Tuaighe), or simply Teileann: in English, the Slieve League, Slieve Tooey, or Teelin peninsula. Teileann has had a famous Irish college for most of this century and is a beautiful spot with very little of the peninsula's population. It had lost its Irish predominance before 1957 and nowhere was Irish then in more general use than English or in equal use. The long narrow 'tongue' which linked its Gaeltacht with that in mid Donegal was a pious fiction then and remains so now, at both times bolstered by the work of local schools and small numbers of supporting families. The little two-teacher Mínte na Dé/ Meentinadea school is run by a husband-and-wife team which works wonders for Irish to the tune of a 41·4 per cent *deontas* score which in 1985–6 was the highest in the whole south-west, a truly unlikely position for what is officially admitted to be an outlier but is real enough now that the 'core' from which it was outlying no longer exists.

There is more basic residual native Irish survival around and especially north of the little school (two-teacher) at Mín an Aoire/Meenaneary, north of An Charraig/Carrick, in the centre of the west of the peninsula. This school survives in part because it has absorbed still smaller schools at Cróibh/Crove and Leargain na Saortha/Largynaseragh, which had more strongly Irish catchment areas farther into the hills. All, however, were weak by 1957 and English was in more general use everywhere. The 34·9 per cent *deontas* score of 1985–6 was much more realistic than the 67·6 per cent of 1981–2 but it is unlikely that as much as a fifth had any Irish from the home on first arrival at school.

Irish-medium instruction did help to maintain the language, and around Mín an Aoire it was laughingly averred that it gave people quite enough to convince the Údarás or Roinn na Gaeltachta officials when the young adults wanted a Gaeltacht grant! There was a current upsurge of interest in Irish because the people wanted a grant for a community hall, and some real evidence that young adults swing back towards Irish when they mature. But in general goodwill towards Irish was not reflected in public or private use with the children and the causes were universal ones, including neglect of the language at secondary level, which merely reflected social and economic priorities over which the schools had no control. There can nevertheless be little doubt that throughout south-west Donegal there is far more Irish used and spoken in all grades of school than there is in the homes.

There is considerable Údarás involvement in south-west Donegal, centred on An Charraig/Carrick, Cill Charthaigh/Kilcar, and Ard an Rátha/Ardara, with roots in industries going back to the days of the Congested Districts Board. Ardara is not even in the official Gaeltacht and the other two centres are as anglicized as *deontas* figures of 11 and 8 per cent suggest. Returned emigrants play a part in depressing Irish around Mín an Aoire, which is close to An Charraig, but their influence is marginal and late in a decline already far advanced by 1957.

Chapter six

Gaeltachtaí of Connacht (Connaught)

Co. Mhaigh Eo/Mayo

There are three separate Gaeltacht areas in Mayo, according to the official map, and the first such map after the official revision in 1956 distinguished five separate 'cores', describing the rest as included for reasons other than the current strength of the language there (*Límistéirí Gaeltachta* 1956; and see map 9). All these cores were tiny and most did not stand up to detailed investigation, at least as purported 'districts in which Irish speakers formed a large proportion of the population'. The main expanse of the north-west Mayo Gaeltacht is often referred to derogatorily as 'Lindsay's Gaeltacht', as P. J. ('Pat') Lindsay was a Mayo TD and the (first) Minister for the Gaeltacht responsible for drawing the new boundaries – in conjunction with 'Pa' O'Donnell, who, already mentioned in Donegal, was Minister of Local Government. The implication is that the boundaries were drawn wide to include as many beneficiaries of 'Gaeltacht' subsidies as possible, to curry electoral favour.

Local enquiries in 1956–7 revealed a complex linguistic situation in most of Iorras/Erris, the old barony that covers most of the contested territory. Most adults could speak Irish but although a big proportion of children understood Irish on first arrival at school the percentage who spoke it fluently in keeping with their age was very low. One observer could therefore truly gather that everyone in Iorras spoke Irish where another could conclude that little Irish was used.

I was able in 1987 to ask Mr Lindsay, living in retirement on Eanach Bhán/Annaghvaan, in the Conamara islands, for his own views on the subject. He, a former senior counsel (equivalent to QC) at the Four Courts, was pungent in his justification for drawing the Gaeltacht generously. A native speaker himself from Dubh Loch/Doolough, in Iorras, he professed himself sickened by the bureaucratic niggling of Dublin officials, themselves not native speakers, sticking to and abusing the letter of the law in order to refuse grants to impoverished Irish speakers. He wanted to help the maximum number of Irish speakers, including deserving learners on

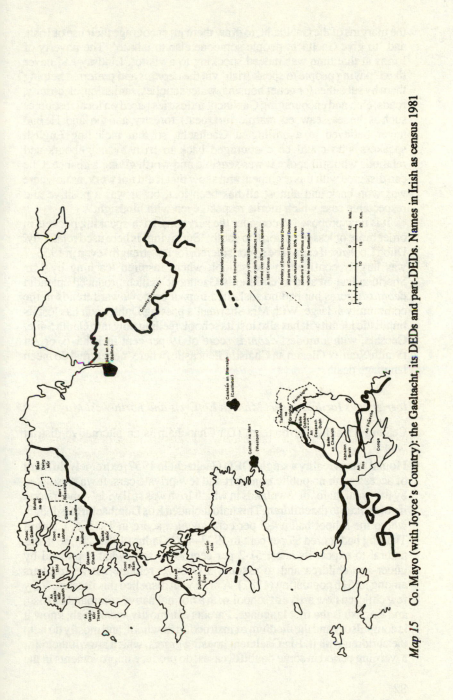

Map 15 Co. Mayo (with Joyce's Country): the Gaeltacht, its DEDs and part-DEDs. Names in Irish as census 1981

Official boundary of Gaeltacht 1956

1956 boundary where different

Boundary of District Electoral Divisions
wholly or partly in Gaeltacht which
returned over 80% of Irish speakers
in 1981 Census

Boundary of District Electoral Divisions
and parts of District Electoral Divisions
which returned below 80% of Irish
speakers in 1981 Census and/or
which lie outside the Gaeltacht

COUNTY BOUNDARY

Béal an Átha
(Ballina)

Caisleán an Bharraigh
(Castlebar)

Cathair na Mart
(Westport)

Béal Deirg
Mór

Maing
na Bó

Barr
Rúscaighe

Gleann
na
hUaidhe

Cnoc
an Daimh

Cnoc
na
Lobhar

An
Maing

Gualá
Mhór

Béal
Mhuir-
thid

Gleann
Chaiseal

Cnoc na
Filín

Gaoth
Mór
Mór
Theas

An
Gaoth
Mór

Acaill

Corrán
Acla

Dumhach
Éige

An Fhódraoi

Conga

An Ros

Abhainn
Bhán

Béile
na Cheasaigh

An
Ceapach
Dubh

Oghbha

Giorraigh

Partraighe

Tuathaigh

the margins of the Gaeltacht, to draw them in, encourage their use of Irish, and 'to give Gaeltacht people someone else to talk to'. The poverty of Iorras at that time was indeed shocking to a visitor. Lindsay had never liked 'paying people to speak Irish' via the *deontas* and preferred helping them by subsidies for better housing, water supplies, sanitation, electricity, roads, etc., and encouraging Gaeltacht industries based on local resources such as the sea, seaweed, marble, turf (peat), forestry, and the land. He had never believed in a unilingual Gaeltacht, so that including English speakers who could be encouraged back to Irish by neighbours and relations who still spoke it was sensible and worth giving a chance. One can disagree with this argument and show that it did not work, as nowhere was won back and almost all has been lost, but it was a positive and respectable case which merits respect, even with hindsight.

It is now proposed to consider the surviving Irish-speaking pockets in order more or less from north to south. 'Surviving' is here used relatively. Dubh Loch itself cannot be so considered, for its 'strength' even in 1956–7 was largely confined to the school, where inspired teaching by Mrs Sheridan had created a 'children's Gaeltacht' which produced splendid *deontas* figures but had no sustained impact on downward trends in the community at large. With Mrs Sheridan's passing Dubh Loch has lost its linguistic identity. It has also lost its school, feeding now into Gaoth Sáile/Geesala, with a modest *deontas* score of 19 per cent in 1985–6, or An tSraith/Srah, or Gleann an Chaisil/Glencastle, where 'no returns' do mean language death.

Iorras agus Iarthuaisceart Mhaigh Eo/Erris and north-west Mayo

Ceathrú Thaidhg/Carrowteige (Dú Chaocháin is an alternative district name)

I found this in reality a single-DED Gaeltacht in 1957, extremely difficult of access, with no public transport and few private cars. It was insulated by the usual 'halo' of townlands in which Irish was still widely understood if not spoken to the children. This halo included Ros Dumhach/Rossdoagh, where the school had a 4·5 per cent *deontas* score in 1985–6. Ceathrú Thaidhg had scored 87 per cent in 1973–4 (Ó Gadhra 1982: 28), so it was natural to expect its latest 51·2 per cent to be somewhat depressed by under-age children and to assume 300 or so reliable native speakers among its 516 population (1981). A brief visit dispelled this illusion. Very few children now arrive at school with a normal native command of Irish, and English is the first language. Parents can mostly speak Irish, know it is compulsory and the medium of instruction in school, and mostly do help the children with it. Big Gaeltacht housing grants, which are withheld for a warning period in some doubtful cases, do produce improvements in the affected homes but only in formal mastery of Irish, rarely in habitual use. Marrying-in and returning emigrants are a problem even here, but abandonment of Irish in the home goes far beyond their numbers.

An Irish summer college is some help to Irish, as is Údarás and other state aid to industry and fishing. But the total area is four square miles of Irish-speaking territory (half of it grazings), whose children inevitably go to secondary schools outside and so are mixed with English speakers whom they are almost bound to meet as marriage partners, with the usual linguistic consequences. Most families have a car, all have a television, all but the most basic shopping involves a trip 'outside', and so on.

There is little prospect of any maintenance of Irish as a first language here, for it is already abandoned by silent popular consensus.

An Eachléim agus An Fód Dubh/Aghleam and Blacksod

Nowhere else in north-west Mayo can be remotely considered as a living Gaeltacht, least of all the village of Belmullet (Béal an Mhuirthead), which has the urban attributes and the secondary schools for most of the district. An Eachléim, towards the southern end of the Mullet peninsula, alone has *deontas* figures comparable with Ceathrú Thaidhg's, almost identical at 51 per cent. They are not identical in meaning, for the Eachléim school area is less homogeneous and gets some of its Irish strength from the children of the farming townlands of An Fál Mór/Fallmore, Glais/Glosh, and Surge View (arguably An Aicill *or* Tóin na hOltaí in Irish), to which the Inis Gé/Inishkea islanders were evacuated after a fishing disaster had destroyed their confidence in 1927. These are tucked away in the extreme south-west corner, away from the long anglicized but tiny former British naval quay at An Fód Dubh/Blacksod. Opinions differ locally on whether they are still habitually Irish-speaking. All adults seem to have Irish fluently and the children have some but they are not notably different from the children of the rest of the district when they first arrive at school, as they certainly were around 1957, when, even so, mothers and grandmothers were already speaking English to the young children in the home.

Good work in the school, with some parental backing, now produces the 51 per cent *deontas* majority, and children coming for the Irish summer college promote greater public and home use of the local Irish during the three months affected. All-English secondary school education at Belmullet alongside children otherwise almost entirely from all-English national schools does not encourage the maintenance of a fully all-Irish programme at Eachléim, and the simple desire to socialize with other children on an equal footing, not as curiosities, tends to draw the children towards English. Job prospects rank high among other anti-Irish influences, none of them unusual, and the Údarás-aided employment is almost all in wholly anglicized Belmullet, because of the same locational advantages which

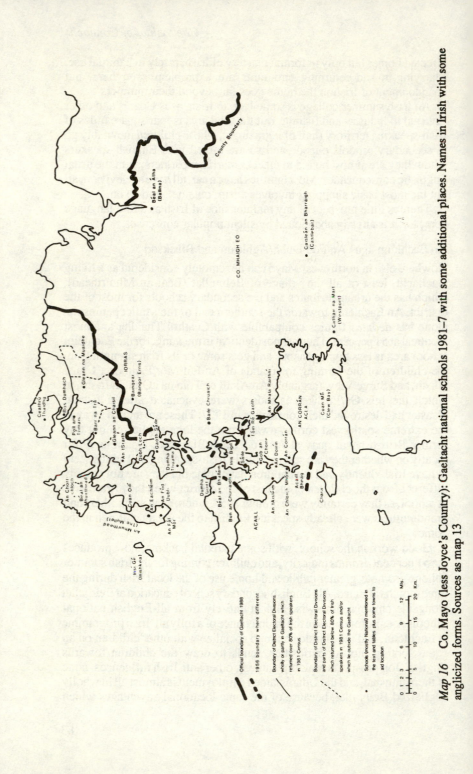

Map 16 Co. Mayo (less Joyce's Country): Gaeltacht national schools 1981–7 with some additional places. Names in Irish with some anglicized forms. Sources as map 13

Legend:

County Boundary

Official boundary of Gaeltacht 1988

1956 boundary where different

Boundary of District Electoral Divisions wholly or partly in Gaeltacht which returned over 80% of Irish speakers in 1981 Census

Boundary of District Electoral Divisions and parts of District Electoral Divisions which returned below 80% of Irish speakers in 1981 Census and/or which lie outside the Gaeltacht

Schools (mostly National) mentioned in the text and tables plus some towns to aid location

Scale:

0 1 2 3 6 9 12 Mls.
0 5 10 15 20 Km.

Place names:

Béal an Átha (Ballina)

CO MHAIGH EO

Caisleán an Bharraigh (Castlebar)

Ceathrú Thaidhg

Dún Dumhach

Gleann na Muaidhe

Poll an tSómais

IORRAS

Barr na Trá

Gleann an Chaisil

An tSraith

Dubh Loch

Bun Geal (Bangor Erris)

Gaoth Sáile

Baile Cruaich

Cathair na Mart (Westport)

An Chorr Chloch

Béal an Mhuirthead

Cuan Oiil

An Eachléim

An Fód Dubh

Dumha Thuama

Dumha Loirg

Béal an Bhalla

Bun an Churraigh

Inis Biail

AN CORRÁN ACLA

An Mhala Raithní

An Ráó Gaoth

Cill Chomáin

Sáile

Acaill Beag

An Cloch Mhór

An Corrán

Cuan Mó (Clew Bay)

An Fál Mór

An Mhuinthead (The Mullet)

ACAILL

An Ainiúm

An Dorán

Cloch

Inis Gé (Inishkea)

drew the secondary schools. Several smaller enterprises at Cuan Oilí/Elly Bay are much nearer but employ few people and are also in an anglicized location. Údarás cannot be blamed for this, with a remit to assist the Mayo Gaeltacht but so little living Irish in it.

Acaill agus An Corrán/Achill and Corraun

The Gaeltacht core here was already defined as four separate pockets in 1956, if one counts Inis Bigil/Inishbiggle as separate. Gob an Choire/ Achill Sound, as the only tangible village, 'central place', and terminus of the railway till 1940, lost Irish early this century and like most of northern Corrán (spelt Currane in English by the youth hostel and others) and the greater part of eastern Acaill was primarily English-speaking well before 1956. About that time around 60 per cent of schoolchildren in the south-western parts of Corrán were estimated to speak Irish for preference and all *could* do so, but the trend was markedly downward among young infants. On Acaill itself the western, more 'remote' parts went English years ago under the influence of the mid nineteenth-century Protestant missionary settlement (founded 1834). The surviving Irish pockets in 1957 were around Sáile/Salia, An Doirín/Derreen, and An Chloich Mhóir/ Cloghmore in the east of the island. They undoubtedly had big majorities of native speakers, but only at the very southern tip, at An Chloich Mhóir, was Irish the first language of a majority of the children – as much as 80 per cent – but even there the weakening among the younger children was causing alarm.

The *deontas* figures for the schools now show patterns typical of extinction of native Irish among the young. The highest in 1985–6 is 34·1 per cent for Sáile, which compares with 14·6 per cent four years earlier and can only reflect fluctuation in attainment by learners, fluctuation by assessors, the movements of odd families, or variation in the proportions of under-age children. There is no Irish-speaking community here but only occasional families which take above-average interest in Irish and give it some place in the home alongside English, which nevertheless predominates for the usual reasons. Recently high proportions at Tóin Ré Gaoth/Tonragee in north-east Corrán are entirely accounted for by the work of the school, as Irish is too long dead here for parents to help other than with their own school-Irish.

Bun an Churraidh/Bunacurry in north-east Acaill achieved its 27·4 per cent under an enthusiastic Head who is an accomplished Irish author and playwright, a capable and inspiring organizer of Gaelic (*sic* – including Scottish Gaelic) cultural activities for the entire district, but no fanatic: a sensitive and sympathetic leader fully conscious of the attractions of English and the consequential need to cultivate love for and enjoyment of Irish without futile denunciation or attempted prohibition of the popular

The death of the Irish language

use of English. He lives at An Chloich Mhóir, where Irish has now subsided to second-language status as at best everywhere else, and is succeeding in maintaining a certain native Irish survival by encouraging small 'family networks' to meet weekly to chat and generally socialize in Irish and by using little incentives to persuade the children to use the Irish which otherwise they tend to dismiss as 'old-fashioned' as well as generally useless for jobs – or for watching television.

Donncha Ó Gallchobhair, the Minister of State at An Roinn na Gaeltachta under Charles Haughey, is a native of An Corrán, the settlement from which the peninsula derives its name, and still has his home there. The local school *deontas* figures (under 25 per cent) nevertheless speak for themselves. The steady decline of the language has continued. Returned emigrants play some role here but less than at Bun an Churraigh, where over half the top class in 1987 were born in England! The state of Irish in 1956–7 and the lack of widespread return migration before 1971 makes the latter a mere supplement to the other influences which had already led to the general disuse of Irish before moderate prosperity arrived.

There is, in short, no Irish-speaking community in Acaill or An Corrán to maintain and the only hope of a future for the native language lies in small family networks as currently attempted at An Chloich Mhóir. Even there English seems already the first and preferred language of the young and it is a matter of maintaining a native continuity within favourable families, and even there only alongside English, which there is no prospect of displacing as first language.

Maigh Eo–Gaillimh/Galway–Mayo

Dúiche Sheoigheach/Joyce's Country (Dúiche Sheoighe normal locally)

An English approximation of the pronunciation of the Irish name would be *Dookher Hoyakh*, with the *r* silent and the *kh* lightly guttural. It should not strictly be applied to the Lough Mask lake shore as far north as and beyond Tuar Mhic Éadaigh/Tourmakeady but the latter area is an obvious appendage to this mountainous and sparsely peopled Gaeltacht, adding two school districts to make a total of eight. Only 151 children in all earned the *deontas* in 1985–6 and only three schools scored above 40 per cent. (See appendix 3.)

When I visited the district in 1957 I concluded that none of the villages – Tuar Mhic Éadaigh, An Fhairche/Clonbur, Corr na Móna/Cornamona, and Mám/Maum (or Maam) – was securely Irish, the first two having been definitely lost. Clonbur, as it is sensible to call this English-speaking place, had been predominantly English since before the First World War and although most of its natives of middle age or above had Irish from the

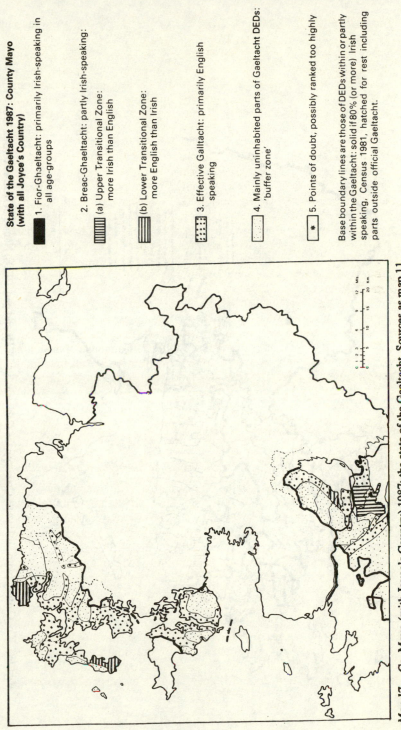

State of the Gaeltacht 1987: County Mayo (with all Joyce's Country)

1. Fíor-Ghaeltacht: primarily Irish-speaking in all age-groups

2. Breac-Ghaeltacht: partly Irish-speaking:
   (a) Upper Transitional Zone: more Irish than English
   (b) Lower Transitional Zone: more English than Irish

3. Effective Galltacht: primarily English speaking

4. Mainly uninhabited parts of Gaeltacht DEDs: 'buffer zone'

5. Points of doubt, possibly ranked too highly

Base boundary lines are those of DEDs within or partly within the Gaeltacht: solid if 80% (or more) Irish speaking, Census 1981, hatched for rest including parts outside official Gaeltacht.

Map 17   Co. Mayo (with Joyce's Country) 1987: the state of the Gaeltacht. Sources as map 11

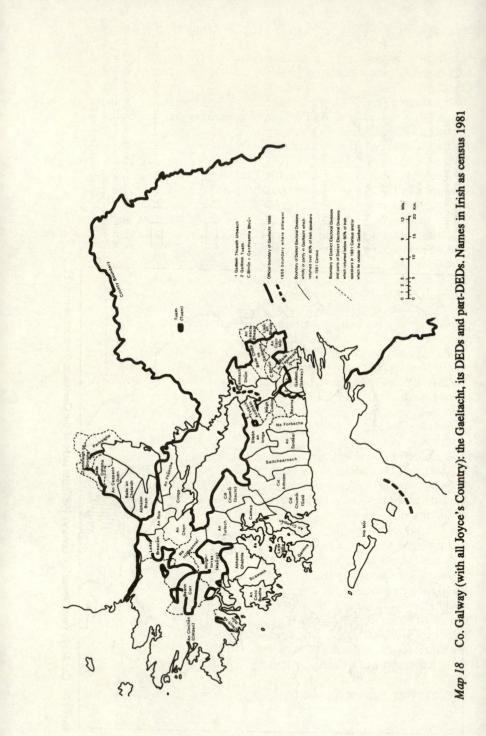

Map 18 Co. Galway (with all Joyce's Country): the Gaeltacht, its DEDs and part-DEDs. Names in Irish as census 1981

County Boundary

Tuam (Tuaim)

1 Gaillimh Thuaidh Urbach
2 Gaillimh Tuath
C.Bhrín = Ceathramha Bhrín

Official boundary of Gaeltacht 1968

1956 boundary where different

Boundary of District Electoral Divisions
wholly or partly in Gaeltacht which
returned over 80% of Irish speakers
in 1981 Census

Boundary of District Electoral Divisions
and parts of District Electoral Divisions
which returned below 80% of Irish
speakers in 1981 Census and/or
which lie outside the Gaeltacht

An Chlochán (Clifden)

An Clochán
Garmna
Leitir Móir
Leitir Mealláin
An Cnoc Buidhe
Scainimh
Abhainn Ghabhla
Maigh Cuilinn
Cill Chuimín (Gad)
Cill Aithnín
Saileearnach
An Spidéal
Na Forbacha
Cill Chuimín (Uacht.)
Camus
An Turloch
An Chorr
Nuigeasna
Beann Corr
Abhainn Bhrain
Leitriún
Breacán
An Ros
Conga
An Fhairche
Partraighe
An Creagach
Cill Bhrin
Baile an Dhaláigh
Oileán
Greigín Teimhleach
An Dúbh
Sliabh an Iolaig
Trasachán Acmhin
Seanchaisidh Dhlúin
An Droim
Baile Chláir Ghaillimh
An Caisleán Gearr
Cill Chiaráin
Gaillimh (Galway)
An Cosán
Inis Mór

0 1 2 3   12   Mls.
0   5   10   15   20 Km.

cradle they made little use of it and there was barely a child in the village to whom Irish was the first language: yet about half received the *deontas*. Tuar Mhic Éadaigh had slid into English more recently and nearly everyone could speak Irish, less than half doing so habitually. There was some pride in having a local *coláiste ullmhúcháin* and satisfaction at having a Gaeltarra Éireann knitwear factory and afforestation scheme, though both the latter operated through English, reflecting normal local usage.

The truly Irish-speaking district in 1957 began south of the village, towards Coill an tSiáin/Killitiane (or Killateeaun), beyond which in the mountain valleys around Seanafearcháin/Shanafaraghaun and Fionnaithe/Finny the bigger threat to Irish seemed total depopulation, which was inspiring a 'bread-and-butter' movement towards the use of English with the children, although most adults were still much more at ease in Irish. The schools at both places have since closed and the remaining children go to Páirc an Doire/Derrypark, which had a 27·3 per cent *deontas* score in 1985–6 and only twenty-five pupils. Its 68 per cent in 1981–2 is surprising and like Coill an tSiáin's recent 50 per cent reflects credit on the schools, which are continuing to bestow a command of Irish on many children whose parents neglect to do so.

At Mám as many as 65 per cent were said to make habitual use of Irish in 1957 but its hold was very insecure and it had slipped to below 40 per cent by 1965. The children from Mám attended Tír na Cille/Teernakill school, with *deontas* scores of 0 per cent and 4·3 per cent in appendix 3. Corr na Móna is a very different and special case, worth more than passing mention.

Already in 1957 the village at Corr na Móna had a local reputation, based largely on experience in its pubs and shops, for anglicizing tendencies and its church used English for most sermons and notices. A keen local language worker took the author into the adjacent Dúros/Dooros peninsula to visit a real little Gaeltacht then recently recovered for Irish as the result of buying out a number of emigrating families which had long used English, but Wagner, whose Irish dialect survey is a model of its kind, was unconvinced that any was spoken in Dooros. He summarized Corr na Móna as '? Irish probably spoken in a few homes', and later elaborated by adding that in some mountain valleys near by Irish was still spoken, at least by the older generation (H. Wagner 1958a: map 1; 1958b: xiii).

Wagner was seeking fluent native idiomatic Irish and was often criticized for his dismissal of 'school-Irish' as clear evidence that English had become the vernacular of a place: which was usually the case but did not allow for the influence of the schools on the younger section of the population, some of whom were still making everyday use of Irish even if also of English in a diglossic relationship. This author heard well-dressed young women conversing in Irish in Corr na Móna post office in

1957, so could not accept that it was entirely confined to the upper valleys or in general disuse. The village and its vicinity were plainly bilingual but weighted towards English, in which case an 81 per cent *deontas* score in 1985–6 denotes exceptional success over thirty years when almost everywhere else in the Gaeltachtaí has suffered conspicuous decline.

What has happened at Corr na Móna has been a transformation in *public* 'public attitudes' (*sic*) towards Irish brought about by successful industrial development under the aegis of Údarás na Gaeltachta (and its predecessor, Gaeltarra Éireann) operating through the local co-operative, Comharchumann Dhúiche Sheoigheach, the manager of which is Eamon Ó Cuív, grandson of President de Valéra and son of Professor Brian Ó Cuív, a leading Irish scholar. Dynamic leadership and exceptional local awareness of the bureaucratic and technical processes for securing state grants are here combined with genuine enthusiasm for the language in the leadership and sufficient personal charisma to attract a major local following and discourage any organized and articulate opposition. The school is well staffed and ensures that the children quickly attain fluency. There was no Údarás-supported ógchlub (youth club) in 1987 but an active Irish-language cultural life was associated with the *comharchumann*. An 'Irish night' I attended drew a good number of all ages, and all formal activities were in Irish and evidently fully understood; but plenty of the young people were chatting in English to each other or switching language according to whom they were addressing. Conversation elicited mixed opinions as to the usefulness or frequency of the use of Irish in the district, as well as the allegation that much of its pretended cultivation was 'hypocrisy', intended to extract state funds.

Elsewhere in Dúiche Sheoigheach there was admiration of the improvement in the status of Irish at Corr na Móna but no belief that it was really any more used in the home than had previously been the case. The 53 per cent *deontas* return of 1981–2 was felt to be generous and the real state of the language considerably worse than at nearby An Chloch Bhreac/Cloghbrack (63 per cent *deontas* 1985–6), where the position among the children was felt to be approaching terminal and there was no active local drive to reverse the trend.

A cause of concern to the author was that the *coláiste samhraidh* (summer college) was placing its students in only a tiny number of homes, so tiny that it must be assumed that lack of reliably Irish-speaking families was as much a consideration as lack of space and facilities in the homes. There were grants available to help provide the space, etc.

There was a note of jealousy in comments about Corr na Móna in adjacent districts. Eamon Ó Cuív was defeated in his 1987 and 1989 attempts to enter the Dáil for his grandfather's party and there is little sign of widespread emulation of his language work even in the immediate area. That jump from 52·7 to 80·6 per cent *deontas* score between 1981–2 and

1985–6 lacks verisimilitude with a stable school population and no tangible social movements to explain it. Attitudes to Irish may well be better and it may be appropriate to reward greater efforts; but it is more than a generation since Irish ceased to be the first language of the home for a clear majority of Corr na Móna children, and that was before most families got a motor car and all a television set. Galway city is now less than an hour's drive away and is visited often.

Before leaving Dúiche Sheoigheach some mention should be made of An tSraith/Srah, at the northern extremity of the official Gaeltacht. The school had an excellent Irish teacher a generation or more ago but the language was certainly dying by about 1947 and little was spoken ten years later. Perhaps because of its 'border' location it has maintained a certain pride in still having some Irish, but this is almost entirely from the school and its wildly fluctuating *deontas* returns, from 12·5 to 37·0 per cent in recent years, cannot be taken as indicative of native Irish in habitual use. There would be very few *deontas* awards in Dúiche Sheoigheach if that was required and none if Irish was required to be *the* language of the home. This is scarcely surprising, given that the four central DEDs all saw their populations halved by emigration between 1926 and 1981, the two most Irish down to 36–7 per cent of 1926, and even Conga/Cong DED, which includes Corr na Móna, fell to 48 per cent by 1981. Emigration may not be seen as a great problem here now but it was behind everyone's thoughts when the crucial decisions were made to turn to English in everyday life for the sake of the future of the children.

Mismatch between DED boundaries and the catchment areas of the schools which returned *deontas* majorities in 1985–6 makes it difficult to estimate maximum and minimum numbers of habitual native speakers, except in the case of Corr na Móna, whose DED had 586 people in 1981. The other DEDs with significant native Irish had many fewer than this and in view of the doubts expressed about Corr na Móna somewhere around 600 should be the maximum for the whole district, the minimum depending on whether one believes there is anyone left at normal working age who does not use English more than Irish. There is nowhere with a *deontas* score reliably over 70 per cent (remember Corr na Móna's 53 per cent in 1981–2) and it must therefore be presumed that all Irish speakers in Dúiche Sheoigheach are living or growing up in a predominantly English-speaking environment even at home. Any hard core of Irish is in individual families, not in any geographically defined community.

Co. na Gaillimhe/Galway

Galway maintains in Conamara/Connemara by far the largest and most populous of the surviving Gaeltachtaí, one to which it might seem logical to attach Árainn but for the fact that the islands' only all-year ferry is to

91

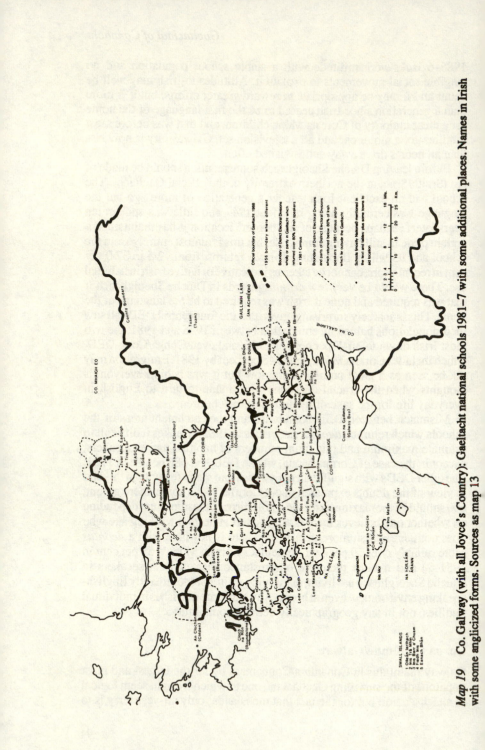

Map 19 Co. Galway (with all Joyce's Country): Gaeltacht national schools 1981–7 with some additional places. Names in Irish with some anglicized forms. Sources as map 13

anglicized Galway city. There is also an area officially defined as Gaeltacht east of the city, including the airport, but this is one of the least credible in the country and is very far gone compared with Dúiche Sheoigheach. The regional name Conamara, which is somewhat flexible in application, will here be used to cover all of Co. Galway west of the city and Lough Corrib, excepting only the portion already dealt with as Dúiche Sheoigheach.

Conamara Theas/South Connemara

This is undoubtedly the strongest and most secure Gaeltacht in all Ireland, the only one sufficiently large and diverse to divide into discrete sub-regions, though the latter are individually very small. There is as usual a 'halo' of official Gaeltacht which is hardly Irish-speaking at all but here the halo is noticeable only at the eastern and western extremities, for in general the northern interior boundary is roadless and uninhabited bogland across which normal anglicizing social contacts with neighbouring communities could not develop. Such contacts have therefore been concentrated at either end of the coastal road and especially in the vicinity of Galway city, within whose borders there were Irish-speaking enclaves until World War II. Commuter developments in recent years have nevertheless wreaked havoc with Irish as far west as An Spidéal/Spiddle, swamping it utterly round Bearna/Barna and Maigh Cuilinn/Moycullen. At the western end there is no such metropolis to pose a threat and the roads from the Clifden and Maam Cross direction are relatively unfrequented. Decline has therefore been relatively slow without the impetus of inward movements and rapid daily access to a city. Non-Irish readers may be reminded that 'city' here meant 47,008 people in 1986, such is the relevant scale.

In much of the Gaeltacht English is encroaching more from the little 'central places' of the Gaeltacht itself, notably Carna but to some extent Cill Chiaráin/Kilkieran, where the presence of the odd hotel, pub, post office, shop/s, Guards' post, factory, or other industrial enterprise is characteristically associated with anglicizing influences, which also go with the presence of a secondary school (at Carna a new community school), even where the latter gives every prominence to Irish and teaches through it. These things give superiority over the 'back' districts, and a pride which rarely seems to centre on Irish. The Carna peninsula does function as a social unit and may be considered first, as in appendices 3 and 4.

Leithinis Charna/Carna peninsula

Recess, in Irish Sraith Salach, lies to the north of the peninsula on the main Galway–Clifden road and the former railway (closed 1935), and has not spoken Irish outside individual homes for a couple of generations or more. Some of its catchment area is not even officially Gaeltacht and much of the rest was included in 1956 only because the language still lingered in a few mainly elderly homes lying back from the road. Recess and Maam Cross (An Teach Dóite) form an unconvincing 'bridge' between the Dúiche Sheoigheach and Conamara Gaeltachtaí, not really there but not too misleading because almost uninhabited. The area for several miles to their south is completely uninhabited, so effective links with Carna and any other Irish-speaking area are few, all major linkages being the obvious ones west to Clifden and east to Galway via Oughterard. Zero *deontas* awards in 1981–2 and 25 per cent in 1985–6 do not denote a presence of living Irish nor sudden real recovery. A recent prolonged dispute involving the status of Irish in the church at Recess seemed unnecessary, as the language lost its role in the community so many years ago.

The Carna peninsula itself has strong pockets of Irish and could be accounted secure in terms of ability to speak the language. The Gaeltacht outliers north and west of Bertraghboy Bay were lost by 1957, as was Bun na hAbhann/Bunnahown and everything south to Gabhla/Gowla. In the rest of the peninsula Irish seemed secure except for depopulation, which had removed nearly 30 per cent of the population of An Cnoc Buidhe/ Knockboy DED (which included Carna village) in the preceding thirty years and by 1971 had taken 38 per cent of the 1926 total plus all the natural increase. A tendency towards English was already remarked upon among the young but there was no abandonment of Irish to cause serious concern. Now this has changed and a situation similar to that in Gaoth Dobhair prevails, though with much less industrial development to explain it and no major population increases from 1971 to 1981. Returning emigrants are a factor, as is marrying-in, but universal influences such as the family car, the television, and rising expectations are necessary to explain a general falling off of the use of Irish as the main or sole language of pre-school children.

Naíonraí at Carna and Glinsce/Glinsk are one reaction to this but the *deontas* figures for Carna (as low as 33·3 per cent in 1981–2) and Cill Chiaráin, in the lower 60s or worse, can only be viewed with misgivings. They have the bigger schools, the only post-primary school, and almost all the industrial employment. There are Irish-language *ógchlubanna* supported by Údarás at both places but the secondary pupils from Carna whom I met in an entirely rural part of its catchment area were chatting together in English and when asked why said they always did so. They were fluent in Irish and their lessons were mostly conducted in it. This also used to happen thirty years ago but when the teenagers matured they reverted to speaking Irish if they stayed in the district. However, they had all started with enough Irish to earn the *deontas* without question and in 1957 few families had cars and none had television. There is an active

Irish-language social life at Carna and a well known summer college; but if the children are turning increasingly to English they cannot be doing it on their own.

Mórthír Láir/Central mainland

The central mainland section of south Conamara still had large numbers of near-monoglot Irish speakers thirty years ago and I had to abandon an attempted townland survey because so many people could not or would not risk an English conversation with a stranger. That was near Casla/ Costelloe and the most impoverished place I have ever visited. The northern parts around An Gort Mór/Gortmore, Scríb/Screeb, and Ros Muc/Rosmuck are still as soundly Irish as almost anywhere, partly because new industry is farther away, though again the old signs of poverty have vanished. South from Scríb, which is only thirty miles from Galway, so at most an hour's journey by a much improved road, weakening becomes noticeable. There were only five monoglot English speakers at Ros Muc thirty years ago, including the two women in the post office, one of them married in. The three children got fluent Irish at school and were assimilated into the Irish-speaking community. This is less common now because local people speak much better English and speak it more often, and one hardly meets a child who feels ill at ease in English. Pressures to socialize in Irish are thus much weaker and the television and rapid access to the city make English even more 'modern' and 'with it' for the young. A summer college, a *naíonra*, an *ógchlub*, and the association with Patrick Pearse (first president in the Easter Rebellion – he had a cottage here) maintain a good level of national consciousness at Ros Muc, neverthe-less, and Gael-Linn showed confidence by sending seven children (1986), a high number for a school with a roll of forty-nine in 1985–6.

The weakening of Irish south of Scríb is not yet obvious to a visitor and is masked both by 1981 census Irish-speaking percentages above 95 for its two DEDs and by *deontas* figures ranging in recent years (appendix 3) from 62 per cent to 90 per cent. It was in a high-scoring school here that the head was kind enough to ask the upper class in my presence to put up their hands to indicate honestly which language they spoke at home. The lesson was being conducted in Irish and there was good Irish-language display work, most of it by the children, all over the walls and in the corridor. When what looked like nearly all put up their hands for English I asked for an Irish count: it was four or five out of about thirty and all admitted that English was the normal language of play. All spoke Irish fluently, largely thanks to the school and to their Irish-speaking parents, who were willing to help with their children's school work. I had been badly misled because on arriving at the school the young mothers who were waiting for the release of the infants' class all spoke Irish in my hearing, except when I spoke to them. Of course I arrived in a big car, alone, a stranger calling at the school: that to a native of the Gaeltacht is a clear sign of an inspector or official, my clean 'professional' anorak being a transparent disguise almost verging on a uniform, and therefore a signal to speak Irish unless various grants are to be put at risk. This is no joke but sociolinguistic reality, and had I arrived with my wife and stopped simply to ask the way they would almost certainly have been chatting in English.

In the same school all instruction was in Irish, except for three hours per week specifically for English, but because of textbook problems and necessary explanations some English was used for a much higher proportion of the time. The amount visible on the wall was no more than appropriate in an all-Irish school, which in one sense this still was but which in the basic essential of the first language of the children on reception it certainly was not. There was no belief here that these children would transmit Irish as mother tongue to their own children: this in an area over 95 per cent Irish in 1981, with no 1985–6 *deontas* figure below 68 per cent, all schools listed to receive Gael-Linn children, and three Irish summer colleges close by – including two at An Cheathrú Rua/Carraroe.

An Cheathrú Rua is the principal village of the area and not notable for its frankness about Irish. The proportion of infants under 6 is held to depress the *deontas* percentages unduly (they were down to 62·4 per cent in 1981–2). Major industrial developments in the 1970s brought problems with returning emigrants and their families but the children of the returnees and other 'blow-ins' (incomers) are claimed to have been fully assimilated, with only one or two exceptions who are struggling in their Irish-medium classes. But again textbook problems seem to cause resort to English ones in two or three subjects and full bilingualism is assumed as the target, as in all Gaeltacht schools.

Two *coláistí samhraidh* are conducted at An Cheathrú Rua, for both boys and girls aged 10 to 18 years. The village is widely criticized in neighbouring districts for 'making a Gaeltacht industry out of the language', especially in relation to the alleged lodging of sixteen or more children in individual Irish-speaking homes the extension of which was paid for out of the profits of the previous summer's boarders plus a hefty grant from the Gaeltacht housing funds of An Roinn na Gaeltachta. How much natural and homely Irish such children encounter in that setting may be imagined. There is no doubt at all that the colleges help local pride in the language and reinforce it with powerful material support which in most places is heavily weighted towards English. In An Cheathrú Rua itself English is not without weight in the factories.

In 1957 the village had about seven shops, in two of which the shopkeeper had little Irish. Electricity had just arrived that year. A vocational school (teaching through Irish) gave status, and there was more English in use than in neighbouring districts: but Irish was the habitual language of the overwhelming majority. A minor tourist interest brought in some English but was hindered by bad roads, water and power supply problems, poor telephone links, and lack of accommodation. A trawler was based here (then very rare in Conamara) but there was no modern industrial employment. Despite serious setbacks since about 1980 there were eight Údarás-assisted enterprises listed in the 1985 report and although some were very small (e.g. a hairdresser and a restaurant) they have contributed to a modernization of outlook which mostly tends towards anglicization. Failures after the euphoria of the mid 1970s had that effect more violently by weakening confidence in the local economy and reviving old convictions that emigration (to English-speaking areas) was the best hope.

An Cheathrú Rua is a community in linguistic transition, with an active Irish-speaking leadership struggling to hold the dikes, not so much opposed as ignored by widespread apathy. Total ignorance of Irish is happily rare at school reception age and a *naíonra* makes up for some parental neglect; but teaching through the medium of Irish is not becoming easier as English increases its ascendancy among the young of this fluently bilingual district.

The importance of An Cheathrú Rua to Irish language maintenance is to be seen in the fact that its DED (An Crampán/Crumpaun) is the sole incontrovertibly Irish-speaking one in the entire country to have increased its population to as much as 106 per cent of the 1926 figure, and if one omits the Galway commuting fringe which includes An Spidéal/Spiddle it is one of only two in the Conamara Gaeltacht to have increased at all. An Turloch/Turlough, which includes Ros Muc and Gort Mór, has dropped to 57 per cent, which allows little anti-Irish influence by inward migration and largely explains the continued strength. Yet the Crampán increase to 1981 was all the work of the previous decade with its sudden jump from 87 per cent of the 1926 figure in 1971; and however much local people may blame returned emigrants and 'blow-ins' for the weakening of Irish it is obvious that the previous long continuous decline had conditioned everyone to the need for English for emigration, here as elsewhere, and blow-ins ignorant of Irish or weak in it only added to existing reasons for its disuse.

Na hOileáin/The Islands

Linked to central Conamara by a series of bridges which reach the mainland at Béal an Daingean/Bealandangan is the string of inshore islands known as Na hOileáin/the Islands, not to be confused with Árainn/Aran, visible further out to sea. This looks the archetypical Conamara Gaeltacht, all rock-strewn land and sea mixed up together. The main road is good in relation to traffic volume but industrial employment is minimal and the *comharchumann* at Tír an Fhia/Teeranea has failed. *Deontas* figures ranging from a lowest 60·3 per cent at the latter in 1985–6 to an unchallengeable 90 per cent seemed to denote stability, especially as reliable outside informants thought Tír an Fhia as soundly Irish as the rest of the islands, so the figures aberrant. I was hoping to find a rock of stability, so toured the islands briefly. Enquiry made clear that Tír an Fhia (on Garmna/Gorumna island) is as English-inclined as the figures suggest. The tiny, dispersed 'village' feels comparatively metropolitan, with a convent, several shops, and an Údarás factory and 'wants better than Irish' ... Hence English comes first for many of the children, most probably the majority. The school teaches through Irish and has the usual textbook problems.

Greater shocks came elsewhere on Garmna and Leitir Mealláin/ Lettermullen, and I left with the impression that English has taken over as the language of infant play and also as the preferred language for most uncontrolled childish pursuits. This is usually less advanced in the schools off the spinal road, but that sort of differentiation is much less than it used to be now that television penetrates every home, however poor the road access. All the little single-teacher schools which it used to be a pleasure to visit on the lesser islands have closed since the 1950s: Inis Barr a'Chuain/Inishbarra, Inis Tra Mhín/Inishtravin, and across the bay Fiadh Inis/Finish and Oileán Iarthach/Illauneeragh. Most involved a walk across a tidal strand and served barely self-sufficient communities. How to get to a secondary school was no problem, as none could afford to. Reasons for closure need not be recited but they have an uncanny resemblance to reasons for abandoning Irish, centring on opportunities, accessibility, and communications. There is no danger of total depopulation on the islands with bridges. It used to be argued that they needed only the provision of modern employment to save their Irish, but that now lacks conviction.

Cois Fharraige

What is often regarded as the main continuous bloc of Irish-speaking territory in the country is Cois Fharraige (sometimes -Fhairrge), the twenty-mile coastal strip west of Galway city, ending at Cuan Chasla/ Cashla Bay. Its name means 'beside the sea', i.e. seaside, but it is never translated or even rendered in English. *Cush Arrigger* is the approximate pronunciation, and as the ecumene is almost entirely a narrow strip with soils made by laboriously mixing shell sand from the beach with peat from the bog which reached down to the shore and blankets the interior the name is apt. Thirty years ago the coast road (the only road) west of An Spidéal was poor and unfrequented, with a bus twice a day and industry unheard of. Petrol stations had just begun to appear. Traditional whitewashed cottages were closely scattered along the road, like unplanned urban ribbon development but here on a poor agrarian base with none of the usual services. Everyone spoke Irish and there was no tourist use of the long southward-facing sandy beaches looking out to the Aran Islands and the Burren.

Now the atmosphere is one of an ill-planned seaside bungaloid straggle of new houses indistinguishable from the 'council' model elsewhere. There is water, electricity, and telephones, and many of the houses are weekend or holiday cottages belonging to Galway city people and others from farther afield, many of them former local residents until work drew them away. Signs to the beaches are now common but almost always in Irish only, as are virtually all road signs and most notices, except at garages and 'B & B's. New industry is often in evidence, from the fishing port of Ros a'Mhíl/Rossaveel in the far west (with a summer ferry service to Árainn) and round Baile na hAbhann/Ballynahown, Indreabhán/Inverin (or Inveran), An Spidéal/Spiddle, and Na Forbacha/Furbogh. Proximity to Galway city makes this a favoured area for Gaeltacht investment, access to markets being well above average. Even Bearna/Barna, now undeniably a Galway suburb and with only 4·3 per cent of *deontas* earners in 1981–2, had six minor enterprises in receipt of Údarás grants in 1985, all having presumably satisfied the language requirements.

The encouragement of industrial growth along this coast was sensibly intended to forestall over-concentration in Galway city and a resultant reduction of the coastal communities to mere commuter functions fatal to the maintenance of Irish (Mac Aodha 1969; Gaeltarra/SFADCO 1971; Hanly 1971; Ó Riagáin 1971). It has largely succeeded and although commuting takes place along the whole length of the coast it is not of major proportions west of An Spidéal. Population increases in every DED between 1971 and 1981 reflected modest prosperity which has been fairly well maintained; but what has been lost for Irish is the old self-sufficiency and relative isolation. Employment independent of the city still brought cars, high purchasing power, a desire for urban-style entertainment, and therefore far more frequent visits to the anglicized metropolis, which till the 1960s was remote for most people west of An Spidéal. Now it is at most 40 minutes' drive away and the linguistic consequences are apparent everywhere, perhaps less in the *deontas* figures than when talking to the young in the westerly districts.

Little time need be occupied pondering Bearna and Na Forbacha. Except among a few enthusiastic professional people there is no pretence that these are really still Gaeltacht places. Conscientiously Irish-speaking families exist at both, but not in much greater concentration than in the professional Dublin suburbs. Their Irish also tends to be the secondary literary Irish acquired at school, not from 'the hearth'. *Naíonraí* at both are effecting remedial action but can do nothing about *native* Irish in places where most of the people are urban incomers. Na Forbacha, which had a good reputation for Irish thirty years ago, has seen its teaching staff double with recent residential growth. Irish remains the principal medium of instruction and is readily absorbed by children of 5 years of age, but it would be foolish to pretend that more than a handful come with it from home as distinct from the *naíonra*. Effective second-language teaching is evident here.

Na Forbacha is a place of some linguistic sensitivity, because its industrial estate includes the national headquarters of Údarás na Gaeltachta, the Gaeltacht Authority, and the central Gaeltacht office of Roinn na Gaeltachta, the Gaeltacht Department (i.e. ministry), whose head office is of course with the minister in Dublin. Údarás's predecessor, Gaeltarra Éireann, was often criticized for being based in Dublin and therefore out of touch with Gaeltacht needs which it was meant to serve, and An Roinn received similar brickbats. When after much debate both set up at Na Forbacha, under eight miles by car from the centre of Galway city, cynicism abounded among Gaeltacht Gaeilgeoirí. There were many good reasons for choosing a 'green field' site near an existing central place with basic infrastructure such as a telephone system, roads, residential accommodation, schools for officers' and staff's children, etc. It is the dominant lore of the immediately adjacent Gaeltacht that few of the officers and higher staff are native Irish speakers and that even fewer of their wives and families speak Irish in normal circumstances. I was further assured that all the upper echelons drive into Na Forbacha each morning in big cars from Galway or from its wealthy and nearer seaside suburb Salthill (Bóthar na Trá: but wholly anglicized) and that the lowly secretaries and ancillaries cycle in from the Irish-speaking districts to the west.

There can in fact be no doubt at all about the language competence in both organizations, which conduct all their internal work through Irish and have a high proportion of native speakers in their upper ranks. As many of them were previously working in or promoted to Dublin, because they are good and it is the capital, many found wives there and/or produced children there, so many must have families which in part come from an English-language background and would not be at ease in Irish. However, from a middle-class background, even 'learner' wives and children are commonly keener to use Irish than the average Gaeltacht native speaker and almost all are less frightened that bilingualism and especially learning Irish may ruin job prospects. I first heard the expression 'Gaeltacht chauvinism' (see p. 164) here when provocatively quoting some of these generalizations and inviting comment from a well-qualified officer with a native Irish-speaking wife. The reality exists and does make difficult some attempts to help the Gaeltacht from outside. But even if the accusations were true, which does seem to be more so when it concerns the directions of travel, then the dire consequences for the Irish language in the Gaeltacht are much reduced compared with what would have happened if the choice of location had put the wives and families into the centre of the Gaeltacht – say at An Cheathrú Rua (which I had favoured in principle) – instead of settling them harmlessly in anglicized Galway, feeding children into already anglicized schools or into a *scoil lán-Ghaeilge*, designed for non-native speakers.

It is generally understood in Cois Fharraige that the high-technology industries which have been introduced find more difficulty maintaining the use of Irish in their work-forces than those based on local resources. This is not so much because more 'key men' are brought in as because of reluctance to use 'new' Irish coinings of vocabulary (the English ones are new too) and a general feeling that such very modern concepts cannot be expressed through the traditional language which the workers often still speak at home. There is a psychological blockage, as if love of the 'old' language itself precludes its use for 'modern' technological wealth-creating purposes.

An Spidéal, long the main village of Cois Fharraige (162 people in 1956), has an old reputation for anglicizing tendencies which are usually blamed on the presence of a police barracks and a coastguard station 'under the British', plus the presence of a 'big house' which is still there and active. Independence and the language movement weakened the trend, converting the schools to the Irish medium and building a good 'Irish college' tradition, but in 1957 English was more spoken than Irish in the shops and bars, and country people who came to market here often used English in the village, much as they put their best clothes on to go to church: it seemed proper. Younger women and senior schoolgirls were said to be leading a 'fashionable' drift towards English, under the influence of proximity (ten miles) to the Salthill dance halls – by bus. A 35 per cent increase in the DED population between 1971 and 1981 hardened existing trends and although the schools still maintain the language one would never guess the *deontas* figures (52 per cent in 1985–6) by listening to any age group of the children or teenagers outside school hours. The latter speak (and shout) fluent idiomatic English and on enquiry admit no normal habitual use of Irish, though all profess fluency, as is natural after a full education in it.

Native-speaking parents are not now to be assumed, for marrying in, which was always found in the village, has become common from the Galway side, additional to whole families from Galway who choose to live here. Hostility to Irish is again rare but was well articulated on utilitarian grounds by one informant. A group of young workers (aged about 30) who gave me their time were certain that theirs would be the last generation to speak Irish naturally. An older incomer with many dealings said most could speak Irish but did not. There was little to be heard in the busy street, and then only among the elderly. A rough consensus among young people I consulted was that the real Gaeltacht (where most spoke Irish) began at Aille, about three miles 'back' to the west. This is a fair approximation and in this language transition zone mainly means that children who learn their

Irish at school west of Aille find plenty at home with native-speaking parents (who did not teach it to them), so often develop a natural use for it which lasts into later life – or has done till now. Around Spidéal and farther east this is unusual.

Sparse as was interior settlement in Cois Fharraige, the years since 1950 have seen continued depopulation, masked statistically by coastal accretions in the same DEDs. All four former interior schools have closed, from the very remote north-western pair at Seana Phéistín (a new forestry settlement of *c.* 1926) and Gleann Mhic Mhuirinn/Glenicmurrin to Buaile Uisce/Boliska behind An Spidéal and Leamh Choill/Laughil on the minor road to Maigh Cuilinn/Moycullen. In the last two cases the feeding of their remaining children into bigger schools in the anglicized villages, with transport provided, has inevitable linguistic consequences in socialization in the playground.

Ceantair imeallacha/Marginal (or border) districts

The northern and north-eastern fringes of Cois Fharraige include a number of Gaeltacht-border districts whose schools occasionally appear in the *deontas* tables but which are in no way native Irish-speaking. They are listed together in appendices 3 and 4. Most are on or near the main Galway to Clifden road, which was the main line of English penetration early in the century, and none makes any normal use of Irish. Interest in the language waxes and wanes, often reflecting a change of school staff (more especially the head) and otherwise a sudden awareness among parents that a neighbour has secured an attractive Gaeltacht housing grant. In such cases applications for the children to be tested for the *deontas* begin to come in from schools which have submitted none for years and it may be assumed that if there is a decent showing of Irish such returned prodigals will be treated favourably and given reasonable time to prove themselves. (See pp. 55–6.) That there is no absolute standard applied uniformly to schools in different linguistic circumstances is illustrated by the fact that Na Tuairíní/Tooreeny's 53·1 per cent cannot be regarded as proportionate to Tír an Fhia's 60·3 per cent. Much as the language is weakening at the latter, it is dead as a native language at Tuairíní; but good work is being done for it in school.

The absence of *coláistí samhraidh*, *naíonraí*, or eligibility for the placement of Gael-Linn children is diagnostic of the state of the language. There is an *ógchlub* at Maigh Cuilinn, denoting some sustained interest after school.

Conamara summary

Despite the weaknesses noted as developing among the children the south Conamara Gaeltacht remains by far the strongest in the country, with a total of 10,610 Irish speakers in 1981 if the figures for DEDs returning 80 per cent or more of Irish speakers are believed. These exclude Árainn. Ten thousand and forty were living in DEDs which had *deontas* majorities in their primary schools in 1985–6, i.e. almost half the total for all Gaeltachtaí. (See appendices 4 and 5.) If the adjacent Árainn is added there is a clear majority. There is no other Gaeltacht to compare when account is taken of the population living in school areas with 70 per cent or more of *deontas* earners: 4,835 (5,691 with Árainn) is 51·8 per cent (61 per cent) of the national total. North-west Donegal and west Corca Dhuibhne have fewer than 2,000 each, so it is clear that the fate of the native language will be decided here.

Distilled still further, the future lies with the twenty-four primary schools (two at An Spidéal) with simple *deontas* majorities in 1985–6; but it has been shown how little a simple majority can mean in terms of living native Irish. Anything like security on a substantially home-Irish base requires *deontas* majorities of 70 per cent or more. These are confined to sixteen schools, mostly very small, with a total of 735 pupils in receipt of the grant in 1985–6. Including Árainn, there are twenty schools and 817 pupils. All are within fifty miles of Galway city and none of the schools in the principal villages qualifies for inclusion.

Gaillimh Láir/Mid Galway

There is little to be said of this little Gaeltacht east of Galway city except that it is dead and that Irish was nearly dead thirty years ago as a language of normal conversation. There were nevertheless plenty of native speakers still alive, forming majorities even at Mionlach/Menlough, within three miles of the city centre and within its boundaries. All the legally defined Gaeltacht had habitual Irish speakers but these were ageing and no *deontas* figures I heard exceeded 40 per cent. Now none exceeds 21 per cent and that reflects as usual the work of the school and little else. The rest are minute. Sixty-one primary children received the *deontas* in 1985–6, including thirty-two in Galway city schools. The city has expanded its built-up area enormously in the past thirty years, swamping Mionlach in housing estates and turning most of this nominal Gaeltacht into commuter settlements. It is a standing joke that Galway's municipal Terryland estate has 2,000 potential voters in the elections for Údarás na Gaeltachta – but the great majority there are not interested and neither care nor vote.

Census claims of ability to speak Irish reach as high as 67·1 per cent (1981) in the odd DED but mean nothing at all for the living language. Knowing the area quite well, I was inclined to ignore it in 1987, but An Carn Mór's 20 per cent *deontas* score merited local enquiry, if only to confirm suspicions. The school has an interesting background of dogged effort for Irish, mixed up with political conflict in earlier years. This and recent desires for Gaeltacht grants have helped maintain language consciousness to a fair extent and the school teaches substantially through Irish. I heard its infants at work in Irish, though English was audibly their natural language of play and only a handful had Irish from home. Secondary education, of course, takes all primary children into the city and involves little or no further use of the Irish medium. This is hardly a point of criticism where scarcely any pupils have Irish as a native language and where textbook shortages cause a resort to English ones even in the heart of the real Gaeltacht.

Na hOileáin Árann/Aran Islands

With only one DED and 1,368 people (1981) the three islands may not seem to merit classification as a separate Gaeltacht, but their situation makes them separate and from some points of view they can even be regarded as three distinct units. Inis Oírr/Inisheer at one time looked likely to be the first to subside into English, as during the British period the presence of coastguards, lighthouse keepers, and their families had a disproportionate influence on a small island population quite close to the Clare mainland and dependent on Ennistimon fair in its economic life. This brought early bilingualism but had not reached the stage of transition to English as first language before the withdrawal of the coastguards and the inter-war depression reduced these external contacts and was replaced by all-Irish policies in school and church.

Thirty years ago strong signs of anglicization were confined to the Inis Mór/Inishmore village of Cill Rónáin/Kilronan, the only port which can offer some shelter to the ferry boats which are still the main contact with the mainland, though the airstrip is anyway only two miles away through Cill Éinne/Killeany. H. Wagner (1958a) had already written off the whole of the main island as predominantly English except for some houses and part of the older generation, but this seemed premature. The school inspector was doubtful of the children's fluency at Cill Rónáin, but gave all the *deontas*, and Irish was the medium of instruction in both the primary and the vocational schools. The parish priest thought about a quarter of the entire population of Inis Mór (including Cill Rónáin) to be habitual English speakers but almost all could speak Irish if the need arose, which it did not in the course of shopping in the village. Nevertheless Irish was the only vernacular language used in the church, in parish meetings, and in all other branches of public life. The main difference between Inis Mór and the inner Conamara Gaeltacht was that whereas officials and priests sent to both almost invariably perfected their spoken Irish, which was absolutely essential for their work, the wives and children of officials coming to Cill Rónáin were under no such pressure from neighbours, bilingualism already being well inclined towards English first.

The 1985–6 *deontas* figures demonstrate that earlier weakening at Cill

Rónáin has developed into collapse, only slightly assisted by 'blow-ins' associated with tourism. The combined population of the DED had fallen by 1981 almost to 60 per cent of the 1926 total. Where in general English used to predominate on the streets and Irish in the homes, now English prevails in both and the 1985–6 *deontas* score of 41 per cent is much closer to reality than the 87·5 per cent recorded in 1981–2, astoundingly higher than Eoghanacht/Onaght's 64·1 per cent in the far west of the island, which may have been influenced by Gael-Linn children and was back to 84·8 per cent, i.e. all except the under-aged, within four years. The summer college on Inis Mór sensibly avoids Cill Rónáin, which could do with a *naíonra* to bolster its pre-school Irish. Either there must be too little demand or no suitable accommodation, but it is odd that the only *naíonra* in the islands is on Inis Oírr, with one of the highest *deontas* scores in the country (92·4 per cent), possibly explained by the *naíonra's* drawing off infants who might otherwise be in school to depress the *deontas* figures until they reach six.

The efforts of the state to support the Irish language in Árainn may be seen in the provision of post-primary education, which when left (as is usual in most parts of Ireland) to voluntary bodies – i.e. the Church – meant that only a few wealthy families could afford to send their children to the mainland for it, and this almost inevitably involved anglicization through residence in an English-speaking place. Cill Rónáin has had a *gairm-scoil* (see above, p. 39) for many years, but since 1967 free secondary education for all has necessitated provision for islanders who previously had none, either by building new island schools or by hostel or other boarding provision on the mainland.

The desire to avoid the usual linguistic consequences of the latter resulted in the opening of a new secondary school on Inis Oírr in 1985–6, with an initial intake of twelve pupils. The island primary school had forty on the roll. It is nearly three miles by stormy sea, pier to pier, from Inis Meáin/Inishmaan (twenty-seven primary children on the roll). The new school obviously reduces direct exposure to anglicizing pressures but it may be doubted whether parents who are aware via the media of opportunities elsewhere will be convinced that the range of subject choice and other stimuli in so tiny a school does not cancel out the language benefits. The children may also think themselves cheated and see the language itself as prison bars which keep them in the island, deprived of opportunities available to most other Irish children. Such a school seems a gamble and one hopes it works, but whether it was built or not the consequences for Irish would seem likely to be adverse. The alternative would be boarding provision, presumably at Cill Rónáin or Galway. It is all too easy to see the snags and hard to suggest viable alternatives. How can one possibly maintain linguistic separation at secondary level for a three-island primary school population totalling 228, of whom 44 per cent

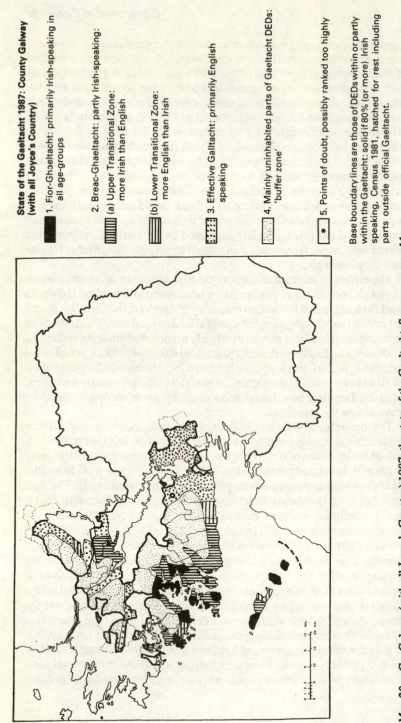

State of the Gaeltacht 1987: County Galway (with all Joyce's Country)

1. **Fíor-Ghaeltacht:** primarily Irish-speaking in all age-groups

2. **Breac-Ghaeltacht:** partly Irish-speaking:

   (a) Upper Transitional Zone: more Irish than English

   (b) Lower Transitional Zone: more English than Irish

3. **Effective Galltacht:** primarily English speaking

4. **Mainly uninhabited parts of Gaeltacht DEDs:** 'buffer zone'

5. Points of doubt, possibly ranked too highly *

Base boundary lines are those of DEDs within or partly within the Gaeltacht: solid if 80% (or more) Irish speaking, Census 1981, hatched for rest including parts outside official Gaeltacht.

Map 20 Co. Galway (with all Joyce's Country) 1987: the state of the Gaeltacht. Sources as map 11

attend a school whose catchment area mainly speaks English?

Údarás na Gaeltachta's annual report for 1985 listed seventeen minor industrial enterprises in receipt of grants in Árainn, only five of them on Inis Mór and almost all of them (fourteen) concerned with fishing or boat repairs, i.e. exploitation of indigenous resources. For effective language support this is commendably distributed and chosen, and compares well with only ten minor industrial grants in the much more populous but non-Irish-speaking mid Galway Gaeltacht. Nevertheless the grants to the latter were much larger on average and five major industries (including a partly owned associate company) were supported, as against only one in Árainn on Inis Meáin. In defence of Údarás it must be noted that it has to wait to be asked before giving aid, which is normally proportionate to the amount put into the enterprise by the applicant: so the record on Árainn is encouraging, regardless of the linguistic merits of any Gaeltacht investment in mid Galway.

Chapter seven

Gaeltachtaí of Munster

Co. Chiarraí /Kerry

Kerry is in the province of Munster, the Irish dialects of which are the basis of modern literary Irish because this was the richest part of the country to maintain Irish widely to the nineteenth century and here had been the necessary wealth to support a literate class to create a literature for revivalists to rediscover. Unfortunately this same relative wealth provided more impetus to English on the petering out of the Penal Laws and by 1926 the Gaeltacht Commission could find only small areas in which Irish was at all secure. There is no evidence that the use of the Munster literary dialect as the basis of modern standard Irish as promoted through the schools has been of any special benefit to the maintenance of normal daily use among native speakers in the province. Rates of decline slowed everywhere after 1922, but as Munster's was most advanced at the beginning there was less to lose. (See p. 205.) Today it is generally accepted that if the rules for the award of the *deontas* were applied strictly in regard to the requirement for Irish to be *the* habitual language of the home then at most a single handful of schools would show a majority, and possibly none at all.

Only 592 primary school children in all the Munster Gaeltachtaí received the *deontas* in 1985–6, scattered through twenty-seven schools only nine of which showed majorities, including three of around 70 per cent or over. Detailed consideration should bear these stark facts in mind.

Corca Dhuibhne/Corkaguiny

This is the south Conamara of the Munster Gaeltachtaí, compact and beautiful in the western ends of what to tourists is the Dingle peninsula but is properly Corca Dhuibhne/Corkaguiny. The districts in which Irish may be heard in normal daily use have not changed much over the past thirty years and remain bounded by the low ridge north-west of Dingle (An Daingean), with a 'grey area' west around Ceann Trá/Ventry which was

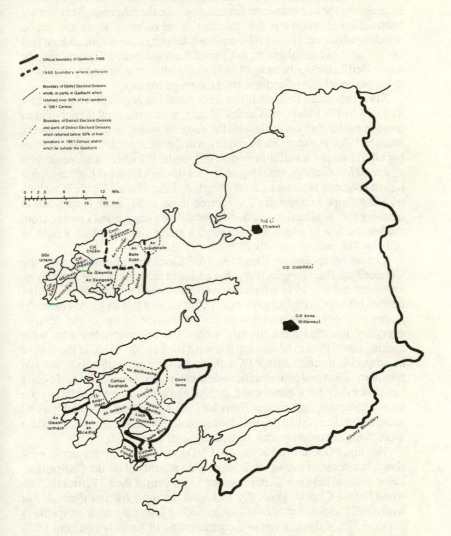

Official boundary of Gaeltacht 1988

1956 boundary where different

Boundary of District Electoral Divisions
wholly or partly in Gaeltacht which
returned over 80% of Irish speakers
in 1981 Census

Boundary of District Electoral Divisions
and parts of District Electoral Divisions
which returned below 80% of Irish
speakers in 1981 Census and/or
which lie outside the Gaeltacht

0 1 2 3   6   9   12 Mls.

0   5   10   15   20 Km.

Trá Lí
(Tralee)

CO. CHIARRAÍ

Cnoc
Bréanainn

Cill
Chuáin   An Clochán

Dún   An
Urlann   Baile
                               Dubh   An Sráidbhaile

Cill
Mhic a'   Caorach
Cháraigh   Na Gleannta

Dún   An Daingean
Chaoin
        Múrbhach

Fionntrá   Cinnáird   Minfhir

Cill Airne
(Killarney)

Na Beitheacha

Cathair
Saidhbhín   Ceanúig   Doire
                                                         Ianna

Tír
Amair-   Máistir
theach   Gaoithe
        An Iimleach

An   Loch
Gleann   an Choiseáin
Iarthach

Baile
an
Sceilig

                              Baile Bhric

Doire   Cathair
Fhionáin   Domhnall

County Boundary

County Boundary

Map 21 Co. Kerry: the Gaeltacht, its DEDs and part-DEDs. Names in Irish as census 1981

noted for its anglicizing aspirations even before the First World War but got no worse for many years. The inclusion of the town of Dingle in the official Gaeltacht in 1926 and again on its contraction in 1956 was barely warranted by any normal use of the language there but manifested a desire to recapture the one dominant central place for the language. This has not been achieved, except at the 'tokenist' level of street signs and public notices and one excellent café-cum-Irish-language-bookshop. About half of Údarás's industrial grants in Corca Dhuibhne were in Dingle and the anglicized district to the east in 1985, accessibility and centrality providing more powerful considerations than language loyalty.

Six rather small DEDs with an Irish-speaking population enumerated as 2,014 in 1981 form the Gaeltacht core, with a nominal 90 per cent or more in each. They coincide with the *deontas*-majority school catchment areas of 1985–6, except for the addition to the latter of Na Gleannta/Glens (or Glin) two and a half miles north of Dingle, for which it serves in part as a *scoil lán-Gaeilge*, teaching as it does through Irish to children whose native language is almost entirely English. Like Minard Castle (Caisleán na Mine Airde in appendix 3), referred to on p. 54, there is no point in classing this as effective Gaeltacht, for the language is not coming from the homes, few of which now preserve a native fluency which would be of help. The parents are school-learners too.

The same applies to Cloghane (An Clochán), north-east over the Connor Pass from Dingle, in an area added to the official Gaeltacht by an extension order in 1974 which made no sense at all in terms of the area of normal Irish speaking but gave equity of treatment and access to Gaeltacht grants to populations which were no more given to the use of Irish in everyday life than most already within the boundary, but who were making fair efforts to encourage it among their children, under the lead of an inspiring teacher: Minard Castle and Glens are both inside the old boundary. Electoral considerations doubtless also played a part and cynics insist that they were paramount, though again the desire to help anyone known to be making serious efforts for Irish was validation enough if one accepts that decline had devalued the meaning of *Gaeltacht* already, so no more damage could be done by making it still less Irish.

The inner Gaeltacht, i.e. the six DEDs which occupy the north-west shore, has some of the worst demographic records of all the Gaeltachtaí, being down to between 38 per cent and 55 per cent of their 1926 totals. The worst is Dún Chaoin, generally reckoned the most Irish of them all but with a 1981 population of only 179, including fourteen non-Irish speakers over the age of three. Even in the prosperous 1970s only one core DED halted its decline, with an increase of one person at Ventry (Fionntráigh in the census reports). Only one other of the thirteen in the entire official Gaeltacht showed an increase, significantly Glin (Na Gleannta: see appendix 2), which jumped by 27 per cent as Dingle town expanded into

110

it. This lacked the linguistic consequences of Galway city's expansion westwards, for Glin was already habitually English.

Local enquiry revealed general pessimism about the prospects of the language in Corca Dhuibhne and mutual recrimination between natives and 'blow-ins' on where to lay the blame. Intelligent and well informed people spoke hotly on both sides. Despite population decline there are large numbers of people married in and rearing families without Irish, alongside others who show more enthusiasm for Irish in their homes than do many natives. As there are undoubtedly far more natives and the language is being abandoned among the children generally it must obviously be unjust to blame one or the other for what is evidently the result of a wide consensus. Gaeilgeoirí agree that most parents in all districts except possibly Dún Chaoin are now speaking at least as much English as Irish to their pre-school children, and that the Irish which is spoken lacks idiom and expressiveness, reflecting the fact that the speakers are thinking in English or saturated in English ideas absorbed from television. This is so even at An Fheothanach/Feohanagh, which has a 79 per cent *deontas* return (i.e. all who were eligible), a *coláiste samhraidh*, a *naíonra* close by, and is good enough to receive Gael-Linn children for three months at a time. It was mentioned in this area that the scholarship children were not always well enough prepared in Irish to benefit fully from their period of all-Irish instruction; but they did no harm in mixing with the local children, because the latter usually preferred to speak English outside school.

An influence noted elsewhere but marked here, perhaps because it is a holiday area, was the presence at Easter of large numbers of visitors, especially from Dublin, staying with relatives who live here. The demographic record of decline of course means that every native family has large numbers of relatives who left for a city life and in most cases married and settled down to raise a family in a city. With modern prosperity and mobility they can afford to come 'home' regularly, bringing their English-speaking families into their parents', brothers', or sisters' Irish-speaking family homes for weeks at a time. These visits are reciprocated and Irish-speaking families trip off to Dublin and even England for one of the vacations. When the guests come to the Gaeltacht, the language of the home turns English while they are here, for the non-native spouse and children are rarely fluent in Irish and the Gaeltacht children love to show off their English to prove they are not country bumpkins. When the Gaeltacht family goes to Dublin, etc., the same applies, reinforced by the added thrill of being in the city. This is an inescapable part of the modernization and mobilization of society, reinforced locally by the crowding of local beaches with day or half-day trippers from anglicized Dingle any sunny weekend or school holiday from Easter onwards. The strongest Gaeltacht districts form an arc north

111

and west of the town, which is never above eleven miles away, i.e. a twenty to thirty minutes' drive. Even without the television in every home and videos in many it would be difficult to save Irish from this.

Widespread complaints about the alleged tendency of Údarás to help mainly outsiders who flit into the Gaeltacht and flit out when the grant is spent have some substance, based on a deficiency of local venture capital and enterprise for Údarás to encourage. It has little bearing on the fate of the language. Comharchumann Chorca Dhuibhne, the producer co-operative on which great hopes were based in the 1970s, has shrunk to a shadow and chiefly confines itself to cultural activities, including the summer school and good-quality 'heritage' work, heavily assisted by the state. There are recriminations about that, too, centring on the alleged inability of Gaeltacht people to work in co-operation with each other. This is placed in the wider context of general lack of confidence in economic prospects at home on pp. 179–81. Many younger informants think this is new but it was universal in the 1950s, long before the *comharchumannaí* achieved their short-lived fame and raised ill-founded expectations. The demographic record which reflects experience since the Famine is sufficient explanation without considering recent misfortunes, alleged management deficiencies, accounting failures, or the like, and the relationship of this background to the fate of the language is also clear enough.

Dún Chaoin's 55·2 per cent *deontas* score in 1985–6 is very misleading, because there were always four or five Gael-Linn children present (this school received nineteen of the Corca Dhuibhne total of forty-eight in 1986) and the school has more than the usual proportion of children under 6. If they are discounted the score becomes 100 per cent. The unique feature here is that there was a long-running attempt by the Department of Education to close the school in the 1970s and to transfer the children to Baile an Fheirtéaraigh/Ballyferriter, almost four miles away. This sparked a national protest which was the culmination of many rumblings about the 'rationalizing out' of small schools and alleged resultant destruction of traditional communities on grounds of educational efficiency, greater opportunities and stimuli for children, etc. (see pp. 205–6.) Baile an Fheirtéaraigh had had some anglicizing tendencies years ago, mostly centring on the parish church and its priests, but these had long been rectified. More emotive was the aura of Dún Chaoin as the mainland home of the Blasket Islanders of literary fame, finally resettled here in 1954. In short, a major *cause célèbre* blew up, Gaeltacht 'civil rights' and language supporters rushed to the aid of the threatened school, the community split between those who accepted the logic of amalgamation and those who did not, and for some time the school subsisted on voluntary contributions. Eventually the Department of Education gave in, so the school survived, with two teachers and twenty-nine pupils on the roll (1985–6), the second teacher secured since 1981–2 as the result of the augmentation of numbers

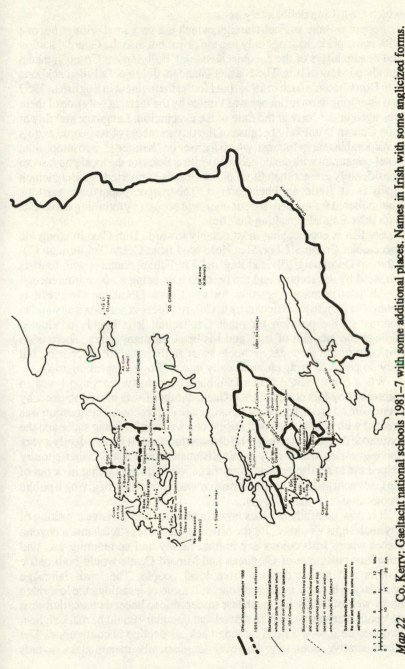

Map 22 Co. Kerry: Gaeltacht national schools 1981–7 with some additional places. Names in Irish with some anglicized forms. Sources as map 13

which Gael-Linn deliberately assists.

People at Baile an Fheirtéaraigh, which is a very small village but one with some pride, as it not only has the priest but also the Guards' station and headquarters of the *comharchumann* ('Ballyferriter Co-op'), take a jaundiced view of this. The Blasket Islanders did inject a little backbone into Dún Chaoin's Irish in 1954, but I found them fluent in English in 1957 and their long-term influence was limited by the fact that only one of them was aged under forty at the time of the evacuation. Language stability at Dún Chaoin is unlikely because of the tiny numbers of its people and its considerable tourist interest, which focuses on 'Kruger's', a cosmopolitan hotel-restaurant with dance hall whose attractions for the local youth seem considerably greater than those of the Údarás-supported *ógchlub*, which again is at Baile an Fheirtéaraigh. The native population must be outnumbered for much of the summer, and not just by returning emigrants with their English-speaking families.

English is encroaching most notably towards Dún Chaoin along the spectacular Ceann Sléibhe/Slea Head road from Ceann Trá through Cill Mhic an Domhnaig/Kilvicadonig and Fán/Fahan, contacts with tourists attracted by the scenery and the beehive huts being a major influence.

All post-primary education for the Corca Dhuibhne Gaeltacht is centred in Dingle town or nearby in Coláiste Íde, but paradoxically and in contrast to the position for other Gaeltachtaí it is largely conducted through the medium of Irish and has been for many years. There is no criticism of the secondary schools as an anglicizing influence here, but they do perforce bring children daily into an English-speaking town.

When I first visited Corca Dhuibhne over thirty years ago I was so impressed by this compact little Gaeltacht that I was moved to ask why there were no proud boundary signs to mark its presence. The question was greeted with polite incomprehension or a wry and knowing smile and the assurance that there was as yet no demand for them. It was evidently a very naive question which only an Englishman would ask. Further enquiry helped me to realize how ambivalent people felt about being in or out of the Gaeltacht and how deeply sensitive was the question of giving it public recognition on roadside signs.

It is now painfully obvious how contentious and divisive the siting of any such signs would be, for the official boundaries stretch miles beyond places where Irish enjoys any normal family and community use, and boundary posts east of Cloghane and Minard Castle would both baffle visitors and attract derision from local people. The 'real' language boundary is in fact a transition zone, still more or less along the low ridge north-west of Dingle but much less susceptible to linear demarcation west of Ventry harbour. And if an agreed real boundary could be marked, how long before it would need moving back, as decline is continuous? The administrative boundary, however linguistically meaningless, avoids such issues – so long as it too remains visually unmarked, eschewing public provocation and contentiousness: out of sight, out of mind.

Uíbh Ráthach/Iveragh

The inclusion of attenuated portions of the ancient barony in the official Gaeltacht in 1956 was an act of faith in the survival of Irish there, but practical limitations to that faith were expressed by the sensible exclusion of the one recognizable central place of Waterville, utterly anglicized and never referred to naturally as An Coireán. Only four DEDs and parts of eight more were classed as Gaeltacht and the official map (*Límistéirí Gaeltachta* 1956) showed only half the area as having large proportions of Irish speakers, distributed in four separate pockets. (See map 9.) Local enquiry reduced this still further.

Native speakers in 1957 abounded in Baile an Sceilg/Ballinskelligs, in the upper Gleann na hUíne/Inny Valley around Caisleach/Cashlagh, and most could speak Irish in the former fishing village of Lóthar/Loher, south of Waterville, but few did. Everywhere English was predominant among the children. The position resembled that in much of Iorras/Erris. Pádraig Breathnach, a respected language activist, admitted to me his own difficulty in assessing the extent to which Irish was habitually spoken. All spoke Irish to him but many of the children were 'not so fluent' when they entered school. Only about 100 families were estimated to maintain Irish in the entire Inny valley and intermarriage with more numerous anglicized neighbours was eroding them fast. Shopping and marketing were entirely in anglicized places and shopkeepers at Dún Géagáin/Dungeagan, the principal nucleus in Baile an Sceilg, had led the drift to English there. The *coláiste samhraidh* which still meets there was criticized as not very helpful because so many of its students came mainly for a holiday or to advance careers for which an Irish qualification was essential but unloved, and the local children, three-quarters of whom would emigrate, were keen to practise their own English. Its survival till now is remarkable, given the 15·6 per cent *deontas* score in the local school (1985–6), but the presence of a *naíonra* shows there is at least some popular desire to preserve the language. In general in Uíbh Ráthach even the pretence of maintaining Irish has worn thin and Baile an Sceilg was the sole full DED to return my Breac-Ghaeltacht minimum of 80 per cent of enumerated Irish speakers in 1981. There were no pretended 'Fíor-Ghaeltacht' scores above 90 per cent.

Enquiries in 1987 confirmed a disastrous situation suggested by the *deontas* figures. Most of the little schools which had formerly helped to sustain the language by giving it to the children had closed in the intervening years. Five had gone, their areas now mostly feeding into the big (110 pupils in 1985–6) new school at An Chillín Liath/Killeenleeha,

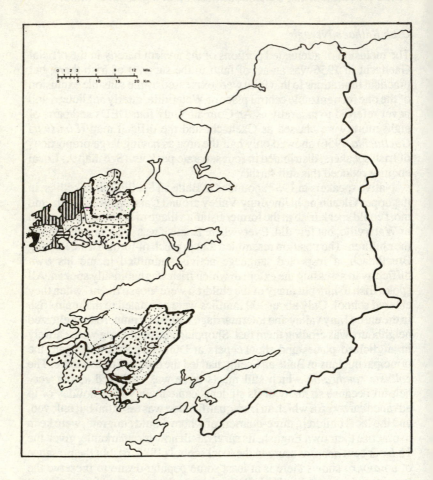

State of the Gaeltacht 1987: County Kerry
1. Fíor-Ghaeltacht: primarily Irish-speaking in all age-groups
2. Breac-Ghaeltacht: partly Irish-speaking:
    (a) Upper Transitional Zone: more Irish than English
    (b) Lower Transitional Zone: more English than Irish
3. Effective Galltacht: primarily English speaking
4. Mainly uninhabited parts of Gaeltacht DEDs: 'buffer zone'
5. Points of doubt, possibly ranked too highly

Base boundary lines are those of DEDs within or partly within the Gaeltacht: solid if 80% (or more) Irish speaking, Census 1981, hatched for rest including parts outside official Gaeltacht.

Map 23   Co. Kerry 1987: the state of the Gaeltacht. Sources as map 11

which is central in the upper valley but near nowhere at all, alone at a crossroads. Its 28·2 per cent of *deontas*-earners came mostly from the Caisleach direction, where the old school is now a Mass centre, but people there admit that the children's Irish lacks the practice of talking to the old people who have died off since I called in 1957. Here again *deontas* awards primarily reflect achievements by the school, as is also the case at Baile an Sceilg and Lóthar, the *naíonra* deserving credit at the former too.

In short, the language is almost as dead in Uíbh Ráthach as in Tralee, Cork, or Dublin. There are no normal habitual Irish speakers of working age, other than teachers and a few professional people who are formally required to use it, and to the children it is almost as foreign as French. Údarás nevertheless has a wholly owned subsidiary company running a big hotel, and has given major industrial grants to three surviving companies and minor ones to eleven different enterprises, including two in Waterville. One recipient I met in Baile an Sceilg told me he hated Irish, though he spoke it. He had had all his primary education through it, then got nothing but English as the medium in secondary school, and the confusion drove him mad. Everything modern and useful comes in English, he declared. It is not irrelevant to note that Baile an Sceilg DED was down to 42 per cent of its 1926 population by 1981, Doire Ianna/ Derriana in the upper valley was on 44 per cent, and Máistir Gaoithe/ Mastergeehy, lower down, on 37 per cent; and a grand total of fifty-six primary school children had enough Irish to qualify for the *deontas*.

When in 1957 I queried the definition of the entire area as Gaeltacht and suggested that it should be downgraded to Galltacht I was impressed by the point that, with so much English already being spoken in the homes, to remove its Gaeltacht status would fatally discourage the minority of parents who were making serious efforts to foster Irish in their homes and so hasten its death, removing all hope of revival. Only a mystic dreamer could still harbour such hope in Uíbh Ráthach and it is a chastening thought that most of the people have left since independence.

Co. Chorcaí/Cork

There are two official Gaeltachtaí in Co. Cork, one small and the other minute. Múscraí Uí Fhloinn/West Muskerry is the only official Gaeltacht in the country that is entirely inland – ignoring the planted colonies in Meath – and Oileán Chléire/Clear Island is the only one confined to one island and half a DED. Both lie well west in the county but Múscraí's position astride the main Cork–Killarney road and the tourist route to Gougane Bara must make it the most frequented of all Gaeltachtaí, and in quality of land and amount of industrial employment it is probably the richest. Their combined populations in 1981 were 3,050, including 2,865 Irish speakers, as usual a much inflated figure. Only 103 primary school children earned the *deontas* in 1985–6 and they were scattered among eight schools, only two of which can be taken seriously in respect of native Irish. There were 641 national schools in the county and city.

Múscraí Uí Fhloinn/West Muskerry

This Gaeltacht consisted of five DEDs and four part-DEDs until 1982, when a government order extended it eastwards towards Macroom, incorporating all or most of the rest of two of the part-DEDs. The idea of the language expanding challenged investigation, and proved once again to be justified by equity and encouragement. The newly incorporated townlands spoke no less Irish than those already included, the schools showed fair language results with some parental support, and the case was made that they ought therefore to be able to share full access to Gaeltacht grants and scholarships, etc. This is not a matter of native Irish in natural everyday use, and the schools' figures (appendix 3) show erratic fluctuations typical of areas where marginally justifiable awards are made 'on trial', to see what results encouragement may bring. This applies to all the schools in the Gaeltacht, the only two with a significant native base among the parents being Cúil Aodha/Coolea and Barr Duínse/Bardinch in the upper Sullán/Sullane valley. They had sixty-six children on their rolls in 1985–6, thirty-eight of whom qualified for the *deontas*.

Barr Duínse is a dispersed rural community a couple of miles higher up the valley than Cúil Aodha and thirty years ago was more reliably Irish in habitual speech. It is barely accessible except through Cúil Aodha, which does have a village-like cluster around its church, school, and post office, so its *deontas* score of 38·1 per cent in 1985–6 seemed odd and challenging compared with Cúil Aodha's 66·7 per cent (appendix 3). English does not usually 'jump' villages to swamp their rural hinterlands. Nor has it done so here. The explanation is sad for the future of the language. A tradition of 'good teaching' of Irish at Cúil Aodha was a major local explanation: 'not so good' at Barr Duínse; but, when asked about what the people themselves spoke, initial evasion usually gave way to admission that there was little difference. There are, as appendix 3 shows, a *naíonra* and an Irish college at Cúil Aodha, denoting pro-Irish leadership and organization, and cultural activities centring on Irish are well supported.

When I visited the district in 1987 almost all the local activists were absent in Dublin for a televised festival in which they played a prominent part, but it is important to give the scale by saying that they and their supporters would fit in a couple of motor coaches, though of course most use cars. It must also be added that emphasis on folk song and music is a usual symptom of language death, as exemplified in the Highlands and Brittany, for they demand no native fluency from exponents or audience. The final, terminal symptoms are pipe music with no words at all and gala

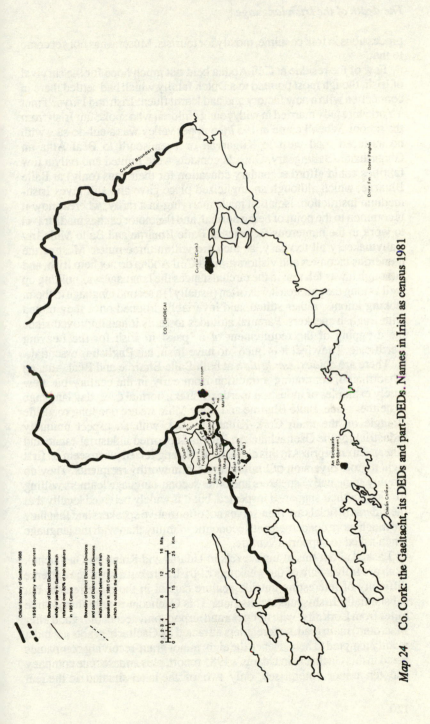

Map 24   Co. Cork: the Gaeltacht, its DEDs and part-DEDs. Names in Irish as census 1981

Official boundary of Gaeltacht 1956

1956 boundary where different

Boundary of District Electoral Divisions
wholly or partly in Gaeltacht which
returned over 80% of Irish speakers
in 1981 Census

Boundary of District Electoral Divisions
and parts of District Electoral Divisions
which returned below 80% of Irish
speakers in 1981 Census and/or
which lie outside the Gaeltacht

0 1 2 3 4   8   12   16   Mls.
0   5   10   15   20   25   Km.

County Boundary

CO. CHORCAÍ

Cúirlí (Cork)

Macroom

Doire Fm.· Doire Finghín

Cúil
na
Mullac

Réidh na
Doirí
Báinseach

Gort na
Tiobraataid

Cúl
Átha
Gaoithe

Cill
na
Martar

Béal
Átha
an Ghaorthaidh

Réal Atha
an Ghaorthaidh
(Mag.)

An Sciobairín
(Skibbereen)

Oileán Chléire

processions in folk costume, mostly for tourists. Múscraí has not yet come to that.

Few of the residue at Cúil Aodha held out much hope for the survival of Irish, though most pointed to a Dutch family which had settled there in connection with a new factory and had learnt fluent Irish and I myself met a Yorkshire lady married in with young children who spoke fair Irish from the school. When I came in 1957 the upper valley was a cul-de-sac, with no surfaced road west to Kilgarvan or even south to Béal Átha an Ghaorthaidh/Ballingeary. Outside contacts were limited and only a few families could afford secondary education for their sons (only) at Baile Bhuirne, which although an anglicized place gave and still gives Irish-medium instruction. Isolation made marrying-in a rarity, whereas now it is common to the point of being normal, and the motor car has made travel to work in the numerous factories at Baile Bhuirne and Baile Mhic Íre/ Ballymakeery all too easy, as they are within three miles. Most of the numerous incomers and visitors around Cúil Aodha do not help Irish, and although it was felt that in the circumstances the language was holding up well among the children it was often (usually?) a second language to them, lacking idioms, rather stilted, and invariably dropped once they mixed with English speakers. Parental attitudes towards it had improved since the dropping of the requirement of a 'pass' in Irish for the Leaving Certificate. They feel it is 'nice ' to have Irish, but English is essential.

There are *coláistí samhraidh* at both Baile Bhuirne and Béal Átha an Ghaorthaidh, continuing a tradition from early in the century but now surely examples of industrial inertia. Irish is a normal everyday language in neither place. Baile Bhuirne and Baile Mhic Íre are one long roadside straggle on the main Cork–Killarney road, with an aspect uniquely industrial for the Gaeltachtaí. An Údarás-supported industrial estate and other such enterprises in this almost entirely anglicized place seem on first sight a gross diversion of limited funds to unworthy recipients. They do employ some native speakers and other second-language learners willing to 'sing for their supper' if inspected, but it is widely believed locally that the Údarás officials are themselves not often native speakers and that they are much more concerned with economic viability than with the language when asked to support a venture.

I asked about this at high levels in Údarás and Roinn na Gaeltachta. Both are fully aware of the weakness of Irish here but also of the extreme difficulty of interesting outside venture capital in the more remote but substantially Irish-speaking districts. This Gaeltacht is only thirty-three miles from Cork city, with its docks and airport, on a decent (*not* good after Macroom) main road, so foreigners attracted by Gaeltacht grants are most readily tempted to here. Hence the eight major grant-receiving companies listed in this Gaeltacht in Údarás's 1985 report, plus an associate company and ten minor enterprises, only two of the latter situated in the real

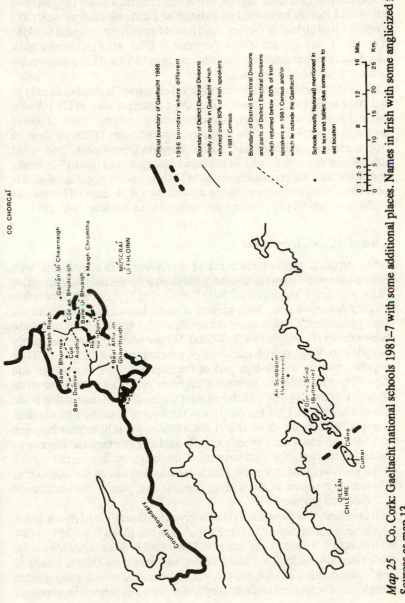

CO. CHORCAÍ

Official boundary of Gaeltacht 1988

1956 boundary where different

Boundary of District Electoral Divisions wholly or partly in Gaeltacht which returned over 80% of Irish speakers in 1981 Census

Boundary of District Electoral Divisions and parts of District Electoral Divisions which returned below 80% of Irish speakers in 1981 Census and/or which lie outside the Gaeltacht

Schools (mostly National) mentioned in the text and tables; plus some towns to aid location

0 1 2 3 4   8   12   16   Mls.
0 5   10   15   20   25   Km.

Sliabh Riach
Baile Bhúirne
Cúil Aodha
Garrán Uí Chearnaigh
Cúm an Bhuacaigh
Barr Duínse
Réidh na nDoirí
Baile Uí Bhuaigh
MÚSCRAÍ UÍ FHLOINN
Béal Átha an Ghaorthaidh
Magh Chromtha

An Sciobairín (Skibbereen)
Dún na Séad (Baltimore)
Cléire
Cuan
OILEÁN CHLÉIRE

County Boundary

Map 25 Co. Cork: Gaeltacht national schools 1981–7 with some additional places. Names in Irish with some anglicized forms. Sources as map 13

Gaeltacht core up the side road at Cúil Aodha. The economic sense of this is obvious but the linguistic sense less so. (See pp. 170–1.) Nevertheless it would be hard to believe that placing the bigger factories at Cúil Aodha would have helped Irish, and experience at Gaoth Dobhair suggests that this would merely have sped its extinction. I did pay random visits to a couple of Baile Bhuirne factories and found English their normal working language. I was assured it was the same at Béal Átha an Ghaorthaidh, which was predominantly English-speaking in 1957 and has a most recent *deontas* score of 12·8 per cent.

With the utmost generosity the Múscraí effective Gaeltacht can only be reckoned as five or six square miles, the catchment area of Cúil Aodha national school, with its thirty *deontas*-earning children, some of whom are English speakers in first language. The relevant DEDs of Gort na Tiobratan/Gortnatubbrid and Doire Finghín/Derryfineen had 1981 populations down to 65 and 54 per cent respectively of their 1926 totals. I estimate the total census-enumerated Irish-speaking population within the *deontas*-majority area as 202, as against the 1,854 returned for the five DEDs in which 80 per cent or more were said to speak Irish in 1981.

Oileán Chléire/Clear Island

Cléire supports the last remnants of south-west Cork Irish and with fourteen *deontas*-earners in its twenty-children school is naturally defensive on the subject. I had immense help here in 1957, about the time when Wagner described it as 'Irish spoken in some houses and by part of the older generation, English being the vernacular'. He considered Irish to be dying rapidly (H. Wagner 1958, 1958a). My own evidence was that nearly everyone could speak Irish and about 60 per cent spoke it habitually. They preponderated in the eastern part of the island, around the school and church but away from the harbour at Cummer, once nicknamed Cumar an Bhéarla ('of the English'). Irish had been the medium of instruction in the school since about 1935 but only six of the twelve families with children in it qualified for the *deontas* in 1958, causing great bitterness between families who knew each other's speech habits better than the inspectors did and some resentful abandonment of the language in rejected homes. In the previous year it was decided to turn to English as the medium of religious instruction in the school, because that was better understood . . . Need one say more?

It is notable that the *deontas* is now given to 65 per cent of the children, i.e. thirteen out of twenty, and the population has fallen from 253 to 164, with occasional evacuation 'scares'. The island is three miles long by at most one mile wide. Two small enterprises received Údarás grants in 1985, one making cheese, the other a co-operative which among other things runs a restaurant and a pottery and repairs machinery. Dependence

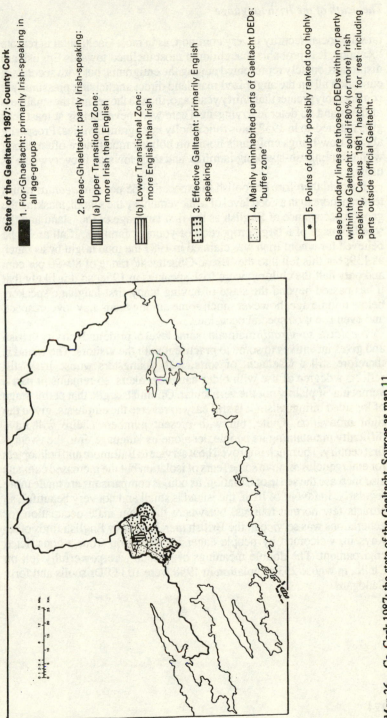

State of the Gaeltacht 1987: County Cork

1. Fíor-Ghaeltacht: primarily Irish-speaking in all age-groups

2. Breac-Ghaeltacht: partly Irish-speaking:

(a) Upper Transitional Zone: more Irish than English

(b) Lower Transitional Zone: more English than Irish

3. Effective Galltacht: primarily English speaking

4. Mainly uninhabited parts of Gaeltacht DEDs: 'buffer zone'

5. Points of doubt, possibly ranked too highly

Base boundary lines are those of DEDs within or partly within the Gaeltacht: solid if 80% (or more) Irish speaking, hatched for rest including parts outside official Gaeltacht.

Map 26 Co. Cork 1987: the state of the Gaeltacht. Sources as map 11

on state social security is very common, as in most Gaeltachtaí in remote locations. It is probable that children most inclined towards English are disproportionately represented among the emigrants, but with secondary education all on the anglicized mainland direct anglicizing pressures are considerably greater than thirty years ago, though the sea and the smallness of the island do deter marrying-in. There were nevertheless at least four girls married-in in 1958, plus four wholly immigrant families. Prosperity abroad now brings emigrants home on holiday much more often, along with their English-speaking families, and the television is everywhere as usual.

It would therefore be foolish to expect that 65 per cent *deontas* return to mean more than a good level of achievement by the school, masking the general acceptance of English as the first language of the island and the sole language of a large proportion of younger families. If all are to be believed for whom Irish was claimed in 1981 the total might be as much as 139; but this fell into the 'Breac-Ghaeltacht' range of 80–90 per cent and only half the children were Irish speakers in 1958, so it is likely that it has passed beyond the stage of having many first-language speakers below middle age, however much some among them may love, respect, and even use it on special occasions.

A *coláiste samhraidh* maintains some level of pride and activity in Irish and gives incentives to some to practise it with the visitors. The island is therefore still a Gaeltacht of sorts, with youngsters whose Irish still reflects a degree of use with older native speakers, so remains in part a vernacular if plainly not the vernacular. Optimists argue that at this stage of lopsided bilingualism it is still easy to reverse the emphasis, given the right motivation. Quite, but with present numbers Cléire will have difficulty maintaining its people, let alone its language, into the twenty-first century. The much improved boat service to Baltimore and helicopters for emergencies remove some fears of isolation but the increased contacts also increase the sense of isolation, as odious comparisons are made more regularly. In favour of Irish, the island is small and not very beautiful, so attracts few normal tourists, but where the main male occupation for generations was service in the British merchant navy English finds other ways in, welcomed by people eager for liberation from a constricted environment. The double meanings of 'insular' are powerfully felt on Cléire, in whose 253 population in 1958 were 103 O'Driscolls and forty Cadogans.

Co. Phort Láirge/Waterford

Na Déise/Decies: An Rinn/Ring

The first name is the proud but disused one of the ancient barony which retained Irish strongly for many years after it had died in most other districts so far east. A wide area west to the Blackwater still had 80 per cent majorities in 1925–6 but almost all was lost in the next thirty years, by which time the official Gaeltacht boundaries had contracted to parts of two DEDs at the eastern end of the broad peninsula south of Dungarvan. An extension order of 1974 took in more of the same DEDs and parts of another in the adjacent An Sean-Phobal/Old Parish area. This had certainly not turned more Irish after 1956 but decline had gone so far in the initially defined area as to make the exclusion of nearby townlands with some keen families unjust, especially where they sent their children into the Gaeltacht for Irish-medium teaching. Nevertheless English is dominant everywhere in normal daily use.

H. Wagner (1958a) already considered English the vernacular of the young at An Rinn and my own investigations in 1957 showed no more than half the people making habitual use of their Irish, which was clearly falling into disuse. English was the language of sermons and notices in the church, to ensure that they were understood, and what status Irish maintained was mainly to the credit of the schools, inspired by Séumas Ó hEocha, 'An Fear Mór' ('the Big Man'), the president of Coláiste na Rinne/Ring College, a famous Irish-language boarding school which takes very few local children, serves a wealthy nationwide community with great influence in the language movement, and runs prestigious *coláiste samhraidh* courses which draw large numbers to An Rinn. This fosters local pride and encourages cultural activities which the 'exclusive' or 'elitist' sound of the college might not suggest. An Fear Mór was a great Irish scholar, a member of the Gaeltacht Commission of 1925–6, and greatly loved locally for having 'put Ring on the map'.

He was not a native speaker himself, having learnt Irish in Dublin during the 'revival' led by the Gaelic League. In his closing years he confided to me a deep pessimism about the state and future of the language at An Rinn. English was the language most spoken on the streets and in the homes, and the children were not much worse than their parents. Attitudes were principally in favour of Irish but there was no real enthusiasm and emigration had led most to the view that Irish was no longer 'any use': 'Irish would probably be dead in the area were it not for the work that was being done in the schools' (MS. 13 February 1957).

The success achieved by the schools in maintaining a degree of bilingualism to the present day must not be underrated. Irish remains the principal medium of instruction in the primary schools here and at Baile

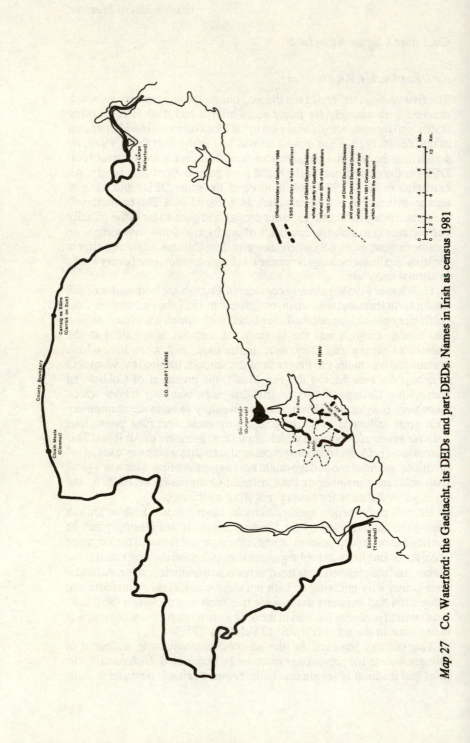

Map 27 Co. Waterford: the Gaeltacht, its DEDs and part-DEDs. Names in Irish as census 1981

Port Láirge
(Waterford)

Carraig na Siúire
(Carrick on Suir)

County Boundary

Cluain Meala
(Clonmel)

Dún Garbhán
(Dungarvan)

CO. PHORT LÁIRGE

AN RINN

BAILE MHIC ÁIRT

An Seanphobal

Ard Mhór
Máigh

Eochaill
(Youghal)

Official boundary of Gaeltacht 1956

1956 boundary where different

Boundary of District Electoral Divisions wholly or partly in Gaeltacht which returned over 60% of Irish speakers in 1981 Census

Boundary of District Electoral Divisions and parts of District Electoral Divisions which returned below 60% of Irish speakers in 1981 Census and/or which lie outside the Gaeltacht

10   Mls.
0 1 2 3 4 5 6 8
0 1 2 3 4 6 8 12 Km.

Mhac Airt/Ballymacart, which latter lacks the sprawling nucleation of An Rinn and is a dispersed farming district. The same is true of the small (fifty-three pupils in 1985–6) secondary school at An Rinn but many children go instead to secondary schools run by religious Orders at Dungarvan, which is only seven miles away, has no school with fewer than 299 pupils, teaches through English, and evidently carries more prestige. The families of teachers are notable among the best young native speakers, just as Fear Mór had said, and the old Gaeilgeoirí I met recently were deeply pessimistic about the lack of fluency and the predominance of English idioms in the 'Irish' which young people spoke to them and in local *feiseanna*. If they insisted on speaking Irish most people would answer in it, but for most English was obviously the first language. It was good that some parents were speaking Irish to their children, but it was not 'real' Irish.

Among the children it is clear that the language of play out of school is English and in the odd home I visited where the young mother was trying to speak Irish to her pre-school child it answered in English. At Easter half the children at play seemed to be visitors, usually on holiday from the Galltacht and staying with relatives. Most of An Rinn does now look like a modestly prosperous seaside resort and as it is only half a day's drive from Dublin it is very easy to visit for those emigrants who only got as far as Dublin before settling down. I met children on holiday from Carrick-on-Suir (thirty miles) and Waterford (thirty-seven), not just here for the day, and parents otherwise keen on keeping up Irish admitted that when their nieces and nephews were present their children spoke little but English. A high proportion of permanently resident young families have one parent married-in.

People around Baile Mhac Airt were very disparaging about the amount of Irish spoken naturally at An Rinn, and those at the latter were dismissive of Irish at Baile Mhac Airt. *Deontas* figures of 41 per cent and 18·2 per cent seem to favour An Rinn and show that 'encouragement' (51·7 per cent) at Baile Mhac Airt four years earlier gave disappointing results. There is not so much difference between the two in normal everyday use of the language. It is a minority language at both, but An Rinn has more professional residents, so more activists, more cultural support (including a thriving Irish pub), and a bigger, well equipped school. All public notices are in Irish, so its 'visibility' is better. There is hardly anywhere to put a notice among the farms and cottages of Baile Mhac Airt; and of course there is no college, no Irish-medium secondary school, and there are no Gaeltacht industries: little to be proud of at all. An Rinn knows it has appearances to keep up, so slides into English more furtively, keeping enough Irish for ceremonial occasions and enough to support Irish dramatics and to be able to clap in the right places. But in ordinary everyday life English comes first and more often alone.

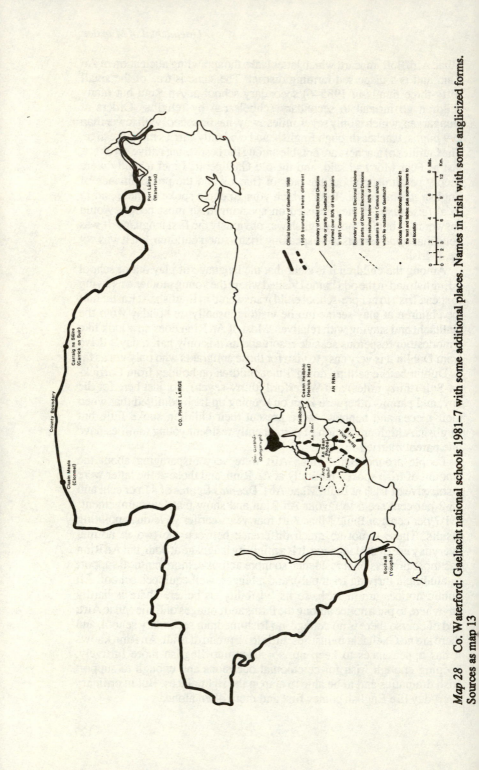

Map 28 Co. Waterford: Gaeltacht national schools 1981–7 with some additional places. Names in Irish with some anglicized forms. Sources as map 13

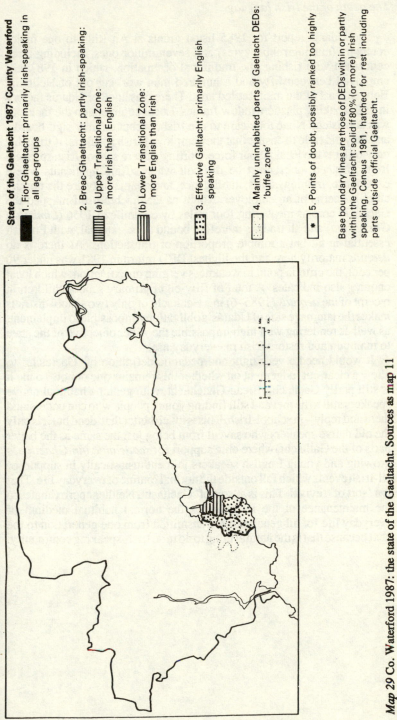

State of the Gaeltacht 1987: County Waterford

1. Fíor-Ghaeltacht: primarily Irish-speaking in all age-groups

2. Breac-Ghaeltacht: partly Irish-speaking:
   (a) Upper Transitional Zone: more Irish than English
   (b) Lower Transitional Zone: more English than Irish

3. Effective Galltacht: primarily English speaking

4. Mainly uninhabited parts of Gaeltacht DEDs: 'buffer zone'

5. Points of doubt, possibly ranked too highly

Base boundary lines are those of DEDs within or partly within the Gaeltacht: solid if 80% (or more) Irish speaking, Census 1981, hatched for rest including parts outside official Gaeltacht.

Map 29 Co. Waterford 1987: the state of the Gaeltacht. Sources as map 11

The Údarás report for 1985 listed grants at An Rinn to one major company (making rubber tyres) and seven minor ones, including three concerned with fishing, the traditional occupation, which in 1987 still employed between fifty and a hundred men working out of Heilbhic/ Helvick, east of the main settled area. There was another Údarás factory in 1987 making plastic window frames. Local comment on the factories was consistent. None took care to use Irish, except on their sign-boards, and they did little to ensure that they employed Irish speakers. If true, this only reflects the local labour force. Sorting sincere school-Irish speakers from insincere ones must be difficult when sifting applicants where experience, training, skills, intelligence, and adaptability are the normal chief concerns of an employer. Roinn na Gaeltachta itself mapped the Gaeltacht core as measuring four miles by one mile in 1956 (*Límistéirí Gaeltachta*) and all trade is therefore bound to be external, with English essential in all but a minute proportion of transactions. As there is no *deontas* majority here and the highest DED return in 1981 was under 90 per cent, the criteria point to weakness verging on extinction, which local enquiry also indicates. A total of fifty-eight primary school children in receipt of the *deontas* (1985–6) in a Gaeltacht of only two school districts makes the language side of Údarás's obligations impossible to implement, as well as rendering well nigh impossible the wider objective of the state to maintain and restore Irish in everyday use.

It would need a very tight and pedantic definition of 'Gaeltacht' to allow a clear-cut judgement on whether this remains one or not. To me it is still partly Gaeltacht, Breac-Ghaeltacht, with genuine habitual native speakers still to be met and still finding young people who can understand them and reply – in school-Irish. This is much better than dead but it is only the old native speakers who save it from being just the same as the better parts of the Galltacht, where elite support for *scoileanna lán-Ghaeilge* is growing and young English speakers join enthusiastically in support of all-Irish events which fall outside the normal routine of everyday life. That is a 'sort of' revival. This is a 'sort of' Gaeltacht. Neither approximates to the maintenance of the language as the normal habitual medium of everyday life for all generations, transmitted from one generation to the next because that is the natural thing to do in an Irish-speaking community.

Chapter eight

Gaeltachtaí of Leinster

Co. na Mí/Meath

Na Coilíneachtaí Gaeltachta/The Gaeltacht colonies

Maps 5 and 6 will serve to indicate that the Irish language was near to death as a native medium in Leinster by around 1900. It lingered near Omeath (north Louth) until the 1950s, but only because the death of the last few native speakers came much later than disuse of the language for social intercourse.

A notable attempt at revival by transplantation began when between 1935 and 1940 three 'Gaeltacht colonies' were established in Co. Meath. The Land Commission 'migrated' 122 families comprising 772 persons from various congested parts of the Fíor-Ghaeltacht and resettled them in family holdings on 2,929 acres allotted from eight estates which had previously been acquired for redistribution. Parts of five townlands were involved but contiguity made them three units, quite widely separated from each other. The average holding was twenty-four acres and a turbary plot, splendid in those days for people from the impoverished west but a different matter now with Dublin at most thirty-five miles away.

The smallest colony, Allenstown, was assimilated early because it only had twenty-three families (112 people) and they had to feed into the existing local school and church, with no special provision for the Irish medium. Baile Ghib/Gibstown, the biggest, with fifty-nine families (373 people), received much more official attention in Dublin but was badly planned linguistically, for it drew colonists from six different Gaeltacht districts with mutually 'difficult' dialects for which English formed the easier lingua franca. In addition some of the sources were suspect in their adherence to Irish (e.g. Bantry in west Cork) and so were plenty of the settlers. The resultant mix never really jelled, though the school under dynamic headship and using the Irish medium kept the language alive among the children, few of whom went on to mainly English-medium urban secondary schools at Navan or Kells (officially An Uaimh and

Ceanannas Mór). Nevertheless all jobs for the young meant leaving or travelling out of the colony, for the family farms were adequate only for parents and schoolchildren, not young adults as well. Marriage too was almost inevitably outside, as was most daily shopping, except for the little post office and general store at Gibstown.

Ráth Cairn/Rathcarran (or Rathcarne), about thirteen miles south-west, between Trim and Athboy, was more fortunate in drawing all its forty families (287) people) from south Conamara and alone deserves the use of its Irish name. It also had its own school and a dedicated head who, much less of a publicist, drew far fewer visitors from Dublin and probably thereby did much to assist the better survival of the language to the present day, though the homogeneous Gaeltacht roots of the colony are a more certain cause.

By 1957, when most of the original colonists were still alive, evidence of weakening of Irish among the young was abundant, admitted flatly by some and baldly denied by others. The same applied in 1970–1, refusal to recognize decline seeming a normal psychological defence against it. (See pp. 177–8.)

The state in 1956 omitted the Meath colonies from the new Gaeltacht and when I asked about this in several departments the explanation was plainly that the language was almost dead or, evasively, that their inclusion would have been too difficult administratively. The former could not be said in public for fear of an outcry by language 'fanatics', which did nevertheless take place, and in 1967 Baile Ghib and Ráth Cairn were added to the Gaeltacht as eastern outliers, parts of four DEDs in three different rural districts, with a total population in 1981 of 948, only 54·8 per cent of whom were returned as speaking Irish. Unfortunately the age-grouped figures for the two colonies are not separated but it is notable that in 1981 only 46·1 per cent of people aged 65 and over claimed to speak Irish and a mere 9·1 per cent (i.e. one girl and one boy) of infants aged 3–4 years were returned as doing so. Both percentages compare strikingly with the 70·5 per cent aged 15–19. These proportions are probably inflated by sentiment but the distorting effect of school-Irish is apparent. The 70·5 per cent is not a lie, for these youngsters have had years of Irish-medium instruction which they have not yet had time to forget. The figure is 40·2 per cent for those aged 34–44, who have had more time.

The most recent *deontas* scores, 1985–6, are in the low range for normal expectation of true survival in everyday use. 32·8 per cent at Baile Ghib would be low anywhere and, allowing for some generosity, accords with apparent trends sixteen years ago. There is a *naíonra* to help the infants. Ráth Cairn also has a *naíonra* and a much higher score, at 58 per cent, which merited a visit. The true position was surprising. About a third of the pupils were ineligible because of age, so from that point of view far more than 58 per cent received the grant. But eighty-one of the ninety-four

(May 1987) on the roll were bussed in from non-Gaeltacht districts such as Athboy and the great majority of infants arriving at school came with English only. There is good support from the colony parents but their children are heavily outnumbered in school and one could hear that the language of play of the junior children was English. It takes about six months to bring the little ones to sufficient fluency to speak and to understand the lessons in Irish, though odd ones have problems for as much as two years or more. Lack of good, well-illustrated textbooks in non-technical Irish causes some resort to English but popular English-language television programmes influence the children much more. They know all the characters in 'Dallas', 'Emmerdale Farm', and 'Coronation Street'.

Ráth Cairn has an active *comharchumann* (co-operative) under sensitive and intelligent local leadership and in 1986 this opened a new all-Irish post-primary school under the Meath Vocational Educational Committee. Virtually all the primary leavers have opted to go to it and numbers should build up to a total of about ninety. The Athboy and Trim vocational schools had rolls of 186 and 229 in 1985–6, with English as their normal medium. A new community centre (*Árus Pobal* on its signs) has also been built and piped water provided for the colony, which also at last completed its own church in 1986. This demonstrates a lively atmosphere but employment is once again proving a difficult problem, many men travelling to work for Tara Mines near Navan and others to Dublin, within an hour by car.

The *comharchumann* played a part in promoting the extension of the local Gaeltacht boundary in 1982, when four townlands were added round Ráth Cairn and one at Baile Ghib. The state required evidence that the areas concerned had a majority of Irish speakers and favoured inclusion, and there was some surprise when this was produced. There were, however, very few inhabitants involved and a factor was the purchase of adjacent farms by descendants of former colonists.

The original colonists are all now dead, apart from some children they brought with them. Some colonists themselves sold their land or let it to outsiders and departed, but there is no doubt that a pride in this colony exists and is shared by many local Meath people; hence their use of its school for their children. This must not, however, be exaggerated, for the great majority of parents who could do so do not send their children to Ráth Cairn and do not want an Irish-medium education for their children. Similarly, the 1981 census statistics for the aggregate colonies give no confidence in the soundness of any evidence that the Meath Gaeltacht merited extension on language grounds.

Old people I spoke to in 1987 included some who had arrived with their parents in 1935–7. They were unhappy with the children's Irish, which was definitely weakening, as they were speaking 'a lot more English'. No one had anything good to say about Údarás's local associate company,

Turmec Teo. (engineering and metalwork). Allegedly it did not use Irish at all, even on its office and toilet notices, and it employed many (or mostly) non-Irish speakers. It was founded by foreign capital and had difficulties, so perhaps had other priorities. An engineering works in Meath can have little occasion to use Irish for trading purposes, and with everyone fluent in English resort to Irish would be little better than tokenism. Údarás is nevertheless criticized for failure effectively to monitor use of the language in an industry it continues to support. Yet one wonders what the local reaction would be if backsliding workers were dismissed just on language grounds or the factory closed because support was withdrawn for the same reason.

It was never likely that so small an infusion of native Irish speakers could trigger the reanglicization of eastern Ireland or even long survive so heavily outnumbered. 'Curiosity value' has been of some help in drawing support and there has always been a *coláiste samhraidh* at Ráth Cairn or Baile Ghib. Gaeltacht grants have certainly helped transform the quality of housing, diversify employment, and improve education and communal facilities, so given material value, which Irish could never previously offer in competition with English. They have not changed the basic setting, either socially or economically. Within forty miles of the centre of Dublin city, with such things as marriage and jobs to think about, there is not much hope of confining either of those to the tiny colony communities, even if in principle anyone wanted to. Only 9·1 per cent of pre-school infants were claimed for Irish in 1981 and only 46·1 per cent of the elderly still thought it worth bothering to claim, so it is evident that Ráth Cairn and Baile Ghib are reaching the stage when no purpose will be served by pretending there are still habitually Irish-speaking communities here. There is good work for Irish and through Irish, and some genuine native speakers, especially among the elderly, the best from Conamara. Much the same could be said of Dublin city, though the rural setting in Meath enables city Gaeilgeoirí to undertake trips here much as Americans head for their nearest Indian reservation – which puts on a show because being Indian is the main source of income.

The Meath lowlands do not compare in scenic beauty with the western coastal Gaeltachtaí and their fine archaeological monuments are well outside the colonies, which are in no danger of attracting the ordinary anglicizing tourist. Nevertheless the cultivation of pride in being 'different' runs counter to the dominant current of feeling which one senses in most Gaeltachtaí: people (especially young children) don't want to be different and feel self-conscious and embarrassed when they find their use of Irish distinguishes, divides, or separates them from neighbours, friends, and relations (see p.209), which in these little 'inland islands' is extraordinarily normal. Some are proud when visitors from Dublin come to see them because of their Irish. The President of the Republic himself had called at

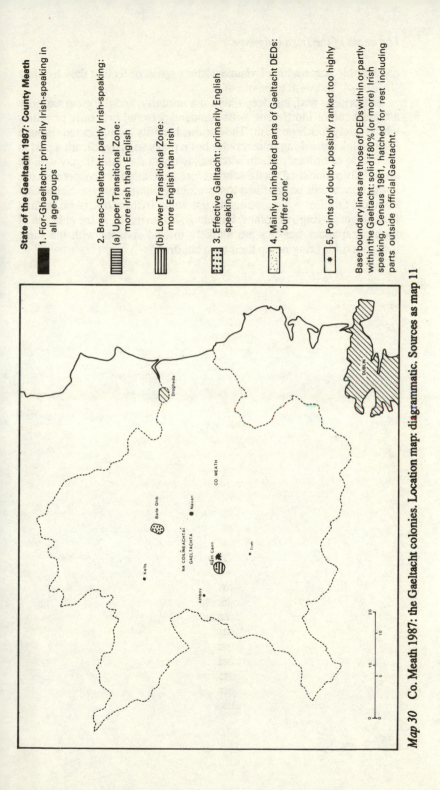

State of the Gaeltacht 1987: County Meath

1. Fíor-Ghaeltacht: primarily Irish-speaking in all age-groups

2. Breac-Ghaeltacht: partly Irish-speaking:

   (a) Upper Transitional Zone: more Irish than English

   (b) Lower Transitional Zone: more English than Irish

3. Effective Galltacht: primarily English speaking

4. Mainly uninhabited parts of Gaeltacht DEDs: 'buffer zone'

5. Points of doubt, possibly ranked too highly

Base boundary lines are those of DEDs within or partly within the Gaeltacht: solid if 80% (or more) Irish speaking, Census 1981, hatched for rest including parts outside official Gaeltacht.

Map 30 Co. Meath 1987: the Gaeltacht colonies. Location map: diagrammatic. Sources as map 11

one humble home which I visited. Others speak of feeling they live in a 'fish-bowl' and wish to be out of it.

The pride is real, but deep only for a minority, and the great majority are apathetic or indifferent, with mundane personal or family priorities which rarely touch on Irish. The various benefits to be secured through Irish weigh something in its favour but it plays so insignificant a part in the course of ordinary life in Meath as to count for little. It may well be artificially maintained via the schools for a generation or two more but use in the homes will be confined to a shrinking number of conscientiously bilingual families who continue to use some Irish in otherwise normal first-language-English homes. Shrinkage is inevitable, as the children of such exceptional families are unlikely to find spouses with the same inclination for bringing up their own children.

Chapter nine

Nua-Ghaeltachtaí? New Gaeltachts? Irish in the Galltacht/English-speaking Ireland

The *Galltacht* will be treated here in two divisions, beginning with the non-Gaeltacht parts of the Republic of Ireland, in which efforts to revive or restore the language have been great, and in which hopes are sometimes expressed that Irish-speaking communities or at least family networks may eventually emerge. There has been no state support for Irish in Northern Ireland, except for the continuation of pre-1922 British policies in the schools and a few additional permissive developments, and the fact that revival efforts have therefore been left very largely to the voluntary sector makes a useful contrast to the results of 'compulsory Irish' policies in the South, so merits separate attention.

It should also be remembered that the promotion of the language has attracted support from all sections of opinion in the Free State/Republic, including the small (under 10 per cent) Protestant minority, whereas it has been very largely confined to the Roman Catholic third of the population of the Six Counties, at least since the Gaelic League adopted the Sinn Féin republican banner from 1916 onwards. The language is much more than usually a symbol of Irish national identity in the North and *ipso facto* repugnant to many or most who consider themselves British. This again gives a 'sharp edge' to support for Irish among ordinary working people in Catholic areas. Such support is largely absent in the South and it will be valuable to compare the extent to which this genuine voluntary nationalist sentiment achieves results different from those in the linguistically anglicized areas which are ruled from Dublin.

The Galltacht in the Irish Republic/Twenty-Six Counties

Chapter 3 reviewed the general trends of language revival in twentieth-century Ireland, and because so little of the country was or is Irish in normal everyday speech most of that review applies to developments and situations in the Galltacht. Table 3 provides a superficially cheering point of departure for this chapter too, showing as it does the near doubling of the numbers of Irish speakers since 1926. This increase was unfortunately brought about by the replacement of genuine native Irish speakers by much larger numbers of second-language learners. Table 6 focuses on Leinster, linguistically the least Irish of the four provinces but which contains the capital, Dublin, and which has achieved the greatest increases in numbers. The province was the only one with no strong Gaeltacht as early as 1891, though a tiny one of Breac-Ghaeltacht strength was certainly there in the Omeath district of north Louth until the 1920s. Leinster is thus the province which had little to lose and everything to recover once the Revival arrived.

Table 6 Irish-speaking population 1891–1981: provinces of Leinster and Connacht, and Co. Dublin[1]

	Leinster		Co. Dublin		Connacht	
	No.	%	No.	%	No.	%
1891	13,677	1·2	3,472	0·8	274,783	37·9
1901	26,436	2·3	12,998	2·9	245,580	38·0
1911	40,225	3·5	17,743	3·7	217,087	35·5
Age 3 years and upwards						
1926	101,102	9·4	39,409	8·3	174,234	33·3
1936	183,378	15·9	86,585	15·7	183,082	36·7
1946	180,755	15·1	92,381	15·6	154,187	33·2
1961	274,644	22·2	140,876	25·6	148,708	37·6
1971	341,702	24·5	195,059	26·8	137,372	37·2
1981	473,225	28·2	268,243	28·5	155,134	38·8

Note: Including city
Source: Census Reports

Figures for Co. Dublin are also included, to indicate still more clearly the reported language trends for the capital city and much of its hinterland. It might be better if it were possible to include statistics for the city itself, but changing boundaries complicate these too much to make them readily comparable and at the same time most of the county now falls within the commuter zone of Greater Dublin, so the difference is not great. Data for Connacht (Connaught), the province with most native Irish speakers although nevertheless overwhelmingly Galltacht at the present day, provide a useful comparison with trends in the regions which were native Irish in speech and lacked the advantages of an easterly location and possession of the national capital. Dublin is, of course, in Leinster, which partly for that reason had 52 per cent of the Republic's population in 1981 (and 1986).

In assessing these figures it should be recalled that the Republic's total population (aged 3+) in 1981 was 3,226,467, of whom 1,018,413 (31·6 per cent) were returned as Irish speakers. Leinster had 1,675,517 people in the same age range, Co. Dublin 942,411, and Connacht 215,322. Hence 30 per cent of the total population and 26 per cent of all Irish speakers were in Co. Dublin alone and 46 per cent were in Leinster. This helps to explain the importance of the Dublin area when it comes to the question of establishing a sufficient and sound numerical base for the creation and maintenance of primarily Irish-speaking communities in the Galltacht.

The most striking difference between Leinster and Connacht lies in the almost uninterrupted increase in the numbers of Irish speakers in Leinster since 1891 and the much more erratic record of Connacht, where the largest increase, in the decade 1971–81, must surely correlate with a belated growth in prosperity and associated 'bourgeoisification', especially around Galway city. It must, however, be noted that the latter had only 35,499 (39,257 with 'Environs') people aged 3 years and older in 1981 and it is by far the biggest town in the province, Sligo having only 16,209 (or 16,932). The replacement of native speakers by school learners has almost perfectly balanced in Connacht. Munster and the Republic's three Ulster counties, having smaller Gaeltachtaí, fall between the Leinster and Connacht extremes and have ended with 34·6 and 30·8 per cent of census Irish speakers respectively.

The figures quoted may be taken optimistically as an indication of potential Irish speakers, i.e. the numbers and proportions who think (or whose census form completer thinks) they know enough Irish to be able to speak it. It has been shown already (pp. 46–7) that the 4·9 per cent of infants aged 3 or 4 years who in 1981 were returned as speaking Irish are a far better guide to its real use than those for any other age group. For Leinster the proportion was 3·4 per cent and for Co. Dublin 3·5 per cent. These can only be maxima, allowing for the usual optimism, nationalist sentiments, difficulties in assessing speaking ability at any age (how much?), and sheer eccentricity. Opinions are abundant on this subject, so it will be appropriate to examine a few hard facts about the numbers of children whose parents now subject them to Irish-medium education, which has been much more a matter of free choice since around 1973.

Ó Buachalla (1984: 89) has shown how the numbers of Irish-medium national (i.e. primary) schools fell from 420 in 1960 to 160 in 1979. Only twenty-three of the latter were outside the Gaeltacht and their roll numbers were 3,389 from a total Galltacht population of about half a million. More recent figures from the Department of Education show a recovery to (exactly) fifty schools with 'over 6,000' pupils by 1987, but even this compares badly with the 567,086 pupils in all primary schools in 1985–6 and is 1 per cent or fractionally more (7,000 would be 1.2 per cent). 'Attitudes' research by Ó Riagáin and Ó Gliasáin (1984: 12, 26, 34) shows that 24 per cent of the sampled population said they would send their children to an all-Irish primary school if it were available. Nineteen per cent said the same of secondaries, and a more credible 67 per cent said they supported the provision of all-Irish schools 'wherever the public want them'.

Sixteen of the fifty all-Irish primaries are in Co. Dublin, entirely in the city and its suburbs. This is not very disproportionate at 32 per cent of the national total, but is by far the biggest concentration in one small area. Co. Cork has ten, seven of which are in the city and its commuter belt, which extends as far as Cobh, Ballincollig, and Carrigaline. The only other nucleation is three in Galway city and adjacent Salthill, which is the biggest per head of population – figures for individual school rolls are not available – and probably relates to proximity to the Gaeltacht, to the numbers of state officials employed at Údarás headquarters and Roinn na Gaeltachta near by, and to the Irish-medium teaching commitment of University College Galway, which has long required fluency in Irish of all its staff. There are altogether around twenty-six national schools in the city and its immediate environs, so the fact that 11·5 per cent of primary schools are all-Irish is remarkable only in that far fewer of the children will be native speakers, even though 41·3 per cent in the city and its environs in 1981 were returned as speaking Irish.

The contraction of Irish-medium secondary schooling has not quite been halted since Ó Buachalla (1984) showed the fall from 132 schools which in 1968–9 were teaching at least one or two subjects through Irish to a mere twenty-two in 1978–9. That number fell to nineteen in 1985–6, but the number of all-Irish secondary schools held steady at fifteen. Here numbers of pupils are available for accurate assessment. Locations are also significant. Of the fifteen all-Irish secondary schools, four are in the Dublin area and their total enrolment of 1,249 constitutes 37·5 per cent of all pupils in such schools nationally. Of the other three schools located in the Galltacht two are in or close to Cork city and one is in Limerick city. A total of 1,982 pupils in all-Irish secondary schools in the Galltacht constitutes 59·6 per cent of the national total. There are eight such schools in the official Gaeltacht. Three cluster in Dingle or immediately adjacent and the rest are thinly dispersed through four other Gaeltachtaí, only one of them in an Irish-speaking place.

The Department of Education's 1985–6 list shows 214,339 pupils in 504 secondary schools, i.e. an average of 425·3 pupils per school, compared with the all-Irish average of 221·7. This clearly indicates a much lower level of support, whether from the Church, the state, parents, or all, and, however favourable to education smaller numbers may be, subject choice can hardly be as wide in the smaller schools. None of these secondary school figures takes account of pupils who pursue their studies in vocational, comprehensive, or community schools, but except in the

Donegal and south Conamara Gaeltachtaí these do not teach through Irish; in addition, it is the designated secondary schools, commonly run by religious Orders, which carry the prestige in Irish post-primary education and draw most of the children of the middle classes.

The figures give perspective when it is seen that only 1·6 per cent of secondary pupils were in all-Irish schools in 1985–6: 3,326 in all. If the four other schools (two each) with either an all-Irish stream or teaching one or two classes in Irish are taken into account, there is a grand total of 5,258 pupils receiving some degree of instruction through the medium of Irish (other than for learning Irish itself) in nineteen secondary schools. Together they form 2·5 per cent of the national total in secondary schools. It must be self-evident that such numbers and proportions are bound to be a tiny minority in any work situation which they later enter; and that if they are keen on their acquired Irish they are bound to feel either 'odd' or very distinguished, if not 'superior', none of which contributes greatly to effective socialization. The four lower-graded secondary schools are, almost needless to say, in important towns: in Cork, Galway, Dundalk (large by Irish standards, with 23,905 people aged 3 and over in 1981, and nationalist because close to the Border), and Tralee (15,406). In no case can they be serving a mainly native Irish-speaking population.

There is some evidence from other sources that Irish is now tending to become a 'feminine option' in schools, but this is not borne out by the all-Irish secondary school numbers, which show 58·5 per cent of pupils were girls in 1985–6, scarcely more than the national 56 per cent of secondary pupils.

Most significant of all the secondary statistics is the fact that 37·5 per cent of all pupils in all-Irish secondary schools are in Dublin and its immediate environs, though the entire county contains only 26 per cent of the Republic's population. The question naturally arises as to whether this 1,249 nucleus spread through seven different annual age cohorts can form the basis of an effective bilingually Irish-speaking community or several smaller communities, family or social networks, work groups, or the like. Here opinion intrudes, but the best advice is negative, only hope providing a countervailing force.

The first serious weakness is revealed in evidence from R. A. Breatnach (1956: 140–1), a leading university professor and language teacher, that the majority of his first-year students who had been taught wholly or partly through Irish had 'nothing approaching a satisfactory colloquial command of the language'; and (1964: 24–5) not 5 per cent of his students and annual Matriculation examinees could sustain a simple conversation in Irish. He himself had taught 9 year olds Irish but could not prevail against 'the all-powerful influence of home and environment'. School-Irish was 'a travesty of Irish, taught as if it were English' (1956: 136). A neglected British and Irish Communist Organization policy statement (1972: 10–11) put it more pungently but with some justice:

> It is a jargon of the middle class . . . not just because it is incomprehensible to the working class in the English-speaking areas, but because it is also largely incomprehensible to the native Irish-speaking community . . . It was developed by Free State civil servants whose native language was English.

There have undoubtedly been big improvements in the teaching of oral Irish since Breatnach was writing and, confronted by almost universal recognition of the failure of earlier teaching methods to impart fluency in Irish to more than a small minority, much current Irish research is now attempting to improve them with better courses, the use of modern audio-visual aids, etc. But Bord na Gaeilge's Advisory Planning Committee report *Irish and the Education System* (1986: xii) admits that '. . . even twelve years of learning Irish still leaves most people without a speaking competence in the language', contrasting this unfavourably with the common achievement in the different linguistic context of other countries of 'reasonably active verbal competence in two or three languages' by second-level students. The report adds (p. x) that '. . . to go on teaching Irish unsuccessfully may . . . only undermine the very ideological function that such teaching has served in the past'.

Mackey, a sympathetic Canadian observer with abundant experience of language problems, warned in 1977 (p. 10) that the 'immersion' system of teaching children through a language different from their mother tongue could sometimes rebound and perfect bilingualism at the age of 7 be followed by serious reversion and loss of command of the acquired language about the age of 10. This, he felt, '. . . indicated clearly that it is the community, not the school, which controls the language'. This does not, of course, necessarily apply to secondary level, but common sense would expect teenagers to be much more critical (whatever their parents' opinions) of the logic and value of subjecting them to education in a language which is much more deficient in textbook and wider literary and audio-visual support than their mother tongue. They may perforce become fluent, but many are unlikely to accept the necessity or validity of the imposition and also unlikely to transmit the second language to their own children. There is evidence to support this suspicion.

The comprehensive survey of the Committee on Irish Language Attitudes Research (*Report* 1975: 306) showed that only 36 per cent of Galltacht residents who spoke Irish intensively either at home or at work had grown up in bilingual homes: i.e. two-thirds were 'new' to Irish, and transmission from parents was exceptional compared with acquisition at school. This failure of the second-language learners to 'reproduce' Irish families is often mentioned but easy to explain, especially by the probabilities of two people with high language abilities outside the

Gaeltacht marrying each other. The CILAR report (pp. 157, 214) estimated this probability at around 2 per cent in theory but found a higher incidence because of 'selection' (presumably shared enthusiasm and interest) but also because of inexact reporting by children in assessing their parents' respective abilities in Irish. In general, fluency in Irish is unlikely to be a prime consideration in Irish matrimony, especially as the 'pool' of fluent Irish speakers is so tiny. It may be noted parenthetically that Irish conservatism also does not help, in that ten of the fifteen all-Irish secondary schools in 1985–6 were single-sex ones, which must reduce quite considerably the likelihood of tempting opportunities for mutual attraction between Irish-speaking teenagers. The religious Orders who run the schools are the controlling influence here.

Mackey (1977, *passim*) gave an excellent outline of factors which hinder or prevent the transmission of Irish across the generations. Knowing a language was no guarantee of using it, for use depended on a wide range of factors, including opportunity, pressure to do so, the presence of others who did not understand it, fear of ridicule (or blame for pretentiousness), mobility in relation to language networks, stress (e.g. for urgent self-expression), marriage and friendship, and sufficient numbers. CILAR (1975: 214) stressed the devastating effects which may result from simple contact with parents' siblings or with grandparents in provoking debates on the wisdom of speaking Irish to children, and the discouragement to young, enthusiastic Irish-speaking parents of the scarcity of books, records, or games in Irish. There is great current emphasis on producing such material, as also greater radio and especially television coverage in Irish, but this is very marginal to the fundamental problem from which most others stem, namely the grave lack of numbers and the lack of any substantial territorial base in which Irish has unchallenged dominance. Mackey went on to opine that diglossia could not be attained in Ireland because the numbers of competent speakers were too small and their distribution random (1977: 5). That is not quite true in relation to the urban and economic geography of Ireland but it is more or less true within the towns and cities, except again in so far as the highest percentages – which will still be low in absolute terms – are in the middle-class districts where academics and state employees congregate. He agreed with Máirtín Ó Murchú (1970: 31) that Irish had no more than a marginal position in any domain of Irish life. Certain groups used Irish for certain purposes but its effect was diluted by constant contact with others who were using English for the same purposes. Diglossia at any Galltacht workplace was impossible because most workers had insufficient Irish, and intermarriage made it very difficult to establish in many homes (Mackey 1977:7).

The geolinguistic point that the use of Irish is not territorially based because Irish speakers in the Galltacht are dispersed throughout the rest of the population has been echoed by Helen Ó Murchú (1984: 8), who points out that there are therefore not two distinct speech communities. There are no areas of life in which either language cannot be used, but English tends to predominate. Fennell had made a similar point (1977: 8) when arguing that it is the natural social group that speaks a language, '... generally a group of people living together *in a certain locality*'. He went on to remind us (p. 11) that 'not a single street, not a single pub or shop or café in Galway – not to mention any other Irish city – has become even predominantly Irish-speaking'. This again is logical, given Mackey's list of linguistic influences and the fact that all keen Galltacht Gaeilgeoirí have a full command of English, usually far better than that of the average monoglot English working man, for all of them need and use it regularly at work and recreation.

There have been periodic attempts to initiate and promote an all-Irish satellite town, garden suburb, or at least a professional residential area in or close to Dublin for exclusive occupation by committed families who would thus create a prestigious territorial base for the language as well as a real community. Ó Sé (1966) warmly advocated 'An Baile Gaelach, the Irish-speaking town', with a minimum population of 2,000 and with Irish as the language of the streets, shops, schools, administration, and church. It could begin at village size, but an earlier attempt to create a suburban 'Gaeltacht Park' had failed because of internal weaknesses plus inability to exclude English-speaking families ... Ó Sé outlined the policies he thought necessary to achieve success and based great hopes on participation by members of city-based language organizations such as Na Teaghlaigh Ghaelacha (The Irish Families) and Glór na nGael (Voice of the Irish, Speech of the Gael, etc: not often translated). Nothing substantial came of this or of similar proposals and there is scarcely any need to spell out the adverse pressures either of normal everyday social and economic life in Dublin or of the normal internal family stresses which stand in the way of success for any such venture. Parental enthusiasm for Irish for the children yet again cannot be reliably correlated with according it the highest ranking in adult priorities. It is also highly questionable whether the children involved could be expected to share their parents' enthusiasm for deliberate sociolinguistic segregation, once old enough to be aware of it and to think about it.

Ó Riagáin and Ó Gliasáin(1984: 10–11, 33) found in their 're-run' of the CILAR survey that the social norms inhibiting the use of Irish had intensified in the previous ten years. CILAR (1975: 38) had found that between 67 and 70 per cent of Irish speakers at all levels above command of a few simple sentences admitted to not liking to speak Irish if a non-Irish speaker were present, and the highest diffidence (at 70 per cent) was among those claiming native-speaker ability. The report commented that this limits opportunities for use to a 'relatively homogeneous and closed circle of intimates', which again begs the question of how this can be achieved and *maintained* with such small numbers and proportions in a modern mobile society. Generation losses are seen in the fact that 3 per cent of Galltacht respondents in each survey claimed to have native-speaker ability but only 2 per cent made the same claim for their eldest child, compared with 5 per cent in 1973 (Ó Riagáin and Ó Gliasáin, 1984: 16).

Bord na Gaeilge's *Action Plan for Irish 1983–1986* (1983: 2) estimated the 'basic community' of Irish speakers as about 4 per cent of the population of the state, including the 1 per cent assumed to be using Irish as their normal day-to-day language in Gaeltacht areas. That allows 106,116 people 'who use Irish extensively in daily life' in Galltacht areas (on 1986 population figures) and 35,372 in the Gaeltacht. I have shown elsewhere in this work that the true Gaeltacht figure is unlikely to exceed 10,000. *Irish and the Education System* (Bord na Gaeilge 1986: vii) accepts that 5 per cent use Irish as their home language, but this is based on CILAR data and is exaggerated by the over-optimism of self-assessment. The figures for parents actually (as distinct from hypothetically) opting their children into all-Irish schooling in the Galltacht seem more reliably indicative at about 1·1 per cent of primary schoolchildren and 1·6 per cent in secondary schools, and even those are likely to be exaggerated by nationalistic sentiment and career ambitions for the children concerned. This author, however, cannot claim authority or expertise in rebutting the assertion that 3 per cent (or more) of Galltacht people use Irish regularly in the home but notes Dillon's authoritative 1966 estimate of 'nearer 1 per cent' of the national population using Irish as their principal means of communication (quoted in Streib 1974: 73–4). Universal acceptance of the fact that such Irish-speaking families are too thinly dispersed in the English-speaking mass is far weightier in prediction of future language prospects than any attempt to pin down a figure which must be somewhere between 1 per cent and 5 per cent and which is impotently minuscule in either case.

D. Fennell (1977: 9) estimated that the Dublin Gaeilgeoirí comprised 'at most four of five thousand enthusiasts ... scattered through a large city whose cultural role in the last few years has been to lead a reaction against the Irish-Ireland ideology' – referring to the successful movement to abolish compulsory Irish for the Leaving Certificate and for entry to most branches of the civil service. Matsuoka, a perspicacious Japanese observer (1982: 5), based his view of Dublin Irish on the 1,113 families who in 1976–7 sent children to all-Irish primary schools. Betts (1976: 226) had reduced this to 200–300 families who were bringing up their children Irish-speaking, i.e. 0·5 per cent of the city population. A salutary gloss on all this is Harris's (1984: 122) discovery that of the 216 second-grade (i.e. year) pupils in Galltacht all-Irish schools that he sampled, 128 (59 per cent) heard only English at home and a mere eleven (5 per cent) heard only

Irish there. The rest came from homes which used both languages. This of course proves that actual Irish users are less than half the already tiny minority which sends its children to all-Irish schools and that even this esoteric group suffers conflicts between what it thinks 'good for the children' at school and what on the other hand it finds convenient and sensible for itself at home.

Harris (1984: 122) also shows that of his 2,217 sample of second-grade pupils who were following the Irish courses in ordinary schools only twenty-seven (1·2 per cent) spoke any Irish at home and twenty-six (96 per cent) of them used it together with English. His test results of pupil performance after subjection to the *nuachúrsaí* (new audio-visual conversation courses for teaching Irish, introduced around 1970) show a depressing degree of failure to attain the specified objectives and, for instance (p. 8), 30·4 per cent of fourth-grade pupils in all schools failed to attain *any* of the specified varied objectives laid down. In a broad-ranging review of possible solutions to constant high levels of failure in teaching Irish he warns against the dangers of disturbing good teachers by over-hasty and ill-prepared changes of course and whilst pointing to successes achieved by the use of Irish in schools for 'real communication' admits that the significant minority support for Irish-medium instruction is too widely spread to be realized in actual bilingual programmes (pp. 138–44). So he too advocates all-Irish education as most effective in developing speaking proficiency, and favours it wherever there is sufficient parental support. This again sounds familiar as the triumph of hope over experience, and in any case is only a question of promoting the acquisition of fluency in Irish as a second language.

If, as seems obvious, the Gaeltacht is fading to extinction, it is pertinent to ask what the revivalist effort in the Galltacht is now for, as scarcely anyone remains to whom it is necessary to speak Irish and the great majority who can speak it speak English better, whatever their level of attainment or dedication. One cannot but assume that the 7 per cent nationally whom Ó Riagáin and Ó Gliasáin (1984: 18) reported as claiming to read Irish as well as or better than English were being more than 'economical with the truth' or that their range of reading was infinitesimal and almost incredibly specialized. They simply cannot be believed, and all my numerous Irish-speaking friends and acquaintances admit that one of their own major difficulties is the constant need to turn to English-language sources for information and entertainment in every field of interest and professional activity except the loved and valued minority ones which specifically concern the Irish language.

Streib (1974) closely examined attitudes to Irish in a small Galltacht town of 3,700 people and found that none of its thirty-one 'community leaders' (public officials, businessmen, doctors, lawyers, etc.) ranked the restoration of Irish as first among seven national objectives they were asked to rank-order and only three of seven who declared themselves as 'ardent' about the language gave it more than low priority (pp. 80–2). From his survey and wider travels he concluded that 'there is no particular prestige attached to the use of Irish by the business or intellectual elite of the country' and, perhaps most cogently: 'They [the Irish] are a communicating people, and are too pragmatic to adopt practices that would impede communication in everyday affairs' (pp. 85, 87). It would be difficult to dispute this.

Relative success in promoting Irish among the middle classes, whose children enjoy longer years of instruction and the inducement of university studies and professional advancement at the end of it, has been shown by Mackey (1977: 10) to cause resentment among lower-income groups who cannot use Irish, and Bord na Gaeilge (1986: vi) warns of the 'tendency towards the social polarization of Irish in our society', rather naively regretting in relation to Irish that 'pupils in general now adopt a very calculating attitude towards school subjects'. One would hope that education would constantly seek to inculcate a capacity for informed choice, and 'the declining saliency of Irish for career purposes' and the 'tendency to by-pass Irish . . . in the rapidly expanding areas of both second and third-level education' show all too clearly what has long been known – that Irish is 'increasingly regarded . . . as mainly the preserve of an academically educated middle class' (ibid.).

The British and Irish Communist Organization (1972: 15) acidly dismissed the revivalist movement in the South as 'part of an elaborate system of graft and state patronage' and 'a ladder for social climbing'. This may be extreme, but Breatnach (1956: 34) had criticized state policies much earlier for their emphasis on 'pressure, preferment and projection' and it is inevitable that those who secure least preferment for their Irish – because of their lack of educational opportunities – will tend to resent it. Macnamara (1971: 85) elaborated on the same point, stressing that the Revival brought material advantages to the middle classes and none to most of the workers. By 'projection' Breatnach meant visualizing and regarding the ideal (Irish revival) as an objective reality (pp. 134–5), which again has never been very practical and in the worsening economic conditions of the early 1980s has led Bord na Gaeilge's Advisory Planning Committee (1986: xii, xiv) to anticipate an intensification of the tendency of pupils in secondary and tertiary education to by-pass Irish and other non-vocational subjects and to downgrade Irish as 'a more appropriate subject choice for girls'.

Dependence of the Revival on the teaching of Irish in schools in any case has one fatal flaw which Ó Catháin (1973: 319), among many others, has pointed out. It necessarily associates Irish in the mind of the child with childish things, and in growing up the child will naturally want to be rid of it, like all the other marks of childhood. Children copy the language they

147

hear on the lips of all grown-ups who are about their ordinary business: 'It is a mistake to believe that the schools can change society.' Or at least they 'cannot mould society against its will' (ibid.: 320). Ó Catháin (p. 317) also warns against the anti-Irish consequences of sending schoolchildren to the Gaeltacht to improve their Irish and give it a native colloquial idiom. He admits the advantages of well organized visits by well supervised and well prepared children but advises consideration of what they find there:

> Irish, they see, is the language of the poor, of the struggling small farmer, of the fisherman, of the oddly dressed people, the sort of people, for example, from whom families such as theirs used to get a servant girl 'to help the children with their Irish', ... the conclusion is there that the people who speak Irish are not, well, their sort of people.

This is rather 'dated' but was very valid when I began my visits to the Gaeltacht in the early 1950s; and social divisions in Ireland tend to be wide, or to seem so because the relatively small population makes them more obvious. He agrees with Streib (1974: 85) that there is no prestige in using Irish, even among the Galltacht elite, but it must be added as a further negative influence that its use is commonly regarded as pretentiousness, showing a desire to be 'different' and 'superior', 'holier than thou' in adherence to Irish national sentiment. Like Ó Catháin with his caveats, I report this not to agree with it but because it exists as one of many language attitudes which people are rarely frank about in public, preferring 'patterned evasion' of the logical behavioural consequences of the universally attested high degree of popular approval of almost all *voluntary* methods of promoting Irish revival.

Harrison (1976: 35) expressed this light-heartedly and well in summarizing CILAR (1975): 'although we are all *for* Irish as we are for cheaper bus fares, heaven and the good life, nobody of the masses is willing to make the effort'. Indifference to and lack of interest in Irish is consistently attributed to around 80 per cent of the population (e.g. Ó Riagáin and Ó Gliasáin 1984: 14) and, again allowing for a proportion who feel decently ashamed of admitting it, it must be the inner view of far more – especially if judgement be based on action rather than overt attitudes.

D. Fennell (1977: 10–11) ascribed the invincible advance of English to the invaluable aid it gave to the universal craving for power and status, with the emphasis for ordinary people on economic advance. Mackey substantially agreed and reminded his academic audience: 'all language survival probably has a price-tag'. He added:

> To me the crucial question appeared to be, if you have all those people in favour of the survival of Irish, what are they willing to pay for it? It is going to cost something more than money . . . In other words how much economic advancement are individuals willing to forego in

return for greater cultural and linguistic identity?   (1977:12)

He had already stressed the great economic advantages of English and the fact that Irish was not used in industry or commerce. One would wish to except parts of the Gaeltacht from that remark, but not much of it, and it is entirely true of the Galltacht, in which the great mass of the population live. Since 1922 the state has succeeded in conferring material advantages on some of the middle classes who have cultivated Irish, but it has failed to do the same for ordinary working people. Hence (Macnamara 1971: 86) 'The *Gaeltacht* people, and the working classes, then, by their behaviour, cut through a deal of middle-class wishful thinking and exposed it for what it is.' Hence also the very small numbers who ever attain real fluency in Irish through the school system.

A conclusion to this pessimistic survey of the state of Irish as a living language in the Galltacht of the Twenty-six Counties may be derived from two comparatively recent reports. The *Action Plan for Irish 1983–1986* declared sadly, 'It is not an easy task to devise a set of policies which would be supported by the community at large and which, in the longer term, would lead to a viable bilingual society' (Bord na Gaeilge 1983: 3). Bord na Gaeilge's Advisory Planning Committee (1986: ix) elaborated: 'A major problem . . . is the distribution and mobility of Irish speakers. It is very difficult for such a small minority, scattered throughout the population, to maintain Irish-speaking networks over time.' Because CILAR studies had shown that only 25 per cent of those who grew up in Irish-speaking homes later established such homes themselves it estimated that:

> . . . the maintenance of the present level of bilingualism in the State requires each school-going cohort to contain about 20–30 per cent of highly competent bilinguals. This is . . . probably somewhat higher than that arising from the performance of school cohorts in recent decades.
>
> (ibid.: ix)

Given the marked decline in all-Irish education, its massive failures when widespread in the past, and the general reluctance of Irish speakers to speak Irish when non-Irish speakers are present, optimism as to the attainment of mere maintenance must appear weakly founded. The position of Irish is greatly improved by the presence of the 30 per cent or so of 'census Irish speakers' whose mainly passive support for the language makes them terribly invisible and inaudible to the most attentive visitor; but they have little bearing on the creation of new Gaeltachtaí in the Galltacht, 'the creation of a Gaelic microcosm in the English macrocosm' which was a major target of early state policies and which the creation of the Gaeltacht colonies in Co. Meath was intended to promote.

It is now incontestably apparent that the revival of Irish based on abstract ideas such as national identity, culture, tradition, and heritage, divorced as they are from the forces of everyday reality for ordinary people (Edwards 1984c: 288, in close agreement with Ó Catháin 1973: 311–2) has finally failed. There seems ample support in the Galltacht for the study of Irish for its symbolic value, but totally insufficient support for its restoration to communicative use. And the tiny minority who favour the latter also have other priorities which render three-quarters of them incapable of transmitting it to their own families. A few ephemeral family, workplace, and other social networks may emerge from time to time, but they have no hope of stability, permanence, or expansion to community or local territorial dominance in modern mobile urban industrial conditions, which include international relationships which again make English indispensable and many other languages more valuable for communication purposes than Irish. Language exists primarily to communicate.

Northern Ireland/The Six Counties: a forgotten Galltacht?

Most non-Irish observers tend to forget that Northern Ireland has continued to be involved in the movement to revive the Irish language, and it is not generally realized that native speakers were still to be found here until very recently. I was mainly indebted in 1955–8 to M. J. Murphy (a noted folklore collector for the Dublin Commission; wrote in Irish as M. S. Ó Murchadha), Pádraig Mac Conmidhe (secretary of Comhaltas Uladh, the Northern branch of the Gaelic League), Lewis Hanna, Donald Savory MP, and Frank McAuley (farmer, of Layde, in the Glens of Antrim) for introducing me to the last individual survivors who retained Irish as their native tongue and to work still being done to promote its knowledge and use.

Rathlin Island had about eight elderly native speakers in 1955, if one included islanders retired on the mainland. Rathlin Irish had passed out of any everyday use about 1940. The last native speaker in the Antrim Glens died about 1953. Sixty native speakers survived in the Sperrin Mountains of mid Ulster in 1950, the youngest aged 55, but they were scattered through twenty-three townlands, with never more than five in any one. Only one of the twelve who were interviewed by Wagner could speak Irish as fluently as English (H. Wagner I, 1958: xiv; Ó Murchadha 1951: 1–3). By 1955 they were down to a dozen. Elsewhere there were reputed to be four or five elderly survivors above Castlederg in the far west against Donegal.

I received thrillingly lively accounts of the last days of native south Armagh Irish from Tomás mac Cuileannáin (Thomas Hollywood), born about 1883 and a founder member of Connradh na Gaedhilge's Irish classes at Dundalk. He was the last semi-native speaker of south Armagh Irish, for although his parents never used their Irish in front of the children he lived for a number of years with his maternal grandmother and picked up the basic phrases and sense of Irish when listening to her conversations with her old friends. He was a shopkeeper with no 'professional' interest in the revival. Similar assistance was received from his old friend in the language movement Peadar Ó Dubhda, who made a name for himself openly attacking the Catholic Church for its neglect of Irish (see Ó Dubhda 1943) and was in the same foundation class as mac Cuileannáin. His background, however, was Leinster, though his knowledge extended well north of the Border.

In brief, I developed an interest in Irish in the North just in time to observe its last fatal illness and to benefit from the opinions of the last survivors as to what had killed it. It was not an experience which prepared me for any roseate assessment of statistical or other claims of 'progress in the schools', in evening class work, in local Irish music festivals, etc., which inevitably have been most of the story of the language in the North since its real extinction as a native language occurred. Most of what has already been said about the fate of Irish in the Galltacht of the Twenty-six Counties also applies in the North – with the obvious exception of any major state support or of a major role for a Gaeilgeoir middle class. The dominant middle class in the North is Protestant and British, and that controls the central administration (except at local government level) and most business.

A slightly mixed blessing is also that there are no semi-fictional self-assessed 'official' census returns to challenge interpretation and to mislead the unwary or the wishful-thinkers. There are occasional demands for these, for 'parity' with Welsh and Scottish Gaelic, which are enumerated within their own respective countries (but not in England). They, however, are indigenous native spoken languages, whereas Irish is either immigrant or a school-acquired tongue in Northern Ireland. It is certainly regrettable that no census enumeration took place after 1911, for, as has been shown, the language was still native if moribund until presumably the 1960s; but it is equally certain that any such enumeration in the North would produce fantastic claims to Irish fluency by many or most of the Catholic minority (now approaching 40 per cent), to whom the language is chiefly a symbol of resistance to 'Britishness', without having any serious attractions at all for purposes of daily communication, acquired by long hard study and practice.

The British and Irish Communist Organization (1972: 15) dismissed 'the myth that "Irish is oppressed" in the North' and acknowledged state support for Irish teaching in both primary and secondary schools there, where it is wanted – which is rarely in non-Catholic schools. It pointed out that Gaelic League clubs and halls had always been eligible for grants as social and community centres, and that Irish could be heard on Ulster radio every week: '. . . not the revivalist tripe, but genuine Irish which is invariably related to the Donegal Gaeltacht' (ibid.: 14–16). The governing body of Comhaltas Uladh was said to consist of Roman Catholic clergy and schoolteachers, but was admitted to have considerable working-class support because of 'the diversion of the militancy of the Catholic working class into nationalist channels'; and 'it is dominated by petty-bourgeois idealists of the civil service and small-shopkeeper variety'. Irish membership of the Communist Organization was reportedly less than minuscule, but it was certainly not a supporter of British or anti-Irish attitudes and in this case its comments were apposite.

Breatnach (1956: 45) too pointed out that Northern Ireland schools had introduced oral examinations in Irish before the Republic and also imposed the rule that teachers of Irish must spend a period of residence in the Gaeltacht. As always, however, this must be put into the context that the Free State/Republic is a poorer and more rural country than Britain and because of its low tax base usually lags behind in introducing modern methods. The power of religious Orders in education and the reluctance of Irish politicians to disturb the Church tend in the same direction. Northern Ireland opinion (Catholic included) usually resents falling behind British standards, which devolution does indeed allow, whereas Republic opinions more often resent any 'slavish copying' of advances made in Britain and tend to 'make a virtue' of any increased differentiation – most easily achieved by inertia in Ireland while Britain proceeds to advantageous (and some disadvantageous) change. It is admittedly unusual to find UK authorities doing more for the spoken Irish language than the South, and this difference has been rectified, but it is typical that language teaching methods there should have been more conservative than in the United Kingdom until very recent years.

There is a certain amount of official assistance from the South for language support activities in the North, and Gael-Linn and a few more southern-based organizations are active there, in addition to the Gaelic League.

School statistics on the teaching of Irish in the North are plentiful but as tricky to interpret as in the South. Department of Education (Northern Ireland) figures for December 1950 showed 151 of a total of 1,631 primary schools were teaching Irish, i.e. 9·3 per cent; and 13,878 out of 189,220 primary schoolchildren were learning it, i.e. 7·3 per cent. Thirty-one of seventy-nine recognized secondary schools were teaching Irish (39·2 per cent), but it was not usually compulsory for the 7,720 children in them, who formed 27·2 per cent of the province's secondary rolls. In fact 2,078 pupils entered for Irish in the Junior or Senior School Certificate examinations in 1951 (equivalent to the English Ordinary and Advanced levels of GCE). Only two out of twelve intermediate schools (more or less secondary moderns in the old English system) taught Irish. They had 522 pupils, and 159 entered for Irish-language examinations. None of twenty-eight technical intermediate schools taught Irish. The combined school totals are probably most significant in showing that, much as in the Republic, only 17·3 per cent of all schoolchildren were in secondary education of any sort, from which it follows that exposure to prolonged instruction in Irish was confined to a small minority of the approximately one-third minority who were Catholics. Comhaltas Uladh gave me figures for 1955 which showed 153 out of 1,600 primary schools teaching Irish and, more important, this included only 22·2 per cent of the Catholic schools and none of the non-Catholic ones.

The Dublin Comhairle na Gaeilge's 1974 report *Irish in Education* (p. 5) used 1969–70 Northern Ireland figures to demonstrate the dangers to Irish of allowing children to choose whether or not to study it. In that year only 12,000, or 6 per cent, of the children attending primary school there were taught any Irish at all; and in Catholic primary schools only about 12 per cent took it. Thus 75 per cent of pupils in all schools which offered any Irish did not take it. The council evidently feared that the same might result from the abandonment of the compulsory teaching of Irish in the Republic, and it is impossible to disagree. Again this is not to contend that the Northern schools system has not produced brilliant individual speakers of 'revival' Irish, several of whom are known to this author. The proverb about one swallow not making a summer none the less applies.

Meic Stephens (1976: 140) quoted 1960 figures to show 7·7 per cent of primary school children learning Irish, adding that it was compulsory only in Catholic schools. He should have specified that this did not apply to most of them. He also quoted a figure of 156 out of 1,332 primaries teaching Irish in 1968 and another that only 6·4 per cent of their pupils were learning it in 1966. His estimate of children taking Irish in secondary schools was about 3,000 in 1957, all of them in Catholic schools (the date may be a misprint for 1967). He also reported that sixty-seven secondaries were teaching Irish.

Comhaltas Uladh's assessment paper *Irish in the Education System* (1988a) and data privately supplied showed no great changes in the school situation, but a fear of deterioration in response to UK Government efforts to specify 'core curricula' in which Irish as a non-native language would be neglected. This fear has recently been removed by the official addition of Irish to the list of languages from which *one* must be selected for compulsory study under the planned national curriculum for the province. Secondary school children will be required to study one language chosen from French, German, Spanish, Italian, and Irish (*Times*, 22 March 1989). Schools must provide one or more of the first four languages – presumably consortium arrangements will be permitted – and may add Irish if they so desire. Non-Catholic schools are unlikely to adopt it on any scale. In announcing his acceptance that Irish could be the compulsory language the Northern Ireland Education Minister stressed his own belief that all pupils should learn one of the major European languages and added,

'Parents who choose to have their children take Irish instead of one of them, at a time when the importance of the European dimension is growing, should think carefully about the future consequences of such a decision.' Comhaltas Uladh data (1988a: 9) seem to show that Catholic parents have already thought this out for themselves. Without specifying dates Comhaltas argues that between 17 and 20 per cent of primary schools now teach Irish '. . . and almost as many thought they might do so in the future . . .' up to a limit assumed to be the 37 per cent of such schools which are Catholic.

More than 20,000 secondary-level pupils now learn Irish, but this is only around 13 per cent of the total, according to my own calculation. A separate Comhaltas Irish-language list of statistics entitled *An Ghaeilge sna Scoileanna Gramadaí sna Sé Chontae* (Irish in grammar schools in the Six Counties) is surely less hopeful for the language in showing that while thirty-three (43 per cent) grammar schools in the North teach Irish (autumn 1987), in all but five of the thirty-three it is optional after the second year and in those it is optional by year 4 – judging by the numbers in each year. Seven hundred and thirty-seven pupils in all were taking it in the GCE year and 185 in the A-level year. The grand total taking any Irish in grammar school in all years combined is 5,962: 10·3 per cent, on my calculation.

Numbers studying Irish may be expected to increase among those secondary school pupils who would hitherto have opted out of language studies but under the new curriculum will be required to choose and study one language, which in Catholic schools could well be Irish. There is no need to go into depth about likely motivations, dynamics, and probable ultimate degrees of fluency to conclude that any such accretion of numbers will have limited relevance to the revival of use of Irish in everyday life in the North.

Table 7 Numbers examined in Irish in secondary education examinations 1987: Northern Ireland

Examination	Total examination entries	Totals examined in Irish	Irish entries as % of total
NI Certificate of Secondary Education	73,706	159	0·22
NI General Certificate of Education, O level	112,847	1,223	1·08
NI General Certificate of Education, A level	22,500	282	1·25

Source: Northern Ireland Department of Education, 24 August 1988 (letter).

Official figures showing the position of Irish in Northern Ireland secondary school examinations in 1987 leave no room for belief in any significant upsurge of interest at that time (see table 7). About 20 per cent of the GCE entrants in both grades failed. The department recorded 105 secondary schools as teaching Irish in 1987. There were 254 secondary schools in the previous year, so around 41 per cent would have been teaching some Irish. Examination entries are perhaps a brutal way of assessing how much and how effectively, but it is indisputable that no attainment in Irish below CSE level can be regarded as a viable basis for eventual fluency of the sort essential for any true language revival; and it is similarly indisputable that the level of Irish attainment displayed in table 7 gives no grounds for optimism.

A shorter Northern Ireland equivalent of the 1975 (Dublin) report of the Committee on Irish Language Attitudes Research was published by Sweeney in 1988 after a well structured survey of modern language knowledge, interest, and ability conducted in 1987 in a European Community context. Sweeney showed that whatever number were studying Irish, only 1,797 were entered for it in secondary school examinations (O level, CSE, and A level) in 1986. This compared with 10,337 for French and 1,048 for German. Entries for Irish in O level and CSE had fallen by over a quarter since 1972, whereas those for French had increased (Sweeney 1988: 8–9). In 1986 Irish entries at this level amounted to 5·5 per cent of the number of 15 year olds in secondary schools, compared with 32·7 per cent for French.

Hardly any Protestants admitted to any knowledge of Irish – a mere 2 per cent, compared with 26 per cent of Catholics. Forty per cent of the latter aged 16 to 24 years claimed 'some knowledge' of Irish, but not too much should be made of this, as 56 per cent of them (Catholics) said the same of French (ibid.: 14–15, 25). Of the 11 per cent of the population aged 16 to 69 with some knowledge of Irish only 6 per cent ranked their speaking ability in it as 'complex' (pp. 25, 31), i.e. 6 per cent of 11 per cent, about 0·66 per cent of this great age range. While claims to linguistic ability are often exaggerated, this is credible and hardly conflicts with the report that 16 per cent of those with some knowledge of Irish in the same group were reported as using it occasionally at home. Only 1 per cent, the same as for French or German, were said to use Irish daily in the home (pp. 25, 33). Only 10 per cent of Catholic children under the age of 11 were said by their parents to have some knowledge of Irish but this increased to over half aged 11 to 15. Sweeney (1988: 20–2) comments that Irish is often compulsory in the junior forms of Catholic secondary schools but not to secondary examination level. Hence the disparity with examination entries.

Over half of adults (16 to 69) reported with a 'knowledge' of Irish admitted they had no ability to speak it and 39 per cent had no ability to understand the spoken language (pp. 23, 32). Discouraging as this may seem, the survey also showed that more Catholic children knew French

155

than Irish, and French was considered 'important' by more Catholic parents (p. 24): 48 per cent of Catholic parents thought a knowledge of Irish important for the children, compared with 78 per cent for French. The same proportion of Protestant parents agreed on French – and 3 per cent on Irish (pp. 20, 34). Other 'attitude' questions revealed that 25 per cent of Catholic adults felt that knowing Irish was important but just as many thought the same of German, and more than double, 51 per cent, gave that ranking to French (p. 28). Even among what might be expected to be the young Catholic 'activists', aged 16 to 24, the 'important' ranking was given to Irish by 34 per cent, with 59 per cent for French.

Ability levels in Irish are generally lower than in French and Sweeney concludes that although it is widely 'known' it is little used or experienced outside the educational context in which it is learnt (p. 24). There is room for some optimism in that interest in further knowledge of Irish was expressed by 34 per cent of Catholics aged 16 to 24, almost as many as the 37 per cent professing interest in furthering their French (pp. 16, 27); but this is very noncommittal and experience suggests that very few will transform their interest into the sustained effort needed to master either language.

There is no need to repeat doubts already expressed about the viability of figures like these as a basis for language revival or maintenance in the Republic; but in the North the numbers and proportions which might provide a basis are invariably less. Also there is no wide 'pool' of population vaguely familiar with Irish as a result of universal subjection to the compulsory teaching of it in all recognized schools to act as a mildly encouraging environment for the minority of really keen Gaeilgeoirí.

It may of course be argued that in the 'ghetto' situation of the Northern Catholics, especially in Belfast and (London-)Derry, the mental walls of the ghetto will in fact provide a protective cocoon within which the language will thrive. Stephens (1976) adduced some evidence for this, quoting the claim that 'the largest *Gaeltacht* in Ireland is in Belfast'. He went on to add:

> By this is meant not that entire communities speak Irish on an everyday basis but there are thousands of native Irish-speakers, some of the third generation, together with others who have learned the language at school or as adults, living in the city. (Stephens 1976: 138)

This sounds very like Dublin and the 'thousands' must be put in the context of Belfast's estimated 303,600 people in 1986.

The same must be said of his description of the ten families who built themselves a housing estate on the Shaw's Road where they spoke only Irish together and for which they built a two-teacher all-Irish primary school which the state at first refused to support (p. 138). The school did 'catch on' and since it achieved minimum numbers for official recognition has been granted state support. It functions like a Southern all-Irish school, perhaps for a rather more politically conscious parentage, and if (as I assume) it is the Bunscoil Phobal Feirste (Belfast Community Primary School) of the 1987 Comhaltas list it has grown to 300 pupils, or 0·1 per cent of the population of Belfast – though obviously a multiple of that for the primary school population.

Cumann Chluain Ard (the Clonard Association), which Stephens mentioned as the principal language organization in Belfast, had about 400 members when he wrote and a hard core of sixty workers. He cited a Belfast total population of 416,679. The Cumann was contemptuous of the 'pusillanimous' Gaelic League and made spectacular claims about the exclusively Irish regimen of members' homes, whose children allegedly listened only to Raidió na Gaeltachta and watched television only for the occasional all-Irish RTÉ programme (Stephens 1976: 139). This 'lacks verisimilitude', assuming the universality of human nature and normal social pressures but one needs to know what happened to the children after 1976. Stephens's account of all-Irish activities in the south Armagh border town of Crossmaglen (1,300 people) is realistic enough in relation to the teaching of Irish in all the primary schools and secondary schools, the weekly use of Irish in the Mass, and perhaps in its assertion that 'the language is spoken every night in several pubs' (p. 141). But again one needs relative quantities and some indication of the context of Irish usage: greetings, odd sentences for 'show', or real natural conversations?

Most descriptions of successful revival in west Belfast, Crossmaglen, 'Free Derry', and similar places are entirely consistent with tokenism rather than normal everyday communicative use. There is ample anecdotal evidence of some Provisional IRA units using Irish to baffle the British police, army, and the Gardaí (cf. pp. 244–5). But one does not need much Irish to baffle people who have little or none – the Guards have it 'on paper' but have little practice in using it – and there is no reason to believe that more than a handful of either branch of the IRA are noteworthy Irish speakers.

Support for pre-school nursery groups (*naíonraí*) conducted in Irish is increasing. There were seven in Belfast in December 1987, with a total enrolment of 182, one hundred of whom were in the one Shaw Street *naíonra*. No numbers were available for the only other one, in Derry city (Comhaltas Uladh data, 1988). One other Irish-medium primary school has now been established in Belfast and there is one with an Irish-medium stream throughout the school at Steelstown, Derry. A total of 393 primary school pupils receive their education through the medium of Irish but the fact that the number is increasing and may eventually lead to the establishment of an all-Irish secondary school (Comhaltas 1988a: 8) is overshadowed by the consideration that the 393 constitute only 0·22 per cent of the primary school population.

Around 3,500 adults were attending Comhaltas Uladh evening classes in Irish in 1987: 0·22 per cent of the total population but perhaps half as much again if children are excluded from the base population.

Among Comhaltas's requests to the Secretary of State are several which suggest serious weaknesses in the popular demand for provision for Irish, notably:

1. that enrolment figures required to gain recognition [i.e. financial support] for the establishment of schools should be reduced to a more realistic level; [This refers to new all-Irish schools.]
2. that Irish should be given protected status at A-level so that schools can provide a course in Irish . . . even though the class numbers are small;
   3. that peripatetic teachers of Irish should be employed. [There is not enough demand for full-time ones everywhere.]

(Comhaltas 1988a: 13)

Most requests are reasonable and one would hope that most will be granted, but there is little reason to believe that any of them will contribute significantly to the revival of Irish as an everyday spoken language in the linguistically entirely anglicized socio-economic environment of Northern Ireland.

Considerable attention was paid in Dublin language circles in 1985 to the successful launching in Belfast of the Irish-medium daily newspaper *Lá* (Day), for no such venture had ever been successful in the South. Nor was it here. By August 1986 it was being commended as having been published 'until recently' and having sold 'over 1,000 copies' each weekday (James 1986:3). Its office at least was again referred to in the present tense in June 1987 (D. Breathnach 1988: 4) but whatever one's admiration for the publisher and journalists the figures may be left to speak for themselves. One must also allow for a fair degree of loyal support in inflating the 'readership', rather than assuming a multiplier of additional readers among the purchasers' families and friends.

Breathnach (ibid.) also quoted a fairly authoritative estimate that in 1987 only thirty families used the language as a sole means of communication and only twenty of these were having their children educated through the language. The context was ambiguous but presumably Belfast.

James (1986: 3) credited the BBC local Radio Ulster with about two and a half hours of weekly broadcasting in Irish, whereas Ladurner (quoted by D. Breathnach 1988: 5) reported only fifteen minutes per week for 1987. Improved provision is expected as a result of the 1985 Anglo-Irish Agreement, as part of the measures to meet the legitimate cultural needs of the minority community, which in this regard remains largely dependent on RTÉ and the services of Raidió na Gaeltachta that do include special Belfast reportage.

It is impossible to see how any of these figures may be taken as a basis for optimism about the prospects of Irish language revival in the North or any part of it, for in every case both numbers and proportions favouring Irish are plainly unviable, given normal socio-economic competition with English. Attitude surveys in the North are as treacherous a guide to reality as in the Republic. One carried out by the independent Ulster Television in 1985 found 20,000 people claiming to speak Irish, a further 20,000 wishing for fluency in it, and 70,000 who 'expressed an interest in television programmes in the Irish language' (D. Breathnach 1988: 4). Even if this is accepted at face value, the total population of the Six Counties in 1986 was 1,566,800 – of which 70,000 is 4·5 per cent. It would be a very naive planner who could accept such favourable attitudes as an index of potential viewing if considering the expense of preparing programmes in Irish. Again experience in the Republic suggests that a very cautious view should be taken of 'attitudes', which themselves may be no more than tokens or symbols of broad nationalist sentiment. It is also far too easy for interviewees to forget the cost and effort involved in transforming their attitudes into action and in the case of language far too normal to think that the responsibility and work will fall on someone else – especially teachers and children. It would also be difficult to demonstrate that any amount of radio or television broadcasting in Irish could be expected to help restore it to popular use among the Catholic masses in the North. Such thinking neglects the fundamental reasons which caused the language to fall into disuse in the first place.

It is commonplace for friends in the South to place hope on the strong anti-British sentiments of Northern Catholics as a powerful basis for the revival of Irish there and even to believe the more extravagant claims made for revival already achieved there. This is facilitated by the general rarity of exchange of visits between Dublin and Belfast, as earlier noted between different Gaeltachtaí. General linkages are indeed west to east, even across the Irish Sea. The hope is anyway foolish because it assumes the continuation of hostile sentiments in perpetuity and it largely assumes that Catholics will stay in their ghettoes and introspectively speak Irish to each other. Common sense, let alone the school figures which demonstrate parental choice of language for the children, should suffice to show how unrealistic this is.

Northern Catholics will certainly use Irish to irritate the Protestants (real 'Brits' quite like it) by writing it on walls and by voting to change street and place names into it, but this is no more than what older-generation Southerners used to call 'painting the pillar-box green'. It is too easy and too utterly trivial to make any difference to the language of the Northern Irish Galltacht, which will remain Galltacht whatever the outcome of the current troubles. The removal of anti-British tensions must

inevitably result, as it did in the South, in a relaxation of pro-Irish language
motivations, and among all the needs for economic and social reconstruction
in the North it is difficult to see the language featuring higher in rank order
than it has in, say, Leinster or most of the Republic's Galltacht.

Finally it should be noted that one reason sometimes adduced for the
Republic's abandonment of most of its 'compulsory Irish' policies in
recent years has been the increased attention paid to the North (e.g. Ó
Buachalla 1984: 75). In other words, it is felt worthwhile to attempt to
attract the Unionist majority by dropping the less strongly supported
distinctions which separate North and South. The language is thus
negotiable, like the divorce laws, but whereas the Republic's people
acquiesced (almost) silently in the ending of compulsory Irish for state
examinations, they rejected permission for divorce. There is surely little
more to be said. If it helps to win the Protestants in the North for a united
Ireland, Irish will be dropped: but that would not help, for everyone knows
it has effectively been dropped long ago and that it is nowhere near the
centre of disagreement. Indeed, if it ceased to be used as an 'offensive
weapon' by extremists there is every reason to assume that Protestants
would once again appreciate it for its cultural value: to study it, but not to
learn it to talk to anyone, and certainly not to devote to it the time and effort
which the great majority in the South have also proved themselves
unwilling to allow. The little networks in west Belfast, etc., are noteworthy,
admirable in their way, but are not credible in terms of language revival,
maintenance, or sustained bilingualism. The voluntarism of the North is
as much a failure as compulsion proved in the South and there is no point
in either Galltacht hoping to recoup its own disasters by emulating the
failed policies of the other.

Part 3

Can Irish Survive?

Chapter ten

Aids to survival

The future of the language is so clearly in the balance that it is appropriate to outline the factors and issues mentioned as influential by Gaeltacht informants, adding others which the author over thirty years of study considers important and which are often so fundamental that they are commonly overlooked in a review of day-to-day problems or deliberately glanced over because of their sensitivity. Aids to survival will be considered first, to emphasize that they do exist and are noteworthy, though liable to be forgotten if preceded by or mixed in with the much longer list of hostile forces.

It is impossible entirely to separate positive from negative linguistic influences, for some become anti-Irish in certain circumstances and others have anti-Irish side effects. Such negative effects will be mentioned here but dealt with more fully in the following chapter.

The order of presentation only roughly reflects the author's evaluation of the relative strengths of each influence. Sub-headings under major influences may be trivial except in special circumstances and are included to enable the reader to make an independent assessment.

Nationalism, patriotism, identity

These inspire large numbers outside the Gaeltachtaí to learn Irish, to teach it to their children, and to support the economy of the Gaeltachtaí by sending their children there on courses and (more substantially) by voting to sustain the whole range of support policies which distinguish this primarily English-speaking country. Irish is universally accepted as a badge of national identity but except for a small minority 'token' recognition and respect suffice and there is no serious attempt to proceed to functional or instrumental use of it in everyday life.

This qualified recognition and support has done much to diminish the deep-seated Gaeltacht shame in speaking Irish and being 'Gaeltacht' (pp. 207–8 below), but the identification of nation and language is greatest among professionals and intellectuals in anglicized urban Ireland. The

Gaeltacht in general is cynical about it because it sees no change at all since 1922 in the language of ordinary working-class Ireland, to which its people almost all belong; and it finds the tokenism transparent and patronizing.

What active linguistic nationalism exists in the Gaeltacht has constantly to fight counter-pressures resulting from the inability of the state and nation to employ young native Irish speakers profitably at home. It is little help to the language if the Gaeltacht young become keen Irish nationalists in the UK or the USA.

Irish entry to the EEC is often mentioned as having 'shamed' Irish politicians into awareness of their lack of a language of their own, compared for instance with the Danes, and has stimulated revived attempts to increase the (negligible) use of Irish in the Oireachtas. This has no tangible effect in the Gaeltacht.

'Gaeltacht chauvinism'

Anti-'Dublin', anti-centralist attitudes are in evidence among many Gaeltacht native speakers, including language activists, and have helped the survival of ordinary spoken Irish in its dialect forms. Native speakers resent and resist the promotion of (to them) an artificial, standardized Irish spoken only by second-language learners, especially officials. This attachment to regional variants is one facet of the conservatism which has preserved the living language. Native speakers identify warmly with their *own* Irish, much less often with an all-Ireland Irish which of course the modern state sees the need to promote. This inward-turning particularism may have helped save Irish so far but its negative aspects are now more obvious, especially to 'outsiders' trying to help and even to speak modernized Irish themselves. Conservatism which hinders modernization hinders survival in a modernizing and mobilizing society. See pp. 100–1, 108, 208–15 for closely related parameters.

Remoteness, poverty, apathy

These undesirable attributes were major aids to Irish survival thirty years ago, when agrarian subsistence at a low level predominated, education was effectively limited to primary level in the local national school, private cars were rare, and 'bibulous lassitude' (to quote a Gaeltacht priest) was a major cultural characteristic. Natural selection processes removed the ambitious and discontented, and remoteness and poverty themselves repelled outsiders who might otherwise have brought in English. Marrying into the Gaeltacht was rare. See p. 73.

These negative supports still operate to some degree, for the Gaeltacht is still usually more remote and economically disadvantaged than its neighbours, and even now has fewer visitors because it is typically 'the end of the road'. This reduces outside contacts and makes it slightly easier for Irish to survive than in the very exposed Meath colonies. The sea is a linguistically neutral neighbour for most Gaeltachtaí and so limits the contact zones. Nevertheless the hopeless apathy and indifference of grinding poverty have disappeared since 1956 and modern personal transport, radio and television, increased and diversified employment, and improved social security provision have reduced the relative remoteness and poverty in such absolute terms that apathy and indifference no longer operate against English but much more against the maintenance of Irish in the homes. The former hopelessness and squalor made it hardly worth while to learn English, which for Irish is fatally associated with hope and opportunity. It now more often demands effort to 'keep up' Irish (cf. pp. 209–10).

Schools

This specific term is preferred to 'education' because it is schools rather than broad educational influences which have done the key work for Irish. In the Gaeltacht the national schools (all-age primary schools till 1967) carried almost the whole burden of maintenance and restoration, directed and encouraged by the Department of Education in Dublin. The counties have no responsibility for primary education in the Republic: hence *national* schools, which in the Gaeltacht are all managed by the Church.

National schools

These impart a fair Irish fluency at primary level to the great majority of children in Gaeltacht districts, i.e. excluding the most marginal, which have turned to English-medium instruction. Save with exceptional teachers they cannot give true native fluency unless supported by (some) use of native Irish by parents at home.

They sometimes impart such fluency and love of Irish to first-language English children as to turn neglectful bilingual parents back to the use of Irish once they are assured that their child's English is sound and under no threat. This is a minority achievement and it is doubtful if it often extends to making the child a natural speaker who would wish to pass on the language as mother tongue to its own children.

The teaching of Irish as a second language in schools outside the Gaeltacht has made bilingualism possible if people want it. Educated Gaeltacht Irish speakers agree that it is now possible to shop in Irish in, for instance, Dungarvan, Dingle, Galway city, or Dungloe – 'so long as you know your shop!' This is a real advance but it does not seem to affect ordinary working-class Gaeltacht people, either because they feel embarrassed to try or because the shopkeepers snub them if they do. Their native dialect is unlikely to be what the shopkeeper learnt at school.

The 'all-Irish' Gaeltacht national schools are all much less so than thirty years ago and devote around three hours per week specifically to teaching English. They also use it more in explanation and resort more openly to English-language textbooks for other subjects. This has greatly diminished parental fears that neglect of English in school was ruining their children's prospects in life, so bilingual parents who spoke English at home to counter this are now said more often to be prepared to speak Irish as well. It is impossible to quantify this but it sounds exceptional, and as it always takes place in a bilingual home in districts tending towards English for other reasons it is doubtful if it makes much beneficial difference.

Post-primary schools

These are much the same as secondary schools in England, and include ordinary secondary schools, vocational schools, comprehensive schools, and community schools. The secondaries were traditionally academic and fee-paying until 1967. The rest are different ways by which the state circumvented the Church's monopoly of provision, which for the Gaeltachtaí till after 1960 was in general an absence of provision.

New Irish-medium secondary schools (all types) have been built in or to serve the main Gaeltachtaí during the past twenty or thirty years. Those in Irish-speaking centres, as at Gaoth Dobhair and An Cheathrú Rua, protect the Gaeltacht from their former 'beheading', which resulted from the removal of the brighter or privileged children to schools in towns. It certainly eliminates the sharp transition to English-medium instruction which 'ends Irish' when Gaeltacht children in south-west Donegal, west Mayo, or (most of) An Rinn go on to secondary education. However, when parents have a choice of secondary school for their children it is evident that many or most opt for the English-medium alternative at that level. The provision of Irish-medium secondary education is nevertheless a clear advance and may well defer the ultimate decline considerably in the case of the tiny little school just opened to serve Inis Oírr (Árainn: see p. 105), whose Irish-speaking children would otherwise be swamped in Galway schools. Where secondary-trained children go for employment is another matter, so this may only be deferring the move to English and should not be overestimated as an influence.

Some secondary schools perfect their children's command of Irish and send them out fully bilingual into universities and colleges from which they emerge to occupy senior executive posts. Trained Irish speakers can cope easily with the regional dialects and move from one Gaeltacht to another without difficulty. They provide the native-speaking core of the

Gaeilgeoirí, the part of the elite that the Gaeltacht is inclined to look up to. This is good for the prestige of Irish and encourages children at school to see some future in it; but because Ireland is a highly centralized country and the Gaeltachtaí are small most of the best jobs are in Dublin, which thus creams off the Gaeltacht elite and alienates it from native speakers in their home environments. Training people well in Irish and then demonstrating that success always means leaving the Gaeltacht is self-defeating, however logical the progression, unless they can be shown to be truly regaelicizing Ireland.

Thanks to secondary education and improved employment opportunities there are now many more well educated people in the Gaeltacht keen on maintaining Irish and appreciative of other dialects and the need for a modern literary standard. They provide a readership and authors for Irish-language books and journals which before 1960 were rarely read outside anglicized towns, and they provide leadership for Gaeltacht Irish speakers. This enhances appreciation of the value of bilingualism, for such people are highly literate thinkers and doers; but for obvious reasons the bulk of their reading is in English, the language of 99 per cent of commercial publishing in Ireland, which also imports the normal range of Anglo-American scholarly and other literature. It is difficult to avoid becoming more fluent in English than in Irish in such bilingualism, the maintenance of which demands very conscious efforts to uphold Irish. A good education encourages this but probably tends towards Irish as only second-language in practice, if not in perceived or sentimental status.

'Compulsory Irish'

This covers a multitude of Irish language requirements for state, semi-state, and local government employment and because hardly anyone questions its justice for employment in the Gaeltacht it has never been an issue in this broader application. 'Compulsory Irish' for many years meant the requirement of a 'pass' in Irish for the (secondary) School Leaving Certificate, the equivalent of an English GCE. Like the old English School Certificate this came as a package, some components of which were essential. The Leaving Certificate required a pass in English, too, but this caused little resentment compared with the insistence on a pass in the 'difficult' and comparatively 'useless' language. Even in the Gaeltacht this was seen as a prime cause of antipathy towards Irish, more especially, of course, in the anglicized districts which were the only ones with access to secondary education and the certificate (cf. p. 213).

It became impossible to maintain the Irish requirement after the provision of free secondary education and the raising of the school leaving age admitted many less able pupils to secondary school, and many teachers now declare that this has helped to transform attitudes to the language from hostile or panicky to broadly favourable. It remains compulsory to study Irish in all grant-aided schools but not to take the examination. A pass remains essential for entry to the National University. It is impossible to measure the practical effects of these improved attitudes but examination entries in Irish show major proportionate declines (Bord na Gaeilge Advisory Planning Committee 1986: 12–14). Whether they were ever relevant to the amount of Irish in normal everyday use is doubtful and the 'better attitudes' are probably no more relevant, either, to the language in the Gaeltacht, tending as they usually do towards contentment with painless token amounts of Irish in place of the effort and difficulty in mastering the real thing. The Gaeltacht native speaker is hardly concerned with this argument, but the evidence suggests that the minority of Gaeltacht children who had access to secondary education were helped in their careers when the state insisted on higher standards in its Irish requirements. 'Better attitudes' to Irish seem simply to reflect less pressure to learn or teach it effectively.

Roinn na Gaeltachta/The Gaeltacht Department (i.e. Ministry)

This gives broad material support to the language through the Scéim Labhairt na Gaeilge, which distributes the £10 grant (*deontas*) to school children, but the financial incentive is much greater because this provides the 'key' to housing grants worth up to £3,000, compared with a limit of £2,000 in non-Gaeltacht areas (figures for 1987). If the children 'fail the *deontas*' the parents do not get the housing grant. This does stimulate some continued use of Irish in homes where bilingual parents are inclining towards English for the children, so helps maintain the native idiom for another generation.

Incentive grants have also been introduced (since about 1980) whereby housing grant applicants who have failed to prove competence in Irish can be given £800 if they become proficient within two years, £600 if they take three years, or £400 if they take the maximum permissible four. This was introduced to encourage returned emigrants and their spouses, key workers, managers in the new industries, and other 'blow-ins', and works quite well. I was told in Iorras (Mayo) of a returned emigrant married to a good Irish speaker but himself poor at Irish yet wanting a £500 improvement grant. He was warned by the inspector that he was not good enough to qualify and to try to improve within six months. He did so with ease and collected the grant, declaring he would happily learn Russian for £500! The child at school from this family already earned the *deontas*, so perhaps it was not so short-term a gain as might be expected.

Roinn na Gaeltachta also gives financial support to Irish summer colleges (*coláistí samhraidh*) the provision of community halls, co-operative development, water and sewerage schemes, road improvements, and marine works, over and above normal state provision. The communities concerned have to demonstrate their native competence in the language and submit to public inquiries to check their language credentials, which An Roinn already knows well enough through the annual testing of the schoolchildren.

I have sometimes sensed excessive generosity in grant-aiding places which have effectively abandoned Irish for their children but the officers of An Roinn see it as a prime duty to encourage communities to conduct themselves so as to deserve such assistance as is available in Irish-speaking areas. If this is interpreted as merely 'putting on a show' of Irish fluency, etc., then at least the people are still capable of that 'show' and but putting it on refresh their use and fluency and demonstrate that the cultivation of their native (or semi-native) language can be advantageous. One may doubt the long-term benefits and fear a consequential growth of cynicism, but as long-term benefits for native Irish are nowhere to be found it is sensible to make the most of any possibilities of re-advance or short-term local recovery. A 'purist' policy could only expedite alienation and the progression from current English-weighted bilingualism to complete English unilingualism. The current policy undoubtedly slows this transition.

Devolution of administrative control of An Roinn's Gaeltacht operations from Dublin to Na Forbacha, actually in a Gaeltacht, has done something to diminish Gaeltacht hostility and suspicion, but the fact that Furbogh is a Galway city suburb which now speaks little Irish removes most gains in this respect (see pp. 99–101). Additionally the fact that the regional offices for Donegal and Munster are (or were) outside the Gaeltachtaí, at Letterkenny and Tralee respectively, maintains cynicism, making visiting officials who in fact are native speakers always seem 'outsiders'. The original reasons for these locations included ease of communication above all, plus a desire not to seem to favour any one of the many provincial Gaeltachtaí by locating in one of them, which would undoubtedly annoy the others.

Removal of the Donegal office to Gaoth Dobhair in 1988 was logical, as the other Gaeltachtaí there were moribund and Gaoth Dobhair's communications are now quite good. Tralee, however, remains the obvious centre (other than Killarney?) for the widely scattered, delicately poised, and tiny Munster Gaeltachtaí, and removal to Corca Dhuibhne, where alone the language is reasonably strong, would only add to the expense of administration (i.e. travel) and cause more cynicism if the offices were placed in the 'obvious' place there, the anglicized town of Dingle.

Location of offices is not entirely a cosmetic matter but is so relatively trivial as to have no significant bearing on the maintenance of Irish as a living language for ordinary working people; but it must obviously have some bearing on the ease of maintaining Irish as a first language in the families of state officials, which cannot be immune to dominant influences outside the home.

Údarás na Gaeltachta/The Gaeltacht Authority

This semi-elective body comes under the Minister for the Gaeltacht but has so far been mainly concerned with support for industrial development, previously the responsibility of Gaeltarra Éireann, which it replaced. State-aided industrial growth transformed the economies of the two main Irish-speaking Gaeltachtaí during the 1970s, virtually halting emigration and thus making possible for the first time in modern history the maintenance of prosperous Irish-speaking communities with diverse employment, free from the debilitating pressures of the paramount need of English for emigration or seasonal migration. There were serious initial errors in overemphasis on attracting foreign 'hi-tech' firms which brought in too much outside labour and proved quick to leave once the tax holiday was over, but replacement by local, more resource-based enterprises has been largely successful. Restored confidence in an economic future for the Gaeltacht has unfortunately been undermined as a linguistic benefit by 'reverse emigration' and numerous side effects. (See pp. 184–6.)

The location of most Údarás-supported enterprises outside the truly Irish-speaking parts of the Gaeltachtaí (Hindley, 1989) is a recurring theme, resulting from faulty definition of the official boundaries in 1956, questionable later extensions, and continued language decline. All enterprises receiving Údarás support have to demonstrate ability and willingness to make maximum use of Irish in their operations and to give preference to Irish-speaking applicants for employment when they are otherwise suitably qualified. Non-Irish-speaking appointees are expected to attend courses (provided by Údarás) to learn the language to the required level. Performance after grant has been paid is difficult to monitor effectively, though this is provided for. Random visits to a handful of enterprises in places including An Rinn, Baile Bhuirne, and Daingean/Dingle found English alone in use, confirming the local opinion of dedicated Gaeilgeoirí.

It may be noted that the principles of industrial location as normally applied elsewhere will almost always favour a central site in a place with existing infrastructure (e.g. roads, water supply, power) as against one where all these things must be provided new at extra cost – unless comparative land values cancel the latter disadvantage. In the Gaeltacht centrality always favours the more anglicized towns and villages, and until the private car became general scanty public transport made travel to work by Gaeltacht Irish speakers hardly possible except to such places. Údarás does, however, subsidize company transport to help get over this difficulty. What it has not succeeded in doing is to avoid disproportionate investment in official Gaeltachtaí such as mid Galway, most of Múscraí (Cork), eastern Corca Dhuibhne (Kerry), and central Iorras (Mayo), where Irish fell out of normal use twenty or more years ago. All these areas fully merit investment aid, but not under Irish language policies or out of funds intended to help preserve the Irish-speaking communities.

In face of the linguistic circumstances of most official Gaeltachtaí, Údarás decisions on industrial location must always be 'wrong' for Irish. Absence of aid kills it by neglect and continued emigration, stressing the absolute necessity of English, while promoting industrial growth draws back emigrants, skilled workers, and managers who bring English into the heart of the Gaeltacht. Any raising of purchasing power and aspirations increases links with the anglicized outside world.

The general conclusion must be that Údarás tries to help Irish, not least in many officially Gaeltacht places where little Irish is normally spoken. These efforts enhance the status of the language to some extent but have little effect in increasing its everyday use where it is already disappearing. The language then tends to be most prominent on the factory sign boards, some office notices, and the company letter heads, but not where it matters, on the shop floor or in routine operations. It is, however, largely thanks to Údarás that Irish has a prominent place in many of the big factories in Gaoth Dobhair and at An Cheathrú Rua, Baile na hAbhann/ Ballynahown, Indreabhán/Inverin, and other places in Conamara where without Údarás incentives industrialization would have resulted in immediate and unequivocal anglicization of the workplace. Corr na Móna in Dúiche Sheoigheach (pp. 89–90) is an even clearer example of a place where Údarás has been successful in helping to arrest what seemed an advanced and irreversible slide into English and to restore Irish to public prominence.

Údarás has done much to offer opportunities and incentives for the promotion and use of Irish in Gaeltacht industries and all this is gain. No more than in any other field can the state save Irish if the people themselves fail to do so and cynically evade the obligations they accepted when seeking state aid.

The Culture and Language Section of Údarás does considerable work for Irish by supporting Irish-language pre-school playgroups (*naíonraí*), youth clubs (*ógchlubanna*), cultural competitions, adult education courses, and a wide range of community development activities. It supplies Irish Mass leaflets to churches and supports the preparation of Irish-language television programmes for RTÉ (Raidió Teilifís Éireann), preparing short videos itself. It has now begun training community leaders and is hoping to augment its work with assistance from the EC Social Fund.

This varied activity helps the ordinary voluntary and professional language workers in the Gaeltacht to feel they are not alone and gives them

171

valuable support in all fields of language activity not already assisted by Roinn na Gaeltachta, Roinn Oideachais, etc. Its subsidies help keep costs down and thus stimulate both the supply of and demand for Irish-medium 'events' which keep Irish in the public eye and ear. Critics may carp about the alleged ineffectiveness of this work in competition with Anglo-American 'admass' and 'pop' culture, but without Údarás and related bodies it is reasonably certain there would be hardly any provision for Irish at all. Again it is not the fault of Údarás if Gaeltacht people fail to use the opportunities it presents and prefer mass entertainment in English.

Other state, semi-state, and voluntary bodies

Almost all Irish-language organizations receive state financial support. There are many more than those mentioned below, but these are the only ones mentioned to me in the Gaeltacht recently.

Gael-Linn

This is very helpful to Gaeltacht schools and communities, to which it sends three-month scholarship children to improve their Irish. The parallel but older Comhdháil Náisiúnta na Gaeilge organizes the summer colleges, which bring a considerable income to the Gaeltachtaí and also encourage some pride in the language. Both have been criticized for sending ill-prepared children who came badly motivated and helped to anglicize the schools or homes in which they were placed, but more rigorous selection should have cured this by now and serious negative influences are rarely mentioned in the case of Gael-Linn. The summer college courses do seem more widely to be regarded as a free or heavily subsidized holiday and when held in non-Irish speaking districts, as is often the case, cannot be helpful to the survival of the native language, whatever they may do for revival as a second language.

Oireachtas na Gaeilge, feiseanna, etc.

This Oireachtas is the Irish equivalent of the Welsh National Eisteddfod (Eisteddfod Genedlaethol Cymru), as distinct from An tOireachtas, which is both houses of the Irish parliament. *Feiseanna* are local cultural festivals which tend to feed into it. Both help to keep Irish a place in society, but it must be stressed that they are a minority interest not dissimilar to amateur dramatic and choral societies in northern England, or the Yorkshire Dialect Society, of limited interest to the young, who tend to find them boring or old-fashioned compared to the exciting and professional offerings of Anglo-American television or the wide-screen cinema.

Non-Irish readers must also be reminded that most language organizations are (Dublin) city-based, small in membership, and especially so among native speakers in the Gaeltacht. Their influence on the Gaeltacht is therefore indirect, in helping to press the state to help the language there.

Publishing

State subsidies to the production of books in Irish are very important in maintaining a modest flow of literature which would dry up almost completely without them, as demand is so small and the rewards for authors and publishers are negligible, even with the subsidies. All Irish-language periodicals survive on state support but, judging from the past thirty years, they do not usually survive long. What is achieved is remarkable, given that there cannot have been more than 30,000 habitual native speakers at any time since 1956 and that few of those were habitual readers in any language. The most important impact of book subsidies in the Gaeltacht is that on school textbooks, which with such small numbers of pupils could not be available without subsidy. This is an invaluable and indispensable aid to the maintenance of Irish, whatever the criticisms of the textbooks currently available. See above pp.73, 135 and 186–9.

Raidió na Gaeltachta

One of the few strongly beneficial outcomes of the Gaeltacht civil rights movement of the late 1960s and 1970s, in addition to Údarás, was Raidió na Gaeltachta. RTÉ had initially opposed it as uneconomic, which of course it was and is. State finance easily overcame this objection, but unfortunately at a time when most people had turned instead to watching television. There are regional broadcasting stations in each of the three main Gaeltachtaí, broadcasting on medium wave to them and on VHF to the whole country, using the RTÉ network. It seemed suspicious that it collected no audience figures (1987) but my own enquiries showed that it was widely listened to for local news – it broadcasts births, marriages, and deaths, and reports all local 'events' – but not for much else, and even teachers confessed to switching off when programmes were in other than their local dialect (see p. 63.) Classes who were asked in my presence to name a programme that was listened to in their home could only mention 'Nuacht' (the News) and teachers were generally critical of the low-budget approach, which was said to be simply to send a tape-recorder to anything that happened to be going on. A week's programme schedule shows there is some truth in this, but the low budget is real, as is the dialect problem.

Television

It is hardly possible to mention television as an aid to Irish, because the amount of it on either of the two RTÉ channels is trivial, confined to short news programmes and the occasional play in 1987. I was reliably informed that surveys reveal an almost universal switch-over to BBC or ITV (UK) when an Irish-language programme is televised – though not, of course, those centrally involved with singing or dancing. An Irish-language television channel would in theory vastly assist the survival of the Gaeltacht by removing the major anglicizing influence on every child in every home. Why this is unlikely to materialize, and why, if it did, it would not achieve the hoped-for success, are discussed among the negative influences later in this chapter.

The best hope now would seem to lie in more subsidies for more and better Irish-language programmes from RTÉ, but the English-language competition is so overwhelming that hardly anyone I met thought it would make much difference save for some useful job creation and encouragement for the small keen minority, not for the man, woman, or child in the bóithrín (country lane).

It is thus difficult to assess whether the small amount of Irish-language television is a net asset or a blatant demonstration of how insignificant a place Irish occupies in the modern mass media of communication, so tending to influence against it rather than for it. It is probably an asset to the thinking minority but the opposite for ordinary people outside the cultural elite.

The Church

Thirty years ago the (Roman) Catholic Church, which manages all national schools in the Gaeltacht, was often subject to criticism because of priestly insistence on the use of English for catechization and religious instruction in Gaeltacht schools, and for the sermons in churches where most but not all the congregations could speak Irish. Such criticisms have not entirely subsided with the passing of the old generation of priests who were trained 'under the British', but since Vatican II 'vernacularization' has worked in favour of Irish in nearly all cases where it is warranted and where the congregation want it. The priests I met in 1987 were all favourable to the use of Irish, as is the Cardinal Primate, and apart from odd local grumbles that the priest spoke 'terrible' Irish which made his English preferable, the evidence suggests that the Church is consistently supportive of the language in the Gaeltacht and in no way to blame for its continuing decline. Where a church abandons Irish it is invariably because the people have done so already and have made their feelings clear.

Another reason for the change in priests' attitudes is the economic advances since 1956. Then many felt that their pastoral duties included preparing the young in their flock for the inevitable emigration by giving them practice in English, which was then seriously neglected in Fíor-Ghaeltacht schools and which they knew was vital for success in life abroad. Relaxation of the schools' Irish regime of course helped, too, as fluency in English is now invariably attained in the normal course of a school career. It was unjust to call such pastors 'anti-Irish', for many of them loved the language and promoted it in numerous other activities.

Certain teaching Orders have earned a fine reputation in their work for Irish in schools, the most prominent being the Christian Brothers. However, the distribution of their schools, never in truly Irish-speaking places, makes it plain that their main contribution must be to Irish as a second language, a partial exception being anglicized Dingle, where the Brothers' secondary school provides Irish-medium education for the boys of the town and also most of those from the nearby Gaeltacht, which it serves and officially is in. The same applies to the girls' school of the Presentation Sisters, and between them they provide the only powerful assistance to the language in Dingle. Irish-medium secondary schooling is also maintained in the schools run by religious at Baile Bhuirne (or – Mhúirne) in Múscraí and Tuar Mhic Éadaigh in Dúiche Sheoigheach, both places much in need of support for the language.

'Family networks'

This is a relatively recent development in the Gaeltacht and involves families of Gaeilgeoirí meeting together informally in small numbers in each other's homes at fairly regular intervals (e.g. weekly or more) to chat together, play games, hear short readings, and to do everything else in Irish together with their children, as part of an effort to maintain and transmit to the young a use and affection for the language in districts where it is seriously threatened. South Acaill is a prime example. The scale is small. Children often protest that they would sooner watch the 'telly' and they also react against it when they socialize with their school cohorts, not wishing to seem 'different'. However beneficial, such networks are plainly a symptom of decline.

Social class influences

The strongly middle-class and professional/intellectual background of the current Irish-language leadership in the Gaeltachtaí compares strikingly with the days when the middle classes led the way to English and may be reckoned a clear gain, reflecting the high status of Irish under the state and in education since 1922. The commercial sector, especially small shopkeepers, has not so obviously been won over but does not provide a rival leadership, merely subverting the language by using English at work and in the family.

Whether the 'bourgeoisification' of Irish in Gaeltacht society, traditionally egalitarian and suspicious of social pretensions, helps maintain the language or not depends greatly on the personality of the individual aspirant 'leaders', their family background, the degree of 'influence' used in their advancement, and so on. Gaeltacht society is tiny and intimately personal, everyone has known everybody's business and background for generations, and outsiders who move in with the intention of showing the way are unwelcome unless very rich and generous. 'He has done well out of Irish' is a common resentful comment from native speakers, even to an English observer, and is usually coupled with a remark that Irish is all right for those clever enough to go in for the state service but useless for 'the rest of us' whose children can only seek an ordinary living.

Away from the Gaeltacht core, where Irish is no longer a community language and it is only professional people who speak Irish, there is more widespread resentment against the alleged 'closed Order' of Gaeilgeoirí, a sort of Masonic Order of initiates who use language qualifications to exclude others from the competition for jobs. The elitism and 'more patriotic than thou' attitudes of such activists do not help the living language at all and to ordinary people make Irish seem something to 'put them down'. This is horribly unfair, for even the most gauche of the elite sincerely wish the entire population to follow them; but their own close networks do look closed from outside and threaten to reduce Irish to a sectarian argot or cult language with no resemblance to a natural community vernacular, which needs ordinary 'uncultured' native speakers to sustain it.

It is good to have middle-class support for Irish but it is vital to recall that the middle-classes moved out of Irish to establish their own socio-economic superiority when the people spoke nothing else, and to beware lest Gaeilgeoir elements in the present bourgeoisie are not doing exactly the same thing in reverse now that most of the masses have dropped Irish. 'Patriotism' can conceal many motives and it is not self-evidently patriotic to insist upon the use and cultivation of Irish in all circumstances when the great mass of the Irish people find it variously inconvenient, difficult, unnecessary, or unhelpful, much as they love and respect the language. The extreme *lán-Ghaeilge* ('all-Irish') element in the bourgeoisie does keep Irish alive in many unlikely places and should be honoured accordingly, but its impact in the Gaeltacht tends to be negative because the Gaeltacht is much poorer than the city suburbs and tends to see the all-Irish movement as something which only well-off city folk can afford and dare risk on their children, who are secure with English as their first language already, and have fine social contacts in Ireland when it comes to looking for jobs.

This again is unfair, for the current impression is that jobs in Ireland are harder to find for graduates than for the less well educated, and statistical evidence on comparative emigration rates by social class is lacking. Such prejudices do not need a statistical base so long as there is a kernel of truth to grow on, and there is a large enough kernel perceptible here. All healthy societies enjoy a degree of what Marxists call 'class warfare' but the native Irish-speaking community is too small to survive divisions threatened by the appropriation of the language by one class or by resentful lumpen-proletarian (and peasant) assumptions that that is going on (see pp. 211–3). Such internecine conflicts seem characteristic of the last stages of decline and it is difficult to see how to avoid them.

Bluff and the 'brave face'

Almost everywhere in the Gaeltacht the first reaction to a visitor asking about the state of the Irish language is to assert that there is 'a lot of it about', that 'everyone' speaks it, and that the children love it: even where the most perfunctory further investigation shows it to be dying with the elderly as a native language and surviving among the young only because of the work of the schools. This is not self-delusion, for the same people will admit to the weaknesses once it is clear that the questioner is sympathetic and not an official 'snooper' out to remove Gaeltacht grants. The entire population seems to share in this deception, regardless of class, occupation, or age, but it is only a brittle façade and seems designed to uphold morale in a difficult situation as well as to serve material ends by safeguarding grant aid. A certain class of language activist maintains the deception with such fervour as to suggest self-delusion or what I call 'loyal lies'. They need to convince themselves in order to convince others and some wishful thinking is helpful where the obstacles to be overcome are immense. Unsurprisingly, school heads and organizers of summer colleges fall disproportionately into this category.

The good effects of this include inspiring other people to join in maintaining or reviving the language: people who would not join if immediately exposed to the usually profoundly discouraging facts. It does help morale and to keep up enthusiasm, recruiting young people who are vital to carry the language into future generations. Illusion and delusion are both necessary at this stage of decline, and as both are normal in everyday life and social psychology there is no need to apologize about them. The majority of people do not respond to this morale-boosting except at token level and remain indifferent in benign neglect or 'patterned evasion' (Streib 1974) of organized language activity.

The bad effects of revivalist 'bluff' and deception are not easy to assess but were met in several schools where teachers who were working hard to maintain Irish were delighted to meet an English scholar who knew the

Gaeltachtaí and who, having no vested interest in concealment, could tell them how other areas were performing: 'When we talk to other people we feel it must only be us that are failing. What are we doing wrong? ' Or: 'Everyone seems to be doing well but us!' This applied most commonly in relatively remote school districts but was encountered even in the heart of south Conamara; and I was even asked at one Raidió na Gaeltachta station how the language was really doing in the local schools. It is sometimes only the reception class teacher (or the *naíonra* supervisor) who can give a sure answer about the first language of the homes.

Lack of frankness over real difficulties does discourage sincere and sensitive workers by giving them a sense of failure, when they are doing as well as anyone else and often better than some 'shop-window experts'. It also prevents co-operation in devising schemes to overcome weaknesses which are universal in the Gaeltacht and not confined to odd schools honest enough to admit them. The conflict is of course between idealism and realism, perfectionism and relativism, which lie in the individual temperament. It is, however, utterly impossible to be inwardly idealist or perfectionist about the status or future of Irish in any Gaeltacht today. Any apparent lack of realism is only a façade or 'public image', designed to encourage or deceive others. Its best defence is that it does help maintain a continued flow of outside funds into the Gaeltacht, *qua* Gaeltacht, does win converts to the language movement, and discourages only people who would be discouraged anyway by the facts of language decline. It does not matter that the emperor has no clothes so long as many wish to believe that he has and continue to act accordingly (cf. pp. 214–5).

My own suspicion is that utterly cold materialistic realism applied to the Gaeltacht would result in the rapid abandonment of Irish-medium instruction in almost all national schools, i.e. all in which the children now first arrive at school or *naíonra* speaking English as their first language, reflex language, or otherwise better than Irish. If I am correct a degree of illusion and self-delusion is the last strong human defence for the Gaeltacht as an institution and the language itself. Illusions did more than material calculations to create an independent Ireland: but in this present matter the struggle for the language is not with the distant British but internal to the Irish people themselves, who live with the day-to-day reality of an English-speaking country and enjoy the ideals and illusions only on the grand occasions when symbols and tokens of nationhood are appropriately displayed, the more grandly because of their unfamiliarity and irrelevance in everyday life.

Chapter eleven

Causes of decline

Most causes are interrelated and many are themselves effects of more deep-seated causes. Some could just as well be classified under other headings and others may be aids to the language as well as posing threats. The order of presentation is therefore somewhat arbitrary, with cross-referencing where needed.

Economic weakness of the Gaeltacht, and emigration

The present Gaeltachtaí, excluding only tiny An Rinn and Cúil Aodha, were the poorest core areas of the impoverished Congested Districts defined by the UK government as in need of special assistance in 1891, and Freeman's map of surviving 'congestion' in 1936 (1950: 126–7) delineates the present official Gaeltachtaí, with a few additions and very few omissions. This association of the Irish language with deprivation is deeply rooted, and thirty years ago old Gaeltacht native speakers constantly repeated folk sayings which drummed this into the young: 'Irish will butter no bread', 'Irish is tied to a donkey's tail', 'Irish belongs to the age of the foot-plough and the sailing ship'. All were said to me in explanation of why the children had not been brought up in Irish. An old man on Árainn Mhór told me, half laughing, that the only successful Gaeltacht industry would be a suitcase one, and his view expressed the fatalistic attitudes which resulted from over a century of mass emigration caused mainly by poverty and lack of opportunity at home. This is the essential background and primary cause of most other secondary causes of Irish decline.

The long tradition of emigration and male seasonal migration for work created a popular need for English, and lack of remunerative employment in the Gaeltacht devalued Irish. The struggle to survive put all emphasis on material considerations in everyday life (not of course in religion), making language no more than a means of communication, an economic tool to be used in seeking a livelihood. Hence, once the schools had provided basic bilingualism at popular demand, it seemed logical to drop the old inefficient tool (Irish) and adopt the new and much more effective

179

one (English). 'Irish is all right for people who are well-off and secure in life' is still a common attitude, justifying the use of English with the children in the home and leaving the schools to give them Irish.

Returned emigrants who have come back to new Údarás-supported industries as quite young parents still say how embarrassed they were in London, Chicago, etc., looking for a job with broken English, fit only for unskilled labouring, and express determination that their children will never suffer like that for lack of English. And no one is confident that large-scale emigration will not return, many citing evidence of recent school leavers to prove it has done so. That parents' first priorities centre on job prospects for their children is not peculiar to poor regions but the emphasis is extreme and often exclusive there.

That emigration from the Gaeltacht 'means' English results from long dependence on English-speaking parts of Ireland and countries overseas as those most receptive to Irish immigrants, so long as they spoke English eventually. It is an elementary point that the few who went to France, Spain, Latin America, etc., adopted other languages. The 'Union' to 1922 can be blamed for the economic tie with Britain but hardly for the overwhelming choice of the English-speaking USA by more far-sighted emigrants avoiding the British flag. This still applies, but an argument I heard recently for Gaeltacht secondary school children preferring French or German or Spanish to Irish in school was that the foreign languages would aid their ambition to travel without being restricted to English-speaking countries. This is not a silly argument, for job opportunities in the Gaeltacht are even now infinitely fewer than outside or overseas for well educated Gaeltacht children. Except for the survival of the language, is this regrettable?.

Whatever the number of emigrants, there have always been many more thinking of emigrating who never got round to it but shaped their views and language practices accordingly, influenced still more later on by letters from their emigrant siblings and the remittances which thirty years ago financed many of the cars then on the road. Reported successes of emigrants abroad never helped Irish but the actual return of the emigrant is usually much more damaging.

Emigration in response to local deprivation can sometimes entirely depopulate a district, leaving no one to speak any language. This has emptied Na Blascaodaí/the Blaskets and the Donegal Gaeltacht islands of Inis Oirthir/Inishsirrer, Inis Caorach/Inishkeeragh, and Gabhla/Gola in the author's lifetime, and fears of depopulation have caused periodic 'panics' on Toraigh, Árainn Mhór, and Cléire, always casting doubt on the usefulness of Irish.

Moderate depopulation in mainland Gaeltachtaí is a major cause of the closure of small schools and the bussing of their children to larger ones, often more central and less isolated, with more anglicized catchment areas. This is dealt with under education (pp. 205–6).

The weakness of the Gaeltacht economy includes a rural agrarian dominance which whilst now considerably shaken is yet relatively intact where the language is strong. The Doirí Beaga–Bun Beag district of Gaoth Dobhair is the sole major exception, a real 'rural town'. Rural dominance implies almost total dependence on nearby anglicized villages and towns for all but the most elementary shopping requirements, for entertainment, for hospitals, and often for employment. Frequent travel to English-speaking central places is therefore normal and even daily, as for many secondary school children. The principles of industrial location (p. 170) rarely favour a true Gaeltacht site. This reinforces the association of Irish with lack of amenities, if at a higher level than traditional 'deprivation'. It is not enough to be able to find some shops (p. 165) in which Irish is welcomed.

Weak economies with a rural basis and lack of employment diversity prevent the different Gaeltachtaí supporting each other by intermarriage and mutual exchange of visits, except in connection with sporting and cultural competitions, the latter supported by Údarás. Even then, economics plays its crippling part, and when An Eachléim in the little Mullet Gaeltacht welcomes a rival Gaeltacht team it has to do so at entirely English-speaking Belmullet, as it has no adequate changing facilities of its own. Each Gaeltacht looks to its own village or town, usually anglicized, or to Galway or Cork cities, or to Dublin, but never to another Gaeltacht, and in most cases there are closer linkages between each Irish-speaking part of any one Gaeltacht and its town, than with each other. The people of the Gaeltacht most often meet in its anglicized town or central village. This is normal to rural structures throughout the world but has linguistic consequences here because the relativities of economic progress and stagnation turned most Gaeltacht central places English first.

Because the same economic influences locate all entertainments in more anglicized centres, the 'pull' of the latter for the young is enhanced and their association of Irish with boredom and having 'nothing to do' is intensified. It also enhances the attractions of television, with its immense anglicizing influence and promotion of city-based culture unapproachable through Irish.

The poor provision for Irish on television and the low funding of Raidió na Gaeltachta are both functions of population numbers which render them uneconomic. (See pp. 174–5, 184–5, 199–203).

The failure of large numbers of companies which invested in the Gaeltacht in the 1970s and of many of the *comharchumannaí* which raised high hopes then has confirmed residual Gaeltacht pessimism and the belief in the necessity of emigration – and English, but more especially among older people who developed their prejudices earlier. The young are not so discouraged, but are fluent in English.

English as 'liberator'

Having often been reproved as a child for speaking debased Lancashire dialect which my grandparents spoke beautifully but which my mother thought would ruin my career prospects, I may be forgiven by Irish readers for pointing out that, to most Gaeltacht people for generations, a command of English was the liberating key enabling them to escape from the poverty, deprivation, disease, isolation, and boredom of life confined within the walls of the Irish language. It is naive to believe that they did not yearn for English or that this yearning ended with 1922. The Treaty gave political independence but made no difference at all to the economically depressed state of the Gaeltacht, almost certainly worsening it by ending Westminster support of the Congested Districts Board, which Westminster could far better afford than Dublin. A country which cannot adequately support at home the people who speak its dying national language will have grave difficulties in sustaining it into the future.

Prosperity in the 1970s: industrialization, modernization, and mobilization.

These form one interrelated theme, with 'mobilization' used in a narrow sense relating to personal travel rather than migration and emigration, just considered.

Successful industrial growth in the 1970s, and especially the industrial estate in Gaoth Dobhair and similar growth in central south Conamara, caused major re-immigration by former Gaeltacht emigrants and their 'outsider' families, plus managers and 'key' workers who were primary English speakers. This almost ended emigration and removed the former main cause of Irish decline, replacing it with a much more effective constant presence of non-Irish speakers in the midst of Irish-speaking communities already bilingual and inclined to use English whenever a stranger was present. The children of the incomers caused a drastic modification of the all-Irish policies of many schools and frequently transformed the language of play. Most schools of the inner Gaeltacht claim to have remedied this and to have absorbed the incomers, and there is no doubt that the infant children of incomers are readily absorbed into Irish-medium classes so long as they arrive at 'reception' age. Children who arrive at an older age present and suffer difficulties. In general children born or brought up abroad excite the admiration of Gaeltacht children because of their experience of city life and the world portrayed on the 'telly', and because of their fluent command of English.

Thirty years ago a stranger in the Gaeltacht was a rarity. Now many live there, and few are native speakers, even though numbers are keen to cultivate and use Irish. In general 'blow-ins' and returned emigrants are the most powerful new force against Irish in this generation, their presence reflecting unaccustomed economic success which was meant to help Irish but on balance has harmed it far more.

Almost universal private transport and much better roads are other results of increased prosperity which act against Irish by improving access and destroying isolation. Not only do most families have a car but they also have money to spend, so visits to 'town' are frequent instead of limited to the great fairs, and visits to and from emigrants who have settled in Dublin, Britain, and even the USA are annual instead of once in a lifetime, with families and children making the exchange visits. Even in devotedly Irish-speaking families with which I stayed the return of Dublin-based relatives on holiday always meant English dominating the home during their stay, if there were children. (See, for example, p. 127.) In any case all the children were already watching the same English-language television programmes, so had that in common.

The other major anti-Irish result of better private transport is the growth of commuting in the Gaeltacht: as from An Rinn into Dungarvan, Cúil Aodha into Baile Bhuirne and Macroom, Corca Dhuibhne into Dingle, Cois Fharraige into Galway city, and so on. In addition better transport has not merely brought English-speaking centres into the daily reach of Gaeltacht workers but has also made several attractive Gaeltacht districts desirable dormitories for English-speaking townsfolk. The nearby Cois Fharraige coast is very attractive to Galway city dwellers, who have degaelicized everything west to Na Forbacha and most round An Spidéal. The Irish-medium schools are one prime deterrent in keeping them out, but in time it is the language of the school which changes.

This mobilization of the population also helps destroy the old sense of community which could survive when movement was unilaterally and definitively outwards in emigration. Now the functioning family normally extends at least as far as Dublin in its daily thought and seasonal visiting, whereas Irish to all intents and purposes ceases to function twenty or thirty miles away at most. The family visitors and returned emigrants are the more powerful anti-Irish influence because they 'belong' with the Gaeltacht, know its limitations, and can speak with evident authority about life outside, dispelling any illusions which may survive about the status and value of Irish in Dublin after over fifty years of 'revival'. When they damn Irish they tend to be believed, and their children rarely look 'deprived' as a result of their ignorance of it.

The new prosperity coincided closely with the arrival of colour television (pp. 199–203) in almost every home, bringing a much greater impact on the young than the radio, which thirty years ago was almost wholly in English too but had yet to penetrate the many very poor homes. The dominance of Anglo-American English-language television in Gaeltacht homes is unquestionable, including the homes of keen but busy

Gaeilgeoirí who like everyone else use the 'telly' to pacify and tranquillize their fractious offspring of all ages. (See pp. 174, 176). Most teachers rank this with returned emigrants as the worst blow to Irish in recent years, but the television is in every home all day.

Prosperity has indirectly reinforced the anti-Irish power of the television by provision of much more employment for young married women with children. This was non-existent in 1956 and is still not as widespread as in England, but it does mean that more mothers are more busy, so have less time to talk to their children, who are left to watch the television when mother is at home or are entrusted to others who also leave them in front of it – unless there is a *naíonra* within reach. More employment for adults of either sex has an adverse influence on family conversation, and as this is the only communication normally in Irish outside schools the seriousness of its decline should not need stressing. This seems to hit middle-class professional Gaeilgeoirí's homes worse than those of ordinary workers, for the professionals, especially teachers, are those who bring work home.

Rising living standards and rising expectations given visual reinforcement by television have further destabilizing effects on remoter parts of the Gaeltacht, especially the islands, because nowadays (not in 1956) everyone expects immediate access to medical attention in cases of emergency, e.g. childbirth complications, appendicitis, coronaries, and at less vital levels dislike the children having to go away for secondary schooling even when the state does finance their boarding on the mainland. For shopping, women want the choice offered in a supermarket and resent the high prices of a single local shop. The old island fear of inability to launch the boat during weeks of bad weather has virtually gone, but the helicopter is only for emergencies, hopelessly uneconomic for normal daily needs, and can be grounded in extreme weather, which is quite frequent.

Women in particular respond to this group of influences and especially to the lack of remunerative employment for women on most islands, other than in ill-paid domestic knitwear or hosiery. They want modern conveniences and modern opportunities, so want to move to where they are. This is a major stimulus to depopulation and the move from Irish, and is fundamentally economic in origins, as the lack of 'mod. cons.' and employment choice is a normal economic consequence of life in small and isolated communities, especially if insular. (See below.)

Small absolute and relative numbers of the Gaeltacht population

These combined with hitherto low purchasing power form a major explanation of why Irish is generally reckoned of little use and production of anything in Irish as uneconomic.

The small numbers of native Irish speakers, now probably a Gaeltacht maximum of 20,000 (appendix 5), ever tempted to read in the language and the number who ever buy a book a tenth of that, mean minuscule markets for Irish-language books and journals and much higher unit costs than for the English equivalents. This in turn leads to lower quality of product in the effort to reduce costs. The same applies to the demand for Irish-language programmes on radio and television, reinforcing the popular association of the language with inferiority.

Limited numbers of native speakers mean limited numbers of potential writers and producers of high quality. If, say, such people are 0·01 per cent of an average population, 0·01 per cent of 20,000 is 2 and of 56 million is 5,600; of 239 million (USA 1985) it is 23,900. The ratio of talent to numbers in a source population is not so rigid, but these figures do make clear a fundamental aspect of supply and demand where Irish is concerned. It must again be remembered that even in Ireland the entire population of 3,537,195 (1986) in the Republic are fluent English speakers, excluding only a few infants; and of the 1,018,413 enumerated as Irish speakers in 1981, few outside the Gaeltacht make any normal use of Irish or resort to it in reading, listening, or viewing.

This much greater number of second-language learners, concentrated as it is among the better educated section of the population (Census 1981, vol 6: xix), has relatively high numbers of talented people and does a disproportionate share of Irish writing, giving a heavy and 'Dublin-Irish' bias to the publications and programmes which state subsidy sustains. This applies to Irish-language textbooks for schools as well and, as has been seen, the further subdivision of the small numbers of native speakers into three distinctive dialect groups makes matters worse, with Donegal worst provided for because its Irish is furthest from the standard.

Limited potential customers must limit the supply of writers and producers who if Irish-speaking must also be fluent in English and well aware that the rewards for writing or producing in Irish are infinitesimal compared with those if they use English. The state subsidies to Irish-language publication in any form are too small to affect this seriously and for a *good* author or producer to write in Irish is an act of self-sacrifice. Some therefore write in both languages but it is the English version which earns the wide, sometimes worldwide, reputation and financial rewards.

It is conversely liable to be the case that a poor or indifferent writer will secure state support for publication in Irish when much greater competition would preclude publication in English. Only readers of Irish will be able to judge how far this applies but it is normal in the Gaeltacht to hear the Irish-language product described by educated Gaeilgeoirí as discouragingly inferior to the English alternative. 'Culture' is heavily affected by supply and demand.

The supply of literature is particularly constricted in technical and professional subjects, e.g. medicine, science, and engineering, in some branches of which there is nothing in Irish. AnCO, the state training body, supports some provision in Irish, as in computing at Baile an Fheirtéaraigh, but there has been a level of demand for computer training far in excess of the normal one for, say, electronic or medical textbooks. Keen Gaeilgeoirí who are specialists in almost any subject inevitably have bookshelves on which there is a massive predominance of non-Irish and usually English texts, from which it must follow that they will be more fluent in English than in Irish in their 'own' subject.

The effect of numbers in minority demand also more generally helps to explain why the vocational schools (see above, pp. 39, 259) have a poor reputation for Irish. For one thing their pupils are less 'academic' and averse to language studies as such, but in this present context it is more significant that textbooks in Irish on most vocational subjects are few and there is no choice between one and another. Lack of choice is important in determining the preference for English, though for the pupils themselves likely job locations (reflecting Gaeltacht economy and size) will be far more forceful determinants.

Heavy dependence on state support for publication and media production induces non-commercial attitudes which constrict audiences further. Irish writing tends to be literary, historical, anthropological, i.e. thoroughly serious and 'respectable' and at its most light-hearted 'folksy' and nostalgic. Some is strongly political too, but that is little in evidence in the Gaeltacht and is read mainly by second-language linguistic nationalists in the towns, especially Dublin and Belfast. There is a lack of slick, modern, well produced 'rubbish' in Irish, far too little to reflect the 'pop' culture which fascinates so much of Gaeltacht youth and is cheerily entertaining to their parents as well. There are no 'Disney'-type cartoons in Irish (efforts are being made to produce some) and no Irish-language equivalents of the popular BBC or ITV television 'soap operas' (cf p. 67) which the entire Gaeltacht admits to following or admits that its children follow. No language can command the loyalty of its people if it produces only high-minded material for them.

Doubtless because there are few material profits to be obtained through Irish there are few ambitious entrepreneurs or profit-seekers in the language movement, willing to debase the language as English is every day debased by floods of 'thrillers', salacious paperbacks, and 'girlie' magazines which would be unthinkable in Irish. The moral dilemma is obvious, especially to the many nationalists who see Irish and the Catholic religion as the two twin pillars of national identity and actually wish to keep Irish unsullied by most of the things which characterize 'pop' and 'admass' culture, yet which the vast majority of Irish people seem to prefer when offered a choice by the media.

This elitism is a self-defeating anti-economic phenomenon, partly economic in origin because used by a sector of the economically secure bourgeoisie to elevate itself above the common herd. But again, can any language survive if it fails to cater for everyone with thoroughly bad taste? The point is serious but should not be overemphasized, if only because the economic logic already used strongly suggests that any Irish-language 'rubbish' which might be produced would be inferior to and uncompetitive with the flood of English-language rubbish. The latter does not need to be profitable in Ireland, having made its profits in the vaster markets outside. Anything earned in Ireland is a welcome 'extra'. Irish-language products are entirely dependent on the tiny Irish market.

Small and decreasing numbers make it increasingly difficult for native Irish speakers to find others to marry, and increased mobility, including travel into towns and large villages for secondary schooling, brings increased opportunities and temptation to marry 'outside the language'. The loss of the language in such mixed marriages is not automatic but it is usual as regards Irish as a first language. Because most of the Gaeltacht is now in daily intimate and sustained contact with non-Irish-speaking places almost all young Irish speakers are exposed to the likelihood of a mixed marriage .

Small numbers of Gaeilgeoirí make it easy for comparatively small numbers of incomers, whether as spouses, industrial workers, or tourists (including town-based relatives) to 'swamp' the language in its erstwhile strongholds. It does not need an actual majority to make Irish speakers feel overwhelmed, as they normally feel this already in relation to their position in the country as a whole.

Small size and fragmentation of the Gaeltachtaí: scattered distribution

The roughly 20,000 maximum of Irish speakers living in *deontas*-majority areas (appendices 4 and 5) is shared between eleven geographically discrete units which are little Gaeltachtaí of their own, separated from each other by predominantly English-speaking districts. Several amount to no more than one or two school districts, e.g. An Rinn, Cúil Aodha, Cléire, An Eachléim, Ceathrú Thaidhg, and Tír Chonaill Láir (Baile na Finne/Coimín). Some that I have classed as a unit are internally fragmented, notably Dúiche Sheoigheach, where doubtful nominal majorities are separated by minorities. There are only three substantially Irish-speaking Gaeltacht core areas: in north-west Donegal, south Conamara, and west Kerry (Corca Dhuibhne). I include Árainn here with Conamara. All have more anglicized parts within them and the largest, south Conamara, measures at most twenty-four miles by ten in a straight line only if its uninhabited interior is included. Ten miles by ten encompasses all that is mainly Irish-speaking in north-west Donegal and twelve by six in Corca Dhuibhne. Farther than that, as one native speaker put it, 'you drive out of Irish'.

In modern Ireland such distances are inadequate to contain the daily needs and movements of the Irish-speaking population, whether for local employment, secondary schooling, weekend and even daily shopping, or medical care. Even primary schooling is liable to cross the real language frontier where schools have had to be amalgamated. Where there is factory or professional employment, promotion is almost bound to be away from the Gaeltacht or at least from the Irish-speaking part of it. Thus the clever and ambitious Irish speaker tends to be 'creamed off' by the inducements of better prospects elsewhere, where in most cases (except in teaching) Irish is unlikely to be useful to them. What poverty used to do in promoting emigration the relativities of affluence and opportunity continue more pleasantly.

The small sizes of the surviving Gaeltachtaí have rendered them parochial in most senses of the term. There are virtues in the close intimacy of parish life, with its warmth and personal values, but it is difficult to maintain it *and* secure the advantages of urban industrial society, as projected into every home by television. Because it is impossible to attain the latter within the constricted bounds of the little Gaeltachtaí the attractions of English for the life outside continue to grow.

If the language were allowed to be a priority it would severely limit both the choice of work and the possible places of work. English gives choice and mobility, and as English can equally be used in a bilingual Gaeltacht except where rules are deliberately erected to exclude it this certainly weakens the cause of Irish maintenance.

The perception that Irish is inadequate in its geographical range and utility has led to full bilingualism being attained before most children reach school, whereas thirty years ago large proportions in the present Gaeltacht cores arrived there monoglot Irish. (See pp. 194–5, 216). Without monoglots there can never be an insuperable need to speak Irish.

The small size of the Gaeltachtaí causes a 'fishbowl effect' or 'native reservation syndrome', as native speakers perceive that they are being visited as museum pieces or historical survivals by urban people who find them quaint and make embarrassing attempts to emulate the very archaisms which native Irish speakers have dropped from their Irish in recent years. The diminutive pockets of survival are fascinating as such – hence this study – but the inhabitants do not in general feel flattered by the attention, do not want to be treated as 'different' (unless by favours equally open to others in need), but wish to play a normal part in the life of modern, increasingly urban-industrial Ireland. This at least means playing down the role of Irish, though it need not if the rest of the country were serious in absorbing the revival into the routines of everyday life.

The greater preference of many secondary school children for French, German, Spanish, etc., over Irish as an examination and 'career' subject (see p. 180) reflects their contrasted geographical ranges. Irish seems to hinder rather than help travel.

The scattered distribution of the Gaeltachtaí helps to isolate them from each other and to make interlinkages between them rare. The only close interlinkage is between Árainn and Conamara, which latter has traditionally supplied turf to the fuelless islands, a mere six or eight miles offshore. Otherwise closer linkages are always with intervening or interior anglicized towns and villages, and otherwise directly with Dublin because of Irish centralization. Hence there is little mutual support among the Gaeltachtaí and travel between them, except by officials, is rare. Teachers are one of the few groups quite frequently drawn from other Gaeltachtaí but my impression is that this is less frequent in Donegal.

The wide thin scattering raises distribution costs for Irish-language journals and also by preventing them from sharing any perceived community of interests distinct from that of anglicized neighbours makes it difficult for such journals to identify and develop themes to attract an adequate readership.

Their small size brings every part of every Gaeltacht to within one hour's drive of an anglicized town or city which is metropolitan in function and status for it. Conversely, the Gaeltacht part of the urban hinterland is almost always the poorest and least favoured. The mainly English-language regional newspapers which the Gaeltacht people read reflect this in their choice of 'news', but there is no need to be able to read to perceive that this is so.

The fact that the nearby towns and villages are usually English-speaking itself reflects economic forces in that anywhere with central-place functions needed English for its external links before its rural hinterland did so. Most were still predominantly Irish-speaking a century or less ago, their non-Irish speakers being then concentrated in the commercial class. 'Out-reach' of any sort demanded English, then as now, but with bilingualism in Irish worth while so long as some of the hinterland was monoglot Irish. The shrinkage of the true Gaeltacht as well as its poverty long ago marginalized it as an incentive to town or village shopkeepers or market dealers to keep up Irish. The total disappearance of Irish monoglottism has removed the incentives completely, save for a small specialist trade focusing on the needs of the small Gaeilgeoirí *literati* class; and that never supports more than the occasional small bookshop with splendid but low-demand Irish material heavily outnumbered by English stuff essential to earn a living. Small size and population make it impossible to earn a living in any of the Gaeltachtaí through Irish alone.

Small size is a major cause of the absence in the Gaeltacht of Irish-speaking town–village–rural networks which might enable native speakers to maintain an integrated community in partial independence of English. This is impossible at community level and exists only in a few sectors and interest groups such as the school system and parts of officialdom. Even there because of background training, high literacy, and linkages with Dublin the network can never in practice be all-Irish. The most dedicated Gaeilgeoir who wishes to keep informed must read an English-language daily newspaper.

Relatively small size and population of Ireland, and its location

These play little or no part in the conscious evaluation of their language by ordinary native speakers but to me seem absolutely fundamental to their thinking. The total population, at 3,537,195 (1986) without the Six Counties, and about 5,095,000 (1985–6) with them, is not small in absolute terms and the latter figure is almost the same as Denmark's, is the same as Finland's, more than Norway's, and dwarfs Iceland's 242,089. The autonomous Faroe Islands maintain a separate language for 45,728. I discount the example of the revival of Hebrew in Israel, whose Jewish population of 3,516,000 (1985) within the 1949 frontiers is virtually the same as that of the *de facto* Republic, for circumstances are entirely different and the Israel case is unique. Summarizing briefly the discussion in chapter 12, all the other countries mentioned maintain their own language without difficulty, yet, with the exception of Denmark, were subject to foreign states and linguistic dominance for as long as Ireland. Finland was never independent before 1917, having been most influenced by centuries of Swedish rule. Norway became independent in 1905 and in main language shows ample evidence of long centuries under Denmark. Iceland became sovereign only in 1918 and finally broke from Denmark in 1944. The Faroes have never been independent.

The Irish language problem therefore does not relate simply to late independence but more to the fact that the language had been substantially abandoned by the mass of the population and all the main towns before independence arrived. The other countries all had a bilingual middle class at independence but except marginally in Finland their mother tongue was still the native language. This may be taken as showing that the British (or English) were much more effective oppressors than, say, the Russians in Finland (who in a century converted none to Russian), the Swedes in Norway (a similar short time), or the Danes in Iceland and the Faroes. Consideration of economic history suggests as more probable distinguishing factors the enormous expansion of economic opportunities in the United Kingdom during the nineteenth century and the negative influences of the agrarian revolution on rural populations, especially in Ireland. This helped to subvert Irish because the worst effects were felt in Irish-speaking Ireland and the fine ones were immediately 'next door', within the same state, in places to which there was complete freedom of movement. The additional factor that the greatest demand for labour overseas arose in

English-speaking North America, notably in the independent USA, put the same premium on English for nationalist Irishmen and women seeking freedom abroad. Daniel O'Connell, a native speaker from Cathair Saidhbhín/Cahersiveen in Uíbh Ráthach had declared his views on the liberating value of English well before the Famine convinced most of the last doubters.

The fact that since 1922 passports and similar identification have remained unnecessary for Irish people moving to the United Kingdom, save in times of emergency, and that ever since 1922 Irish citizens have retained the right to vote in British elections on virtually the same residential terms as British citizens, indicates how closely integrated the two states are as well as how little the Irish Republic's 3·5 million pose a potential immigrant threat to the over 56·5 million in the United Kingdom, from which they are divided by no cultural barriers of any significance, religion included. This is surely an inestimable benefit in times of difficulty at home and could not exist so readily if a major language divide made the absorption of Irish immigrants troublesome because of demands for separate schooling, as for Hispanics in the USA, where illegal Irish immigration, well attested in the Gaeltacht, causes little concern and is quietly overlooked.

Because Ireland is so relatively small in area and resources and its people are closely integrated with the English-speaking world, proud of its US presidents of Irish ancestry, and with every family (including all Irish speakers) with dozens of relatives in Britain or the USA, the 'natural habitat' or ecumene for ordinary Irish people has grown much larger than the state to include most of the English-speaking world. This numbers well over 320 million native English speakers if Australia and most of Canada are included, i.e. about ninety-one times the population of the Republic and 10,000 times a generously inflated maximum of 30,000 native and partly habitual Irish speakers. No consideration with an economic element can ignore this question of scale, which explains why English always wins any economic argument with Irish.

It is the comparisons between Britain and Ireland and between the USA and Ireland which have been shattering to Irish and it is vital to note that Wales, which is much closer to London than Ireland ever was, has retained its language more successfully (though now terminally threatened) because it had the coal, iron, slate, lead, copper, and other industrial resources which enabled it the better to employ its people at home with rising living standards throughout the industrial revolution and into this century (cf. pp. 223–4). So it is foolish to overemphasize proximity and political inclusion in the United Kingdom till 1922. Wales has been under direct English jurisdiction for centuries longer than Ireland and is a smaller country with no maritime defences in England's direction. Some specific consequences of Ireland's size, population and location include the following:

All Irish people appreciate the essential part played by the English language in the freedom of movement they enjoy outside their own country, and all Gaeltacht native speakers add to that their own ability to move more freely within Ireland itself.

The country, the population, and the economy of Ireland are so small that they are highly dependent on external markets, especially in the United Kingdom, but also in the United States. In the European Community, now providing additional outlets, no one can understand Irish, so all external trading links and most political ones depend on the use of English. The Gaeltacht is fully alive to this and responds accordingly. Its position is the same in relation to its external linkages with the rest of Ireland. Trade of any sort has long promoted the use of English.

Even with 'compulsory Irish' for state and semi-state employment, job prospects for most well qualified Irish-speaking people are better in other countries, mostly English-speaking ones. And at that elementary level a child who wins a Gaeltacht scholarship to University College Galway to pursue Irish-medium degree studies in, say, German or Spanish will find text-books in Irish next to non-existent because of the impact of minute demand upon supply.

The relative insignificance of Ireland in size, numbers, and purchasing power makes Irish people at least subconsciously aware that Ireland and matters Irish are of no great consequence to Britain or the United States, except as an occasional irritant or a source of pleasant diversion. Their part in the English-speaking world is not therefore one of reciprocal give-and-take. They themselves have retained their religious and political identities but have given away a major distinguishing feature, the Irish language, in exchange for most of the benefits of membership of that world, i.e. access to greater wealth and everything now classed as mobilization and modernization. No such price was ever stated but the Church understood it when from their foundation in 1831 it made English the working language of its Irish national schools, except in MacHale's Tuam (Connacht) archdiocese, where opposition died with him.

Small numbers in Ireland partly explain why all but one passenger ferry links (to Brittany) from Ireland are with Britain and why most transatlantic airliners fly over without landing. The way from Ireland to much of the outer world is still via Britain. From the Gaeltacht it is always via anglicized parts of Ireland first, except for the new little airport at Carrickfin, which serves Gaoth Dobhair – and is on former 'planted' land. The position for freight traffic is similar but less relevant to language, though transit instructions in Irish would be unlikely to get a load as far as an Irish port if entrusted to a non-Gaeltacht carrier.

It is impossible in any Gaeltacht to be more than Baile an Sceilg's 233 miles from Dublin by main road and that (in Uíbh Ráthach) is only ninety-eight from Cork city. Gaoth Dobhair is about 190 miles from Dublin but only 120 from Belfast and within fifty of (London-)Derry. South Conamara is within 140 to 170 miles of Dublin and has Galway city within ten to forty. In short, every Gaeltacht core is within an easy day's drive of the capital and most habitual Irish speakers are within half a day. Now most have cars and can afford to use them the old isolation is broken and English is much more needed and used, as during frequent exchange visits with town-based relatives. (See pp. 183.)

For the same reason of small size and distances all attractive Gaeltacht districts are now in easy day or half-day trip distance for anglicized townsfolk. Corca Dhuibhne is a summer playground (fine winter days too) for Dingle and Tralee; Conamara for Galway; Gaoth Dobhair for Letterkenny and Derry; An Rinn is both a day-trip and weekend resort and commuter residence for Dungarvan, as well as having longer-stay holidaymakers. Evening trips from the towns affect many of them, for they are so close. Granted, some pubs make a living by offering an Irish-language atmosphere, usually in musical form, but the clientele speak English in the main and 'fishbowl' self-consciousness is strong.

Sport is enthusiastically followed in Ireland, and in April 1987 everyone in the Gaeltacht seemed to be watching the British snooker final on television. Children in Irish-medium classes, asked by their teachers what sport they best enjoyed watching, said soccer, mentioning especially Manchester United and other British teams with strong Irish player-membership. Because of small numbers it is obvious that able Irish sportsmen will always achieve greater fame and rewards outside Ireland. In Britain they are near enough to home for few supporters to feel they have left or that British teams are less interesting because 'foreign'. This they are for 'international' matches but for nothing else. Gaelic football and hurling do have a following but the role of the language in them is slight and the old Gaelic Athletic Association anathema on Rugby is an embarrassing memory.

Some older people still regard Manchester United, Glasgow Celtic, Liverpool, and (Edinburgh) Hibernians as Irish teams, but again there is no linguistic association and such points merely re-emphasize the degree to which the Republic, while independent, remains integrated at the level of working-class sporting culture. Almost all major British sport is relayed in English to Ireland, except on Raidió na Gaeltachta, and of course for all important games the English-dominated television has no competitor. The lack of 'rubbish' in Irish is thus paralleled by a general absence of sport, including racing, which occupies an inordinate amount of time on Irish television.

Limited numbers contribute (*sic!*) to the constricted tax base which restricts the ability of the state to subsidize its Irish-language programmes or the Gaeltacht to a level which might be sufficient to achieve success. The high proportion of small farmers and self-employed people in family businesses with incomes it is difficult to prove makes matters worse and causes very high income-tax levels for those in paid employment as well as making taxes on consumer goods, including petrol, very high. This makes living costs high, as do sparse rural distributions which add to transport costs, with the combined result a high-cost/low-wage economy which encourages emigration now that most are prosperous enough to pay taxes.

It is arguable that the Republic can less afford to help the Gaeltacht (pp. 182, 199) than 'the British' could and did in the days of the Congested Districts Board and special state aid to the railway system. All the Gaeltacht railways were built with British state aid and all have been closed by independent Ireland. The basic network in Welsh-speaking Wales and the ex-Gaelic Highlands still survives as loss-making parts of British Rail, with massive subsidies which the Republic cannot hope to equal.

Welsh and Highland roads in general are much better, too, again mainly paid for out of revenues from the more prosperous and well populated parts of England, plus the Edinburgh region and of course the North Sea. The underdeveloped regions of both states benefit from EC funding but this too illustrates dependent status. It is hoped shortly to secure support for aspects of the language programme from the European Social Fund but the need for this is a symptom of the many weaknesses which for generations have turned people from the language, from the Gaeltacht, and from Ireland itself.

Much of what has already been said will be understood as aspects of normal 'centre–periphery' relationships. That each individual Gaeltacht is peripheral to its own wider region, which in turn is peripheral to Ireland, which in turn is peripheral to the British Isles, again provides a basic context unfavourable to Irish survival and contributing to the 'minoritization' of the native speakers. That Britain itself is peripheral to the European Community affords no relief, because political membership of the Community has so far had no tangible effects on the prevailing directions of Irish emigration, which remain linguistically English-wards. Peripheral location also contributes to a sense of being marginalized, which is much the same thing and leads to similar low self-evaluation, which bears most severely on the language.

Failure of the language 'revival' outside the Gaeltacht

It is this above all which has left the Gaeltacht as isolated residual pockets in an English-speaking Ireland and enhanced its sense of separation, deprivation, and inadequacy. The failure fosters disbelief in the sincerity of official language policies, which are seen as imposing serious obligations only on schoolchildren. There is satisfaction for those who receive them in the special benefits which Gaeltacht people can receive as Irish speakers and some satisfaction in the privileges reserved for attested Irish speakers in the public service; but as these are drawn heavily from second-language learners who secured a university education – rare indeed for Gaeltacht children before the 1970s – this is as often as not a cause of bitterness. The bourgeois bias of the 'revival' has been mentioned already (especially pp. 175–77).

Gaeltacht people are, in short, disinclined to see good reason why they should risk disadvantaging their children with Irish as a normal daily medium when none of the more prosperous parts of Ireland shows any widespread inclination to do so. 'Token' gestures and constitutional platitudes do not convince them, for they know that business and commerce care nothing for Irish. They no longer believe in the possibility of a language 'revival', for it began in earnest in 1893 with the foundation of the Gaelic League and the decline of the language as an everyday medium has continued uninterrupted, if creditably slowed. Not a single community, however small, has been regained for Irish after losing it among the children.

This is important, but it is not primary, for the failure of the revival in the Galltacht results from fundamental weaknesses appropriately considered under other headings or in their own right. (See chapter 9.) It is certainly unjust to try to blame the state or any sector of Irish society for the failure, as hindsight enables us to be confident that no amount of effort expended since 1922 could have halted or reversed continued decline. Independence did not make Ireland an island sufficient unto itself, and socially and economically hardly anyone wished to weaken the links which the Irish adoption of English as effective first language had forged. They still do not, despite a certain schizophrenia among some intellectuals who find bilingualism easy, enjoyable, and rewarding, so cannot understand why the masses of Ireland avoid it while always voting in its favour. There are few practical advantages in bilingualism with Irish compared with, say, Dutch or Danish. Most inducements to acquire Irish are artificially contrived and do not impinge on ordinary people, who in every country will always be the great majority.

It is failure outside the Gaeltacht which has created the 'fishbowl' which so many of its inhabitants wish to be out of.

Communication, communications, and transport

These all concern moving things about, whether goods or ideas. A language as a medium of communication has much in common with a packhorse or an aeroplane as a means of communication. The one does not get you far compared with the other. Similarly people who have a horse will not use it for normal everyday transport once they have acquired a private car: it will not take them far enough fast enough. Comparison may also be made with what (information, etc.) different languages carry. The sheer bulk of information carried by Irish compared with English resembles the load of a packhorse compared with that of a modern container lorry. In sum, for purposes of communication, whether over distance or for handling or receiving a wide or bulky range of subject matter, Irish cannot compete with English. It has an impressive history behind it and is a legitimate subject of national affection, but its lack of communicative use is rendering it a museum item, very like the steam locomotives which operate on the preserved Worth Valley Railway at my own home and which attract hordes of visitors because they are remembered with great affection by people who nevertheless appreciate that modern technology has rendered the 'iron horse' functionally obsolete. A handful of experts in steam locomotion now suffice to satisfy the public interest, which is occasional-recreational rather than based on need, marginal rather than essential.

This is another way of making the simple materialist point that a navvy would be a fool to use a spade when a JCB can do his work in a fraction of the time. The weakness of the analogy is that the latter is too powerful to do the subtle work of the former, so the spade is unlikely ever to be obsolete; whereas English can do anything that Irish can do, plus more, except in fields which are narrowly confined to scholarly studies of the Irish past and a tiny proportion of the present. These are esoteric matters on which most people do not seek communication, other than through smooth, professional, televized glosses – in English.

Transport and communications in the ordinary sense are a major cause of the concentration of so many Gaeltacht secondary schools and Údarás-supported business enterprises in anglicized central places, and of course also largely explain why those places are anglicized. Places with centrality in relation to location and existing transport systems will always be the most convenient for siting services for the wider area and businesses which both serve and draw on the labour of the wider area. Because of their centrality and better communications they will focus external links through themselves and will therefore be first to feel the need for a second language to extend the links and secure related benefits.

See pp. 182–3 on the influence of increased access to villages and towns, daily commuting, exchange of family visits with the Galltacht and abroad, etc.

Language as a means of communication is not just a general principle, and the maintenance of a language implies that it is needed to communicate with someone somewhere. The death of the last old Irish monoglots, assumed to have occurred since around 1960, means that Irish is no longer necessary to talk to anyone. Given that learning any language demands effort, this is a serious loss of natural incentive and is regarded by many as a fatal step towards language death. Complete bilingualism by speakers of a minority language is by this logic merely a transitional stage towards abandonment of that language, for it has thereby lost its communicative *raison d'être*. (Compare pp. 216 and 218.)

Unilateral bilingualism is an inevitable result of the gross imbalance between the advantages to be derived from learning English and those of learning Irish, as well as of daily exposure to 'the media', which give Irish speakers constant practice with English outside the inhibiting constraints of the classroom and conscious learning. To native Irish speakers who fifty years ago chiefly met English at school and thereafter rarely encountered it in farming, English could remain difficult throughout life, so, if an English speaker did marry in, Irish stood some chance in the home because difficulty was mutual. Above all because of the television this has now changed and almost all Irish speakers are confident and fluent in their English, which also 'comes at them' far more through daily contacts with non-Irish speakers at work, as neighbours, and in all other ramifications of socio-economic advance since around 1960.

English speakers, by comparison, remain in the normal position of learners of a foreign language acquired only at school. Irish plays little part in economic life and when Irish speakers are encountered socially they are always fluent in English and switch to it immediately they note a flaw in the learner's Irish. The ordinary learner is unlikely to encounter the urban minority of dedicated Gaeilgeoirí, which would justly except itself from this generalization and which indeed itself largely consists of middle-class professional learners of Irish. Irish is too weakly represented in the media to be noticeable unless one makes a conscious effort to seek it out, and there are few normal, everyday, non-idealistic or non-academic incentives to do that.

Hence Irish bilingualism with English is almost always effective at levels of ordinary everyday use, basic perceptions, and popular idioms, whereas English bilingualism with Irish is commonly ineffective, bookish, stilted, and at best hyper-correct instead of relaxed, idiomatic, and natural; but usually it is halting and wrong, for sheer lack of regular practice. The English speaker is not exposed to sufficient Irish to become ordinarily fluent in the way that the Irish speaker, with so many environmental aids and incentives, readily does in English. Bilingualism in Ireland is therefore usually unbalanced in favour of English and any minor problems of intercommunication are always solved by recourse to English, which is always understood. With such universal unilateral bilingualism can Irish survive?

It need only be mentioned in passing that the communicative weakness of Irish does not imply any alleged lack of expressiveness for inter-personal communication. Dialect differences within Irish do, however, limit its useful range for Irish speakers themselves (cf. 'Geordie' English) and it is clear from a tour of Gaeltacht schools that many teachers of Irish can only with difficulty understand Irish-language texts on subjects which are semi-technical but which they understand readily in English, e.g. mathematics. The wider communicative weakness is a matter of geographic range and reflects the broad spatial, economic, and demographic factors already outlined, plus a few more still to be considered.

Mass (?) media of communication

It is conventional to give this a heading of its own, but it is here held forcefully that the impact of the media is only secondary to economic and other forces and only an aspect, albeit very important, of communications and transport. The query (?) in the subtitle serves to remind that 'mass' is a scarcely appropriate adjective in Ireland and is never appropriate for communication in Irish.

The press

The Irish-language press is severely restricted by limited readership, peripheral and sparse population distributions, conflict of interest between Gaeltacht native speakers and urban second-language learners, dialect divisions, etc. Hence the inability to support an enduring daily newspaper and the tendency for periodicals to be irregular and ephemeral in their appearance; hence also, despite state subsidies, relatively high costs and low quality. Lack of demand is of course the main key. Ordinary Gaeltacht readers complain that 'the news is not new' in Irish-medium publications. The same negative factors influence authorship and publication of books in Irish. (See pp. 185–6.) State aid makes numbers available at very fair prices but their circulation again reflects lack of demand in the Gaeltacht and (chicken or egg?) the almost total lack of shops selling serious books there.

Reading of any sort in the Gaeltacht is therefore largely or exclusively in English and all popular newspapers are in English. Intellectual and professional Gaeilgeoirí read much more in both languages but even their bookshelves show more in English. One reverts here to the crude economic point that any great Irish scholar who wants an audience for his works will find a much larger one, even for a work on the language itself if it is published in English (p. 185).

The cruder point is often made that Gaeltacht people 'are not great readers' anyway. This is as true as of most rural populations anywhere, discounting pseudo-rural commuters, 'drop-outs', craft-colonists, and country cottage retirees. Nevertheless any who do read have little option but to do so mainly in English, and if their bent is technical–scientific–commercial there is scant choice at all. Hence the bias towards English is obvious to all and influences everyone with aspirations. I am not convinced that the dedicated Gaeilgeoirí must be excepted, for their fluency in English is admirable and the anglicizing pressures bearing on them are felt in their homes and families despite their own personal paramount sentimental preference for Irish. Education 'opens windows' and the view through any educated Gaeltacht window has to be towards English or some other language. Any reading which communicates widely cannot be in Irish. This is a hard material fact, not a matter of opinion or preference.

Radio

Overshadowed by television, radio now plays a minor part in subverting Irish and includes in Raidió na Gaeltachta a significant aid. (See p. 173.) Most Irish radio broadcasting remains in English and much BBC broadcasting is heard in the Gaeltacht. Irish local commercial radio, a modern phenomenon, is as English as commercial considerations make necessary. There is no profit in an advertisement which few can understand, though the occasional 'token' Irish one can help in a few specialist fields where the aim is to appeal to nationalist sentiment. It is easier to do this on television, where the visual image can help to overcome the nationalist viewer's weakness in spoken Irish. In general, radio is only one of many influences against Irish and it is rare to hear it mentioned as such.

Television (See also pp. 174, 183–4, 186)

Restricted demand has the usual consequences for supply, as does the limited number of potential writers and producers. It is a common Gaeltacht assertion that RTÉ's English-language programmes are inferior to those of the BBC, which many prefer to watch, and the very few Irish-language ones are not widely admired for their interest or professionalism. Costs and fear of low quality rule out hopes of an all-Irish 'channel' like Sianel Pedwar Cymru (Channel 4 Wales), which the Irish state seems unlikely to be able to support, and most in their hearts know that Irish speakers would not watch it unless it were good, i.e. as good as the English alternatives.

The ministerial Working Group on Irish Language Television Broadcasting which reported in 1987 was clearly constrained by considerations of cost, potential audiences, and potential programme producers in rejecting proposals for a separate Irish language channel:

> A credible dedicated Irish language network would require a minimum of three hours output per night involving capital costs of some £8·5 m. and estimated current costs of £18·5 m. per annum. The Working Group formed the opinion that such a service would be counter-productive ...   (*Irish Language Television ... Report* 1987: 30)

Apart from the costs, it would first be necessary to establish in RTÉ 'a strong commitment to achieve the output proposed on a gradualist basis but within clearly defined time limits', and to do so now or even in the medium-term future might well ghettoize the language. There would also be a need for 'an infrastructural, financial and human resource capacity to generate the quantum of programming required to constitute a credible channel . . .' (ibid: 21).

The Group recorded mildly RTÉ's repeated failure to live up to its earlier professed commitment to increase its Irish-language output to specific target levels (pp. 3–4, 11–12) and substituted its own quite low targets (p. 29). No one I have spoken to expects any serious changes to take place, for it is quietly admitted that very few people really want to watch Irish-language programmes and that the numbers competent to write and produce them at a professional level are minute, further limited by their own ranges of personal interest – which are normal, perfectly creditable at the individual level, but collectively narrow because the collectivity of qualified Irish-speaking professionals in this field is itself incomparably tiny. The inescapable comparison is with the competition through the English language.

Regardless of its effects being rooted in more deep-seated factors, television is everywhere reckoned the most potent current influence against Irish among the young. I have already termed it the universal tranquillizer of pre-school infants for busy mothers and noted its similar palliative effects on fractious teenagers (p. 183–4). As a killer of family conversation it is unprecedented. Grandparents' tales which used to entertain the children tend now to be an unwarranted distraction from some soap opera, and one wonders if the English-language television does not now talk more to Gaeltacht children than their parents do, assessed in hours per day. Certainly it talks to them long enough to help guarantee their fluency in English by the age of 5 and to provide prime subject matter for conversation with their friends. This is not at all peculiar to Ireland but has linguistic consequences here which it lacks in Britain, where parents are just as negligent and both parents more likely to be gainfully and distractingly employed.

This said, another brutal point must be added. Television has been a great mental liberator for rural Ireland, including the Gaeltacht, and makes up for the absence of modern sophisticated entertainment which was formerly normal. Selective use also takes valuable broadening and educational programmes into homes which never encountered such material except for a few early years in an often one- or two-teacher national school. Few teachers could offer the sophistication or the visual illustration that modern colour television for the Anglo-American market can offer to Ireland at prices far below what would be possible if marketing was limited to Ireland's combined 5·1 million or the Gaeltacht's minuscule figure.

To mention the television as liberator may seem almost as offensive as having said the same for English, but it is pure intellectual escapism, elitism, snobbery, and self-delusion to deny this self-evident truth. The experienced observer can *feel* the opening of windows which has occurred over the past thirty years. The people have not had this foisted on them against their will and in most cases retain some balance between it and outdoor sports and a fair degree of support for Irish-medium cultural activity in their area.

The television does none the less give an exaggerated idea of the quality, variety, and excitement of life 'outside' and has the greatest effect on the immature and inexperienced young who (like the aged) are also the ones most likely to be left with the telly as company. It is their prolonged exposure to this English medium which is doing most to make bilingual Gaeltacht children more fluent in English than in Irish on first arrival at school. It remains to be seen whether a few hours a day at a *naíonra* will suffice to counter it. Again, the fact that the television takes English into every home as a constantly welcome guest is something entirely new. On its own it makes English the effective first language of the home of all the undiscriminating, and it seems inevitable that children growing up with this background must mature as first-language English speakers, conditioned to transmit that language as mother tongue to their own children.

It was suggested in the Ráth Cairn colony in Meath that television is so effective in giving the children fluency in English that many parents now feel it 'safe' to speak Irish to them, there being no fear that they will not get sufficient English. Judging by reactions when I suggested as much in other Gaeltachtaí, this must be rare. The general opinion is that parents are similarly affected by constant exposure to English, but when they are native speakers old bonds of tradition and affection help them to keep up Irish among themselves, but less so when talking to the children.

The official assessment of the anti-Irish influence of television is well summarized on p. 13 of the 1987 *Working Group Report*, and is hardly contestable in any detail. However, its premise, the (alleged) 'demand of the Irish-speaking public for a comprehensive television service in Irish', is questionable. All Gaeltacht people I discussed this with were acutely aware of costs and of *what else could be done with the money*, and other competing economic priorities ranked higher for almost all of them. Similarly the concluding reference to the 1966 UNESCO declaration that 'cultural rights are an element of human rights' evades the fundamental difficulty that the vast majority of Irish people show no strong inclination to exercise this right in relation to the language which they honour as a symbol but have little practical use for. No one challenges the right to Irish-language television. The serious questions are about true market demand, likely programme supplies and competitive quality, and costs in relation to competing claims on finite national resources.

It would be unfair to ignore as too fanciful the occasionally expressed view that 'the British' have deliberately boosted BBC and ITV transmissions to Ireland to promote a policy of cultural domination; but it *is* fanciful, and support from at least one United States professor (Schiller 1978) must not be allowed to give it credence or respectability. The 'powerful transmitters' which were complained of were in Wales and Northern Ireland, both of them either mountainous or with ample uplands to interrupt television reception from the earlier conventional transmitters. I have long conducted field courses in Gwynedd (North Wales) and all my friends there complained of the appalling reception which they got in return for their television licence in the 1950s. (I was working mainly in Snowdonia and on its margins.)

One has to be paranoid and/or blindly Irish ethnocentric not to realize that because Ireland is relatively small, flat, and close to Britain broadcasts relayed for upland Wales, lowland Môn/Anglesey and Llŷn, could not miss Ireland if they wanted to. The westerly location of the Connacht Gaeltachtaí gives them some protection, but there is no way in which modern transmissions for the Six Counties/Northern Ireland can avoid reception in north-west Donegal, or those for Devon and Cornwall miss much of Munster, in much of which my (ordinary) car radio readily picks up local radio from Plymouth. As early as around 1960 I queried the unusual (for Britain) height of television aerials on Dublin houses, only to be told that they were to secure decent reception of BBC television. The advent of ITV only intensified Irish popular preferences and with greater prosperity of course these spread to the Gaeltacht. The idea that this represents a British 'plot' is as futile in the elucidation and assessment of a difficult problem as most 'conspiracy' theory. Indeed, it is a facile xenophobic evasion of thought, an attempt to blame the 'foreign enemy' for cultural choices which are freely made in Ireland, by the Irish people.

Pages 184–7 have pointed out how difficult it is for a country of 3·5 million people to maintain a quality and volume of 'media' production to compete with the output of the United Kingdom's 56·5 million. The latter are in a similar position in relation to the United States' 239 million (1985). Need more be said about likely provision by and for the effective Irish-speaking population, natives or learners?

One of the earliest Irish government proposals for a second Irish television channel in 1973 was simply to relay BBC1, BBC2, or ITV. This would have had great advantages of economy but fell before a combined assault from nationalist groups, including the Gaelic League and labour organizations such as the Irish Transport and General Workers' Union, who denounced the threat to jobs in the Irish media (Schiller 1977: 4). The point here is surely that the Irish state made the proposal, knowing that the entire population watched British television frequently and by choice, and acutely conscious that separate media provision for the Republic is costly. It underestimated the anti-national symbolic significance of its proposal, but it is symptomatic of the normal complexity of both language and national attitudes in Ireland that the public which jumped to the defence of independent Irish television broadcasting continues to watch British programmes for much of the time. It might be easy to do something about this if it were the result of an anti-Irish plot instead of being a result of comparative population statistics, purchasing power, geographic proximity, a common language, and Irish consumer demand.

The contribution of Irish 'media personalities' to British and United States television merits mention, but sadly not for their projection of Irish culture so much as in demonstrating that the rewards for talented Irish people are far greater outside Ireland – yet again. The implications for speakers of the Irish minority language are plain.

Educational policies and schools

The schools have done so much for Irish and so much of the burden of the revival has been left to them that it may seem churlish to class them with adverse influences here. (See pp. 165–8.) Most of the anti-Irish influences are now in the past and many have been dealt with as by-products of beneficial policies or as scarcely avoidable consequences of spatial, economic, or demographic factors. The following range from the fundamental to the trivial, though the latter have sometimes served as the crucial 'trigger' or last straw which caused the abandonment of Irish somewhere.

The national schools were the medium whereby Irish-speaking children were given fluency in English and, by inference if not directly, taught to identify it as the key to a successful career. They are still the main source of correctly spoken and written English and none would pretend that the aim of Gaeltacht education is not full bilingualism rather than the maintenance of 'Irish only'. This sounds damning but has developed as basic policy because of universal popular demand, reflecting social and economic pressures for English. Schools are a public service and can override parental wishes only with difficulty: hence the failure of teaching through the Irish medium to convert a single school area or more than unrepresentative families back from English to the everyday use of Irish in the home.

Over-dependence on schools for the revival of Irish and its maintenance in the Gaeltacht made it something children expected to 'grow out of' on leaving school, as it had so little status outside and in non-manual occupations. Those which required Irish all required long training, so seemed bookish and still school-oriented to the normal person, as well as being irrelevant to most Gaeltacht children, who had few opportunities of secondary education before 1967.

Neglect of secondary education for the Gaeltachtaí compelled young people to emigrate to inferior unskilled and low-paid jobs in English-speaking districts and countries, thus accentuating their perceptions of the inferiority and uselessness of Irish.

Provision of secondary and vocational education both before and (much more) since 1967 often takes Irish-speaking children into anglicized towns or villages where even if the school uses Irish the external social influences are adverse and it becomes obvious that 'better-off' places do not speak Irish or confine it discreetly to the home.

Universal provision of post-primary education involves training for skills which facilitate emigration to better jobs which demand much more fluency in English than traditional gang work. And because the Gaeltachtaí are so small, and lack 'central places', attainment of high qualifications inevitably leads to high positions outside, i.e. the creaming off of potential leadership.

Changes in post-primary education since the dropping of the Irish pass requirement for the Leaving Certificate have resulted in far less teaching of and through Irish. The raising of the school leaving age and the end of much secondary selection had the same result by putting into academic schools many more children who did not respond to second-language learning, let alone to instruction through Irish, which had previously been common in 'good academic' schools in the Galltacht. Now it is very common for Irish-speaking national school children to progress to English-medium secondary schools serving their district. The transition from Irish medium to English disadvantages some, alienates others, and often annoys parents, who think it unfair that their children are placed in competition with others from places where they have been used to English instruction already. This affects small Gaeltachtaí most and should not be over-stressed, for many Irish-speaking children choose (or are sent to) the English-medium alternative if there is one. (See pp. 70, 76, 125, 127, 166.)

A tendency towards the use of more English in the work of nominally 'all-Irish' Gaeltacht primary schools is sometimes blamed for a weakening of Irish among the children but is usually a result of it, because of far more children enrolling with little or no Irish. Otherwise it results, in part, from rising standards as teachers are less willing to tolerate inferior Irish-language textbooks and resort to English ones where they are plainly much better. There is no evidence that they do this lightly. The lack of choice of good Irish textbooks in different subjects has been mentioned enough, including the difficulty that they may also be in the wrong Irish for the district. Hence the efforts of Cloch Chionnaola and Gaoth Dobhair primary teachers to produce their own (p. 68).

The emphasis on official, standardized Irish in Gaeltacht education until around 1970 or later is difficult to evaluate as an anti-Irish influence but has been mentioned so often by teachers and some officials that it must have been serious, and Donegal worries about textbooks show that it is still troublesome. The main argument is that it makes native speakers feel their Irish is inferior and not even school books are written in it; and this, as they dislike 'Dublin-Irish' or 'New Irish', helps destroy their traditional attachment to the language and gives impetus to their preference for English. Dublin is usually perceived as alien and interfering, and the idea of long-anglicized Dublin determining what is correct or incorrect in Irish arouses the utmost disdain – even though the best Irish scholars are usually, for professional reasons, based there.

Gaeilge B'l'Áth (Dublin-Irish), or Nua-Ghaeilge (New Irish), was based on the Munster dialects, which alone had significant literary representation when the town-based Gaelic League began the modern revival. It was the only model available to the keen second-language learners who laid the bases of modern educational policies and they promoted it regardless of the fact that there were far more surviving native speakers of both the Connacht and Donegal dialects, imposing it through the schools and state-supported literature. It is not surprising that many good Irish speakers resented having to learn another useless dialect when they felt they had Irish already and really needed English. Adjustment of Modern Irish towards Connacht Irish, which prevails in the main residual Gaeltacht in Conamara, was left dangerously late, until after 1960, by which time most of the Munster Irish pockets were hovering on the verge of extinction.

Native Irish-speaking Gaeltacht teachers deplore the closure (or transfer to other use) of the *coláistí ullmhúcháin* (preparatory colleges) through which many of them entered the profession. Before 1967 these colleges were one of the main means of entry for Irish-speaking children, to whom they gave privileged admission.

Their abolition accompanied the general widening of access to secondary and higher education and the move to make teaching a graduate profession. The colleges in question – one survives in Dublin – were in or near the Gaeltacht, as at Tuar Mhic Éadaigh/Tourmakeady, Salthill (known as Bóthar na Trá, but Galway city's very anglicized 'seaside'), and Coláiste Íde, near Dingle, and gave an all-Irish education in near-monastic conditions. They achieved a high degree of linguistic success for their non-native Irish students too, and it is questionable whether these standards are now attained in the normal English-dominated colleges and universities.

The closure of small rural schools is often blamed for helping to destroy the social cohesion of small communities and so impelling them towards English. The school was often their only central focus (the parish being much bigger) and the school head was their natural leader – after, but sometimes in place of, the priest. In fact closure often resulted from depopulation, with rising standards and growing appreciation of the disadvantages of having a child's entire education from 6 to 14 in the hands of one or two teachers only. If the teacher was good, the small school could work wonders, but if merely average or poor. . . Again, the non-linguistic advantages of larger schools are obvious. Language alone cannot be the sole consideration, least so where shrinking school populations actually show that everyone has been leaving for the outside world. Nevertheless it is equally obvious that bussing rural children into large, better staffed, and better equipped schools in the more central villages must harm their Irish, as well as making them familiar with village amenities which used to be beyond walking distance and which also help to associate English with being better-off. Secondary education will of course normally do this anyway.

There is now great reluctance to close true Gaeltacht schools because of this and appendix 3 will indicate many which would long ago have been closed in England. It is a serious question whether the results of keeping children in such schools will increase or reduce their chances of eventually remaining in the Gaeltacht but it should at least ensure that they stay for a few more years in a predominantly Irish school environment.

Thirty years ago the heads of Gaeltacht schools usually lived in the adjacent school house and were constantly and inseparably attached to the school. This no longer applies. The influence of the head, who now may live miles away and come in by car, is correspondingly reduced. The influence of a good head is of course also spread far wider by the car, so there are gains in this, but the loss of intimacy and immediate sustained daily contact in setting an example in the constant use of Irish are real losses which have led to the relapse of many districts into English. If the school-house system had survived, the increased mobility of the people as a whole would have tended to the same result, for driving past each other does not involve speaking. This is simply more modernization and mobilization.

Similar influences include the much wider employment of young married women in schools, rare thirty years ago. They include excellent teachers and numbers of Gaeltacht school heads but family commitments and other priorities, plus sometimes living twenty or thirty miles away, do reduce their linguistic impact on the school catchment area. Again, greater prosperity in the Gaeltacht has reduced the social prestige of teachers of either sex or marital state and made everyone more independent of each other, as well as of Irish.

Gaeltacht teachers are sometimes criticized for their poor quality and failure of leadership. The gist of this is that education in the Gaeltacht is so poorly supported in buildings and staff that no ambitious teacher could possibly settle there. All the promotion prospects are elsewhere. This was said publicly of the Guards in an official submission to the Gaeltacht Commission in 1925–6 (*Minutes of Evidence*, 21 May 1925: 2, 7, 10), and it has certainly been a factor in the closure of small schools. I have not seen much evidence to support it as a general point and assume that there are many good reasons why an intelligent Irish speaker (especially a native one) should choose life in the Gaeltacht to the prospects of Dublin, Cork, or emigration. But I live by choice in a Pennine valley, admittedly more handy for a city than any Gaeltacht except Cois Fharraige! Some Gaeltacht teachers are community leaders. Others are not. This seems perfectly normal.

Increased co-education in post-primary schools does probably promote 'mixed marriages' by Irish speakers because of the larger catchment areas of such schools and colleges: more mobilization.

The fall in vocations for the religious Orders has contributed to an apparent reduction in the number of dedicated celibate Irish teachers in their secondary schools, which now employ large numbers of lay staff. It is difficult to assess whether this has had any effect on the incidence of Irish as an ordinary spoken language, but it sounds unlikely. Both the fall in vocations and the decline of Irish appear related to increased employment opportunities, travel, and related material considerations.

That Irish-language courses for schools tend to be aimed at beginners rather than native speakers and therefore unhelpful in truly Gaeltacht schools simply reflects the lack of the latter and the normal operation of supply and demand – just like the 'Dublin-Irish' problem.

Limited provision for Irish for native speakers in RTÉ's education broadcasts invites the same comment, but in Gaeltacht schools in Donegal I was surprised to find the BBC's English-language schools' programmes (including Saturday mornings) commended and followed. There are of course far more resources behind them.

Parents sometimes admitted thirty years ago that they spoke English to their children to make up for neglect of it by the schools, declaring their conviction that English was essential for their success in life. I have not encountered this in recent years and attribute the fact to more sensible school bilingual policies (cf. p. 166) plus the influence of television (pp. 199–203).

Some adverse side-effects of the *deontas*, Gael-Linn children, and Irish summer colleges have been referred to earlier (e.g. pp. 53, 57–8, 172). Most are to be rated as irritants rather than real causes of Irish decline, and anyone who gave up Irish for a declared reason like this must have been on the verge of doing so for much stronger reasons.

Social psychology

The following represent attitudes of mind or prejudices which for the most part are effects of the accumulated linguistic experiences of generations of Irish speakers but are still encountered. Shame in speaking Irish, being a native speaker, and/or coming from the Gaeltacht is still quite common and presumably derives from past poverty and deprivation plus encounters with better-off monoglot English speakers at home and abroad. (See pp. 179–81.) The old inferiority complex about Irish dies hard, and to call someone a 'Gaeltacht' remains a personal insult.

Lack of pride in the Gaeltacht is almost the same thing but not quite as negative. The demoralizing effects of long continued language decline leave little to be proud of, and the failure of almost all efforts at preserving or reviving Irish causes general pessimism, defeatism, and cynicism about the motives, intelligence, and possible success of continued efforts by those who refuse to be discouraged. At best apathy and indifference ensue.

Frequent enquiries in different Gaeltachtaí as to why there were never any boundary markers or 'Welcome to the Gaeltacht' (in Irish) signs on approach roads elicited the admission that no one wanted any. The idea had been discussed but raised no enthusiasm anywhere. People think of themselves as Donegal people, Kerry folk, Cork people, people from Mayo or Galway, but never as Gaeltacht people. This may be rationalized in terms of the fact that the counties are fairly ancient, though only Donegal (as Tír Chonaill) dates in any real sense from before the English Henry VIII. None the less Gaeltachtaí are by comparison mere residual fragments surviving unplanned from the wreck of much larger districts whose boundaries have been contracting throughout the generations since at least 1800 so have never had the stability to attract loyalties or much sense of identity. More serious difficulty at an elementary level would arise the moment a Gaeltacht sign was erected, because there would be sure to be disputes about the justice or otherwise of its location.

It has been shown elsewhere (Hindley 1989) that the official boundaries of the Gaeltachtaí are usually through entirely English-speaking districts and include places with few or no *deontas* awards. There can be little sense in marking the Gaeltacht boundary except to indicate that Irish is in regular and normal use immediately it is passed. This is never the case. To mark a boundary which for most normal non-administrative human purposes is unreal would provoke derision and acrimony, but any attempt to define a more meaningful alignment would cause an unprofitable wrangle which would further dissipate the limited energies currently available for constructive language work.

I have often suggested that Gaeltacht boundaries should be redrawn – usually withdrawn – to make them linguistically meaningful. Responsible local people have usually argued that it would only discourage keen individuals and families, who would have to be excluded because of the manifestly anglicized character of their communities, and lead to their abandoning the already unequal struggle . . . Or would it? Residence in the Galltacht does not discourage thousands of people throughout Ireland from cultivating Irish. One must nevertheless concede a likely psychological difference between having never (in modern times) been part of the Gaeltacht and finding oneself pushed out.

Lack of pride in belonging to the Gaeltacht is still notable among most residents, if not so openly expressed, and it will take more than two decades of qualified prosperity to dissipate it – if indeed the language does not die first. The economic bases of the old fear of being considered 'Gaeltacht' may largely have disappeared but the social psychological legacy appears to have become fixed as a tradition.

The extension of the Gaeltacht boundaries in 1967, 1974, and 1982, all in response to local demand, may seem in flagrant contradiction to what has just been said, but relate to the different plane of a desire to share in preferential Gaeltacht grants. Less sophisticated people among the new undeserved beneficiaries usually argue that their use of Irish is at least as good as that of their neighbours who were within the older (1956) boundaries, and at the same time show ill-concealed delight at having hoodwinked officialdom. This is nothing to do with 'Gaeltacht pride', and the same informants will commonly simultaneously transmit an impression of feeling rather ashamed of their need for the grants and benefits. The latter often also applies to popular feelings about the welfare payments which support the inner districts which are usually farther from factories and businesses, for they show the Gaeltacht as somewhere with special needs, still rather indigent, a place you have to pay people to go to or stay in. Such ambivalence again denotes attitudes of mind which do not point towards robust language maintenance.

Dislike of being or seeming different by speaking Irish is closely related and a familiar part of socializing in any community. Few want to feel out of the main stream, unless they are very secure in life, and only elites enjoy minority status and the 'fishbowl' effect. Hence the 'rule' of always speaking English to strangers and in the company of any non-Irish speaker. 'Politeness' and 'obsequiousness' are other descriptions, the latter unnecessarily offensive. Smallness of numbers contributes strongly to this, as does low evaluation ('shame') of Irish and its social status.

In the weakening parts of the Gaeltachtaí this attitude now leads some to see the maintenance of Irish by a family, especially in public, as an affectation, as if admitting that it is something one could be proud of but should not. This is probably just one reflection of a stultifying egalitarianism which tends to deplore people trying to do better than their neighbours and which formerly helped slow the drift towards English. It is only coincidental that it here affects language.

The sense of being remote, isolated, out of the main stream, is much greater than modern reality warrants. (See pp. 164–5, 182–3 and map 1). Possibly the separate language does help to reinforce it and thus adds to the reasons for its own removal. The fact that the Gaeltacht is geographically peripheral is unquestionable. (See also p. 188 on the 'fishbowl' syndrome).

It has long been the fashion among Gaeltacht teenagers to speak English together as a sign of maturity and modernity, like smoking and drinking. Parents say that they were the same but returned to Irish as they settled down, and they expect their children to follow. This seems optimistic, for in their day there were few cars, no television, and the old Irish-speaking grandparents were still at home. Much has now changed. The young do indeed find Irish old-fashioned, prefer everything 'outside' to what they see in the Gaeltacht, want to be 'with it', and speak too little ordinary vernacular non-school Irish for 'return' to it to be much in question. Compared to the 'pop' television culture, Irish is boring. Can they grow out of this?

Villages such as Carna, An Cheathrú Rua, Tuar Mhic Éadaigh, An Spidéal, Cill Rónáin have long spoken English in public even though most people could speak Irish. This pride in English, which they did acquire before their rural hinterlands, is only the reverse of the 'shame in Irish' coin. (See pp. 207–8 above.)

Dependency on state welfare payments is widely held by Gaeltacht professional people to kill or reduce initiative and entrepreneurship, as well as explaining the failure of most of the *comharchumannaí* (co-operatives), which were heralded as a panacea for economic ills in the 1970s (cf. pp. 179–81). This sounds suspiciously like an elite viewing the plebeians and any truth in it centres on inactivism and resignation to failure. However, the ambitious and dissatisfied have long tended to emigrate, so 'natural selection' may well have had some effect. Specific effects, even assuming the justice of the stigmatization, are difficult to discern where the language is concerned. On the whole one would expect it to aid survival as a result of indifference to 'improvement'. There is precious little evidence of this to be extracted from the industrial revolution of the 1970s, which brought plentiful change and plentiful movement from Irish.

The egalitarian tradition of the Gaeltacht, where only the priest had authority, may have contributed to the weak management and financial control which lay behind the failure of many co-operatives. If these failures have contributed to weakening belief in a future for the Gaeltacht they must to some extent have weakened adherence to the language.

It seems somewhat paradoxical that dependence on 'Dublin' is accompanied by widespread hostility to it, even among the elite. Rather than a paradox, this might be construed a universal rule, exemplified throughout the Third World and in most families. It masks a desire by the dependent to attain independently the status, etc., of the benefactor.

Language 'fanatics' bear the brunt of much criticism of where the revival movement has gone wrong and it is usually alleged that the compulsory imposition of Irish 'tests' for state office and public examinations has alienated far more than they have won over. This must be more true of the Galltacht than of the Gaeltacht, but the fact that so many language enthusiasts were not native speakers has embarrassed and annoyed many real Gaeilgeoirí, who felt 'put down' by the (to them) impracticably idealistic and 'purist' claims advanced allegedly on their behalf. (See pp. 175–80.) There is a cleavage between the revivalist outside enthusiasts and the Gaeltacht native speakers, and it unfortunately tends to centre on the willingness of the latter to allow the language to die now it has ceased to serve any practical purposes for them.

Most so-called 'fanatics' I have met would merely be termed enthusiasts on any other subject. The term is used sweepingly to denote anyone who asks Irish people who are broadly in favour of the revival to do something about it personally instead of confining sympathy to voting for children, civil servants, and other people to learn and use Irish: i.e. a fanatic is one who demands the communicative use of Irish, however inconvenient, in place of or as well as its universally acceptable symbolic or token use. Such people are usually regarded as well intentioned nuisances but are seen as dangerous if their policies threaten children's career prospects by imposed language requirements and as hateful if they threaten one's own. The loss of clear linkage between the language and Irish national identity now that under 1 per cent are habitual Irish speakers makes them deeply offensive to many when they proclaim it unpatriotic not to speak Irish, but sincere token acceptance of the ethos of revival causes psychological confusion here and explains why public opposition is muted and the masses proceed by 'patterned evasion' to circumvent what they feel unable to resist directly.

The role of the language as a banner of identity in the nationalist movement from 1893 and especially under Pearse as leader in Easter 1916 makes it psychologically very difficult to drop except by inadvertence. Most people know that in reality it has been dropped and it was never strong enough even by 1893 to be a weapon as well as a banner, most having lost it long before then. The 'fanatics', through ignorance, lack of perceptiveness, closed minds, or excess of zeal and idealism, refuse to accommodate to the reality of an English-speaking Ireland and by their determination, dedication, and well intended obtuseness do indeed keep Irish prominent, though it is doubtful whether they do much to keep it alive in any normal, natural, communicative, and community sense, for there are few of them resident in the Gaeltacht core areas. There local native-speaking enthusiasts are invariably realistic, as they live with the practical problems of language maintenance in their natural setting among the working people whose conflicting priorities they appreciate in human terms.

The role of the revival myth is an interesting one in social psychology, of great importance to the study of the modest revival of Irish in the cities and Galltacht areas; but the Gaeltacht has been so little affected by belief in the myth, except in reacting against unreasonable demands placed on it by outside believers, that it need not be explored in any depth here. It always depended on idealism, and idealism does not thrive on the barely subsistent living standards to which the Gaeltacht was accustomed until around 1970. The benefits of Gaeltacht aid were appreciated but idealistic pontification on the virtues of all-Irish Gaeltacht policies by well-off and well placed persons who were obviously English speakers beneath their adopted Irish rarely struck the right note and was usually discounted as the excess of the typical 'convert'. The failure to reconcile romantic nationalism and nationalist myth with the realities of Gaeltacht life has been a conspicuous element in the failure to save the language. It would nevertheless be foolish to believe that some different approach might have succeeded, given that the methodology is entirely circumscribed by economic and social circumstances beyond any but limited control by the Irish state. And there is little common ground between Gaeltacht workers who see language as a tool, to be discarded for a better one when it becomes obsolete (p. 196) and nationalists who believe Irish people should speak Irish just because they are Irish and regardless of utilitarian considerations.

The depths and origins of Gaeltacht hostility to non-native language enthusiasts who are trying to save both the language and the Gaeltacht deserve profound psychological investigation beyond this author's expertise. I sense that by 1922 (and probably by 1893) Irish had become the key distinguishing feature of a Gaeltacht subculture which was also the anti-culture of an underclass in relation to anglicized Irish middle-class society. In this it resembles broad Cockney in east London. Its speakers still do not regard it as 'respectable' but it shows their independence of middle-class values and 'high' culture, bringing a sense of integrity and collective privacy which 'Gaeltacht chauvinism' reflects (p. 164). This is not incompatible with a sense of shame about it (pp. 207–8) but the language is their own possession, it is part of themselves, and there is a deep psychological 'class-war' element in their resentment of and resistance to its appropriation by (to them) 'upper-class' outsiders. The appropriation of their lands in earlier generations had caused not dissimilar reactions.

What has happened in the course of the attempted revival is that a section of the anglicized upper class (middle class really, but it is the upper one in Ireland) has adopted the lower-class *patois*. The lower-class reaction is exactly what would have been expected in London if the West End 'toffs' of the 1920s had presumed to combine with their 'slumming' improving lectures on the virtues and desirability of maintaining Cockney English, and then went on to try and talk it, finally offering instruction to the Cockneys on how they should talk it 'correctly'.

Intellectual Gaeltacht native speakers will see this as a caricature but it is not so for ordinary non-contemplative Irish speakers for whom the language is a rare, distinctive possession which hitherto their 'betters' left well alone. If they want to copy the upper classes it will be by aspiring to their material possessions and *their* language. It is embarrassing, disorientating, and unconvincing when the upper classes set out to patronize and adopt the language of the underprivileged, and, like the daft ideas of 'deschooling' which diverted British educationists of the 1960s, smacks of a covert attempt to keep them in their 'proper station' – especially as the Irish elite retains its own fluent native English as the normal vehicle of its continued control of the state and society.

The upper-class seizure and (limited) use of 'the Gaeltacht language' flies in the face of normal class relationships and is repugnant to many ordinary native speakers, to whom it seems insulting: as if they are not good enough to be addressed and dealt with in the 'high' language and cannot even be trusted to use their own without guidance. They do not want to talk it 'correctly', but naturally and easily, because it came that way from their mothers in the cradle and it was what they heard from their grandparents. They do want correctness in their learning of English, which they know full well is the vehicle of upper-class success and the essential key to their own and their children's advancement.

This ignores the 'national language' question, but so for most practical purposes do most Gaeltacht native speakers of Irish.

Seán Ó Conchúir (1984), whose report on the work of the *naíonraí* in the Conamara islands (not Árainn) is a model of objective analysis, quotes without demur the weighty conclusion of a national survey of *naíonra* provision: 'Research into Gaeltacht preschool playgroups conducted by the Comhchoiste reveals that the quality of spoken Irish among Gaeltacht children attending . . . is inferior to that of children attending Irish-speaking playgroups in the cities and towns' (Egan 1981, cited by Ó Conchúir: 9–10). A chapter could be written on the implications of this quotation, from conflicting viewpoints, but no interpretation of it can be held to augur well for native Irish, whatever else one chooses to make of the position where the children of urban learners now speak 'better' Irish than those from a rural native Irish background – or are regarded as doing so.

The state's 'compulsory Irish' policy was designed to create a real need for Irish, to counter, in part at least, the constant need for English. It was assumed that to make it officially essential for employment under the state would have similar effects on the speaking habits of the Irish public as has the unofficial everyday need to use English. This was a fundamental error in social psychology, for making a language 'essential' or 'required' by what the public perceives as artificial measures produces entirely different reactions from what happens when it is seen as naturally essential. In the first case it becomes an unnecessary obstacle perversely erected, so if possible to be circumvented. In the second it is something to be sought after and cultivated. Even Gaeltacht speakers have never since at least 1922 been fully convinced of the need for Irish for much routine business in the Gaeltacht itself, partly for reasons just outlined.

The general lack of local support for the various 'Gaeltacht civil rights' movements and groupuscules of the late 1960s and 1970s follows from what has just been said. Some, like Ceárta Gael in Donegal, are still mentioned with obloquy for their alleged endeavours to hound all non-Irish speakers out of the Gaeltacht, and their excesses are usually attributed to a membership consisting mainly of outsiders and second-language learners. None ever attracted significant votes in elections, and except for provoking unusual vocal opposition on language matters they seem to have had few long-term effects either way. However, it is doubtful whether without them the normal level of Gaeltacht grumbling would have moved the state to create Raidió na Gaeltachta or Údarás, or to put a main Gaeltacht base for Roinn na Gaeltachta at Na Forbacha. Prodding by outsiders has played a major part in shaming the Gaeltacht into support for its own language at many stages since 1922, and there is plenty of reason to doubt whether all-Irish instruction in Gaeltacht national schools would ever have become so widespread or so long sustained without outside 'fanatics' to push it through the Department of Education in Dublin and numerous local management committees.

Left to itself the social psychology of the Gaeltacht, shaped by material pressures and mass emigration, would have killed Irish years ago. It is some tribute to the power of ideals that it is still alive, if also sustained by the less commendable Gaeltacht qualities of apathy and inertia, which on balance now tend to help English more (pp. 174–5).

Fear of denunciation by 'fanatics' makes objective assessment of the problems and failures of language maintenance very difficult and promotes the pretence that all is well (pp.177–8) when most is lost. To tell the truth is liable to attract denunciation for defeatism and lack of patriotism, and teachers who admit that in ordinary circumstances their children speak little Irish are commonly blamed for it themselves and accused of incompetence and/or hostility for saying so. As the language is rarely a first priority in life, it is thus easier and safer to avoid the subject and not to disagree with local enthusiasts who keep saying all is well and deluding themselves (in some cases) while decline continues unimpeded. The language is a sensitive issue because of the conflict between sentiment and material pressures. Hardly any local expert wants quoting about it and the 'loyal lie' (p. 177) is the normal reflex answer to the first question; but everyone knows the language is dying and that its future will be as a second language, maintained by the schools and not in the homes. Large numbers of teachers and officials expect it to 'see them out' but longer perspectives and expectations are rare.

'Fanatics' and local sceptics are for once in full agreement in wishing to suppress the truth about decline. The sceptics, cynics, and materialists who have no time for Irish in other respects still cling to their 'Gaeltacht' grants and though they treat them as a private joke at the expense of the state would bitterly resent their withdrawal if effected by some high-minded local exposure of the objective linguistic situation. The truth could 'cost money', and money ranks higher than truth about the language. I have been offered the semi-apologetic excuse that 'We might as well try and get something out of it' when asking working people about this. Enthusiasts who maintain a similar pretence to help keep up support for their summer colleges may have higher motives, but the result is the same.

There is ample anecdotal evidence that refusal of the *deontas* award has caused some marginally Irish-speaking families to exclude Irish from the home, and that over-generous awards to scarcely Irish-speaking families have caused hitherto loyal ones to abandon it on grounds of 'Why should we speak Irish when they get it [the grant] for nothing?' This sounds far-fetched but the discouraging effects of strict assessment on modest efforts are well attested and in linguistically marginal places where people are dithering about Irish such 'straws' are liable to be the last one, though trivial in themselves. As factors in language change they may be classed as occasions of change rather than causes of change.

Marriage, parents, and families

Marriage is frequently a cause of Irish decline when bilingual native speakers marry monoglot English speakers. Parental decision or consensual action in speaking English first (or alone) to their offspring is the major instrument of decline but is the result of wider economic and spatial causes. (See pp. 180–1, 187, 197.) It is nevertheless important to remember that only Gaeltacht parents can save Irish as an ordinary native language, and the following family-centred points are here extracted from their wider contexts to give them due emphasis.

Linguistically mixed marriages are increasing because of such influences as the closure of small schools, bussing into central places for primary and secondary education, the presence of incomers because of increased employment opportunities, more and better transport (especially the private car), co-education in secondary schools, and above all the fall in the numbers of native Irish speakers (p. 187). Because of the great advantages of English and the prevalence of unilateral bilingualism (p. 197) this usually results in the bringing up of children with English as their first language.

Gaeltacht families have long had large numbers of English-speaking relatives in other parts of Ireland or overseas. Exchange visits are now frequent and bring English regularly into most homes at the personal as well as the universal television level. (See pp. 183–4, 192–3.)

Housing improvements and increased prosperity have made sharing of homes by grandparents and young families far less usual. This reinforces the influence of television by making conversation between infants and grandparents less common or constant and limits the transmission of idiomatic Irish to the young. Grandparents, perhaps because long past worrying about their own prospective emigration, were always a great help here despite their obvious failure to impress their own offspring; and when relapsed into near-monoglottism their aid was inestimable in maintaining the native idiom. Nevertheless a nostalgic and 'deathbed' conversion cannot do much to counter a preceding lifetime of neglect of Irish and preference for English for their own children, the present generation's parents.

The passing of the old near-monoglot grandparents who were numerous in north-west Donegal and Conamara thirty years ago has ended the need for the young to speak Irish in the family (p. 186).

The parental priority is invariably the career prospects of their children. This above all inclines most to give precedence to English in talking to them. Where parents have lived abroad it is difficult for them to think otherwise, unless they belong to a high socio-economic group (p.180).

A tendency to 'leave Irish to the schools' where the latter teach through Irish is another aspect of this and it is likely that pre-school *naíonraí* will facilitate the drift rather than halt it. Parents are not so much hostile to Irish as seeing English as a priority and will be glad if their children speak Irish once they are sure they are secure with sound, fluent English. That still means making English the first language, even if it is much better than abandoning Irish completely. (See pp. 179–80, 203–4.)

The Irish language itself

It is improbable that any inherent characteristics of a language will contribute significantly to its rise or decline in popular use. The following are encountered as secondary reasons for the abandonment or weakening of Irish.

Lack of an agreed standard of Irish acceptable to all Gaeltacht speakers has been a common stated cause of their preference for English other than for local intimate purposes where their own dialect was appropriate. (See pp. 108, 164, 205.) Dialect divisions have hindered writing and publication in Irish and reduce the audience for broadcasts in Irish.

Script and spelling reforms since around 1948 were badly confusing older native speakers in the late 1950s and still make spelling a major problem for many well educated Gaeilgeoirí accustomed to reading both older and modern Irish literature. The formal abolition of the dative case for official writing aroused fury among many native speakers but was sensible enough, as the dative had dropped out of many dialects. The abandonment of the traditional Irish uncial script except for decorative use and its replacement with ordinary letters with substitution of added h for the dots previously used to show aspiration (e.g. ch for č, gh for ġ) also broke with tradition on the practical grounds that to maintain the old system would have needed special typewriters just for Irish and greatly increased costs. To object to such reforms seems silly if it is not recalled that these arguments are practical and utilitarian yet were advocated by people who at the same time were exhorting the Gaeltacht to eschew utilitarianism in matters of language. The fragile state of the language made disturbing its traditional rendering dangerous and further helped to alienate native speakers from it, leading them to argue that 'state Irish' was nothing but an artificial concoction contrived to make learning it easier for non-Irish speakers.

The charge has substance, and a noteworthy Irish educational author told me how he had had a script returned from his publisher with a request to make his Irish less idiomatic so that readers (learners were assumed) could follow it more readily. As learners outnumber native speakers by at least ten to one the point is fair, but it is no way of maintaining the *native* language and is more likely to give wavering native speakers a small extra push towards English.

Lack of modern technical vocabulary in Irish is often cited as a reason why people in 'practical' occupations turn from Irish. This is unjustified, for adequate vocabulary is constantly created and much is available in N. Ó Dónaill's definitive *Foclóir Gaeilge–Béarla* (1977) and T. de Bhaldraithe's English–Irish dictionary (1959), plus specialist vocabularies. Nevertheless these are not owned or used by most native speakers, who get their English technical vocabulary from non-literary sources through normal work channels and just 'pick them up on the job'. The Irish terms exist but are not familiar to ordinary people, who are far more likely (for basically economic reasons) to encounter their English equivalents. This is not a failure in the language but of weakness in the production and distribution of Irish-medium literature on subjects for which there is little demand in the Gaeltacht and a vast amount outside. (See also pp. 101, 185–6.)

The 'corruption' of Gaeltacht Irish by major infusions of 'raw' (uninflected) English vocabulary, full phrases, and even full sentences, and the use of English idioms in direct translation to replace Irish ones which are now being lost cause some to despair of its future, as it seems without actually dying to be dissolving in the English sea. This is a symptom of decline rather than a cause, though it may encourage a few to make the transition to English more directly. The English language itself demonstrates in its overwhelmingly French and Graeco-Latin intellectual vocabulary that it is possible for a language to thrive on such influences, but the circumstances of today offer no hope of such an outcome for Irish.

Numbers of Gaeltacht Irish speakers, including teachers, have asked me whether Irish is not indeed 'the most difficult language' in Europe: a most difficult question to answer. I know enough of Basque, Magyar, Finnish, and Turkish, which as non-Indo-european languages pose unusual problems, to think Irish easier than those, but I must confess to having found Irish much more difficult than Welsh, which has very similar mutations and grammar and much basic vocabulary in common. Irish and Scottish Gaelic both have cumbersome spelling systems which it is hard for a learner to relate reliably to vowel sounds which are commonly a glide; and both are torn by dialects which get the learner confusingly 'corrected' *after* mastering the textbook rules of pronunciation.

The really significant point is the initial question, which shows that native speakers themselves have come to regard their language as difficult, perhaps in the main because the synthetic Irish attempted by many learners is excruciatingly embarrassing to any natural Gaeilgeoir. This also leads to the discouragement of learners by hyper-correction and a mutual desperate resort to English for easier and relaxed communication.

A sensible conclusion is that languages are 'difficult' in inverse proportion to the strength of motivation for learning them. Material self-interest and immediate daily needs for some practical purposes render languages accessible, and purely academic motivation makes any language (including the refinements of their own) difficult for many people. The supposed difficulty of Irish therefore derives mainly from the lack of any natural economic use for it, apart from requirements artificially imposed by the state, which tend to be irritating rather than compelling. This returns us to the economic weakness, lack of spatial range, and perhaps most fatally to the extinction of a pool of monoglot Irish speakers full of national traditions and unable to express them in anything but Irish (p. 196).

It is self-evident that Gaeltacht Irish speakers have far bigger incentives for learning English than have Irish English speakers for learning Irish. In addition the 'media' give them far greater opportunities, an imbalance which the school system cannot alone redress. English comes to the people of Ireland easily, naturally, and all the time, at work and in relaxation in front of the television. Irish is not more difficult, but is more difficult to find and demands conscious effort. This is a fault not of the language but of its situation in Ireland today; and as such it promises to be fatal – soon.

'Internal colonialism', etc.

Despite an anti-colonialist bias this author has not found Hechter's (1975) expression particularly useful in analysing Irish decline, more especially because Welsh has survived so much better than Irish despite much longer subjection to English rule. (See p. 191.) It is politically loaded and ascribes too much to deliberate intent and contrivance.

218

The collapse of Irish seems to have set in firmly with the opening of opportunities to Catholics on the relaxation of the Penal Laws after around 1750. It accelerated once the industrial revolution and the Union gave linguistic force to the lack of coal and iron in Ireland and its abundance in Britain – including Welsh-speaking Wales. And it has continued regardless of Irish independence since 1922. All this seems to indicate causation based on economic forces and opportunities divorced from politically motivated 'exploitation' or planning. Modernization and mobilization of pre-industrial peasant economies afford more convincing macro-explanations, as do centre–periphery considerations. See, for example, Gottmann (1980) and Rokkan and Urwin (1982, 1983). However, not too much should be made of the idea of the English centre growing rich on exploiting the impoverished Irish periphery, for the latter proved so extreme a case of hardship to the Victorians that they here jettisoned *laissez-faire* economics and launched into state subsidies decades before they were tolerated in England. (See p. 194.)

The failure of autarky in de Valéra's 'economic war' of the 1930s so depressed Irish agriculture as to stimulate emigration still further, thus enhancing the appeal of English. It has since become fashionable to denounce 'colonial' exploitation of Ireland by 'the multinationals', some of which withdrew hurriedly by or around 1980, but the parallel fate of numerous local *comharchumannaí* (co-operatives) and small Irish independent businesses makes conspiracy theory largely superfluous here. Economic modernization and mobilization inevitably involve the entire world in interlinkages and interdependence which bring disadvantages to balance the usually greater advantages. Again, they do not help a small local language but they are in no way aimed at it. The decay of English dialect exactly parallels the decline of Irish and with hardly any extra or any fewer reasons involved.

English-language television is not 'cultural colonialism', 'cultural imperialism', or 'cultural hegemonism', for the Irish market is too small seriously to concern the supposed Anglo-American hegemonists of the rest of the English-speaking world (cf. pp. 186–7). Ireland buys in programmes because they are preferred to the native product and Irish-language television fails to develop because demand is too small. It would not distress anyone outside Ireland if the language revival were to succeed. It would even please Ulster Unionists by putting a real barrier between them and the rest of Ireland. (See pp. 198–203).

Social class distinctions still encountered in some Gaeltacht villages are their nearest approach to conventional Marxist 'class war' and have helped to establish the inferiority complex suffered by many native speakers. It is paradoxical that Irish is still perceived as a low-status language in the Gaeltacht, whereas it is a high-status one in Dublin and the cities; but the explanation is simple. The Gaeltacht bourgeoisie differentiate

The death of the Irish language

themselves by cultivating English and sending their children for boarding school education out of the Gaeltacht. The politically dominant city bourgeoisie (not the *commerçants*) differentiate themselves by cultivating Irish and sending their children for Irish-medium boarding school instruction as at Coláiste na Rinne (at An Rinn) or Coláiste Íosagáin (at Baile Bhuirne). It is regrettable that other considerations cause the mass of the people to follow the one lead rather than the other and perspective is helped by noting that it is the petty-bourgeoisie of the Gaeltacht who on a superficial judgement look more effective leaders than their far more numerous, wealthy, and otherwise influential Dublin counterparts. It does not, however, follow that if two groups are going in the same direction the one is necessarily leading the other. It is possible that they draw the same conclusions from similar circumstances. The Irish of the Dublin elite is more 'blue stocking' and if it has a utilitarian element smacks only of elite 'jobbery', jobs through Irish or in the Irish language being far too few to attract a mass following. (Pages 175–6 and 207–15 have explored this more fully.)

220

Chapter twelve

Irish as a West European minority language: some comparisons

Despite its official status, Irish is from all other points of view a minority language, that is to say, one with a relatively small number of native speakers living within the domain of a much more widely spoken language a command of which is generally felt necessary for the pursuit of a full economic and social life. Irish is at the lower extreme of minority language decline in that speakers of Irish only (monoglots) are extinct except among youngest infants and there is not a single town, however small, in which it prevails as the normal community language. Nor does it prevail as the natural everyday speech of any territory comparable in size to an English county or a French department, except at best by summation of its small and scattered Gaeltacht fragments. Its official and honoured status is utterly belied by the inability of the great majority of the Irish people to speak it fluently, easily, and unselfconsciously, however much of it they learnt at school and however much they wish they could speak it as well as they do their real native language, which is English.

Irish shares many problems which threaten its continued existence with many other languages in Western Europe. These will now be reviewed for the parallels they afford, beginning with the rest of the British Isles.

The United Kingdom

Three indigenous languages have died in the British Isles since around 1780: Cornish (traditionally in 1777), Norn (the Norse language of Shetland: *c.* 1880), Manx (1974). Three indigenous minority languages remain but have suffered such decline during the present century as to make their extinction a more or less imminent prospect.

Welsh

Welsh is by far the most strongly placed of the Celtic languages in terms of numbers and is spoken by a majority of the population in about half the total area of Wales. This includes several noteworthy towns, including Caernarfon and Pwllheli in Gwynedd, but the industrial areas are largely anglicized in speech and in general the Welsh-speaking parts are the most rural and sparsely inhabited. The proportion of Welsh speakers in the total population of Wales has fallen from 50 per cent in 1901 to 19 per cent in 1981, and the final figure of 503,549 reported Welsh speakers is inflated to some extent by school learners and limited in survival probability by the fact that large numbers live in areas where the majority do not speak Welsh. Areas with 70 per cent or more of Welsh speakers remain extensive in Gwynedd and Dyfed but the great majority live outside them, i.e. in districts where English is the language of most public intercommunication, as only 0·8 per cent nationally say they speak only Welsh.

Most of the reported local increases in numbers of Welsh speakers between 1961 and 1981 were in heavily anglicized districts where Welsh is not in normal everyday use, and most notably in the Cardiff region, where administrative reforms favouring Welsh have made it valuable for state employment and therefore fashionable in the bourgeoisie that formerly disdained it. A genuine revival of national sentiment is evident, too, though barely visible in parliamentary voting figures or in daily life. In 1981 13·3 per cent of infants aged 3 or 4 years were returned as Welsh speakers in Wales, but the increase from 11·3 per cent in 1971 and 13·1 per cent in 1961 is highly unconvincing, numerous places which were Welsh-speaking in earlier decades having been lost in the interim. It is unlikely that as many as 10 per cent of children in Wales speak Welsh as their mother tongue.

Despite 'paper gains' of second-language learners the territorial contraction of the Welsh-speaking heartland continues inexorably along all the main roads from the English cities and around every coastal and mountain resort, every weekend cottage, every holiday and retirement home. Traditional Welsh 'heartland' areas such as Eryri/Snowdonia, coastal Môn/Anglesey, and even pockets in the Llŷn/Lleyn peninsula now exhibit serious weakening, and no substantial settlement on the Cambrian coast south of Harlech can be classed as primarily Welsh in habitual daily usage. The broad areas of Dyfed (south-west Wales) which do maintain Welsh-speaking concentrations above 70 per cent are already fragmented by areas of weakness. A notable threat lies along the Shrewsbury to Aberystwyth road, where the final territorial break between north and south Welsh appears imminent, delayed only by a sparse population in the relatively monotonous upland marginal farming tract south of Pumlumon. Everywhere it is the unspectacular and less attractive interior marginal farming districts which preserve Welsh best: no coast, no lakes, no jagged peaks or rocky gorges, so minimal catering for visitors. And the highest Welsh-speaking densities are in the formerly slate-quarrying communities of Gwynedd, where unsightly spoil heaps still repel most intruders and the rainfall is notoriously torrential. Lower property prices and constantly improving roads give all this an air of impermanence as defences for Welsh in a very small country where in addition the children's education, even (or especially?) in these geographically 'protected' districts, inevitably points outwards.

Most outside observers are impressed but also misled by the progress justly claimed in recent years for Welsh in the schools and to a lesser extent in public administration. Provision for Welsh-medium teaching to secondary level is now good wherever it is desired and the state supports 'all-Welsh' schools wherever sufficient parents request them in English-speaking districts. Official forms are now generally available in Welsh, signposts and traffic notices are bilingual, the language is used in the courts; and provision for Welsh under Gwynedd County Council is far superior to that under any Irish equivalent. Unfortunately none of this makes the slightest difference to the linguistic consequences of what sociologists term the modernization and mobilization of Welsh society.

Almost everyone is rich compared with forty years ago, most families have access to cars, all children receive secondary education, and far more go on to universities and higher education; far fewer people are now dependent on heavy extractive industries which kept them locally, far more work in service industries which promote mobility, and even at home communicate constantly with outside businesses; almost all have salaries which make trips to the nearest (usually English-speaking) town for shopping and entertainment both a pleasure and a habit; and most can now afford and do indulge in continental holidays on which it is fun to stress their Welsh identity but for which the lingua franca is always English. A wealthy British state can afford to finance Sianel Pedwar Cymru (S4C), the mainly Welsh-language television channel. However, while there is indeed a television in almost every home, its dominant medium is English.

Welsh survived better than Irish because in the early years of industrialism Wales had coal and iron, slate and lead, to support its own industrial growth. It had emigration, as did England, but in general Welsh children could expect a future at home, if that was their choice, so the population in Wales multiplied and so long as employment was in manual trades and skills there was little threat to Welsh. As prosperity rose and expectations with it, so education improved and the mental horizons of the people widened to those previously confined to the early-anglicized gentry. The schools gave bilingualism, but so too did industrial prosperity, which attracted large numbers of less well-off English people to work in the South and North Wales mines and other industries and who of course in time intermarried. English provided the opportunities of work in a much wider geographical area with a much wider choice of job at higher levels of remuneration. When the Welsh became prosperous and mobile, they (often) wished to go to England. When the English became prosperous and mobile, they (often) wished to go to Wales. The balance of numbers, of wealth, and of geographical range entirely favoured English.

The lessons for Irish from the Welsh example are unhelpful, for they indicate clearly that avoidance of the mass emigration and depth of poverty that did much to stifle the Gaeltacht was of only short-term benefit to minority language survival, and that reasonably successful economic development and 'modernization', as planned by Údarás and effected in Wales by regional development assistance since the 1930s, themselves involve a high degree of mobilization which is entirely disadvantageous to a language of limited geographic range. Welsh experience also confirms that benevolent state support may help transform public attitudes to a disadvantaged language but cannot change the socio-economic fundamentals which determine day-to-day habits of language use. There is a further negative consideration in that the overwhelming defeat of the 1979 devolution referendum in all parts of Wales was widely ascribed to fears among many non-Welsh speakers that a Welsh Assembly would be dominated by an 'all-Welsh' professional lobby which would impose language requirements for all public employment and so blight the employment prospects of the majority of the children of Wales. As in Ireland, compulsory revivalist policies excite popular hostility; and as in Ireland voluntary methods do not achieve results, apart from a certain slowing of decline brought about by the removal of at least some pressures against the old language.

There are no reliable estimates as to the numbers of the half million Welsh speakers who in fact make habitual use of the language, but from his knowledge of Wales this author would hazard the opinion that it will be fewer than 250,000. There were (1981) 281,280 in Gwynedd and Dyfed, which have almost the whole of the strongly Welsh areas but even so have many Welsh speakers in anglicized towns such as Llandudno and Carmarthen; and there are no substantial Welsh-speaking communities in the other Welsh counties, except in the Lliw valley of west Glamorgan, which is insufficient to disturb the global estimate. Even so, the latter is at least ten times the likely figure of habitual Irish speakers, and if this is still inadequate for successful language maintenance, it is improbable that the added weight of Irish national sentiment will suffice to compensate for gross lack of numbers. Current belief in the Irish language movement that state support for an Irish-medium television channel, or at least much more use of Irish in existing channels, would radically reduce pressures against the language are not well supported from Welsh experience with S4C, welcome as the latter is, for viewing figures are disappointing and it is perfectly obvious that the normal problems arising from supply and demand – i.e. small numbers of potential viewers, small numbers of potential programme producers – combine to make most Welsh speakers prefer watching English-medium programmes most of the time. My own impression is that this applies even more strongly to young children, who inevitably have not yet developed any countervailing motivations but whose speech and thought habits will determine the future of the language, as of much else.

The comparatively large pool of native Welsh speakers, with comparatively well developed literary traditions and no problems of an unstandardized language to bedevil efforts in modern publication, has nevertheless encountered and failed to overcome most of the other difficulties which impede or limit Irish-language publication. These again centre on comparative costs because of numbers, and perhaps more fatally on the vastly greater choice of material in English at all levels of interest, however depraved and however enlightened or esoteric. And as education advances and foreign travel becomes yet more commonplace, Welsh people too begin to admit that while bilingualism (or better) is excellent, bilingualism in English and French – and/or German, Italian, Spanish, Russian, etc. – is more useful and opens far wider doors than does bilingualism with Welsh. Again, if this is true for half a million Welsh speakers, how much more is it likely to seem true for the minuscule numbers of native Irish speakers?

Scottish Gaelic

The decline of Scottish Gaelic is more directly comparable to that of Irish, so less need be said about it. There are no 'success stories' such as early standardization of the modern language as achieved by the Welsh Bible in 1588, or of modern media progress as in S4C, to suggest ways in which Irish could be more successfully promoted. In addition, Scottish Gaelic lacks any major nationalist impetus, for since the Middle Ages Scottish linguistic nationalism has focused, where it has focused at all, on the 'Scots' (obsolete 'Scotch') or 'Scottish' variants of English which, themselves unstandardized since the Scots accepted the *English* Bible from their own James VI and I, are none the less as English as Lancashire, Yorkshire, or Devon dialect and substantially indistinguishable from the Northumbrian or Cumbrian forms of English. Gaelic was confined to the Highlands by the Tudor period, with marginal and doubtful exceptions in parts of Galloway and Carrick, and died in the main Scottish cities and towns long before Irish lost its major urban footholds. Yet Scottish Gaelic continued to dominate the Highlands until the beginning of the twentieth century and has collapsed only since then.

The relatively long-sustained immunity of Gaelic within the Highlands and Islands was not due to the presence of industrial raw materials to sustain economic growth, as in Wales, though it survived late in a few locations such as Easdale in north Argyll, where slate gave support till the

225

collapse in the Great Depression, and in occasional small fishing villages such as Embo in east Sutherland, where self-sufficiency in a 'noxious' industry excluded tourism and (like slate) never brought sufficient prosperity to raise ambitions to levels demanding the daily use of English. Irish parallels would include Teileann/Teelin in west Donegal or Heilbhic/ Helvick in south Waterford. The main protection for Scottish Gaelic seems to have been poverty and isolation, reflected in late penetration by railways and in most districts on the west coast no such penetration at all.

The Highlands are what their name suggests, and generally lack the cultivable land which characterized most of Irish-speaking Ireland around 1800. Subsistence arable in narrow glens or on coastal strips offered few prospects for commercial transport development and Highland roads had to be state-supported from the time of General Wade (1725 ff.) onwards. The prospect of profit for proprietors was limited to coastal fishery development after 1800 and in the interior to the substitution of sheep – later sometimes deer – for unremunerative subsistence crofter-farmers. Kelp-burning (for explosives) supported great coastal population increases during the Napoleonic Wars but then collapsed in the face of foreign (chiefly Spanish) imports. The potato also sustained high population growth in the crofting fringes, very much as in Ireland, but the blight and famine of the 1840s struck Gaelic Scotland too and added famine emigration to the outward movements caused in many districts by deliberate clearances of tenants by landlords. All this reduced population drastically, as in Ireland, but from a much lower base, and the substitution of pastoral for subsistence arable farming did little to make rail transport economically viable in so sparsely populated a region. Hence population collapse took place without much direct outside contact except for the emigrants themselves, and population densities made distances to schools as bad a deterrent to attendance as the fact that they were not free until much the same time as in Ireland.

The motives for learning English for emigration were thus much the same as in Ireland, at much the same time, and with no religious discriminatory element on the scale that affected Ireland till 1829. Yet Irish collapsed first. It is difficult to escape the conclusion that this relates closely to comparative difficulties of access, intensified by the almost total absence within the Highland area of urban centres above village size to which railways could be attracted or from which English could readily be diffused into the adjacent rural hinterlands. This again relates to basic physical geography, which in general was too poor to sustain urban growth. Most of nineteenth-century Irish-speaking Ireland was better placed than this and only the present Gaeltacht cores in west Galway and north-west Donegal were as deficient in towns. It is also striking that they, when their local population figures are studied in the detail available from census sources, appear to have suffered less depopulation than neighbouring anglicized districts, a feature they shared in common at least till World War I with the surviving Gaelic strongholds in the Western Isles of Scotland. Of course in the latter case extreme insularity may be a much weightier consideration, though it did not protect the one town and major port of Stornoway from subsiding into English well before the 1950s, when the author began to study it. It had a census majority of Gaelic speakers then, but very few Gaelic-speaking children in the schools.

The author's unpublished survey of around 1956–7 assessed the habitual Gaelic-speaking population of Scotland as at most 33,900 (cf. 95,447 in the census of 1951), of whom 26,840 were in the Western Isles and 5,500 in Skye. This represented the loss in the present century of the entire Highland mainland and the rest of the Inner Isles, and compared closely with final estimates of between 29,284 and 42,265 habitual Gaeltacht Irish speakers, the larger figure allowing the benefit of enormous doubts for several small Gaeltachtaí (e.g. Uíbh Ráthach/Iveragh) and the margins of all the larger ones. The minimum estimate for Gaelic was 31,670, so in essence the Scottish and Irish figures were identical. From the point of view of Irish survival this was not so good, for Scottish Gaelic had achieved this without any of the energetic support accorded to Irish by the state since 1922 and without any nationalist fervour to sustain it in the voluntary sector.

An Comunn Gàidhealach, the Highland equivalent of Connradh na Gaeilge (the Gaelic League), was founded earlier, in 1891, but remained non-political in the absence of any great separatist political movement and secured only mild ameliorations of the position of Gaelic in the educational system, publishing, and the other media. There has never been any pretence of leading a 'return' of the whole Scottish people to the Gaelic language, except in a tiny 'lunatic fringe', and even after the upsurge of nationalist feeling in recent decades, with renewed interest in adult Gaelic classes in the towns, the 1981 census showed only 79,307 people – 1·3 per cent of the total – as able to speak Gaelic. This did include increases in the towns which partly balanced decreases where the language is native and alive, but in the absence of any widespread teaching of Gaelic in schools outside the residual Gaelic districts there is no need to discount very much of this 'able to speak' total on grounds of over-optimism or nationalist sentiment as in Ireland. Well over half are Gaelic speakers who now live in English-speaking districts or who otherwise have Gaelic as mother tongue but have not used it with their children.

Gaelic decline has continued uninterrupted since my research in the 1950s and the one major pro-Gaelic change to have occurred has been the creation in 1975 of a new county council, Comhairle nan Eilean (Council of the Islands), to administer the whole of the Western Isles from Stornoway. Hitherto they had been administered in two main blocs by two different county councils centred far away on the utterly anglicized east coast of Scotland, remote across the Minch and the Highland mountain barrier. The new council has adopted a bilingual policy which has serious hopes of success because most of the population affected do indeed speak Gaelic as their native language, so no artificial stimulus need be devised. At school level, however, the prospects are not so promising, as native-speaking children are now a minority.

It can be deduced from figures supplied by the Council that only 43 per cent of all children entering first-year secondary classes in the Western Isles in August 1982 spoke Gaelic as their mother tongue (Macsween 1983). The remaining 57 per cent were classed as learners. In urban Lewis, i.e. Stornoway, 9·3 per cent were classed as native speakers, suspiciously double the 4 per cent found in the town's primary schools in 1957 (Smith 1961: 32), but probably the result of the wider catchment area for secondary schooling. Even in rural Lewis only 62·6 per cent of new secondary entrants were native speakers in 1982 and for the other three island groups the proportions were Harris 57·5 per cent, the Uists 48·4 per cent, Barra 55·0 per cent. Non-native speaking children are of course most concentrated in the minor port market centres, i.e. Tarbert (Harris), Lochmaddy (North Uist), Lochboisdale (South Uist), Castlebay (Barra), and near the military base on Benbecula; but this is no help to long-term Gaelic survival, being part of the normal pattern of decline through increased outside contacts and a degree of marrying in. Irish and Welsh experience suggests that with such native Gaelic figures English must already be the lingua franca at secondary level. The native Gaelic proportions were better in 1976, as high as 100 per cent in Barra and 86·7 per cent in rural Lewis, but already all the rest were under 70 per cent and all the comparisons point inexorably downwards.

I used to hope that the width of the Minch and the high cost of the ferries across it would insulate Western Islands Gaelic sufficiently to enable it to survive like Faroese in the Faroe Islands: though I noted that Faroese still controlled its capital of Tórshavn, whereas Stornoway was lost; that Denmark was remote for the Faroes and the mainland quite close for the Western Isles; and that Danish was a much weaker language than English if it came to powers of attraction to speakers of minority languages. (See also p. 242.) The survival and reassertion of Inuit ('Eskimo') in Greenland in the face of Danish makes that point well enough. Now that regional development aid and outside work on North Sea oil have greatly enhanced Western Isles incomes, the ferry services to the mainland have been greatly improved and shortened by new routes which complement the addition of improved inter-island services, and air services to the Lowland cities have come within the financial reach of much of the population. More need hardly be said, save for the summary comment that once the children of a relatively remote and well integrated community gain access to a much larger one offering wide and relatively luxurious opportunities, they tend to wish to leave, and to leave their native language behind; and their parents, being older, wiser, and more experienced in detecting trends, tend to anticipate this by language decisions taken in their children's infancy. The television, with in this case scarcely any Scottish Gaelic on it, carries its subliminal message regardless of parental or school influences.

Scottish Gaelic is thus plainly dying despite its possession until very recently of a homogeneous native-speaking community in a geographically well defined area, well insulated by the sea and the Highland massif from close contact with English-speaking areas. But, to bring it down to Irish earth, Stornoway was a big Kilronan for Scotland's enormously greater equivalent of the Aran Islands – an English foothold (or cancer) that could not be contained. Recent slight increases in census returns of Gaelic-speaking ability in the younger age groups in Scotland have occurred almost entirely in districts where improved provision for Gaelic in primary schools has led to increases in second-language learning. (See MacKinnon 1985: 6, 10.) There is no more reason than in Ireland to regard this as an indication of revival in everyday use, and the 'bottoming out' of the historic decline in the proportions of Gaelic speakers aged 3 or 4 years since 1961 gives no grounds for confidence, amounting as it does to 0·6 per cent of the age group nationally and under a thousand children in total.

Channel Island French

The impending death of a major world language in a minority language situation affords a striking contrast for Irish, not least because decline occurred under conditions of complete local autonomy with French-medium administration. The States (parliaments) of Guernsey and Jersey did not permit the use of English in debate alongside French until 1898–1900, and French is still an official language of both bailiwicks. Yet it is near to complete disuse as a community language and it is unlikely that any children speak it as first language. Glanville Price (1984a: 207–16) gives a lucid account of its history and decline, relating the latter to the intensification of naval, military, and fishery links with England in the early nineteenth century, the retirement of veterans to Jersey, increased contacts with England through tourism and trade as steamer services developed, and the general provision of English-medium schools by the end of the century. French was nevertheless the home language of the islands until after 1900.

The fact remains that none of the Channel Islands is more than thirty miles from France (Jersey is about twelve), whereas distances to England are between eighty and 100 – to Dorset or Devon. Except in war, travel to and from France has hardly ever been restricted and French exiles such as Hugo found the islands a convenient place of refuge from intolerant regimes. How then could French die here?

It seems clear to this author that the explanations are basically physical geographical in origin, i.e. deriving from the fact that the Channel Islands are south of Britain but north of most of France. They are therefore attractive to British tourists because they are warmer, but of little attraction to the French because they are not. The British political link of course facilitates travel and trade because no passports are required, and French protectionism has not encouraged exports to France. Even so, with scant mineral resources other than rock, a southerly location *vis-à-vis* industrializing Britain in the nineteenth century gave the Channel Islands excellent opportunities for the sale of early vegetables and flowers which they could never have hoped to sell to France, where spring is so much earlier and the northern winter non-existent in the Mediterranean south. Commercial links with England were thus immensely stimulated by climatic relativities – once living standards in England enabled the English to buy such luxuries as flowers and early vegetables or to become tourists, and once the steamship had been invented to make sea links dependable. The Protestantism of the islands also helped to orient them northwards, but again also made them a refuge for French Huguenots, and until the present century the churches remained predominantly French in their language of mission.

Another major factor tending towards French decline has of course been relative population sizes: 135,694 in 1986, compared with Great Britain's estimated 55,196,400. Division between two main islands and two lesser ones of note fragments the potential community and even the two lesser islands have their own parliaments. There is no university or equivalent, so because of the political link higher education is normally in Britain – one can hardly say 'on the mainland' in this location.

Continuing economic and social advances since World War II have reinforced the anti-French climatic influence, as large numbers of wealthier British people have retired to the Channel Islands to enjoy their milder climate and low tax burdens while still under the security of the British flag, and 'tax haven' settlers of younger age have added to the flow. This has been all too late to affect an anglicization which was already far advanced by 1940, when my wife found herself at school in Manchester with some of the many Channel Island children evacuated to Britain to avoid the German occupation. This mass evacuation, which lasted for four years, accustomed many of the last French-speaking children to English for everyday purposes, but it must be emphasized that they were already a minority and this 'last straw' must not be weighed more heavily than that. Ambitious Channel Islanders, once education was widely available to them, naturally looked out of the islands for their careers and had plenty of wealthy English-speaking outsiders among them to point the most profitable direction. Here of course there are few parallels with Irish, for none of the Gaeltachtaí have ever attracted large numbers of incomers, except for the returning emigrants of Gaoth Dobhair/Gweedore and south Conamara (strictly Cois Fharraige and Mórthír Láir) in very recent years. There is no real resemblance here, or with the trickle of literary visitors to Árainn/Aran which Synge initiated.

The fact remains that French in the Channel Islands is effectively dead as the native language and that it has died without political discrimination, religious oppression, evictions, or natural disasters such as the Great Famine. It has died under full 'home rule' (no 'Union' or MPs in London), which has never been disturbed except by German occupation, and as far as printed sources indicate it appears to have been abandoned without major debate, by the unspoken but common consent of those who once spoke it and ceased in this century to transmit it to their children. In this case the lawyers lagged behind and French is still the language of conveyancing in Jersey and Sark (G. Price 1984a: 215) as well as serving various ceremonial functions in the states, etc. There is no evidence that this has any effect in promoting French in everyday use and it serves here merely as a reminder that tokens and symbols of 'ethnicity' or tradition mean no more than that. None the less, despite the vast experiential differences of Ireland and the Channel Islands since 1800 and even earlier, it must be evident yet again that for all languages within the 'culture ray' of English the development of modern urban industrial society has brought the same result, whether their people stayed poor or neglected, or whether they prospered, and whether they developed a vigorous language movement or not.

Feelings like those of 'the shame of Irish dying in a free Ireland!', a cry often heard when I began my Irish studies, doubtless explain the reticence I encountered when I first enquired about French in the Channel Islands and especially when I asked why they had never included a language question in their census enquiries. Self-evidently, they did not want to know, for the loss is deeply regretted but accepted as a price worth paying for prosperity. It is an interesting paradox that now that anglicization is virtually complete it has become necessary to exclude further immigrant settlement except by the wealthiest. Problems here are indeed very different from those of Ireland, but the linguistic outcome is the same; and, almost needless to say, French-language broadcasting has always been easily received in the Islands, as is French television. The dialect distinctions which make Jersey and Guernsey French especially interesting were no impediment to a ready understanding of the standard language, once schooling became common.

Other Western European languages

There are so many minority languages in Western Europe that it would involve writing another small book to compare them all adequately with

Irish. They are therefore listed in table 8 with some relevant data under their respective states and then exemplified where comparisons with Irish seem particularly valid. Minority languages of the British Isles are included, to facilitate comparisons. Most language figures are estimates and population figures are the most recent available from the *Statesman's Year-book*, 1988–9 edition. A number of language estimates are taken from Gunnemark and Kenrick's *Geolinguistic Handbook* (1986), an excellent source for the entire world. Some use has also been made of the EC Commission report *Linguistic Minorities in Countries belonging to the European Community* (Luxembourg 1986) but its figures usually have to be heavily discounted because of their derivation from enthusiastic interest groups. This is always a problem with languages which the respective state (e.g. France) ignores in its census enumerations and in general I have preferred to make my own estimates on the basis of many years of travel and investigation.

Erik Allardt's weighty monograph (1979) with its attempt to rank-order forty-six linguistic minorities of Western Europe by factor analysis, using eighteen variables, challenges emulation, but so many of his variables require estimation (or guesswork) that it is hardly surprising that the deduced ranking often verges on the ludicrous, for instance (p. 63) ranking Manx – which is extinct – seventeen places above Scottish Gaelic in its generalized linguistic, economic, and political resources. One must regretfully conclude that adequate trustworthy data are hopelessly lacking for such a venture and confine oneself to the difficult enough task of estimating basic numbers able to speak and otherwise habitually speaking each language.

It will be seen from table 8 that the official status of Irish ('Full') might appear to class it with languages which are comparatively secure. This is illusory and readily corrected by reference to numbers of habitual speakers and the geographic setting.

Catalan, by far the strongest of the languages enumerated, represents a people with a long national tradition who despite long subjection to Castilian Spain have largely retained command of their cities and towns, including Barcelona and Tarragona, and the loyalties of a bourgeoisie which retains a capacity to assimilate the poorer Castilian-speaking workers who are drawn into their region. Dialect divisions, as in Irish, combine with traditional provincialism to weaken Catalan solidarity in Valencia and the Baleares but a bedrock of six or seven million native speakers gives an incomparably surer base for survival than the figures for Irish. And yet Catalan is under threat from immigration founded on economic prosperity, as the world role of Castilian Spanish cannot be ignored by the Catalans who, already comparatively well-off, are commensurately ambitious. There is nevertheless a considerable modern literature in Catalan and strong support for the language in the other mass

Table 8 Minority languages of Western Europe (including DDR)

State	State population	Minority language	Speaking minority language	Habitual speakers of minority language	Official use of minority language	Geographic setting
Austria	7,555,338	Croatian	24,526 (1971)	Very few	Ltd	R
Belgium	9,864,751	Slovenian	c. 40,000	c. 20,000	Mod	R
		French	4,500,000–	4,500,000	Full	U
		German	50,000+	50,000	Full	U
Denmark	5,156,935	Faroese	?45,728	?45,728	Full	U
(Almost whole population of Faroes speaks Faroese)						
Finland	4,925,644	Sámi	1,726	1,726	Mod	R
		Swedish	298,295	298,295	Full	U
France	55,622,000	Basque	90,000	Few ch.	Ltd/Nil	R
		Breton	?500,000	?50,000	Ltd/Nil	R
		Catalan	100,000	?50,000	Ltd/Nil	R
		Corsican	150,000	?150,000	Ltd	R
		Dutch	c. 50,000	Few ch.	Ltd/Nil	U
		German	1,500,000	1,000,000	Ltd	R
		Occitan	??	?50,000	Ltd/Nil	R
Germany:						
BRD	61,140,000	Danish	25,000	25,000	Full	U
		Frisian	5,000	Few ch.	Ltd	R
DDR	16,639,877	Sorbian	?110,000	?20,000	Mod	R
Ireland	3,443,405	Irish	1,018,413	219,110	Full	R
Italy	57,290,519	French	55,000+	?50,000	Mod	U
		Friulian	?350,000	Few ch.	Nil	R
		German	200,000+	200,000	Full	R
		Ladin[1]	15,000	Few ch.	Ltd	U

Country	Population	Language				
Nether-lands	14,615,125	Occitan	??	Few ch.	Nil	R
		Sard	500,000-	Few ch.	Nil	R
		Slovenian	?76,000	?	Mod	R/U
		Frisian	300,000-	?	Ltd	R/some U
Norway	4,174,005	Nynorsk (Landsmål)	1,000,000	c. 1,000,000	Mod	R
		Sámi	20,000	?20,000	Ltd	R
Spain	37,746,260	Basque	600,000+	400,000-	Full	R/some U
		Catalan	7,000,000+	?6,000,000	Full	U
		Galician	1,500,000+	?1,000,000	Ltd	R/some U
Sweden	8,381,515	Finnish[2]	?20,000	Few ch.	Nil	R
		Sámi	6,000	?6,000	Mod	R
Switz-erland	6,523,400	French[3]	1,300,000	1,300,000	Full	U
		Italian[3]	280,000	280,000	Full	U
		Rhaetian[4]	40,000	?30,000	Mod	R/some U
United Kingdom[5]	56,965,856	C.I.French	?16,000	Few ch.	Mod	R
		Scottish Gaelic	79,307-	?20,000	Ltd	R
		Welsh	503,549	250,000-	Full	R/some U

Abbreviations and symbols

? Doubtful.

?? Very doubtful, usually because of widely varying estimates, and because little encountered on author's own travels.

+ Correct figure probably rather more than this.

- Correct figure probably rather less.

ch Children.

Full Official use as much as reasonable in the circumstances of each case: usually bilingual provision, with main national language as alternative.

Ltd Partial provision only, often limited to some primary school use and token representation elsewhere.

Mod Moderate. Use above minimal level but not approaching equal treatment even in the strongest areas. Usually numbers and proportions preclude this.

R Rural. Minority language almost wholly disused in towns within its area.

U Urban as well as rural. Minority language predominant in many/most towns within its area.

R/Some U Language mainly rural but with some strong urban representation, usually at majority level only in smaller towns.

Notes

1. Otherwise Central Rhaetian or Dolomitic.
2. Indigenous Finnish of the Tornea valley only. There are 134,234 immigrant Finns dispersed throughout mainly southern Sweden.
3. Swiss nationals only. There are considerably more Italian immigrants dispersed mainly through German and French-speaking cantons.
4. Otherwise West Rhaetian or Romansch.
5. Total population, including Northern Ireland, the Isle of Man, and the Channel Islands.

A few tiny indigenous minorities have been excluded from the table because of their insignificance and/or because they are not otherwise represented, e.g. Magyar in Austria, Albanian, Croatian, and Greek in Italy. Luxembourg is omitted because it does not fit the tabulation. Its native language, Letzeburgesch, *pace* Gunnemark and Kenrick (1986: 126), is a German dialect, but has little literary use compared with standard German or French, and the latter is the language of administration, though not often a native language. This is rather like medieval Ireland, where Irish predominated under a veneer of Norman French and English.

Sources

Allardt (1979); EC Commission (1986); Gunnemark and Kenrick (1986); M. Stephens (1976); *Statesman's Year-book 1988–89*.

media. In France none of this applies and the language is giving way rapidly to French. In short, Catalan represents one of the richest parts of Spain and one of the poorer parts of France, and the French language has more 'pull' than Spanish partly because of this. Catalan does have another advantage over Irish in that it is a close relative of its Spanish and French neighbours, so it is relatively easy for Castilian immigrants to pick it up for their own advancement. There is no such gulf as that between English and Irish, which deters so many keen learners of Irish.

Comparisons between Irish and Basque are closer but again the decline of Basque relates centrally to the modern industrialization of the Spanish Basque provinces and the great influx of workers from adjacent and distant Spanish provinces. Basques who themselves did well naturally wished to travel and for that Basque itself was entirely useless. Basques have played an active and profitable role in the development of the Hispanic world and to that Castilian Spanish provided the key. Because the Basque provinces themselves were comparatively rich, and urban growth provided good home markets for Basque agriculture, the rural population enjoyed reasonable prospects of survival at home without mass emigration. Hence Basque rural survival resembles that of Welsh, with a steady loss of main towns and industrial areas which attracted immigration and a slower loss of smaller market towns where the needs of commerce promoted the rival 'main' language but the daily pressures of the constant presence of large numbers of incomers were much weaker or absent. Habitual speakers of Basque greatly outnumber the Irish and there is still a fairly substantial Basque-speaking middle class to provide authentic leadership of a type not easily imposed by second-language learners. In rural Navarra and the French Basque provinces, all much less populous, out-migration dominates and there are few pressures to arrest a Basque decline which clearly follows from the need for wider communication in the search for jobs elsewhere.

Basque 'home rule' in Spain during the past decade has brought Irish-type conflicts about the extent to which a knowledge of Basque should be essential for public employment. Most are agreed on the teaching of Basque in schools but only a third of the population of the titular Basque provinces (i.e. excluding Navarra) can speak it, Basque is exceptionally difficult to learn, and children's job prospects are important . . . Inter-marriage with non-Basques is frequent because of prosperity and normally results in non-Basque-speaking families, for the usual reasons.

Galician (Gallego) in north-west Spain is in a poor area, suffers constant emigration, but is still quite strong in its rural districts because of neglect and poor school provision. Castilian is accepted as the key to the outside world and Galicia has so far failed to develop any important nationalist movement, let alone the 'obvious' one of a secessionist desire to join Portugal, for the standard language of which Galician provided a principal model. Of course Portugal itself is poor and there are purely local cross-border interlinkages. There appears as yet to be no language question in Galicia and the new Spanish state seems by its wise and tolerant regional autonomy policies reasonably sure to prevent one from arising. The Galicians can provide for their language as they like, but as yet they find Castilian more useful for their careers and seem content to leave Galician at home.

A large number of European minority languages are in fact the dominant ones of adjacent countries, so always have those behind them when confronting problems of numbers and the modern media. Thus German in Belgium, Alsace–Lorraine, and the South Tyrol is unlikely to sink into the defeatism and inferiority complexes of fully minority languages such as Breton, Frisian, or Swiss Rhaetian. The same applies to French in the Val d'Aosta (Italy), where nevertheless Italian industrial immigration is swamping it. The minority proportions of French speakers in Belgium (32 per cent nominally but 41 per cent with the inclusion of 'bilingual' but primarily French-speaking Brussels) and Switzerland (20·1 per cent) are made almost irrelevant by firm and generally clear-cut areas of territorial dominance backed by complete administrative devolution. The Swiss Italians as a mere 4·5 per cent are secure in their own canton of Ticino, though demographic movements from the wealthier German-speaking cantons do disturb them and may in time result in language decline. Near-encirclement by Italy and large-scale Italian labour immigration make this less likely than might seem the case.

The Irish equivalent in Switzerland is the Rhaetians, at 0·9 per cent of Swiss nationals, confined to one canton, in which they are a minority, and geographically broken into four separate Alpine pockets which have never agreed a standard language for their dialects. The towns are lost to German, and commune sovereignty, which allows each commune to decide the language of its schools for itself (usually in Switzerland it is the canton), facilitates a steady retraction of the language frontier as the value of German in the international tourist trade progressively advances up the valleys. Official status in the Graubünden is good for the status of Rhaetian but makes little practical difference to its use in the job market. There is no real nationalist movement above a broad 'folkloric' level and utilitarian attitudes prevail. With such small numbers, in scattered pockets, intermarriage with non-Rhaetian speakers is inevitable and frequent, the more 'useful' language passing to the children. Rhaetians who do not wish to stay with the tourist trade migrate to the German-speaking cities of the Mittelland.

The example of Swedish in Finland may in some respects be seen as encouraging for Irish, for this once imperial language has had its proportionate strength reduced by half since Finland's independence in 1917. First-language Swedish speakers were 11·6 per cent in 1910 and 6·1 per cent in 1986. Their numbers have been almost static but Finnish speakers have multiplied and industrial expansion has brought them into almost all the formerly Swedish-dominated coastal towns and cities, usually displacing Swedish majorities. The rights of Swedish are fully protected by a generous bilingual policy which extends to all-Swedish university education, but the relative position of Swedish has greatly declined. A higher standard of living and lower birth rates have played their part, plus a greater tendency to emigrate because of better education and possession of a language which opens the door to Sweden and half opens it to Germany, those being the two countries which (apart from the USA) attract ambitious Finns.

Sheer lack of numbers is crucial in intermarriage and nowadays Finnish speakers tend to take their Swedish learning less seriously, preferring to learn English, which the better-educated Swedish speakers also prefer, though the continued need for Finnish is obvious in Finland. Thus, so far from Ireland, the power of English is a relevant consideration, and one may also add that a high proportion of Finnish academic research material, whether from the Finnish or the Swedish faculties, is published in English. German, French, and Italian Swiss likewise now tend to prefer to learn English instead of each other's co-national languages.

The survival and resurgence of Finnish took place despite Swedish rule, which is commonly dated from 1155, though Swedish settlement may have preceded the arrival of the Finns. Be that as it may, there were no concessions to Finnish as an official language or in schools and universities before the Russians took over in 1808. Yet, as in medieval and early modern Ireland, lack of official status was irrelevant to the speech of the majority population and the small scale of government activity affecting ordinary working people gave few inducements to cultivate Swedish. In short, nominal political subjection was not a major factor in language change. The Russians respected the autonomy and institutions of Finland and from 1863 onwards responded to popular demands for greater recognition of Finnish. The growth of public education by the end of the Russian period in 1917 had broken the Swedish dominance among the middle classes, but this took place in conditions where all were united in a sense of 'Finnishness' against Russian domination, so linguistic tensions never rose to levels of mutual intolerance.

At independence the Swedish Finns were still comparatively 'privileged', but in a democratic Finland with substantial equality of opportunity their statistics were strongly against them. At little more than 10 per cent of the population they were in the same numerical and socio-economic positions as Protestants in the Free State in 1922, and their subsequent loss of relative numbers and status has been for almost exactly the same reasons, though little to do with language in the Irish case. The point here is surely that democratization (as an aspect of modernization) and mobilization of both majority and minority populations tend to have adverse consequences for any minority, whether rich (in the case of Swedish Finns and Irish Protestants) or poor (native Irish speakers); and the causes are largely independent of political pressures, especially if the state is democratic and liberal. Swedish, with under a third of a million native speakers, has difficulty maintaining itself among 4.5 million Finnish speakers, despite having 8 million Swedes closely adjacent and full access to the Swedish media, as well as enjoying generous provision in the latter in Finland itself.

There is in Finland the special case of the Åland Islands, where Swedish is supreme and unchallenged among a total population of only 23,640, well within the range to which habitual Irish and Scottish Gaelic have now shrunk. Here the resemblance stops, for the islands are much closer to Sweden than to Finland, well within a hundred miles of Stockholm itself, closely linked with Sweden economically, and enjoy a high degree of local autonomy negotiated by the League of Nations when they tried to secede to join Sweden after World War I. Official neutrality dates back to 1856 (the Crimean War), so there are no Finnish military forces in Åland, whose inhabitants are exempt from Finnish national service. The sole official language is Swedish, education is exclusively in Swedish, and Finnish may be taught only with the permission of the local commune. Finnish settlers may apply for local citizenship only after five years and without it cannot vote, carry on trade, or purchase land. The islanders depend chiefly on agriculture, fishing, and tourism, and average incomes around 1970 were about 10 per cent higher than in mainland Finland. (See Straka 1970 and Stephens 1976 for further details.)

Population size is clearly not the key factor here but location, relative prosperity, proximity to, and close commercial links with Sweden (which has a much larger population), and above all the securing of autonomy before Finnish or any other alien language had gained a significant foothold. The milder climate might well have attracted numerous Finnish-speaking settlers, especially since 1950 as prosperity has grown, and if that had been allowed on a permanently resident scale Åland could now be on the path pioneered by the Channel Islands. It is notable that the Channel Islands did not until too late to safeguard French choose to use their autonomy to exclude 'mainland' settlers and never undertook determined language policies of any sort. Generalization about the consequences of autonomy as tending in any one direction is therefore untenable. One can only deduce that for basic geographical reasons Swedish retained more instrumental value in Åland than French did in the Channel Islands, for Åland emigrants are more likely to seek employment in Sweden than are Channel Islanders in France. And of course they receive Swedish television direct from Sweden as well as from Finland.

Few monoglot Swedish communities survive on the Finnish mainland

The death of the Irish language

and the only blocs of more than single commune size are two separate ones in Ostrobothnia, i.e. relatively remote from the main urban centres of Finland and still strongly agricultural, located on or near the coast facing Sweden. Elsewhere the attractions and opportunities of urban industrialism make a command of Finnish almost essential, and the pressures of intermarriage in a bilingual community with no violent language consciousness on either side almost invariably operate in favour of Finnish as the language of the new home and its children. This, if in different circumstances *vis-à-vis* socio-economic status, is of course much as in Ireland, where relative numbers are much more disproportionate and the utilitarian advantages of the minority language only minor.

Historic accident has perhaps played a major part in protecting Finnish from Swedish, in the sense that the main force of modern urban industrialism struck Finnish after independence and eventual (after civil war) democracy, and after the Russians had acquiesced in the breaking of the Swedish language monopoly. In Ireland the linguistic side effects of agrarian and industrial progress (or devastation) were immense a century earlier and independence came long after the democratic majority had abandoned its traditional tongue. Another crucial accidental difference is that Irish fell within the domain of English rather than of a language with the relatively limited economic power of Swedish.

None of the Irish Gaeltachtaí have the linguistic homogeneity of Åland or the latter's high degree of prosperous self-sufficiency, nor can they draw on support from a neighbouring pool of speakers of their language in an independent state or in their own.

The Sorbian language, which is the last survivor of a number of Slavonic languages that existed in eastern Germany, presents similarities to Irish in that it is confined to its own country, is spoken by very small numbers and proportions, is surrounded and interpenetrated by areas in which the majority language predominates exclusively, and it none the less enjoys the support of a state which is keen to promote it in part-expiation of former injustices. As in Ireland this support leads to incredible official language statistics which can only at best reflect second-language learning and conceal the true plight of the native language.

Sorbian survived in spite of the lack of any official status from the early Middle Ages onwards and the absence of any developed sense of national identity. It was hardly persecuted, even under the Nazis, who insisted on German for everything and held it in contempt but found no reason to shoot loyal Germans just because of their ancient Slavonic first language. The Sorbian home area was one of variable soils on agricultural land within forty of fifty miles of Berlin and Dresden, with no important towns inside its own linguistic boundaries. Survival evidently resulted from a high degree of agricultural self-sufficiency – after relatively early loss of the market centres because of external trade. The maximum north–south extent of the area with any native Sorbian speech is under sixty miles, and east–west is about twenty. Mellor (1962–3) mapped it as in a dozen different pockets in 1925, but the biggest (in the south) covered half the total area and did include the small town of Bautzen/Budyšin, which is the administrative and cultural centre for Sorbs in the DDR today.

Modern contraction began with the beginning of lignite extraction in the late nineteenth century and the development of ancillary industries which together drew in German-speaking labour and gave the Sorbs themselves rising expectations, further augmented by the advent of state education in German. Fairly reliable estimates showed a reduction in Sorbian-speaking numbers from 141,000 in 1849 to 106,000 in 1900 and 57,000 in 1934. An official post-war census in 1946 recorded 32,000 in areas with a total population of about half a million. Thereafter under Soviet influence enlightened 'national' policies have been pursued in the schools of the minority area, and cultural organizations among and for the Sorbs have been well subsidized. Sorbian is used as a teaching medium in some schools and taught as a subject in more. That probably explains why the DDR census of 1985 found 100,000 Sorbs whereas Straka (1970) could find evidence of no more than 62,000. Somewhere around 20,000 seems probable for the residue of habitual native speakers, for industrialization, urbanization, and the collectivization of farming have all proceeded apace since 1946, bringing more German-speaking workers into the Sorbish area and attracting (or pushing) rural Sorbs into German-dominated towns and industries. Stephens (1976: 415) reported that Sorbs were reduced to a thousand people among the 45,000 in 'their' capital, Bautzen.

There can, in short, be little doubt that state encouragement will have greatly increased appreciation of the cultural value of Sorbian as well as providing employment in teaching in or through it, preparing literature in it, devising radio programmes, and so on; but in the geographic and socio-economic setting of Lusatia (the regional name in English/Latin, *Lausitz* in German, Sorbian *Lužica*) the prospects of survival as a first language can only be extremely bleak and the absence of any formal national autonomous region on the Soviet model makes it plain that any such thing would be utterly unrealistic in terms of comparative numbers. The attempt to form an autonomous Sorbian district around Bautzen and to move population to fit it was apparently made in 1952 and abandoned because of general public hostility. This does somewhat resemble the Irish case, where recurrent demands for separate administration for the combined Gaeltachtaí (i.e. separation from existing county councils and unification under a single Gaeltacht county council or equivalent) have likewise failed for lack of grass-roots support. Neither in Lusatia nor in the Gaeltacht is the language question usually the first priority. This applies under both people's democratic socialism and under capitalism, and should certainly not be surprising to a Marxist versed in the paramountcy of materialist considerations in determining human cultural choices.

General

Irish is unique in Europe as being proclaimed the first official language of the state despite its extreme minority position, for at best all other minorities receive nominal equal status which is usually confined in practice to their actual area of concentration or dominance. The actual role of Irish is similarly constrained, its primacy being symbolic and token, not real.

Almost all the languages listed in table 8 are in decline, the exceptions being mainly those which are majority languages in an adjacent state which by its mere presence affords strong support; and even then the framework which the modern state provides is usually pulling and pushing the border minorities out of bilingualism into exclusive reliance on the 'national' language. In all cases urban industrial growth and increased mobility are associated with minority language decline, and this seems far more important than differences in political status. The relative strength of Catalan in Spain is the sole example of a strong minority language with no other country of its own, but in that case large absolute numbers and economic strength have been shown to be crucial.

The Faroe Islands, autonomous under Denmark, are unique in that unlike Åland in Finland their language is entirely their own (Icelandic is very similar), but midway location between Britain, Norway, and Iceland gives no help to Danish and a fish-based economy does not usually attract Danes northwards. Less than fifty thousand people are therefore enough for safe survival because of geographical context, and autonomy arrived (in 1948) at a time when almost all the people still spoke Faroese and their school-Danish was used only by a minority in trade and administration.

Political autonomy or independence therefore seem able to secure a language only if it has survived strongly until autonomy is secured, and especially only so long as it has retained popular dominance in its towns, which inevitably provide the leadership for the rural community. Even insularity is not sufficient in itself if socio-economic integration with a mainland is advanced (e.g. the Isle of Man and Channel Islands) or if rural poverty becomes linked with rising expectations bred of new schooling and the chance of emigration, as in Corsica and Sardinia. The latter have substantial populations but despite a few local nationalists plainly do not see their future through their local languages, though as late as around 1950 they seemed to have that potential. Now they look outwards, and although their languages are both much closer to Italian, for political reasons the Corsicans look to French and Sardinians to Italian.

There is not a single example of the restoration to a majority position of a language which lost it in its own well defined territory. Even important languages such as Polish and Czech finally consolidated themselves only by mass expulsions of German speakers who were a linguistic threat because their monoglottism was in the context of Polish and Czech elites who were bilingual with German and under Prussian or Hapsburg rule had themselves been drifting towards German as mother tongue. Estonian, Latvian, and Lithuanian had their own compact territories before brief independence was won in 1917–21, but Lithuania quickly lost its capital, Vilnius (Vilna, Wilno) because the city had far more Yiddish and Polish-speaking citizens than Lithuanians. The other two states had German-speaking elites who included aristocratic rural landlords. All this contributed to instability which invited intervention by more powerful neighbours and in the end returned them to effective minority status under Russian domination, and substituted Russians for the expelled German speakers. In Estonia and Latvia Russians and related Slavs now approximate a third of the total.

Outside Europe the two most quoted examples of language 'restoration' are those of Hebrew and Afrikaans. Neither has much relevance to Irish. The need for a lingua franca for the multilingual Jews who refounded Israel has no parallel in Ireland, and for all Ireland's sufferings there is no Irish equivalent of the Jewish reason for abandoning the main Jewish national language, which was Yiddish (Jüdisch), the German Jewish dialect which received the full force of Nazi extermination policies and was also latterly repressed under Stalin. Afrikaans is more relevant because it was subordinated by the British in the Cape and for a short time in the two 'Boer' republics, where English continues to challenge it for supremacy in the main industrial and commercial city of Johannesburg. Nevertheless Afrikaans never lost its overwhelming majorities among the Whites in the entire country apart from the eastern Cape and much of Natal, so its 'restoration' was little more than a removal of mild repression, certainly not a widespread reconversion of Afrikaner backsliders from English to Afrikaans. Restoration was mainly a matter of asserting genuine bilingual policies and enabling bilingual Afrikaners to feel that they need not use English for all but 'homely' purposes. This was easy, with a simple change of national sentiment, and far easier than relearning a lost language which hardly anyone else speaks.

Afrikaans had to standardize itself and fight a battle with Dutch before it succeeded, but the possession of the loyalties of about two-thirds of the White population was a strong starting point and made this a minor technicality compared with the continuing controversy caused by the dialect divisions among the already minuscule numbers of native Irish speakers. In 1980 Afrikaans was the home language of 2,581,000 Whites and almost all the 2,800,000 'Coloureds'. This compared with 1,763,220 Whites with English as home language, and 15,200,000 Blacks whose major home languages numbered nine. The 800,000 Indians usually favour bilingualism with English, as in general do increasing numbers of Blacks. *Apartheid*, or separate development with residential segregation, does at least do more than most other political systems to favour the survival of cultural minority groups but Afrikaner domination of the White-controlled political system is crucial in ensuring the survival and prosperity of the Afrikaans-speaking minority.

In normal European terms this is an archaic survival of a common 'premodern' phenomenon, the control of a state by a dominant minority which imposes its own language through the superstructure of the state while leaving subordinate native languages otherwise largely undisturbed. The Normans achieved this in England and German was in the same position in much of Eastern Europe before 1919. It is interesting to reflect that the Dublin middle-class Gaeilgeoirí (professional Irish speakers) have in effect been attempting to revive and replicate such a situation, imposing Irish as an 'elite' language on a vast non-Irish-speaking majority: but with the added eccentricity (cf. Latin in medieval Europe) that they do not even speak Irish as native language themselves. That Irish still has to work alongside securely established English is, however, paralleled in South Africa, where despite the Afrikaner White majority English is unchallenged as the language of international trade and communication. The ultimate future of Afrikaans as a minority language in the wider setting of South Africa depends very much on political developments which are currently unpredictable and have no parallels in Ireland except in worst-case theory, which could eventually solve the Northern problem by mass emigration by the Ulster Protestants unwilling to accept 'native majority rule' and official parity for Irish but subjected to it by external pressures. Again mass movements may finally settle the future of a minority and one may readily refer back to the Famine migration from 1845 onwards, which undoubtedly clinched the alienation of the Irish people from any great belief in an economic future for their own language.

The example of Hebrew is much more attractive for Irish speakers because it *is* a 'return from the grave', achieved on idealistic grounds and without strong economic motivations. There were no more economic reasons to revive Hebrew than there are to revive Irish, and yet the effort has succeeded. This argument neglects the existence of the powerful utilitarian need, already mentioned, for a common medium for the ingathered exiles assembled in revived Israel. Also Yiddish was written in the Hebrew script and contained large Hebrew elements, and most world Jews were accustomed to the use of the Hebrew liturgy. Refugee camps and compulsory service in the Israeli forces, unavoidable under the constant Arab threat, threw immigrants together in circumstances propitious for the dissemination of Hebrew under pressure. Again there are no useful parallels with Irish, apart from anecdotal evidence of the occasional value of Irish for covert communication by, for example, the Irish peace-keeping force in the Lebanon and IRA units in Northern Ireland. Pressures for Hebrew in Israel have greater permanence – so long as the state survives. It must nevertheless be remembered that hardly any Jews of the great majority who live outside Israel speak Hebrew as mother tongue, and that inside Israel bilingualism is general, rather than Hebrew monoglottism. It is helpful for Hebrew that it is closely related to Arabic and affords an easy step towards a command of the latter, but other historical, political, and economic circumstances explain why the weight of Israeli bilingualism is with English and also why trilingualism (or more) is relatively common among Israeli Jews.

It cannot be argued from this that the Irish are therefore demonstrably unenterprising, despite the ethnic stereotypes readily to hand. More relevant is the fact that Irish migration has been almost exclusively to English-speaking places, so bilingualism in anything other than English has rarely been useful except for the relatively small emigration of the 'Wild Geese' exile elite to Catholic mainland Europe in the seventeenth century. They learnt French, Spanish, German, etc., quickly enough and were quickly assimilated into the appropriate societies and language groups. In general the adoption of a single second language has sufficed for the Irish and their historic experience has not been one of sustained persecution and harassment at a level instilling belief in the need for a wide command of languages for anticipated flight.

The Irish have not been persecuted in modern times simply for being Irish and have usually found the domain of the English language – i.e. the 'language of the oppressor' – more congenial than any others in the world. This in turn relates to the English- (or British-) led industrial revolution and the growth of a British Empire which spawned the Unites States as a superficially anti-British alternative to British/English domination. Opportunities were manifestly better in Britain or the USA in the nineteenth century and usually since. The same applies to mobile Jews and it is for the same 'Irish' reasons that there are now far more Jews in the USA than in Israel and that almost all have adopted English as their native language. It is for the same reason that most Jews who currently emigrate from the USSR after applying to go to Israel in fact go to the USA, unless physically prevented from doing so. The Irish and the Jewish roads are thus not so vastly different and lead to the English language more than to anything else. Israel is too new and the Hebrew revival too short-lived in the span of human history for profound long-term conclusions based on their success to be securely founded.

An added complication which should be remembered is that there are no readily available figures for numbers of native speakers of Hebrew in Israel any more than there are of Irish in Ireland. Gunnemark and Kenrick (1986) assess home-language Hebrew numbers as around 3 million, but given the fact that Jewish immigration has totalled 1,778,460 since 1948 (inclusive), compared with only 482,857 between 1919 and 1948, non-native speakers may as yet predominate, even though they are bringing up their children in Hebrew first. There is a parallel here with keen second-language Irish speakers who bring up their children in Irish in places like Dublin, but it is not a close one, for the numbers involved have no resemblance (see chapter 9) and the other differences in cultural and socio-economic pressures and motivations are vast. The Irish lack most of the Israeli Jewish reasons for wishing to revive their old language and are much more in the position of the 12 million Jews who, living outside the very special circumstances of that new state, mainly confine themselves to learning it at school where that is feasible but in general adhere to the mother tongue of their country of citizenship as their own. Neither the Afrikaans nor the Hebrew revival is sufficiently relevant to the circumstances in which Irish is situated for it to be used to improve the existing methodology of its attempted restoration.

The position of French in Canada is more inclined to that of Irish, as some 5·5 million to 6 million home-language French speakers are outnumbered more than three to one in Canada (total population 25 million) and much more so by the adjacent USA, which is functionally overwhelmingly anglophone and a major source of employment for French Canadians. Nevertheless there is a compact critical mass of 5·5 million habitual French speakers in the province of Québec, in full control of the government and much of the economy, with their own education system complete to the highest levels, ample French media provision, and with inward migration as the principal threat. The relatively greater prosperity of the rest of Canada and much of the USA combines with the vigorous pro-French policies of the provincial government to encourage the unilingual anglophone minority to emigrate from Québec in disproportionate numbers, especially from the more rural southern districts, and belated wider realization of the advantages of bilingualism with French should be reducing the pressures which have hitherto worked against the maintenance of French. That English-speaking Canadians now see a knowledge (and some actual use) of French as helping them to maintain an international distinction between themselves and the US Americans has a bearing on Irish experience but is likely to have no more weight when it comes to mother tongue. A token use of French will surely suffice here.

The basic difference between Irish and Canadian French lies in absolute numbers plus the ability of French Canadians to draw on the cultural backing of 'la Francophonie', but above all on the enthusiastic support of France itself (population 55·6 million in 1987), conscious of the relatively few secure outposts which the language still maintains overseas. Irish has no support from native speakers overseas and it is almost painful to have to point out how total has been the linguistic assimilation by English of the innumerable Irish immigrants who settled in the USA. There is not and apparently never has been an Irish-speaking *community* of any size in North America, even though scores of thousands of emigrants went as native Irish speakers and retained a keen sense of Irish national identity. Even less than in Ireland itself, that identity failed to focus on language, and for Irish Americans Irish scarcely achieves token recognition beyond appearing on banners on St Patrick's Day. That is not a reflection upon the Irish immigrants, for the French established French Canada before British settlers arrived, whereas the USA was thoroughly dominated by English before major numbers of Irish arrived and their acceptance of the English language of the host community has been followed by all other language groups who have joined to form the modern American nation.

It is not surprising that French in Canada and in North America generally should feel weakened by the tendency to unilateral bilingualism with English, where the balance of numbers and of economic power makes the learning of English by French speakers so much more immediately advantageous and remunerative than the learning of French by English speakers. Such a difference will usually mean that equally good teaching and equally serious learning will usually end in greater fluency by those learning English than the other way round, for the background motivations and environmental stimuli will be so much greater. This is the fundamental problem which Irish shares with all other minority languages, including those with substantial regional majorities. All are to varying extents dying or suffering erosion by the free choice of their native speakers, usually because they command insufficient resources and territory to satisfy the ordinary career and (often) daily needs of a modern mobile urban industrial world with sophisticated tastes in media entertainment. Most are declining in apparent apathy, some are declining in the face of patriotic sentiment and nationalistic resistance, but all are declining nevertheless.

Chapter thirteen

Conclusion

There is no room for honest doubt that the Irish language is now dying. The only doubt is whether the generation of children now in a handful of schools in Conamara, Cloch Chionnaola and Gaoth Dobhair, and Corca Dhuibhne are the last generation of first-language native speakers or whether there will be one more. The reasons have been discussed at length and relate primarily to economic forces which have promoted the modernization of the Gaeltacht economy and the mobilization of its people, involving them intimately in much wider and constant social and economic relationships than are encompassed by the language.

Numbers and distribution of surviving Irish speakers are crucial in the progress of decline and as they are less obviously a matter of opinion it may be best to conclude with a few statistical considerations.

First it is necessary to discount the 1,018,413 persons aged 3 years and upwards who were enumerated as Irish speakers in the census of 1981. They constituted 31·6 per cent of the total population, ranging in intensity from 4·9 per cent of the 3 to 4 year olds to 51 per cent of those aged 15 to 19, and 13 per cent of the over-65s. Only 58,026 were enumerated in the official Gaeltacht so could possibly be living where Irish was a normal everyday language, and despite the usual inflation of the figures only 52·8 per cent of children aged 3 to 4 were returned as Irish speakers in the Gaeltacht. This confirms that barely half the official Gaeltacht now claims to maintain Irish as mother tongue.

The detailed survey embodied in this book has shown how in fact the position is much worse when studied in the field and in relation to national school *deontas* figures, i.e. numbers and proportions of children in receipt of the grant for native Irish speakers.

Appendix 3 shows that in 1985–6 there were only 132 national schools with any pupils in receipt of the *deontas*. There were 3,412 national schools in the twenty-six Counties in the previous session. Of the 132 only fifty-six had a majority of pupils in receipt of the *deontas*. Thirty of the fifty-six had only one or two teachers when staffing figures were published for 1981–2 (*Tuarascáil an Chomhchoiste* 1986: 53–8) and the proportion is unlikely to be very different now. These small schools formed a large majority of those with a *deontas* majority in the strongest Gaeltacht of south Conamara with Árainn.

It is assumed that, allowing for a few anomalous *deontas* returns, only children in schools with a *deontas* majority are likely to be growing up in a predominantly Irish-speaking background. This yields the following figures of grant-receiving children for the Gaeltacht counties' national schools in 1985–6:

Donegal: 760 children in 12 schools, in 1 bloc and 2 'pockets',
Mayo: 117 children in 3 schools, in 3 separate 'pockets',
Galway: 1,610 children in 31 schools, in 1 main bloc and 1 'pocket',
Kerry: 277 children in 7 schools,
Cork: 43 children in 2 schools, in 2 distant 'pockets',
Waterford: none,
Meath: 51 children in 1 school.

Because 'encouragement' is so important in boosting these figures a bare *deontas* majority cannot be treated as a reliable indicator. Application of a 70 per cent majority 'test' reduces the numbers of Irish-attested primary children as follows (again 1985–6):

Donegal:[a] 379 children in 7 widely scattered schools,
Mayo: none,
Galway: 903 children in 21 schools, central in Conamara or Árainn,
Kerry:[b] 191 children in 4 adjacent schools,
Cork: none,
Waterford: none,
Meath: none.

Notes:
a Two schools with just under 70 per cent are added to the Donegal total, plus anomalous Toraigh (see p. 68).
b Dún Chaoin is added to the Kerry figures because of special circumstances (see p. 112).

The total numbers of *deontas*-receiving children in 50 per cent *deontas*-majority schools are thus 2,858, and in 70 per cent *deontas*-majority schools a mere 1,473. As I have been assured at some of the 70 per cent schools that most of their children arrive with English as their first and 'reflex' language, I am reluctant to count this smaller figure as too strict an estimate of the grand total of children currently in national schools and likely to consider transmitting the language to their own children – assuming they remain in the Gaeltacht and marry a first-language Irish speaker.

Appendices 3 and 4 attempt to establish a range of estimates of the current habitually Irish-speaking population by using the figures of Irish speakers aged 3 years and over as enumerated in the national census of 1981. The smallest unit for which details were published is the district electoral division (similar to a British civil parish) but, where only part of a DED is in the official Gaeltacht, figures are given for that part. First, it is assumed that DEDs and part-DEDs which in 1981 returned 90 per cent or more of Irish speakers were indeed predominantly Irish-speaking, as argued on p. 47, and may be classed as Fíor-Ghaeltacht. Second, it is assumed that DEDs, etc., returning between 80 per cent and 90 per cent of Irish speakers are only Breac-Ghaeltacht, i.e. partly Irish-speaking, with English in use to a high degree for everyday and domestic purposes. The DEDs, etc., are itemized for each individual Gaeltacht in appendix 4, duly classified as Fíor-Ghaeltacht or Breac-Ghaeltacht and with their 1981 returns totalled.

Units returning less than 80 per cent are ignored in both appendices and regarded as Galltacht, i.e. predominantly English-speaking. Also ignored are various small part-DEDs with under 100 inhabitants aged 3 and over in 1981. Partly because their populations are very small, as little as ten persons, and partly because they are on the Gaeltacht margins, so somewhat sensitive, their Irish returns are among the most incredibly inflated in the country and cannot be treated seriously as regards normal speaking ability or use. Larger part-DEDs show some abnormal inflation, too (e.g. Guala Mhór in Mayo), but their larger populations seem to average out the worst strains on credibility.

Appendix 5 reduces the individual Gaeltachtaí details of appendix 4 to county summaries, retaining a separate entry for the overlapping Mayo–Galway Gaeltacht of Dúiche Sheoigheach. Note that the 80 per cent 'Breac-Ghaeltacht' base reduces the enumerated Gaeltacht Irish speakers of 1981 to a still improbably high 36,209. The 90 per cent 'Fíor-Ghaeltacht' base gives 21,463, which still seems rather high because it includes a number of DEDs which recent investigation has shown to be primarily English-speaking.

The same tables therefore proceed to refine and update the calculation by two further assumptions based on interpretation of the 1985–6 national schools' *deontas* figures:

1. Nowhere with a *deontas* minority (under 50 per cent) in its school or schools can be reckoned as in any way effectively Irish-speaking unless there is evidence to show that the scores were distorted by special circumstances. A rough approximation of the present *maximum* habitually Irish-speaking population may thus be arrived at by applying to a DED's 1981 Irish-speaking population figure a fraction representing

the proportion assessed as residing in those areas which had a *deontas* majority in the schools in 1985–6.

2. Given that a bare *deontas* majority is rarely an indication of Irish predominance and is always in the context of universal fluency in English, a surer *minimum* figure for the hard core of habitual Irish speakers may be derived by isolating from the 1981 Irish-speaking returns those assessed as living in districts which in 1985–6 had over 70 per cent of *deontas* awards or very near to it.

The boundaries of school catchment areas rarely coincide with those of DEDs but there is little difficulty in estimating the proportions of DED populations falling within the two broad *deontas* categories. The *deontas* percentages themselves are used in full appreciation of the caveats outlined in chapter 4, and any special reservations about particular schools' figures are noted in appendix 4.

A calculation was also attempted on the basis of the assumption that, because children aged 5–9 years were 10·265 per cent of the Gaeltacht population aged 3 years and over in 1981, therefore 'effective' Irish speakers should number around ten times the 1,473 *deontas* recipients in the 70 per cent *deontas*-majority schools, i.e. 14,730 or thereabouts, with an upward allowance because of the ineligible 5 year olds. This was rejected as too crude compared with the area-by-area count adopted but it does serve as a useful 'control' and falls quite centrally between the maximum and minimum estimates of the last two columns in appendix 5, second section.

Budding linguistic statisticians should note that 8,751 is the figure finally preferred as the most likely residual of native Irish speakers living in communities with sufficient attachment to Irish to transmit it to a substantial majority of their children as language of the home and community. They alone are living in circumstances in which continued transmission seems possible or even probable in the light of experience. This is all that close scrutiny leaves of the 1,018,413 persons aged 3 years and over who were enumerated as Irish speakers in the census of 1981 and is reasonably proportionate to the 1,473 number of children in 70 per cent *deontas*-majority schools. I do not suggest this dogmatically but feel it safe to set a 10,000 upper limit to the current numbers of habitual native speakers while admitting that many of them share grave doubts about the advisability of continuing to speak Irish and may well end their careers more fluent in English and in normal circumstances no longer using Irish.

There are, as has been seen, only 45,728 people in the Faroe Islands (1985), which maintain a language of their own, and 23,636 in the Åland Islands (Finland), where Swedish survives without difficulties from Finnish. (See chapter 12.) Why can we not accept as comparable the larger figures of Irish speakers, at least the 58,026 counted in the Gaeltacht in the

1981 census, and credit them with the same capacity for perpetuating their language? First, the great majority of census Irish speakers are English speakers who learnt Irish as a second language and show no inclination to use it for normal communication. Second, what now seems a majority of native speakers have failed to transmit Irish to their children as first language, so demonstrate no practical language loyalty. They are alive but they do not see Irish as the language of the future and by neglecting to put it first with their own children they have already ensured its ultimate disuse in their own families.

People who can speak Irish but do not, especially to their children, cannot be counted as a positive factor in language maintenance as regards the natural living language of everyday use and normal inter-personal relationships. Their sentimental attachment to Irish, even if they are only school learners, makes their knowledge significantly different from that of most English speakers who learn French, but the fact that the latter are more likely in time to find their French advantageous for travel and business does not make the comparison entirely favourable to Irish.

There are, in sum, few helpful comparisons to be made between the geographical locations of the more secure European minority languages and those of Irish in terms of language maintenance. The former tend to be insular (as Faroese and Åland Swedish) and/or to have affinities with some nearby larger language group. Whereas the fragmentation of insularity may enhance protection by the sea, the fragmentation of the Irish-speaking districts is caused by the penetration of tongues of English-speaking territory along roads and former railways, absorbing all towns and most villages and imposing a need for English on almost all Gaeltacht interlinkages or socio-economic networks.

It would be hard enough to sustain Irish if all habitual native speakers lived in one core area contiguous to each other. The 19,110 native speakers in simple *deontas*-majority areas are in ten or eleven separate pockets and cannot travel to each other except through intervening anglicized areas. The 9,324 of the 70 per cent *deontas*-majority areas live in three main blocs, 61·0 per cent (5,691) in south Conamara (with Árainn) which itself is penetrated but not yet fragmented by degrees of incipient anglicization, ranging from highly advanced at Carna and Cill Rónáin to muted at An Cheathrú Rua and Cill Chiaráin. North-west Donegal, now with an estimated 1,944 residuum, seemed secure thirty years ago and fairly so around 1970, but its successful industrialization has inadvertently shattered its core and pushed remaining Irish dominance into the most peripheral school areas, with Bun Beag and Doirí Beaga semi-anglicized in the centre between them. Corca Dhuibhne's 'hard core' of 1,689 retain contiguity between their four strongest school areas but in practice most contact is through long-anglicized Dingle or largely anglicized Ventry (Ceann Trá).

In the light of hitherto continuous language decline none of these figures offers any hope of the continuance of Irish as a normal language serving ordinary purposes of everyday social intercourse in the family or the community. They confirm entirely the dominant impression left by field study, that Irish is now hovering on the verge of abandonment by its native speakers in all but a couple of handsful of school areas, most of them so small and comparatively remote that they may be excused for not having yet noticed what has already happened everywhere else or perceived it as relevant to themselves.

It has not been a purpose of this study to prescribe remedies or to suggest what changes in official language policies might seem in logic to follow from this survey and analysis. Suffice it to say that the future of Irish must be as a second language, respected like Latin for *extra*-ordinary reasons. Irish will never be needed like Latin for intercommunication in a multilingual international Church but may continue to be learned up to oral fluency by a minority of nationally conscious devotees. There are numerous questions which cast doubt on this, most notably whether the final draining of the Gaeltacht 'well' of traditional native speakers will not itself end the flow of keen learners.

Much of the romantic appeal of the language will die with the Gaeltacht, for there is no doubt that going to learn Irish there, among native speakers in their (usually) beautiful and exotic environment, is far more attractive than learning it in the classroom, lecture theatre, or study in some English-speaking town. This deserves stressing because it is clear to an outsider that learning and speaking Irish *in the Gaeltacht* gives many non-Gaeltacht Irish people a sense of completeness, of one-ness with Ireland's historic culture and traditions, which they cannot experience through their normal Anglo-Irish speech and reading, and which gives an irreplaceable dynamism to their mastery of the language, lifting it to the fluency which mere second-language learning rarely attains unless it is followed up by sustained and necessary use. The romantic-nationalist element is thus psychologically vital to maintain a flow of future learners and the death of the Gaeltacht would remove its sole material prop.

In more strictly practical terms it is impossible to find an example of a language surviving as a normal daily social medium once full bilingualism has been attained by all its native speakers. Full bilingualism removes any need for a lesser language and thereafter it becomes the property of scholars, a priesthood, or some other special group, never a full social spectrum and never a majority in an open community of ordinary working people. 'What use is it?' is almost unanswerable once there is no one left with whom communication is impossible without the old language. Without 'romantic' idealism, functional utilitarianism prevails.

The Irish language is lost in the midst of a thriving English-speaking world of over 320 million people – by home language alone. Ireland is one of this English-speaking world's economically weakest members, and the

253

Gaeltachtaí are among the weakest parts of the country's weakest regions. If the prosperity of either the great English-language ecumene or of the new and expanding European Community falters, the Gaeltacht may expect to feel it first – and to worry still more about the retention of its Irish language incubus. Already as I write the press carries highly coloured articles about the resumption of Irish mass emigration to the USA (e.g. *The Times*, 17 March 1989).

Much of the appeal of Irish since 1893 has been romantic and it is the tragedy of the language that poverty and deprivation have generally made romance a luxury in the Gaeltacht struggle for survival and improvement, which gave all the priority to the liberating powers of English. Romance thrives on comfort and leisure, so it is no surprise that the future of Irish now appears to lie in the hands of the linguistically long-anglicized urban bourgeoisie, especially in Dublin. That thought alone may provoke some Gaeltacht native speakers to preserve the traditional language for another generation: but it is only an English view, and I should like to be proved wrong.

Appendices

Appendix 1

Glossary of Irish terms

Plurals, where given, are bracketed and indicate the letters to be substituted after the last consonant in the singular form. Other plurals fortuitously unrepresented in this list may be indicated internally and occur in place-names in the text, e.g. *oileán* (island), plural *oileáin*. Also note initial mutations which look like misprints to many readers when in otherwise capitalized names, e.g. An tOileáin (the Islands), Na hOileáin (of the Islands), An tSraith (various Sraith/Srah place-names). This facilitates identification of the nominative form and the use of glossaries. Initial aspiration, e.g. c/ch, d/dh, g/gh, is normal in numerous circumstances and should cause no difficulty except in pronunciation.

Several terms are omitted as obvious, notably *Bord* (Board), *Coimisiún* (Commission), and *Institiúid* (Institute).

Note that accented letters in Irish are also accented when capitalized.

Breac-Ghaeltacht Partly Irish-speaking district, usually with English predominant. Officially defined in 1926 as those whose census returns showed 25–79 per cent Irish speakers. Almost entirely demoted to Galltacht (*q.v.*) in 1956. The term remains in popular use for any weak Gaeltacht district.

Coláiste (pl. *coláistí*) **samhraidh** Irish-language summer college, usually in a Gaeltacht (as officially defined).

Coláiste Ullmhúcháin Preparatory college which prepared Irish-speaking pupils for entry to teacher training colleges. They gave privileged entry to Gaeltacht native speakers.

Comhairle Council.

Comhaltas Brotherhood; Comhaltas Uladh: Ulster regional organization of the Gaelic League.

Comharchumann(-*ai*) Co-operative; usually a producer co-operative active in land reclamation, fishing, food processing, tomato production, and/or miscellaneous manufactures and 'heritage' schemes.

The death of the Irish language

Comhchoiste   Joint committee.
Comhdháil Náisiúnta na Gaeilge   Literally National Convention of
the Irish Language, but never translated. A state-supported
language organization which organizes *coláistí samhraidh*,
etc.
Conradh   League, association, Conradh na Gaeilge: the Gaelic
League (earlier rendered Connradh na Gaedhilge).
Deontas   Grant or award for native Irish-speaking children aged 6
years and over (see pp. 50–1). Resented as patronizing
by some Gaeilgeoirí, who prefer *aitheantas* (recognition).
Deontas is usually not translated and is the normal term in
English.
Feis(-*eanna*)   Festival or fete, always Irish-language.
Fíor-Ghaeltacht   True Gaeltacht, defined in 1926 as those areas in
which 80 per cent of the people were enumerated as Irish
speakers. Now used to distinguish predominantly Irish-
speaking districts from the more anglicized parts of the
official Gaeltacht as defined in 1956.
Foras   Foundation, institute, An Foras Forbartha, the Development
Institute; An Foras Talúntais, the Agricultural Institute; An
Foras Tionscail, the Industrial Institute. The Irish names
are employed when speaking or writing English and are
rarely translated. An Foras Forbartha is sometimes
rendered in English as the National Institute of Physical
Planning and Construction Research. *Forbartha* may also
mean irritating or annoying!
Gaeilge B'l'Áth   Dublin-Irish. A term of opprobrium in the
Gaeltacht. Dublin is Baile Átha Cliath in Irish but
contracted in normal speech. Used by Gaeltacht native
speakers to mean synthetic standard Irish in its modern
simplified spelling, grammar, etc.
Gaeilgeoir(-*í*)   Irish-speaker, whether native or not. Often used
pejoratively in English to denote a language 'fanatic' and
occasionally so used in the Gaeltacht. In the text the
meaning is according to context.
Gael-Linn   Irish language organization active over a broad field,
here noted for its three-month scholarships to the
Gaeltacht. The name is 'made up' and implies 'Irish with
us', etc.; never translated.
Gaeltacht(-*aí*)   Irish-speaking district as officially defined in 1926
and redefined in 1956 within contracted boundaries. *The
Gaeltacht* may mean all the Irish-speaking districts or a
single one, according to context. The plural *Gaeltachtaí* is
employed when referring to several different ones or to

258

make clear that the reference is to more than one where the context does not suffice to do so.

Gaeltarra Éireann   The former Gaeltacht Industries Board, superseded by Údarás na Gaeltachta; *Gaeltarra*: Gael-products.

Gairm-oideachas   Vocational education.

Gairm-scoil(*-eanna*)   Vocational school, in effect secondary technical school. The hyphen is often omitted.

Galltacht   English-speaking districts in which Irish is not normally a native language. Rarely used in the plural, as it is not fragmented and covers most of Ireland.

Meán-scoil(*-eanna*)   Secondary school.

Naíonra(*-í*)   Irish-language pre-school playgroup, supported by Údarás.

Nua-Ghaeilge   New Irish. Modern literary Irish, as promoted by the state, with simplified grammar and reformed spelling. The term is used in the Gaeltacht to mean the same as Gaeilge B'l'Áth, but is less pejorative. Definitely not the normal vernacular Irish of native speakers.

Nua-Ghaeltacht   New Gaeltacht, i.e. the Irish-speaking districts as officially redefined in 1956 and subsequently extended by Orders in 1967, 1974, and 1982. Normally used only when it is necessary to distinguish between the 1926 and post-1956 entities and never seen in plural form.

Ógchlub(*-anna*)   Youth club. *Óg* is youth, *chlub* is club.

Oireachtas   (1) an tOireachtas is the legislature, i.e. both houses, (2) Oireachtas na Gaeilge, literally Assembly/Festival of the Irish Language: the Gaelic League's annual cultural festival, into which regional and local *feiseanna* 'feed'. Same as Scottish *Mòd* and *Eisteddfod Genedlaethol Cymru* (Welsh National Eisteddfod).

Pobalscoil (pl. *scoileanna pobail*)   Community school. Secondary school, hardly different from comprehensives. Alternative form is *scoil phobail*, i.e. *pobal* aspirated and in genitive.

Raidió na Gaeltachta   Gaeltacht radio service, operated by RTÉ.

Raidió Teilifís Éireann   Irish radio and television corporation: RTÉ.

Roinn na Gaeltachta   Gaeltacht Department , in effect Ministry. May be referred to as An Roinn, i.e. the Department.

Roinn Oideachais   Department of Education. *Oideachas* is education, with genitive form in title.

Scéim Labhairt na Gaeilge   *Deontas* scheme, literally 'the Irish-speaking Scheme', operated by Roinn na Gaeltachta; initially by An Roinn Oideachais.

Scéim na Scolaireachtaí Trí-mhí   Three-month Scholarships (to the

The death of the Irish language

Gaeltacht) Scheme, operated by Gael-Linn.

Scoil chuimsitheach   Comprehensive school. There is only one in a real Gaeltacht, at An Cheathrú Rua (Conamara), and a marginal one at Glenties/Na Gleannta (Donegal). Alternatively *cuimsitheach-scoil.*

Scoil(-*eanna*) lán-Ghaeilge   All-Irish school, teaching through the medium of Irish in non-Gaeltacht districts, cf. *ysgolion gymraeg* in Wales. Normal Gaeltacht all-Irish schools are not so termed and do not receive the lán-Ghaeilge schools' additional grants for 'special learning difficulties'. English is taught through English medium.

Teachta(-*í*) Dála (TD)   Member of Dáil Éireann, the lower house of the Oireachtas. Equivalent to MP.

Tuarascáil.   Report.

Údarás na Gaeltachta Gaeltacht Authority. Semi-elective body with wide investment responsibilities and considerable powers of cultural support for the Gaeltachtaí. Originally conceived as a sort of Gaeltacht parliament with wider powers of decision. Subordinate to Roinn na Gaeltachta. Succeeded Gaeltarra Éireann (*q.v.*) in 1979.

Appendix 2

Some problems in the rendering and identification of Irish place-names in the Gaeltachtaí

Any extensive reading about the Gaeltachtaí will quickly reveal apparent discrepancies in the renderings of place-names by different authors and official sources. Sometimes the differences are sufficiently wide to make one fear that one is dealing with different places, e.g. Mulrany in Mayo may be met as Mallaranny in English renderings, or as Maol Raithnighe or An Mhala Raithní in Irish. The latter is official and authenticated by the Place-names Branch of the Ordnance Survey in Dublin, which prepared the 1969 list of Irish Names of Post Towns (*Ainmneacha Gaeilge na mBailte Poist*). Maol Raithnighe preceded the spelling reform of 1948, but one of the leading Ordnance Survey researchers admits that the Maol has 'at least an equal claim' to authenticity (Ó Muraíle 1985: 112). The anglicized forms are old rivals, both currently in use on published maps. The Post Office prefers Mulrany in its own literature but neither it nor the Ordnance Survey claims authority on English renderings and my Ordnance maps say Mallaranny. This is rather an extreme case and applies to a place on the borders of the Gaeltacht, but there are many similar examples which, even if less extreme, may confuse the uninitiated and have at times worried this author. Several basic points need making:

There is a considerable lack of standardization of Irish place-names, especially in the Gaeltachtaí, where any literary tradition is recent and authority for any particular rendering of contested names is difficult to establish.

The Irish Ordnance Survey was founded under the Union and although O'Donovan and O'Curry attempted to collect correct Irish forms of all names in the initial survey the published maps gave exclusively anglicized renderings and there was no attempt to print correct Gaelic forms, as was done (if often imperfectly) in the Scottish Highlands and Islands. In addition the findings of the early survey were left unpublished and had little direct effect on the 'restoration' of the Irish forms of names undertaken by the pioneers of the Gaelic League after 1893. The enthusiasts of that period quite often produced name forms which have now acquired 'tradition' and which local people and some scholars are reluctant to drop

261

despite their being proved 'wrong' by more scholarly research.

There is still no comprehensive coverage in the Irish language of the place-names of the Gaeltacht, let alone the rest of Ireland, on Irish OS maps. The new half-inch to one mile series prints the names of major settlements bilingually but leaves most in anglicized form only. The six inches to one mile series will do better but is progressing slowly and at £30 per sheet (1987) is unlikely to have much impact outside public offices, which are few in the Gaeltachtaí. The Ordnance Survey's 1:575,000 *Éire*, a map of all Ireland in Irish, is too small to cover more than a fraction of places and covers considerably less than its 1938 predecessor. Gaeltacht places tend to be tiny and are very often townlands with scattered population and minimal nucleation to show as a 'place': hence the importance of 'post towns' (places with a post office) and schools as a focus, though in each case there may be no recognizable village in the immediate vicinity. Many Irish names are self-explanatory in Irish, so do not provoke contention, but acceptance of the spelling reform of 1948 is far from universal, particularly when the meaning of a name is uncertain and therefore the application of the rules is doubtful, possibly masking the original meaning still further. (See Mac Lysaght, p. 371, on the same problem as it affects surnames.)

The Irish one inch to one mile map series is badly obsolete and is still for sale from plates prepared in the first decade of this century. It has not been updated or replaced by a 1:50,000 series, evidently because of cost and lack of public demand.

Whilst avoiding grammatical detail it is important to note that many place names in Irish normally take the definite article *An* (The) or *Na* (plural The), and that where these precede an otherwise feminine name its initial consonant undergoes mutation. Hence, for example, Ceathrú Rua or An Cheathrú Rua, both of which are encountered, though the latter alone is strictly correct. It is not always clear whether *An* is an essential prefix to a particular name, and local usage varies with some common names such as (An) Aird Mhór. The contraction of *an* to *a'* in a medial position (e.g. Coill a' tSiáin for Coill an tSiáin) is strictly incorrect in print but usual in speech, so often encountered. Masculine names behave similarly in the genitive singular, frequent in the full names of schools. The gender of some place-name elements is variable between Gaeltachtaí, so adds to variety here. The more exotic changes (to English speakers) are often indicated in print by the use of small and higher-case letters in a way calculated to madden an English typist, e.g. Dún na nGall, Caiseal na gCorr, Ré na nDoirí, or An tSraith. The small letter in essence displaces the capital, which nevertheless gives the 'root' form of the word for dictionary identification. In names like Bun na hAbhann both the h and the A are pronounced but the A gives the root word. Needless to say, poor typing and proof reading often produce errors in maps of such names, as they also do when it comes to the use of accents. Irish uses only the acute (´) accent, but it uses it on capital letters too, unlike French; it is commonly omitted where there are no accents on the typewriter or word processor.

There are also a number of words which seem to attract accents even when they do not deserve one. Aird and Ard are the most common examples but in both cases it was usual until 1948 to put an accent on the A, and the habit persists with anyone trained under the old system. Irish writers do not worry too much about such inconsistencies, so neither should outsiders, except in aiming for some consistency in their own renderings.

The indication of the plural by internal changes, as in English mouse/mice is common in Irish: e.g. *oileán/oileáin* (island/islands). *An tOileán* (the island) becomes *Na hOileáin* (the islands). *Cill/Cealla* (church/es) occur in place-names but not as alternatives for the same place. For those with a rudimentary acquaintance with Irish or linguistics Ó Dónaill's Irish–English dictionary (*Foclóir Gaeilge–Béarla* (1977) will resolve most doubts where, as is commonly the case, a Gaeltacht name consists of ordinary dictionary elements.

Note that appendices 3 and 4 provide bilingual indices of the Irish and English names of current Gaeltacht national schools and district electoral divisions. These names do not feature in the listing which follows except where significant spelling variations in the Irish forms have been noted in the sources cited. Name forms are numbered according to source where apparently exceptional. Letter notations are:

A Normal or acceptable alternative form in local use.
D Deviant, aberrant, but not necessarily incorrect or unjustifiable.
E Assumed error or misprint.
G Correct or generally accepted form now: where two Gs are given to forms, the first has the authority of the OS Place-names Branch. 'G locally' indicates strong local support from other official sources.
NV Normal variant but not in nominative form, so should not stand alone; depends on context (usually implied datives or genitives).
O Obsolete form, antedating simplified spelling of 1948, etc.
? Doubts about categorization or statement.

The glossary is highly selective and consists mainly of names which have more or less worried the author at some time over the past thirty years, beginning as utter novice. Irish speakers should have no difficulty with most, but evidently disagree strongly over many, usually on questions of interpretation of origins and far less on grammar.

It is hoped that the examples chosen will by their variations enable deductions to be made as to other place-name equivalents not cited here.

The general tendencies should be clear from perusal of the listings, and deductions for parallel cases will usually be reliable: but it will always be necessary to check locally and/or with the Place-names Branch of the Ordnance Survey in Dublin. It must also be accepted that two alternative forms may both be held 'correct'.

It is clear that there ought to be a published and readily available official index to the Irish-language forms of the place-names of the Gaeltachtaí, in at least as much detail as is available for English names in the Census of Ireland 1901 *General Topographic Index* (Dublin 1904), which gave an alphabetical index to all the townlands and towns of Ireland. The Gaeltachtaí are now so small that to do this for them as an immediate need should take little time and produce a quite slim publication. Where Irish is no longer spoken there is no such pressing need, at least for everyday use, for guidance beyond the already provided post-town listing. There are nevertheless some 1,820 townlands in the official Gaeltacht and while over half of them no longer use Irish as their normal daily medium no government department would be wise to be first to point this out by selectively omitting them from its listing.

The Place-names Branch of the Ordnance Survey expected to publish a comprehensive list of Gaeltacht townland names in the course of 1989.

Categorization of the name form cited from a particular source as E or D is not intended to be critical of the source, which (as here) probably found it somewhere else, had a printing schedule to meet, had neither time nor expertise for corrective research, and had no ready-reference to correct or officially preferred forms. If my categorization or spelling can be shown at times to be wrong, I must offer the same range of excuses and try to resist blaming faulty accentuation on the typist or printer!

Glossary of various Irish forms of Gaeltacht place-names: a selective listing

Names are presented in geographical order by county and Gaeltacht districts are arranged from north to south and otherwise west to east, varied at times by area groupings, denoted by line spaces. The form preferred by the author is given first and where such guidance is available almost invariably follows the precedents provided by sources 12, 15, 25, 26 or 27. The common English equivalent or equivalents are given last, for cross-reference.

The raised numbers refer to the sources listed at the end of this appendix. Note that Ordnance Survey, Roinn na Gaeltachta, and Údarás na Gaeltachta sources of recent date are usually the most authoritative. The census reports, An Roinn Oideachais, and even the Orduithe na Limistéirí Gaeltachta (Gaeltacht Area Orders) are inclined to maintain obsolete or archaic forms, as are the voluntary language organizations.

The various working papers from all bodies are, not surprisingly, most prone to clerical errors, which are here ignored where obvious but may sometimes be included where the author feels uncertain.

The abbreviation Co. is used throughout to abbreviate Irish *Contae* or English *County* in relation to county names. Up to 1948 the census reports spelled it *Conndae* in Irish.

A few non-Gaeltacht places are included in the list because of frequent mention in publications about the Gaeltachtaí or because they occur in Gaeltacht lists of addresses and are likewise variable. Most names which show only slight variation are omitted and the examples here should suffice to explain them or at least put them into context.

Tír Chonaill (never correctly preceded by Co.) (A); Co. Dhún na nGall or Dún na nGall(both G); Donegal

I prefer the first alternative, on traditional grounds.

Cloch Chionnaola, Gaoth Dobhair, and Na Rosa (north-west Donegal)

Cloch Chionnaola (G); Cloch Cheann Fhaola (G locally); Cloch Chinn
      Fhaolaidh [1,8,MSS] (O); Cloghaneely.

Toraigh (G); Toraí (A); sometimes Torraí (E); Tory Island.

Machaire Robhartaigh[25] (G); Machaire Rabhartaigh[32] (G locally);
      Machaire Uí Rabhartaigh[31] (D); Magheraroarty.

An Fál Carrach (G); sometimes Fálcarrach[33] (D) or Fálcharrach (E), or
      accent omitted (E). Falcarragh, formerly Crossroads in
      English. The DED remains Crossroads, in Irish (An)
      Croisbhealach.

Gort an Choirce (G); sometimes Gort a'Choirce[14 etc] (A); Gortahork.

An Luinneach (G); An Luinnigh[34] (NV); Lunniagh.

Doirí Beaga (G) or Na Doirí Beaga[34] (A); Doire Beag'[11,31] Doire
      Beaga[31] and Doire Bheag[24]: all D or E; Derrybeg.

Na Machaireacha[8,29]; sometimes Baile Láir; Middletown. Name partly
      superseded because place absorbed into Doirí Beaga, but
      still in general use in locality.

Uaigh (G); Oileán Uaighe (A); Oileán Uigh[1] (O or E); Owey Island.

Rinn na Feirste[12] (G); Rann na Feirste[31,34] (common locally); Rinn na
      Feirsde[25] (O/A); Rann na Feirisde[3] (O/A). Rannafast.

An Earagail[15,29] (G); An tEaragal[1] (G locally); An Eiragáil[34] (E);
      Errigal.

Dún Lúiche (G); Dún Luigheach[1] (O); Dunlewy.

Na Rosa[8,21,29] (G); Na Rosann[25] (A locally, from alternative plural of
      Ros); The Rosses.

Cionn Caslach (G); Ceann Caslach (D: arguable G in Donegal dialect);

Kincasslagh.

Croithlí (G); Croichshlighe[1, 11] (O); Croichshlí [8] (contraction from preceding); Crolly.

Loch an Iúir[8, 14, 29, 32] (G); Loch an Iubhair[11, 13, 25] (25 is usually sound but this is O); Loughanure.

An additional complication is that Cnoc na Naomh (Knocknaneeve) national school is sometimes referred to as Doire Chonaire (Derryconor), the first being the hill above it and the second its townland location.

Fánaid, Ros Goill, Gleann Bhairr, An Tearmann, etc. (north-eastern outliers)

Ros Goill[8, 25] (G); Ros Guill[9, 23] (A); Ros Ghuill[3] (E); Rosguill.

Na Dúnaibh (G); occasionally seen as Na Dúine, e.g. 1959 Roinn na Gaeltachta college list (D); Downings, sometimes Downies (O) in English.

Dún Fionnachaidh (G); Dún Feannachaidh[23, 26] (O); Dunfanaghy.

Port na Bláiche (G); Port na Blaithche[11, 24] (O); Portnablagh.

Fothair[25] (G) or Fothar[11, 24] (A); Faugher.

Creamhghort[9, 12] (G); but Crannphort[1, 5, 23], etc (A, frequent locally); Cranford

Duibhlinn Riach[25] (G); Dubhlin Riabach[31] (E, from O Riabhach); Devlinreagh.

An Craoslach or Craoslach (G, A); Craosloch[11, 24, 31] (O or E); Creeslough.

An Cheathrú Chaol (G); Ceathramha Chaol[5, 9, 11, 23, 24, 31] (nevertheless O; spelled both ways in 24); Carrowkeel.

Cill Mhic Réanáin (G); Cill Mhac nEanáin 1 (O); Cill Mhic hÉanáin[24] (O, D?); Cill Mhic Néanáin 8 (E); Kilmacrenan.

Tír Chonaill Láir (Mid Donegal)

An Dúchoraidh (G); An Dubhcharraidh[1] (O); Dubhcharaidh[11, 24] (O but still in use); An Dúchoraigh[9, 20] (D); Na Dubhcharraigh[23] (D); Doocharry.

Leitir Mhic an Bhaird (G); Leitir Mhic Bhaird[31] (D); often given accent in Bháird (E); Lettermacaward.

Na Gleannta (G); Na Gleanntaí[1, 2] (O); Gleanntaí[3] (O/A); Gleanntaigh[24, 27] (?); Glenties.

An tÉadan Anfach[25] (G?); Éadan Fhionnfhaoich[31] (O?); Éadan Fhionnfhraoich[11, 24] (O+E?); Éadan Fhionnfraoch (A, widely used locally); Edeninfagh.

Baile Uí Chiaragáin (G); Baile an Chiaragáin[11, 24] (E?); Ballykerrigan.

266

Bealach Féich (G); Bealach Bó Féich[1] (O); Bealach Bó Féidh[6] (O);
Ballybofey.
An Bhinn Bhán[21]; Binn Boghaine[9, 20, 23] (?former is mountain, latter
DED, but same name and district. Latter O?); Binbane.

Tír Chonaill Thiar-Theas (South-west Donegal)

An Bhreacaigh (G); Breacach[11, 24] (?); An Bhrocaigh[25] (E); Brackey.
An Bhrocaigh[25] seems an accidental transposition from
Brocagh in the Finn valley.
Mínte na Dé[25] (G); Mín Teineadh Dé[11, 24, 31] (O); Meentinadea.
Málainn Bhig (G); Málainn Bheag[23] (G locally); Malinbeg, sometimes
two words).
Cill Charthaigh (G); Cill Chartha[1] (G locally); Cill Carthaigh[23] (E);
Kilcar.
Sliabh Tuaidh (G); Sliabh a'Tuaigh[1] (O); Slievetooey, sometimes two
words in English.
Teileann (G); Teilionn[1, 3, 4] (O); Teelin.

Co. Mhaigh Eo or Maigh Eo (A); Co. Mhuigheo (O); Mayo

Iorras and Iarthuaisceart Mhaigh Eo (Erris and north-west Mayo)

Port an Chlóidh (G); Port an Chlaidhe[1] (O); Port an Chlaí[29] (?);
Portacloy.
Ceathrú Thaidhg (G); Ceathramha na gCloch[1] (O – for Ceathrú na
gCloch): but in fact different adjacent townland,
Stonefield, now quite overshadowed by Carrowteige or
Carratigue.
Port Durlainne (G); Port Durlaíne[18] (D?); Port Urlainne (G locally?);
Port Turlainn[1] (O/A); Porturlin.
Poll an Tómais (G); Poll an tSómais[1] or Poll a' tSómais[24] are A[26];
Pollatomish or Pulathomas.
Barr na Trá (G); Barr na Trágha[1] (O); Barnatra.
Béal an Mhuirthead (G); Béal an Mhuirthid (O but in common use)
(accent often omitted, E); Belmullet.
Oiligh (G); Cuan Oilí (Elly Bay) (G); Cuan Éilí, Eilí (Both A locally);
also Eillighe[1] for the Bay and Árd Ailigh[1] for Elly Head:
(?) (assume last two O).
Inis Gé (G); Inis Géidhe[1] (O); Inishkea Islands: usually singular in
Irish; plural Insí Gé.
Gleann an Chaisil[25] (G); Gleann a'Chaisil[31] (A); Gleann Chaisil[5, 9, 23];
(?) Glencastle.

Baingear (G); Baingear Iorrais[29] (A); Beannchar or Beannchar Iorrais
   A, common locally; Beannchor[24] (E?); Bangor Erris.
Baile Chruaich (G); Baile Chruaigh[29] (D?); Baile Fiodha Cruaich[1]
   (O); Ballycroy.

Acaill and An Corrán (Achill and Corraun)

Acaill (G); Oileán Acla (Achill Island) (A); Achaill[3] (D); Achill.
Béal an Bhalláin (G); Béal a'Bhuláin[31] (?) (contentious); Bull's Mouth.
Dumha Goirt[26] (G); Dú Goirt,[8] (accent omitted); Dubhgort[1]: all
   arguable. Doogort.
Dumha Éige (G); Dú Éige[8, 9] (A, widely preferred); Dumhaigh Éige[1]
   (O); Dumhach Éige[5, 23] (A); Dooega.
An Chloich Mhóir[8, 30] (G); An Chloch Mhór[26] (A); Cloch Mór met
   locally: (?); Cloghmore.

An Corrán (G); Cnoc an Chorráin [1] (A: should strictly be the *place* in
   south-west corner of peninsula); An Corrán, Corrán Acla
   (G) or Leithinis an Chorrain[8] (lacks accent) specify whole
   peninsula; Corrán Acaille[29] (E); Corraun Achill.
Tóin ré Gaoth (G); Tóin re Gaoith[18](E?); Tóin na Gaoithe[31] (?);
   Tonragee or Tonregee.
An Mhala Raithní (G); An Maol Raithní (A); Maol Raithnighe (O);
   Maol Rathnaighe[24] (?); Mulrany or Mallaranny.

Maigh Eo–Gaillimh; Mayo–Galway

*Dúiche Sheoigheach (G); Dúiche Sheoighe[32, etc.] (A: common
   contraction); Dúithche Sheoigheach (O); Joyce's Country.*

Approximate pronunciation *Dookha Hoyakh*
An tSraith (G); An Srath[5] (D); Na Sraithe (NV); Srah.
Partraí (G); Partraighe[1, 9, 23] (O); Partry, Partree, or Portroyal.
Tuar Mhic Éadaigh (G); Tuar Mhic Éadaí[33] (A); Tuar Mhic Éide[1, 13]
   (O); Tourmakeady.
Coill an tSiáin[25, 34] (G); Coill a'tSiáin (A); Coill an tSidheáin (O); Coill
   a' tSídhean[31] (E); Cill an tSidheán[1] (E); arguable re. Coill
   or Cill; Killatiane or Killateeaun.
Fionnaithe (G); Fionnmhuigh[1] (O); Finny.
An Chloch Bhreac (G); An Chloch Breac[24] (E); Cloghbrack,
   Cloughbrack.
An Fhairche (G); the possible Fairche is never seen; an intrusive accent
   on An Fháirche is E but quite common; Clonbur.

268

Conga (G); Cunga (E) often encountered; Cong.
Corr na Móna (G); Cor na Móna[13] (O); Cor na Mónadh[1] (O); Cornamona.

Co. na Gaillimhe or Gaillimh (G); Galway

Conamara Theas (South Connemara)

Sraith Salach (G); Srath Salach[1] (O); Recess.
An Teach Dóite (G); An Teach Dóighte[1] (O); Cros an Mháma[13] (D/A); Cros a'Mháma[16, 24] (A); Cross Bhóthar Mháma (Maam Crossroad)[31] (D/A but should be Crosbhóthar . . .) (Cross, encountered elsewhere, is E in Irish); Maam Cross.
Maíros[25] (G); Maigh Iorras[29] (O); Maighiorrais[13] (E); Muighros[24, 31] (A); Muigh Iorras[5, 9, 23] (O); Moyrus.
Glinsce (G); Glinnsce[1] (O); Glinsc[13] (E); Glinsk.
An Cnoc Buí[9] (G); An Cnoc Buidhe[5, 23, 29] (O: but note odd reversion between 9 and 23); Knockboy.
Carna (G); often Cárna (E, but A locally); Carna.
An Aird Mhór (G); An Árd Mhór[1] (O); Aird Mhór[24] (A); An Aird Mhóir[31] (NV?); Ardmore.
Maínis[25] (G); Maoinis[34] (A); Muighinis[1, 24] (O); Muínis[8, 15] (arguable A); Mynish or Mweenish.

Scríb (G: but often no accent); Scríob[8] (E?); Screeb.
Camas (G); but Camus[5, 9, 23, 32, 33] (D) is at least as common; Camus.
Leitir Mucú (G); Leitir Mucadh[34] (O); Lettermacow, Lettermuckoo.
Béal an Daingin (G); Béal an Daingean[27] (27 has previous too) (E?); Bealandangan or Bealadangan.
An Cheathrú Rua (G); Ceathrú Ruadh[24] (E: hybrid, half O); An Ceathrú Rua[31] (E); An Cheathramha Ruadh[1] (O); Carraroe.
Gleann Mhic Mhuirinn (Roinn na Gaeltachta MS map); Gleann Mhac Muirinn[1, 8] (?); Glenicmurrin.
Casla (G); cf. Coisdealbha[13] (D): translates anglicized name of Costelloe Lodge, using the Irish form of the family name, but Costelloe is here an English corruption of Casla; Cashla or Costelloe, latter O).
Na Doiriú (G but not locally); Doireadha[31] (G locally: contraction ignored); Derroogh, Derreagh.

Leitir Calaidh (G); Leitir Caladh[34] (A); Lettercallow.
Inis Barra[1]; Inis Bearachain[8]; Inis Barr a'Chuain (Roinn na Gaeltachta MS map) (from local usage); Inishbarra.

Tír an Fhia (G); Tír an Fhiaidh[24, 31] (latter spells it both ways) (O);
    Teeranea, Teernee.
Garmna (G); Garomna[1, 13, etc.] (O); Gorumna.
Leitir Mealláin (G); Leitir Mhullan[13, 16] (13 uses both) (E);
    Lettermullan.

Cois Fharraige (G); Cois Fhairrge (O); no English equivalent;
    pronounced Cush Arrigger, with only a touch of i.
An Tulaigh[25] (G); An Tulach[18, 24] (G locally); Tulla[33] (E); Tulla.
Sailearna (G); Sailchearnach[5, 9, 13, 23] (O); Silerna, Selerna, or Salerna.
Na Forbacha (G); Na Foirbeacha[13] (O); Forbach[11, 24] (E); (S N-) Na
    bhForbacha [31] (NV); Furbogh, sometimes Furbo or Forbo.

Doire Oirthir Ghlinna[25] (G?); Doire Glinne[31] (Doire Ghlinne is local
    contraction and A); Derryerglinna.
Tulaigh Mhic Aodháin[25] (G); Tulach Aodháin[5, 9, 23] (A, common);
    Tullach Uí Chadhain[31] (A – but should be Tulach);
    Tullokyne.
Maigh Cuilinn (G); Magh Cuilinn[5, 9, 23, 24] (A: sometimes with double l
    – E, or accent on á – E); Má Cuilinn, occasionally
    encountered, is a misleading contraction (E); Moycullen.

Gaillimh Láir; An Achréidh (Mid Galway)

Eanach Dhúin (G); Eannach Dhúin[9, 23] (O/A); h sometimes omitted to
    give Dúin (E); Eanach a'Chuain[13, 16] (O/A); Annaghdown.
Baile Chláir (G); fuller name is Baile Chláir na Gaillimhe (A);
    Claregalway.
Ceathrú an Bhrúnaigh (G) but published references are to Ceathramha
    Bhrún[5, 9, 23] (O), for which modern Ceathrú Bhrún is
    sometimes rendered.
Mionlach[24, 25] (G); Mionloch[5, 31] (D/O); Menlough, Menlagh.
Cnoc Mhaol Drise[25] (G); Cnoc Maol Dris[24] (E); Brierhill (*sic*).
An Carn Mór (G); Cearn Mór[31] (E); Carnmore.

Oileáin Árann (Aran Islands)

Árainn is used for the entire group but sometimes for the main island
    (Inishmore) alone, and both are correct. Inis Mór (big
    island) is also current, but the DED of that name covers all
    the islands, so is liable to confuse. Inis Mhór is sometimes
    encountered but is E, as a grammatical exception. Inis
    Móir[13] (NV). Aran (-Islands). Inis Mór/Inishmore should

be confined to the larger island, unless DED specified.
Inis Meáin (G); Inis Mheán[13] (E); Inis Meadhóin[1, 24] (24 without
 accent) (O); Inishmaan or sometimes Inishmeane.
Inis Oírr (G); Inis Oirthir[1, 8, 13, 31] (O but A); Inis Thiar[3] (E); Inisheer.

Co. Chiarraí or Ciarraí (G); Co. Chiarraighe or Ciarraighe (O);
 Kerry

Corca Dhuibhne (Corkaguiny)
Approximate pronunciation *Korka Geena* (hard g)
Baile Dháith (G); Ballydavid: often confused with Baile na nGall (e.g.
 on 30 and the well produced Údarás Map of Ireland with
 Gaeltacht Regions, n.d., *c.* 1986, mainly in English); Baile
 na nGall (Ballynagall) is over two miles south of Baile
 Dháith (Ballydavid) but usage is even confused locally and
 is enshrined by duplication on the one-inch map, last
 revised in 1899. Ceann Bhaile Dháith (Ballydavid Head) is
 fixed, near the true Baile Dháith. Coastguards originally
 based at Baile Dháith mistranslated it as Ballydavid and
 took the name with them when transferred to Baile na
 nGall. The use of Ballydavid (or Baile Dháith) for Baile na
 nGall should be avoided.
An Fheothanach (G); Feothanach[25, 33] (A); Feothanaigh (NV);
 Feohanagh.
Baile an Mhoraigh[31] (G); Baile an Mhúraigh (OS MS source *c.* 1970)
 (?); Moorestown.
An Mhuiríoch (G), occasionally Muiríoch (A); Murreagh. The real
 complication here is that the school is called Smeirbhic
 (Smerwick), though the OS maps mark the latter as a
 clachan or hamlet at the opposite side of Smerwick
 Harbour in the townland of Ard na Caithne. Smeirbhic/
 Smerwick seems to have been used in English as a district
 name for the whole area round the Harbour (a large bay)
 but the usage has died and even confuses local people. The
 school is at Muiríoch/Murreagh, which is both the small
 nucleation and the wider townland, which also includes
 Baile na nGall. Smerwick Harbour is Cuan Ard na Caithne
 in Irish *(cuan,* bay) and Smeirbhic is an Old Norse
 derivative, probably originally the name of the inlet (O.N.
 vík) and never precisely attached to one place, unlike
 Heilbhic/Helvick in Waterford, *q.v.* The whole bay used to
 be Cuan Smeirbhic in Irish.

Baile an Fheirtéaraigh (G); Baile an Fheirtéirigh[3] (O); Baile 'n
   Fhirtéaraigh (A, common locally); the school is often
   described as SN (National School) an Fhirtéaraigh[31, 33]
   (NV); Baile an Fhirtéiraigh is A locally; Ballyferriter.
Baile Uí Shé[34] (G); Baile hÉ[18] (D); Ballyhea: alternative name for Na
   Gleannta school, see below. Named Ballyheabought on OS
   one inch map, rendering Baile Uí Shé Bocht, infrequently
   used for the school.
Na Gleannta (G) (and see Baile Uí Shé, above); sometimes An Gleann,
   but correctly Na Gleannta (plural), because there are two
   together and they are usually referred to collectively:
   Glens, Glen, Glin. Na Gleannta/Glin are also confusingly
   but officially employed for the much larger DED, which
   covers Dingle's rural surroundings, including the two Na
   Gleannta townlands.
Dún Chaoin (G); Dún Caoin[5, 23] (E); Dunquin.
Na Blascaodaí[30] (G); Na Blascaoidí[3] (E); cf. An Blascaod Mór[14] (Great
   Blasket, often An tOileán Mór, Big Island); the Blaskets.
Sliabh an Iolair[14] (G); Sliabh an Fhiolair (O); Mount Eagle
   (translation); cf. Cnoc Bhréanainn: Brandon Mountain.
Ceann Trá (G); Ceann Trágha[24] (O); Fionntrá[33] (A but O/E for village);
   Fionntráigh[1, 5, 9, 23, 29] (O); Ventry. Really two different
   townlands confused. The village is in Ceann Trá townland
   and is what is usually meant by Ventry and was intended
   by most non-local users of Fionntrá, etc. Ventry Harbour is
   usually Cuan Fionntrá still. Government officials seem to
   have caused the confusion by transferring the name Ventry
   to what had been Cantra *c.* 1835.
Cill Mhic an Domhnaigh (G); Cill Mhic a'Domhnaigh (A);
   Kilvicadonig.

An Daingean (G); Daingean Uí Chúis (A, fuller traditional);
   occasionally Daingean Uí Chúise (?); Dingle.
An Bhreac-chluain (G); An Breac Cluain[25] (E); Brackluin.
Caisleán na Mine Airde[25] (G); Caisleán na Minairde[31] (A, general
   locally); Minard Castle; NB. Mináird is prevalent, with or
   without the accent, for Minard itself.
Also note Trá Lí (G), Tráigh Lí (O), and cf. Trálí, Tráighlí, both D but
   common; Tralee.

Uíbh Ráthach (Iveragh)

Approximate pronunciation *Eev Raa* (long a).

Doire Ianna (G); Doire Fhiana[1] (O); Derriana.

An Chillín Liath (G); Cillín Liath (A); Killeenleeha or Killeenleagh.

Cill Mhic Ciaráin[26] (G?); Cill Mhic Ciarnain (MSS) (E and/or O?); Kilmackerrin, Kilmakeerin, Kilmackieran.

Dún Géagáin (G); Dúngéagáin (A); Dungeagan: the village in Baile an Sceilg.

Baile an Sceilg (G); Baile na Scealg[3] (O); Baile an Sceillig[5, 7, 8, 9, 23] (O); Ballinskelligs.

An Coireán (G); An Cuirreán[1, 4] (O); An Corrán[14] (O/D); Waterville.

Doire Fhíonáin (G); Doire Fionán[23] (E); Darrynane or Derrynane.

Cathair Dónall (G); Cathair Domhnall[1, 5, 23] (O); Caherdaniel.

Co. Chorcaí (G) or Corcaigh (G) (*sic*); Co. Chorcaighe (O); Cork

Múscraí Uí Fhloinn (West Muskerry)

District name sometimes spelt Muscraí (E); or Musgraí . . . (O); Múscraí without suffixes is G.

Baile Bhuirne (G); Baile Bhúirne[27] (D); Baile Mhúirne[3, 18, 24, 28, 32, 33] . . . (D) (persistent rivals locally, with or without accent); Ballyvourney.

Barr Duínse[25] (G); Barr d'Inse[31, 34] and Barr Dínse are G locally; Bardinch or Bardinchy.

Cúil an Bhuacaigh (G) or Cúl/Cúil a'Bhuacaigh (G locally); Coolavokig.

Cluain Droichead[12, 25] (G); Cluain Droichid[24] (A?: concurrent locally); Clondrohid

Ré na nDoirí[25] (G); Rae na nDoirí[12, 27, 31] (O); Reananerree.

Baile Uí Bhuaigh (G); Baile Uí Bhuadhaigh[1] (O); Baile Uí Bhuaidh (O, locally A) Baile Bhuaidh[5] (O/E); Ballyvoge or Ballyvoig.

Maigh Chromtha[1, 12, 14, 29] (G); Magh Chromtha (A locally), sometimes with accent wrongly added on Mágh[7, 32]; Maghchromtha[3, 24] is variant of preceding (D); Má Cromtha[8] (D), Mochromtha[1, 2] (O); Macroom.

Cill na Martra[17, 23, 25, 33] (G); Cill na Martar[5, 23] (?); Kilnamartery.

Béal Átha an Ghaorthaidh (G); Béal Átha an Ghaorthaigh[34] (E): Béal Átha Ghaorthaidh[7, 9, 24, 31] (D or E); Ballingeary, but Bealanageary in all Census vols.

Co. Phort Láirge or Port Láirge (G), sometimes as one word (A); Waterford

Few names will normally be encountered from this tiny moribund

Gaeltacht, and this residue of *Na Déise* (Decies) is usually referred to
as An Rinn (Ring), its main agglomeration. Ringville, the census's
English name for the DED, is obsolete for normal purposes. Note the
following:

An Rinn (G); Rinn (E); An Rinn Ó gCuanach is fuller traditional form;
    Ring.

Aird Mhór[15] (G); An Áird Mhór (A locally); Áird Mhór[1] (O); Ard
    Mhór[23] (E); Ardmore.

Baile Mhac Airt (G); Baile Mhic Airt[31, etc.] (D; A locally); Ballymacart.

Heilbhic (G) is sometimes rendered Helbhic. This, for Helvick, an Old
    Norse name, is no more authoritative than the anglicisms
    concocted from Irish names: cf. Smeirbhic in Corca
    Dhuibhne (Kerry).

**Co. Na Mí or An Mhí (G); Co. Na Midhe or An Mhidhe (O);
Meath**

Again minute, so few names likely to be encountered. Note only: Baile
Ghib (G), sometimes Baile Gib[e, g, 10] (E or D); Gibstown.
Ráth Cairn (G); Ráth Chairn[17, 28, 33] (E); Rathcarran, Rathcarne, etc.

References

1. *Éire 1:500,000* (1938) Dublin: Ordnance Survey. (Map of Ireland in the Irish language and script.)
2. *Census of Population, Ireland, 1936, vol. 8, Irish Language*, (1940) Dublin: Department of Industry and Commerce.
3. *Memorandum for the Taoiseach: a Board for the Gaeltacht* (1953) Dublin: Comhdháil Náisiúnta na Gaeilge. (With six maps.)
4. *Límistéirí Gaeltachta 1956* (1956) Dublin: Ordnance Survey. (Map, in Irish, of the Gaeltacht areas as defined in 1956. Scale 1:633,600.)
5. *Ordú na Limistéirí Gaeltachta 1956*, Gaeltacht Areas Order, Dublin: Department of the Taoiseach.
6. Comhdháil Náisiúnta na Gaeilge (1957) *Tuarascáil Chinnblianna 1956-57*, Annual Report, Baile Átha Cliath.
7. *White Paper on the Restoration of the Irish Language* (1965) Dublin: Oifig an tSoláthair.
8. *Complete Atlas of the British Isles* (1965) London: Reader's Digest. (First such atlas to give extensive presentation of Irish versions of names on ordinary topographic maps of Ireland.)
9. *Census of Population of Ireland, 1961*, vol. 8, *Irish Language* (1966) Dublin: Central Statistics Office.
10. *Ordú na Limistéar Gaeltachta 1967*, Gaeltacht Areas Order, Dublin: Department of the Taoiseach.
11. *List of National Schools* (1967) Dublin: An Roinn Oideachais (Department of Education). (Arranged alphabetically according to location.)
12. *Ainmneacha Gaeilge na mBailte Poist*, Irish names of post towns (1969) Baile Átha Cliath: An tSuirbhéireacht Ordanáis (Ordnance Survey). (Authoritative.)
13. Mac Aodha, B. S. (1969) *Galway Gaeltacht Survey*, 2 vols., Galway: University College.
14. *List of Recognised Post-primary schools 1969–70* (1970) Dublin: An Roinn Oideachais (Department of Education).
15. *Éire 1: 575,000* (1970) Baile Átha Cliath: An tSuirbhéireacht Ordanáis (Ordnance Survey). (Authoritative map of Ireland in Irish.)
16. Hanly, D. P. (1971) *Planning Report on the Galway Gaeltacht*, Dublin: An Foras Forbartha. (Has list of place-names at end.)
17. Ó Riagáin, P., ed. (1971) *The Gaeltacht Studies*, vol. 1, *Development Plan for the Gaeltacht*, Dublin: An Foras

Forbartha. (Has index of place-names at pp. 120–1, and several useful maps.)

18. Gaeltarra Éireann (1971) *Tuarascáil Bhliantúil 1970*, Annual report, Baile Átha Cliath. Also miscellaneous working papers, including lists of locations of minor industries 1970–1.

19. *Ordú na Limistéar Gaeltachta 1974*, Gaeltacht Areas Order, Dublin: Department of the Taoiseach.

20. *Census of Population, Ireland 1971*, vol. 8, *Irish Language* (1976) Dublin: Central Statistics Office.

21. *Atlas of Ireland* (1979) Dublin: Royal Irish Academy. (Has no Irish versions on ordinary topographic maps; one single-sheet map in Irish, with few names on it; and a one-page glossary of Irish equivalents of anglicized names; cf. Reader's Digest atlas.)

22. *Ordú na Limistéar Gaeltachta 1982*, Gaeltacht Areas Order, Dublin: Department of the Taoiseach.

23. *Census of Population, Ireland, 1981*, vol. 6, *Irish Language* (1985) Dublin: Central Statistics Office.

24. *List of National Schools* 1984–5 (1985) Dublin: An Roinn Oideachais (Department of Education). (Arranged alphabetically according to location.)

25. *Tuarascáil an Chomhchoiste um Oideachas sa Ghaeltacht*, Report of Advisory Committee on Education in the Gaeltacht (1986) Baile Átha Cliath: Oifig an tSoláthair. (Authoritative, though with three or four errors.)

26. Ó Muraíle, N. (1985) *Mayo Places – their Names and Origins*, Dublin: FNT. (Authoritative.)

27. Údarás na Gaeltachta (1986) *Tuarascáil agus Cuntais 1985*, Report and Accounts, with English summary. Na Forbacha: Údarás.

28. *List of Post-primary Schools 1985–86* (1986) Dublin: An Roinn Oideachais (Department of Education).

29. Room, A. (1986) *Dictionary of Irish Place-names*, Belfast: Appletree. (Covers 3,000 names but still omits most Gaeltacht places because they are so small or lack village nuclei.)

30. *Ireland/Irlande 1:400,000* (1986) Paris: Michelin. (Map giving selective presentation of Irish versions of names; far better than most published single-sheet maps of Ireland and than the Ordnance Survey half-inch to one mile series, but selection is arbitrary, e.g. in north-west Donegal anglicized Burtonport is given bilingually and Derrybeg in anglicized form only. Usually follows 12 and 15, unless names on

neither.)

31. *Computer Print-out of List of National Schools and their Heads,*
January 1987 (1987) Dublin: An Roinn Oideachais
(Department of Education). (Block capitals without
accents: references here assume correct accents.)
32. Comhdháil Náisúnta na Gaeilge (1987) *List of Coláistí Samhraidh/*
Summer Colleges, Dublin: CNG.
33. Údarás na Gaeltachta: *Miscellaneous Working Papers*: naíonraí
(1986), ógchlubanna (1986–7), external Irish language
courses (1986), Na Forbacha: Údarás.
34. Gael-Linn (1987) *Miscellaneous Schools and College Lists,*
Dublin: Gael-Linn.

Gaeltacht national schools 1981–2 and 1985–6: numbers and proportions of pupils in receipt of grant (*deontas*) under the Irish-speaking Scheme (Scéim Labhairt na Gaeilge)

Schools are classified according to location in each separate Gaeltacht, in rough geographic order from north to south and west to east, to aid location on maps. Irish-language name forms are given first, as they are official in the Gaeltacht. Variant spellings are nevertheless often encountered in official publications, ignoring the modern simplified versions. Anglicized forms are also given here as a rough guide to pronunciation for readers unfamiliar with Irish orthography. They are not standardized but are the forms normally found on topographic maps of Ireland. Maps before about 1970 hardly ever used the Irish versions of Gaeltacht place-names.

County, Gaeltacht, and location of school	No. on Rolls		No. awarded deontas		% awarded deontas	
	1981/2	*1985/6*	*1981/2*	*1985/6*	*1981/2*	*1985/6*

Co. Dhún na nGall/Thír Chonaill (Donegal)

Cloch Chionnaola, Gaoth Dobhair, agus Na Rosa (Cloghaneely, Gweedore, and the Rosses: north-west Donegal)

Toraigh (Tory)	36	22	17	14	47·2	63·6
Mín an Chladaigh (Meenaclady)	110	97	79	66	71·8	68·0 G
Machaire Robhairtaigh (Magheraroarty)	70	71	52	57	74·3	80·3 C, G
Cnoc na Naomh (Knocknaneave)	143	136	107	73	74·8	53·7 G
Gort an Choirce (Gortahork)	35	33	22	15	62·8	45·5 C
An Fál Carrach* (Falcarragh)	305	357	97	54	31·8	15·1 N, C
Caiseal na gCorr (Cashelnagore)	97	81	77	52	79·4	64·2
An Luinneach (Lunniagh)	207	173	159	120	76·8	69·4 N, G
Doirí Beaga (Derrybeg)	208	228	135	134	64·9	58·8 N, C, G
An Bun Beag (Bunbeg)	188	162	137	92	72·9	56·8 N,G

County, Gaeltacht, and location of school	No. on Rolls		No. awarded deontas		% awarded deontas	
	1981/2	*1985/6*	*1981/2*	*1985/6*	*1981/2*	*1985/6*
Dobhar (Dore)	83	79	57	37	68·6	46·8
Béal Cruite* (Belcruit)	75	75	2	3	2·7	4·0
Anagaire** (Annagary)	197	201	62	57	31·5	28·4 N
Rinn na Feirsde (Rannafast)	101	92	79	78	78·2	84·8 G
Loch an Iúir** (Loughanure)	61	56	34	27	55·7	48·2 N, C
Árainn Mhór I*	82	68	25	5	30·5	7·3 ⎫
Árainn Mhór II (Aranmore)	64	69	29	23	45·3	33·3 ⎬ N, C
An Clochán Liath* (Dungloe, Dunglow)	325	315	17	17	5·2	5·4 N
Mín na Manrach (Meenamara)	17	14	12	11	70·6	78·6

Fánaid, Ros Goill, Gleann Bhairr, An Tearmann, etc. (Fanad, Rosguill, Glenvar, Termon and the north-eastern outliers)

	No. on Rolls		No. awarded deontas		% awarded deontas	
An Caiseal** (Cashel/Fanad)	116	126	77	44	66·3	34·9 N
Na Dúnaibh* (Downings/Rosguill)	147	145	54	20	36·7	13·4
Maigh Ráithe* (Murroe)	52	34	8	6	15·4	17·6
Dún Fionnachaidh* (Dunfanaghy)	76	60	4	1	5·3	1·7
Fothair* (Faugher)	37	NR	1	NR	2·7	NR
Carraig Airt* (Carrigart)	136	NR	0	NR	0·0	NR
Duibhlinn Riach* (Devlinreagh)	101	141	27	16	26·7	11·3
Gleann Bhairr* (Glenvar)	22	NR	6	NR	27·3	NR
Craoslach* (Creeslough)	178	155	2	2	1·1	1·3
An Tearmann* (Termon)	94	101	7	3	7·4	3·0
Leitir Ceanainn* (Letterkenny) (Special)	23	NR	1	NR	4·3	NR
Cill Mhic Réanáin* (Kilmacrenan)	131	NR	0	NR	0·0	NR

Tír Chonaill Láir (Mid Donegal)

	No. on Rolls		No. awarded deontas		% awarded deontas	
An Dúchoraidh* (Doocharry)	33	28	5	4	15·2	14·3
Leitir Mhic An Bháird* (Lettermacaward)	80	69	25	8	31·3	11·6
Baile na Finne** (Fintown)	63	42	48	33	76·2	78·6
Baile Uí Chiaragáin* (Ballykerrigan)	36	NR	0	NR	0·0	NR
Cill Taobhóg* (Kilteevoge)	52	60	10	7	19·2	11·7
An Coimín** (Comeen)	67	51	50	30	74·6	58·8 C, G
An tÉadan Anfach** (Edeninfagh)	52	47	34	19	65·4	40·4

County, Gaeltacht, and location of school	No. on Rolls		No. awarded deontas		% awarded deontas	
	1981/2	1985/6	1981/2	1985/6	1981/2	1985/6
Na Gleannta*						
(Glenties) (2)	199	NR	1	NR	0·5	NR

Tír Chonaill Thiar-Theas (South-west Donegal)

An Bhreacaigh* (Brackey)	80	68	5	1	6·3	1·5
Mínte na Dé**						
(Meentinadea)	34	29	13	12	38·2	41·4
An Caiseal*						
(Cashel/Glencolumkille)	154	145	47	19	30·5	13·1
Mín an Aoire**						
(Meenaneary)	37	43	25	15	67·6	34·9
An Charraig* (Carrick)	166	167	53	19	31·9	11·4 N
Cill Charthaigh* (Kilcar)	180	171	53	15	29·4	8·8 N

Co. Mhaigh Eo (Mayo)

Iorras agus Iarthuaisceart Mhaigh Eo (Erris and north-west Mayo)

Ceathrú Thaidhg**						
(Carrowteige)	71	84	52	43	73·2	51·2 C
Ros Dumhach* (Rossdoagh)	59	66	6	3	10·2	4·5
Poll an Tómais*						
(Pollatomish)	84	NR	3	NR	3·6	NR
Barr na Trá* (Barnatra)	48	44	0	1	0·0	2·3
Gleann na Muaidhe*						
(Glenamoy)	45	52	2	1	4·4	1·9
An Chorrchloch* (Corclogh)	66	NR	5	NR	7·5	NR
Béal an Mhuirthead*						
(Belmullet)(2)	198	186	11	4	5·5	2·2
An Eachléim**						
(Aghleam)	113	104	64	53	56·6	51·0 C
Gleann an Chaisil*						
(Glencastle)	46	NR	0	NR	0·0	NR
An tSraith* (Srah)	56	NR	2	NR	3·5	NR
Gaoth Sáile* (Geesala)	109	117	9	22	8·2	18·8
Dumha Thuama*						
(Doohooma)	118	NR	1	NR	0·8	NR

Acaill agus An Corrán (Achill and Corraun)

Béal an Bhalláin*						
(Bullsmouth)	41	NR	0	NR	0·0	NR
Bun an Churraidh**						
(Bunacurry)	102	106	29	29	28·4	27·4

County, Gaeltacht, and location of school	No. on Rolls		No. awarded deontas		% awarded deontas	
	1981/2	1985/6	1981/2	1985/6	1981/2	1985/6
Sáile** (Salia)	48	41	7	14	14·6	34·1
Gob an Choire* (Achill Sound)	100	NR	0	NR	0·0	NR
An Doirín* (Derreen)	69	43	8	3	11·6	7·0
Tóin Ré Gaoth* (Tonragee)	47	39	9	13	19·1	33·3
An Corrán** (Corraun)	70	69	15	17	21·4	24·6

Maigh Eo – Gaillimh (Mayo – Galway)

Dúiche Sheoigheach (Joyce's Country)

An tSraith** (Srah/L. Mask)	48	46	6	17	12·5	37·0
An Trian Lár*† (Trean Middle)	79	84	14	13	17·7	15·5
Coill an tSiáin** (Killitiane)	46	42	22	21	47·8	50·0
Páirc an Doire** (Derrypark)	25	33	17	9	68·0	27·3
An Chloch Bhreac** (Cloghbrack)	43	43	30	27	69·8	62·8
An Fhairche* (Clonbur)	80	74	5	5	6·2	6·8 N
Corr na Móna** (Cornamona)	74	72	39	58	52·7	80·6 G
Tír na Cille* (Teernakill)	35	23	0	1	0·0	4·3

(Last two rows braced with C)

Co. Na Gaillimhe (Galway)

Conamara Theas (South Connemara)

Leithinis Charna (Carna Peninsula)

Sraith Salach** (Recess)	48	52	0	13	0·0	25·0
Maíros (Moyrus)	51	51	47	38	92·2	74·5
An Aird Thiar (Ard, West)	44	54	33	47	75·0	87·0
Maínis (Mynish, Mweenish)	24	30	24	24	100·0	80·0 G
Carna**	90	89	30	47	33·3	52·8 N, C, G
An Aird Mhór (Ardmore)	45	36	27	30	60·0	83·3 G
Cill Chiaráin** (Kilkieran)	85	92	54	58	63·5	63·0

County, Gaeltacht, and location of school	No. on Rolls		No. awarded deontas		% awarded deontas	
	1981/2	1985/6	1981/2	1985/6	1981/2	1985/6
Mórthír Láir (Central mainland)						
An Gort Mór (Gortmore)	60	50	49	43	81·7	86·0 G
Ros Muc (Rosmuck)	62	49	47	45	75·8	91·2 N, C, G
Camas (Camus)	60	54	41	41	68·3	75·9 C, G
Leitir Mucú (Lettermacow)	68	68	50	60	73·5	88·2 G
An Tuairín (Tooreen)	84	69	76	47	90·5	68·1 C, G
An Cheathrú Rua (Carraroe)(2)	290	293	181	200	62·4	68·3 N, C, G
Ros an Mhíl, Na Doiriú (Rossaveel, Derreagh)	143	117	104	91	72·7	77·8 N, G
Na hOileáin (The Islands)						
Leitir Móir (Lettermore)	53	45	40	35	75·5	77·8 N, C. G
Leitir Caladh (Lettercallow)	38	40	33	36	86.8	90·0 G
Tír an Fhia (Teeranea)	59	58	41	35	69·5	60·3 C, G
An Cnoc (Knock)	28	31	23	25	82·1	80·6 N, G
An Droim (Drim)	54	55	41	44	75·9	80·0 G
An Trá Bháin (Trawbane, Trawbaun)	48	42	41	40	85·4	95·2 C
Leitir Mealláin (Lettermullen)	46	52	40	40	87·0	76·9
Cois Fharraige						
An Tulaigh (Tully)	126	129	88	96	69·8	74·4 G
Sailearna (Selerna) (Inveran)	179	205	108	134	60·3	65·4 N, C, G
An Spidéal** (Spiddal, Spiddle)(2)	291	282	176	146	60·5	51·8 N, C, G
Na Forbacha** (Furbogh)	117	107	15	40	12·8	37·4 N, G
Ceantair Imeallacha (Marginal districts)						
Bearna* (Barna)	254	238	11	17	4·3	7·1 N
Doire Oirthir Ghlinne* (Derryerglinna)	16	NR	0	NR	0·0	NR
Uachtar Ard* (Oughterard)(2)	197	NR	6	NR	3·0	NR
	NR	86	NR	6	NR	7·0
Tulaigh Mhic Aodháin** (Tullokyne)	50	40	0	12	0·0	30·0
Maigh Cuilinn* (Moycullen)	232	235	12	5	5·1	2·1

County, Gaeltacht, and location of school	No. on Rolls		No. awarded deontas		% awarded deontas	
	1981/2	*1985/6*	*1981/2*	*1985/6*	*1981/2*	*1985/6*
Baile Nua, Maigh Cuilinn** (Newtown, Moycullen)	NR	83	NR	58	NR	69·8
Na Tuairíní** (Tooreeny)	58	49	20	26	34·5	53·1
An Bhuaile Bheag* (Boleybeg)	61	84	0	2	0·0	2·4

Gaillimh Láir (Mid Galway) (including parts of Galway city)

Mionlach* (Menlough)	100	110	1	1	1·0	0·9
An Caisleán Gearr* (Castlegar)	105	104	3	1	2·8	1·0
Cnoc Mhaol Drise* (Brierhill)	129	NR	0	NR	0·0	NR
Gaelscoil Dara ‡ (in Galway)	NR	37	NR	7	NR	18·9 ⎫
Scoil Fhursa* (in Galway)	280	276	11	12	3·9	4·3 ⎬ N, C
Scoil Iognáid* (in Galway)	314	446	13	13	4·1	2·9 ⎭
An Rinn Mhór* (Renmore)	109	NR	2	NR	1·8	NR
Eanach Dhúin*/Cor an Dola (Annaghdown/ Corrandulla)	94	NR	2	NR	2·1	NR
Baile Chláir* (Claregalway)	231	287	5	3	2·2	1·0
An Carn Mór** (Cammore)	91	118	22	24	24·2	20·3

Oileáin Árann (Aran Islands)

Eoghanacht (Onaght)	39	33	25	28	64·1	84·8 ⎫
Fearann an Choirce (Oatquarter)	26	28	22	21	84·6	75·0 C ⎬ 1xG
Cill Rónáin (Kilronan)	72	100	63	41	87·5	41·0 ⎭
Inis Meáin (Inishmaan)	30	27	25	24	83·3	88·9 C, G
Inis Oírr (Inisheer)	54	40	45	37	83·3	92·5 N, G

Co. Chiarrai (Kerry)

Corca Dhuibhne (Corkaguiny)

An Fheothanach (Feohanagh)	77	75	56	59	72·7	78·7 N, C, G

County, Gaeltacht, and location of school	No. on Rolls		No. awarded deontas		% awarded deontas	
	1981/2	1985/6	1981/2	1985/6	1981/2	1985/6
An Mhuiríoch (Murreagh)	59	63	42	44	71·2	69·8 N, C, *G*
Baile an Fheirtéaraigh (Ballyferriter)	100	97	79	72	79·0	74·2 N, *G*
Dún Chaoin (Dunquin)	25	29	14	16	56·0	55·2 *G*
Cill Mhic An Domhnaigh (Kilvicadonig)	24	29	10	19	41·7	65·5 C, *G*
Ceann Trá** (Ventry)	66	72	47	45	71·2	62·5 N, C, *G*
Na Gleannta** (Glens)	28	43	22	22	78·6	51·2 G
An Daingean* (Dingle) (2)	260	249	44	46	16·9	18·5 N
Cluain Churtha** (Clooncurra/Lispole)	71	92	33	24	46·5	26·1 ⎫
Caisleán na Míne Airde**† (Minard Castle)	38	25	30	12	78·9	48·0 *G* ⎬ C
An Bhreac-chluain* (Brackluin/Anascaul)	137	NR	8	NR	5·8	NR
An Clochán** (Cloghane)	55	56	26	16	47·3	28·6 C, *G*
Abha an Chaisle*/An Com (Aughacasla/Camp)	124	NR	1	NR	0·8	NR
Uíbh Ráthach (Iveragh)						
An Gleann* (Glen)	29	32	3	4	10·3	12·5
Baile an Sceilg* (Ballingskelligs)	88	95	15	15	17·0	15·8 N, C
An Coireán* (Waterville)	122	130	0	1	0·0	0·8
Lóthar** (Loher)	26	15	10	5	38·5	33·3
An Chillín Liath**/ Máistir Gaoithe (Killeenleeha/ Mastergeehy)	115	110	34	31	29·6	28·2
Co. Chorcaí (Cork)						
Múscraí Uí Fhloinn (West Muskerry)						
Baile Bhuirne* (Ballyvourney)	197	203	29	10	14·7	4·9 N, C
Barr Duínse** (Bardinch, Bardinchy)	32	21	11	8	34·4	38·1 G
Cúil Aodha** (Coolea)	36	45	30	30	83·3	66·7 N, C, *G*
Ré na nDoirí* (Reananeree)	55	49	17	6	30·9	12·2

County, Gaeltacht, and location of school	No. on Rolls		No. awarded deontas		% awarded deontas	
	1981/2	*1985/6*	*1981/2*	*1985/6*	*1981/2*	*1985/6*
Baile Uí Bhuaigh* (Ballyvoge, Ballyvoig)	81	81	26	18	32·1	22·2 N, G
Cúil an Bhuacaigh* (Coolavokig)	9	NR	6	NR	66·7	NR G
Garrán Uí Chearnaigh*/ Cluain Droichead (Garrane/Clondrohid)	111	113	0	1	0·0	0·9
Béal Átha an Ghaorthaidh* (2) (Ballingeary) (one only, 1985/6)	130	133	37	17	28·5	12·8 N, C, G

Oileán Chléire (Clear Island)

Cléire (Clear Island)	20	20	14	13	70·0	65·0 C

Co. Phort Láirge (Waterford)

An Rinn (Ring) (sometimes known as Na Déise, or Decies)

An Rinn** (Ring)§	104	117	60	48	57·7	41·0 N, C, G
Baile Mhac Airt* (Ballymacart)	60	55	31	10	51·7	18·2 N
Dún Garbhán* (Dungarvan) (2)	710	NR	2	NR	0·3	NR

Co. Na Mí (Meath)

Na Coilíneachtaí Gaeltachta (The Gaeltacht colonies)

Baile Ghib**/Domhnach Phádraig (Gibstown/ Donaghpatrick)	61	58	18	19	29·5	32·8 N
Ráth Cairn** (Rathcarn/ Rathcarran)	79	88	57	51	72·2	58·0 N, C

Notes

 * Places where the Irish language is dead as a first and home language for the great majority of children. *Deontas* awards are to the credit of the school and a few adventitious families 'keen on Irish'.

 ** Places where Irish is no longer the first language of most children on first arrival at school and where the *deontas* figures reflect successes by the schools. Parents may be fluent Irish speakers and co-operate with the schools by using some Irish with their children, but most children are more fluent in English.

 Absence of asterisks indicates that the 1985/6 figures seem to indicate well the linguistic balance in the district and in a few cases understate the strength of Irish because of the high proportion of ineligible children on the rolls. Most children will be fluently bilingual up to the percentage indicated for 1985/6 but it must be noted that in most schools with up to 70 per cent *deontas* awards and in many with up to around 80 per cent most children now arrive at school at ages 4$^{1}/_{2}$ to 5 years either speaking English only or more fluent in English than in Irish. Success in the *deontas* examination at age 6 is again commonly attributable to the work of the school but the quality of the children's Irish is usually better and more idiomatic than for schools marked ** because the children hear their parents making more use of it between themselves.

(2) after a location name indicates that there are or were two schools there, their figures here combined, except where none were available for one of them at either date.

† The figures for An Trian Lár and Caisleán na Mine Airde were incorrect as published in the 1986 report. Those given here are as corrected by Roinn na Gaeltachta in 1987.

‡ Gaelscoil Dara in Galway is an 'all-Irish' school for children whose (usually non-native speaker) parents want them to have an education through the medium of Irish in a city where that is not otherwise provided or required. Irish would not therefore normally be the everyday language of their homes, despite the high levels of fluency attained.

§ Figures are given for a second school in An Rinn in the 1986 report, but because it was a boarding school for non-Gaeltacht children they are omitted here as irrelevant to the language of the area.

NR indicates that there was no return in the session. This may be because: (*a*) the school has closed (or opened) since 1981/2; closure will usually be suggested by minute numbers on the roll in 1981/2, (*b*) no applications were received, (*c*) no awards were made. Nil awards are, however, usually given for 1981/2.

C after the figures indicates that a *coláiste samhraidh* (Irish summer college) was to be held near by in 1987.

G after the figures indicates that the school was eligible to receive three-month Gael-Linn scholarship children in 1986. *G* italicized means it actually received one or more.

N after the figures means that a *naíonra* (Irish-medium pre-school playgroup) was functioning in the school area in April 1986. Two *naíonraí* designated Connacht I and II remain unidentified in Co. Galway.

These interpretative comments on the statistics solely represent the views of the author and in no way purport to represent the views or opinions of the officials, teachers, and other Gaeltacht residents consulted.

Sources

Tuarascáil an Chomhchoiste um Oideachas sa Gaeltacht (Report of Advisory Committee on Education in the Gaeltacht), Dublin: Oifig an tSoláthair, 1986, for *deontas* figures 1981/2; P. Ó Durcáin, Roinn na Gaeltachta, Na Forbacha, Gaillimh, 1987, for unpublished provisional *deontas* figures 1985/6 and corrections to 1981/2 figures; Gael-Linn, for data on 'scholarship' children; Údarás na Gaeltachta, for data on *naíonraí* and *ógchlubanna*; Comhdháil Náisiúnta na Gaeilge, for data on *coláistí samhraidh*.

Estimates of effective Irish-speaking populations, based on national census statistics 1981, with adjustments based on *deontas* figures 1985–6

County, Gaeltacht, and DED	Total population 1981	No. aged 3+ Irish-speaking 1981	Estimated Irish-speaking population 1981 resident in:		
			50% deontas-majority areas 1985–6 %	No.	70% deontas-majority areas 1985–6 No.

Co. Dhún na nGall (Donegal)

Cloch Chionnaola, Gaoth Dobhair, agus Na Rosa (Cloghaneely, Gweedore, and the Rosses: (north-west Donegal)

Fíor-Ghaeltacht

Mín an Chladaigh[1] (Meenaclady)	1,456	1,331	90·0	1,198	1,198
Gort an Choirce (Gortahork)	1,756	1,590	90·0	1,431	–
Dún Lúiche (Dunlewy)	733	640	66·6	427	–
Machaire an Chlochair (Magheraclogher)	2,768	2,472	75·0	1,854	–
Cró Beithe (Crovehy)	220	192	90·0	173	173
Fíor-Ghaeltacht total	6,933	6,225	–	5,083	1,371

Breac-Ghaeltacht

An Croisbhealach (part) (Crossroads)	2,145	1,648	0·0	0	0
Anagaire (Annagary)	2,127	1,720	33·3	573	573
Árainn Mhór (Aranmore)	803	683	0·0	0	0
Breac-Ghaeltacht total	5,075	4,051	–	573	573
District totals	12,008	10,276	–	5,656	1,944

County, Gaeltacht, and DED	Total population 1981	No. aged 3+ Irish-speaking 1981	Estimated Irish-speaking population 1981 resident in: 50% deontas-majority areas 1985–6 %		70% deontas-majority areas 1985–6
			%	No.	No.

Fánaid, Rois Goill, Gleann Bhairr, An Tearmann, etc. (Fanad, Rosguill, Glenvar, Termon and the north-eastern outliers)

Breac-Ghaeltacht

Ros Guill (Rosguill)	870	656	0·0	0	0
Fánaid Thiar (part) (Fanad West)	297	242	0·0	0	0
Fánaid Thuaidh (part) (Fanad North)	595	451	0·0	0	0
Cnoc Eala (part) (Knockalla)	161	135	0·0	0	0
District totals	1,923	1,484	0·0	0	0

Tír Chonaill Láir (Mid Donegal)

Fíor-Ghaeltacht?

Baile na Finne (Fintown)[2]	289	248	100·0?	248?	0[2]

Breac-Ghaeltacht

Na Dubhcharraigh/An Dúchoraidh (Doocharry)	99	80	0·0	0	0
Gleann Léithín (Glenleheen)	258	221	0·0	0	0
An Clochán (part) (Cloghan)	530	418	0·0	0	0
An Grafadh (Graffy)	353	300	0·0	0	0
Breac-Ghaeltacht total	1,240	1,019	0·0	0	0
District totals	1,529	1,267	–	248?	0

Tír Chonaill Thiar-Theas (South-west Donegal)

Fíor-Ghaeltacht?

Cró Caorach (Crowkeeragh)	220	197	0·0	0	0

Breac-Ghaeltacht

Cill Ghabhlaigh (Kilgoly)	535	405	0·0	0	0
Inis Chaol (Inishkeel)	181	151	0·0	0	0

County, Gaeltacht, and DED	Total population 1981	No. aged 3+ Irish-speaking 1981	Estimated Irish-speaking population 1981 resident in:		
			50% deontas-majority areas 1985–6 %	No.	70% deontas-majority areas 1985–6 No.
Gleann Cholmcille (Glencolumbkille)	878	666	0·0	0	0
Cill Charthaigh (Kilcar)	701	551	0·0	0	0
An Leargan Mór (part) (Largymore)	423	321	0·0	0	0
Breach-Ghaeltacht total	2,718	2,094	0·0	0	0
District totals	2,938	2,291	–	0	0
Donegal county total	18,398	15,318	–	5,904	1,944
Fíor-Ghaeltachtaí	7,442	6,670	–	5,331	1,371
Breac-Ghaeltachtaí	10,956	8,648	–	573	573

Co. Mhaigh Eo (Mayo)

Iorras (Erris) (only)

Fíor-Ghaeltacht?

Cnoc an Daimh (Knockadaff)	516	464	100·0	464	0

Breac-Ghaeltacht

Muing na Bó (Muingnabo)	389	303	0·0	0	0
Guala Mhór (part) (Goolamore)	143	117[3]	0·0	0	0
Breac-Ghaeltacht total	532	420	0·0	0	0
District total[4]	1,048	884	–	464	0
Mayo County total[5]	1,048	884	0·0	464	0
Fíor-Ghaeltachtaí	516	464	100·0	464	0
Breac-Ghaeltachtaí	532	420	0·0	0	0

Maigh Eo – Gaillimh (Mayo–Galway)

Dúiche Sheoigheach (Joyce's Country)

Fior-Ghaeltacht?

Baile an Chalaidh (Ballinchalla)	276	252	50·0	126	0

The death of the Irish language

County, Gaeltacht, and DED	Total population 1981	No. aged 3+ Irish-speaking 1981	Estimated Irish-speaking population 1981 resident in:		
			50% deontas-majority areas 1985-6 %	No.	70% deontas-majority areas 1985-6 No.
Abhainn Brain (Owenbrin)	323	288	0·0	0	0
An Ros (Ross)	137	120	0·0	0	0
Fíor-Ghaeltacht total	736	660	–	126	0
Breac-Ghaeltacht					
Conga (Cong)[6]	586	489	100·0	489	0
District total	1,322	1,149	–	615	0

Co. na Gaillimhe (Galway)

Conamara Theas (South Connemara)

Fíor-Ghaeltacht[7]

County, Gaeltacht, and DED	Total population 1981	No. aged 3+ Irish-speaking 1981	50% deontas-majority areas 1985-6 %	No.	70% deontas-majority areas 1985-6 No.
Abhainn Ghabhla (Owengowla)	425	371	100·0	371	159
Scainimh (Skannive)	693	628	100·0	628	230
An Cnoc Buidhe (Knockboy)	968	832	100·0	832[8]	358
An Turloch (Turlough)	731	673	100·0	673	673
Camus/Camas (Camus)	424	379	100·0	379	379
Cill Chuimín Uacht. (Kilcummin)	162	141	100·0	141	141
An Crampán (Crumpaun)	2,246	2,033	100·0	2,033	0
Leitir Móir (Lettermore)	870	822	100·0	822	822
Garmna (Gorumna)	1,413	1,323	100·0	1,323	996
Cill Chuimín Gaill. (Kilcummin)	1,182	1,077	100·0	1,077	1,077
Sailchearnach/ Sailearna (Selerna)	990	851	100·0	851	0
Fíor-Ghaeltacht total	10,104	9,130	100·0	9,130	4,835
Breac-Ghaeltacht					
An Spidéal (Spiddle)	1,108	910	100·0	910	0
Na Forbacha (Furbogh)	748	570	0·0	0	0
Breac-Ghaeltacht total	1,856	1,480	–	910	0
District total	11,960	10,610	–	10,040	4,835

County, Gaeltacht, and DED	Total population 1981	No. aged 3+ Irish-speaking 1981	Estimated Irish-speaking population 1981 resident in:		
			50% deontas-majority areas 1985–6 %	No.	70% deontas-majority areas 1985–6 No.
Oileáin Árann/Aran Islands					
Fíor-Ghaeltacht					
Inis Mór (Inishmore)	1,368	1,270	100·0	1,270	856
Galway county					
total[9]	13,328	11,880	–	11,310	5,691
Fíor-Ghaeltachtaí	11,472	10,400	100·0	10,400	5,691
Breac-Ghaeltachtaí	1,856	1,480	–	910	0
Co. Chiarraí (Kerry)					
Corca Dhuibhne (Corkaguiny)					
Fíor-Ghaeltacht					
Cill Chúáin (Kilquane)	517	473	100·0	473	473
Cill Maolchéadar (Kilmalkeader)	589	535	100·0	535	535
Márthain (Marhin)	199	187	100·0	187	187
Dún Urlann (Dunurlin)	377	341	100·0	341	341
Dún Caoin (Dunquin)[10]	179	153	100·0	153	153
Fionntráigh/Ceann Trá (Ventry)	382	325	100·0	325	0
Fíor-Ghaeltacht total	2,243	2,014	100·0	2,014	1,689
Breac-Ghaeltacht					
Na Gleannta (Glin, (Glens)	1,125	904	66·6	602	0
Cinnáird (Kinard)	404	334	0·0	0	0
Mináird (Minard)	356	290	0·0	0	0
Breac-Ghaeltacht total	1,885	1,528	–	602	0
District total	4,128	3,542	–	2,616	1,689
Uíbh Ráthach (Iveragh)					
Breac-Ghaeltacht					
Tír Aniarthach (part) (Teeranearagh)	109	85	0·0	0	0
Baile an Sceilg (Ballinskelligs)	452	371	0·0	0	0
Breac-Ghaeltacht total	561	456	0·0	0	0

County, Gaeltacht, and DED	Total population 1981	No. aged 3+ Irish-speaking 1981	Estimated Irish-speaking population 1981 resident in:		
			50% deontas-majority areas 1985–6 %	No.	70% deontas-majority areas 1985–6 No.
Kerry County					
total	4,689	3,998	–	2,616	1,689
Fíor-Ghaeltachtaí	2,243	2,014	–	2,014	1,689
Breac-Ghealtachtaí	2,446	1,984	–	602	0

Co. Chorcaí (Cork)

Múscraí Uí Fhloinn (West Muskerry)

Fíor-Ghaeltacht

Gort na Tiobratan (Gortnatubbrid)	461	404	50·0	202	0
Béal Átha an Ghaorthaidh Magh Ch. (Ballingeary Mac.)	505	431	0·0	0	0
Fíor-Ghaeltacht total	966	835	–	202	0

Breac-Ghaeltacht

Sliabh Riabhach (Slievereagh)	903	720	0·0	0	0
Doire Finghín (Derryfineen)	241	180	0·0	0	0
Cill na Martar (part) (Kilnamartery)	151	119	0·0	0	0
Breac-Ghaeltacht total	1,295	1,019	0·0	0	0
District total	2,261	1,854	0·0	202	0

Oileán Chléire (Clear Island)

Breac-Ghaeltachtaí

Oileán Chléire (part) (Cape Clear)	164	139	100·0	139	0
Cork county total	2,425	1,993	–	341	0
Fíor-Ghaeltachtaí	966	835	–	202	0
Breac-Ghaeltachtaí	1,459	1,158	–	139	0

County, Gaeltacht, and DED	Total population 1981	No. aged 3+ Irish-speaking 1981	Estimated Irish-speaking population 1981 resident in:		70% deontas-majority areas 1985–6 No.
			50% deontas-majority areas 1985–6 %	No.	

Co. Phort Láirge (Waterford)

Breac-Ghaeltacht

An Rinn (part) (Ringville)	1,042	867	–	0	0

Waterford County total

Breac-Ghaeltacht	1,042	867	–	0	0

Co. na Mí (Meath)

Na Coilíneachtaí Gaeltachta[11] (The Gaeltacht colonies)

Breac-Ghaeltacht?

Ráth Mór (part) (Rathmore)	165	120	100·0	120	0

Notes

DEDs are in geographical order from north to south and west to east, i.e. like words on a page. So are the counties and the Gaeltachtaí within each county.

'Fíor-Ghaeltacht' districts, in which 90 per cent or more were returned as speaking Irish in 1981, are distinguished from and given before 'Breac-Ghaeltacht' districts, which returned between 80 and 90 per cent of Irish speakers. Note that figures in the penultimate column of the table (for 50 per cent *deontas*-majority areas) include all those in the final column (for 70 per cent majority areas). They are meant respectively to represent the probable maximum and minimum figures of habitual Irish speakers living in marginally and reasonably sound Irish-speaking communities.

Place-names are spelled first as in the Census vol. 6, Irish Language. A few approved alternatives are also given and anglicized forms are bracketed.

Census figures for certain part-DEDs on the margins of the Gaeltachtaí are excluded from the table, regardless of high percentages of enumerated Irish speakers, where *deontas* returns for the neighbourhood are minute and the population total in 1981 was below 100. Grotesquely inflated census returns are frequent in these border districts and bear no relationship to local language use. Four such part-DEDs scored above 90 per cent in their census returns, including three which registered 100 per cent.

[1] Mín an Chladaigh's *deontas* proportions, which are within 2 per cent of 70 per cent and depressed by special circumstances distorting Toraigh's figures, are here treated as 70 per cent or above.

[2] Baile na Finne's *deontas* figures are queried for reasons stated in the text. They give statistical support for a high Gaeltacht classification but must be largely discounted.

[3] Guala Mhór's 1981 census Irish score is grossly inflated at 83 per cent.

[4] Outside Dúiche Sheoigheach, which follows, no other Mayo DED attained 80 per cent in 1981. Any small Irish-speaking minority in An Geata Mór Theas/Binghamstown South will be compensated for by the inclusion of Guala Mhór above.

[5] Excluding Dúiche Sheoigheach, part.

[6] Conga includes Corr na Móna, whose 80 per cent *deontas* score is discounted.

[7] The extra space between lines in the Galway Fíor-Ghaeltacht separates its geographical sub-regions.

The death of the Irish language

[8] Probably too high because of the dubious position at Carna.
[9] Excludes Dúiche Sheoigheach. There were no DEDs in Gaillimh Láir/Mid Galway with Irish-speaking returns as high as 70 per cent in 1981.
[10] Dún Caoin's *deontas* figures are unduly depressed by abnormal circumstances and are here treated as in excess of 70 per cent for comparability.
[11] Neither of the DEDs officially designated as Gaeltacht reached the 80 per cent minimum criterion in 1981, but Ráth Mór returned 78·4 per cent, so, exceptionally, is given here.

Sources

Census of Population of Ireland 1981; *Tuarascáil an Chomhchoiste um Oideachas sa Gaeltacht* (1986); Roinn na Gaeltachta (P. Ó Durcáin) 1987.

Appendix 5

Gaeltacht summary, by county Gaeltachtaí

County	Total population 1981	No. aged 3+ Irish-speaking 1981	Estimated Irish-speaking population 1981 resident in:	
			50%+deontas-majority areas 1985–6	70%+ deontas-majority areas 1985–6[1]

Assumed effective Gaeltacht, i.e. DEDs and part-DEDs returning Irish speakers as over 80 per cent of persons aged 3 years and more in 1981

County	Total population 1981	No. aged 3+ Irish-speaking 1981	50%+deontas-majority areas 1985–6	70%+ deontas-majority areas 1985–6[1]
Dún na nGall/Donegal	18,398	15,318	5,904	1,944
Maigh Eo/Mayo	1,048	884	464	0
Maigh Eo–Gaillimh[2]/ Mayo–Galway	1,322	1,149	615	0
Gaillimh/Galway	13,328	11,880	11,310	5,691
Ciarraí/Kerry	4,689	3,998	2,616	1,689
Corcaí/Cork	2,425	1,993	341	0
Port Láirge/Waterford	1,042	867	0	0
Mí/Meath	165	120	120	0
National total	42,417	36,209	21,370	9,324

Assumed Fíor-Ghaeltacht only, i.e. DEDs and part-DEDs returning Irish speakers as over 90 per cent of persons aged 3 years and more in 1981

County	Total population 1981	No. aged 3+ Irish-speaking 1981	50%+deontas-majority areas 1985–6	70%+ deontas-majority areas 1985–6[1]
Dún na nGall/Donegal	7,442	6,670	5,331	1,371
Maigh Eo/Mayo	1,048	884	464	0
Maigh Eo–Gaillimh[2]/ Mayo–Galway	736	660	126	0
Gaillimh/Galway	11,472	10,400	10,400	5,691
Ciarraí/Kerry	2,243	2,014	2,014	1,689
Corcaí/Cork	966	835	202	0
Port Láirge/Waterford[3]				
Mí/Meath[3]				
National total	23,907	21,463	18,537	8,751

Notes
[1] The figures in the final column, although county totals, derive exclusively from the three Gaeltachtaí of Cloch Chionnaola and Gaoth Dobhair/north-west Donegal, Conamara Theas/South Connemara (with

The death of the Irish language

Árainn/Aran) and Corca Dhuibhne/Corkaguiny.

[2] The Maigh Eo/Gaillimh heading refers only to the Dúiche Sheoigheach Gaeltacht, which overlaps the two counties.

[3] No DEDs or part-DEDs qualify for this category by virtue of their 1981 census language returns.

Sources

Census of Ireland 1981 and Roinn na Gaeltachta *deontas* figures.

Bibliography

The sources listed include many which have remarkably little to say about language in Ireland and are included for their contribution to the geographic, economic, political, or social background. In so far as they ignore the language or accord it only passing mention they give silent testimony of their evaluation of it. Spelling and accentuation are intended to be the original author's, as is use of English or Irish names by the same author.

Aalen, F. H., and Brody, H (1969) *Gola: the Life and Last Days of an Island Community*, Cork: Mercier.

Adams, G. B. (1958) 'The emergence of Ulster as a distinct dialect area', *Ulster Folklife* 4: 61–73.

—— (ed.) (1964) *Ulster Dialects: an Introductory Symposium*, Holywood: Ulster Folk Museum. (Includes his 'The last language census in Northern Ireland', pp. 111–45.)

—— (1970) 'Language and man in Ireland', in D. McCourt (ed.) *'Studies in Folklife presented to Emyr Estyn Evans*, Holywood: Ulster Folk Museum.

—— (1975) 'Language census problems, 1851–1911', *Ulster Folklife* 21: 68–73.

—— (1976) 'Aspects of monoglottism in Ulster', *Ulster Folklife* 22: 76–87.

—— (1979) 'The validity of language census figures in Ulster, 1851–1911', *Ulster Folklife* 25: 113–22.

Adams, W. F. (1932) *Ireland and Irish Emigration to the New World from 1815 to the Famine*, New Haven, Conn.: Yale University Press.

Adler, M. (1977) *Welsh and the other Dying Languages in Europe*, Hamburg: Helmut Buske Verlag.

Agnew, J. (1981) 'Language shift and the politics of language', *Language Problems and Language Planning* 5, 1: 1–10.

Ainmneacha Gaeilge Na mBailte Poist (Irish names of post towns) (1969), Baile Átha Cliath: An tSuirbhéireacht Ordanáis (Ordnance Survey).

Akenson, D. (1975) *A Mirror to Kathleen's Face: Education in Independent Ireland 1922–60*, Montreal and London: McGill-Queen's University Press.

Alcock, A. E., Taylor, B. K., and Welton, J. M. (eds.) (1979) *The Future of Cultural Minorities*, London: Macmillan.Alison, W. P. (1847)

Observations on the Famine of 1846–7, in the Highlands of Scotland and in Ireland, Edinburgh: Blackwood.

Allardt, E. (1979) 'Implications of the ethnic revival in modern industrialized society', *Commentationes Scientiarum Socialum Fennica* (Helsinki) 12: 1–81.

Anderson, C. (1815) *Memorial on Behalf of the Native Irish, with a View to their Moral and Religious Improvement through the Medium of their own Language*, London: Gale.

—— (1828) *Historical Sketches of the Ancient Native Irish and their Descendants*, Edinburgh: Oliver & Boyd; 2nd edn 1846, London: Pickering.

Andrews, L. S. (1978) *Decline of Irish as a School Subject in the Republic of Ireland 1966–77: Black Paper on Irish Education*, Dublin: Conradh Ceilteach and Conradh na Gaeilge.

Archer, J. (1801) *Statistical Survey of the County of Dublin*, Dublin: Royal Dublin Society.

Arensberg, C. M. (1937) *The Irish Countryman: an Anthropological Study*, London: Macmillan.

—— and Kimball, S. (eds.) (1940) Family and Community in Ireland, Cambridge, Mass.: Harvard University Press.

Athbheochan na Gaeilge: see (An) *Coimisiún um Athbheochan na Gaeilge* . . .

Attwood, E. A. (1961–2) 'Agriculture and economic growth in western Ireland', *Journal of the Statistical and Social Inquiry Society of Ireland* 20, 5: 172–95.

Auchmuty, J. (1937) *Irish Education*, Dublin: Hodges Figgis.

Barker, Sir E. (1917) *Ireland in the last Fifty Years, 1866–1916*, Oxford, Clarendon Press.

Barkley, J. M. (1959) *A Short History of the Presbyterian Church in Ireland*, Belfast: Publications Board, Presbyterian Church in Ireland.

Barrington, D. (1957) 'Uniting Ireland', *Studies* 46: 379–402.

Barrit, D. P., and Carter, C. F. (eds.) (1962) *The Northern Ireland Problem*, 1972 edn, London: Oxford University Press.

Bartlett, T., O'Dwyer, R., Ó Tuathaigh, G., and Curtain, C. (eds.) (1988) *An Introduction to Irish Studies*, Dublin: Gill & Macmillan.

Batterberry, R. (1955) *Oideachas in Éireann 1500–1946* (Education in Ireland 1500–1946), Baile Átha Cliath: Oifig an tSoláthair (Stationery Office).

Beaumont, G. A. de la B. de (1839) *L'Irlande sociale, politique et religieuse*, 2 vols., 1863 edn, Paris.

Beer, W. R., and Jacob, J. E. (eds.) (1985) *Language Policy and National Unity*, Totowa, N.J.: Rowman & Littlefield.

Betts, C. (1976) 'Irish: scarce better off than under the British', appendix 3: 226–35, of his *Culture in Crisis: the Future of the Welsh Language*, Upton, Wirral: Ffynnon Press.

Bhaldraithe, T. de (1945) *The Irish of Cois Fhairrge, Co. Galway*, 2nd edn 1966, Dublin: Dublin Institute for Advanced Studies.

Blácam, A. de (1929) *Gaelic Literature Surveyed*, Dublin and Cork: Talbot.

Black, R. D.C. (1960) *Economic Thought and the Irish Question, 1817–1870*, Cambridge: Cambridge University Press.

Blaghd (Blythe), E. de (1955) *Briseadh na Teorann* (Breaking the borders),
    Baile Átha Cliath: Sáirséal & Dill.
—— (1972) 'Hyde in conflict', in Ó Tuama, S. (ed.) *The Gaelic League
    Idea*, Cork and Dublin: Mercier.
Blanchard, J. (1963) *The Church in Contemporary Ireland*, Dublin: Clonmore
    & Reynolds; London: Burnes & Oates.
Blaschke, J. (ed.) (1980) *Handbuch der europäischen Regionalbewegungen*,
    Frankfurt-am-Main: Syndikat Autoren- und Verlagsgesellschaft.
Blythe, E. (E. de Blaghd) (1949) *The State and the Language*, 2nd edn 1951,
    Dublin: Comhdháil Náisiúnta na Gaeilge.
—— *Tomorrow is Too Late* (1952 edn) Dublin: Comhdháil Náisiúnta na
    Gaeilge.
Boal, F. W., and Douglas, J. N. H. (eds.) (1982) *Integration and Division:
    Geographical Perspectives on the Northern Ireland Problem*, London:
    Academic Press.
Bord na Gaeilge (1983) *Action Plan for Irish 1983–1986*, Dublin: Bord na
    Gaeilge.
—— (1984) *Action Plan for Irish 1983–1986: Report 1983–1984*, Dublin:
    Bord na Gaeilge.
—— (1985) *Action Plan for Irish 1983–1986: Report 1984–1985*, Dublin:
    Bord na Gaeilge.
—— (1986) *Action Plan for Irish 1983–1986: Report 1985–1986*, Dublin:
    Bord na Gaeilge.
Bord na Gaeilge Advisory Planning Committee (1986) *Irish and the Education
    System: an Analysis of Examination Results*, Dublin: Bord na Gaeilge.
—— (1988) *The Irish Language in a Changing Society: Shaping the Future*,
    Dublin: Bord na Gaeilge.
Boyd, A. (1984) *Northern Ireland: Who is to Blame*? Cork: Mercier.
Boyd, H. A. (1947) *Rathlin Island, North of Antrim*, Ballycastle: Scarlett.
Breathnach, D. (1988) 'Study visit programme. Extracts from reports of visits
    to. . . Northern Ireland', *Contact Bulletin* (European Bureau for Lesser
    Used Languages) 5, 1: 3–5.
Breathnach, P. (ed.) (1983) *Rural Development in the West of Ireland:
    Observations from the Gaeltacht Experience*, Occasional Papers 3,
    Department of Geography, St Patrick's College, Maynooth.
—— (1985) 'Rural industrialization in the West of Ireland', in M. J. Healy
    and B. W. Ilberry (eds.) *The Industrialization of the Countryside*,
    Norwich: Geo Books.
—— (1986) 'Structural and functional problems of community development
    co-operatives in the Irish Gaeltacht', in D. Ó Cearbhaill (ed.) *The
    Organisation and Development of Local Initiatives*, 8th International
    Seminar on Marginal Regions, University College, Galway.
Breathnach, P., and Cawley, M. E. (eds.) (1986) *Change and Development in
    Rural Ireland*, Special Publication 1, Maynooth: Geographical Society
    of Ireland.
Breatnach, R. A. (1947) *The Irish of Ring, Co. Waterford*, Dublin: Dublin
    Institute for Advanced Studies.
—— (1956) 'Revival or survival? An examination of the Irish language

policy of the state', Studies 45: 129–45.

—— (1964) 'Irish Revival reconsidered', Studies 53: 18–30.

British and Irish Communist Organization (1972) *The Irish Language: Revivalism and the Gaeltacht*, Belfast: British and Irish Communist Organization.

Broadcasting Council for Scotland (1982) *Report of the Study Group on the Future of Gaelic Broadcasting*, Glasgow: BBC Scotland.

Brosnam (Ó Brosnacháin), G. (1986) 'Rural Development through a Community Co-op in South-west Ireland' (Corca Dhuibhne), paper given at International Conference on the Role of Local Employment Initiatives in Strengthening the Economy of Less Populated Areas, Kuopio, Finland, June.

Brown, T. (1981) *Ireland: a Social and Cultural History 1922–79*, Glasgow: Fontana.

Browne, C. R. (1893–96) *'The Ethnography of Inishbofin and Inishark, County Galway'*, Proceedings of the Royal Irish Academy, 3rd series, 3.

Brudner, L. A., and White, D. R. (1979) 'Language attitudes, behaviour and intervening variables', in W. F. Mackey and J. Ornstein (eds.) *Sociological Studies in Language Contact*, The Hague: Mouton.

Burga, S. de (1958) *The Irish of Tourmakeady, Co. Mayo*, Dublin: Dublin Institute for Advanced Studies.

Burke, J. F. (1940) *Outlines of the Industrial History of Ireland*, Dublin: Browne & Nolan.

Byrne, A. (1987) *Adult Education in the Gaeltacht* (Report), Dublin: AONTAS.

Byrne, E. (1938) 'Where the Irish language still lives', *Ireland-American Review* 1: 50–1.

Cahill, E. (1935) 'The Irish national tradition', *Irish Ecclesiastical Record* 46: 2–10.

—— (1939) 'The Irish language and tradition, 1540–1691', Irish Ecclesiastical Record, 5th series, 54: 123–42.

—— (1940) 'The Irish language in the Penal Era', *Irish Ecclesiastical Record*, 5th series, 55: 591–617.

Camier, P. (1968) 'The Gaeltacht Colonies in County Meath, Éire', unpublished BA dissertation, University of Leeds.

Campbell, E. M. J., and Donnelly, U. (1947) 'Peasant life in the Glens of Antrim', *Economic Geography* 23: 10–14.

Campbell, J. L. (1945) *Gaelic in Scottish Education and Life*, Edinburgh: Saltire Society (Johnston).

Carney, J. (1955) *Studies in Irish Literature and History*, Dublin: Dublin Institute for Advanced Studies.

Carvalho, C. M. D. de (1962) 'The geography of languages', in P. L. Wagner and M. W. Mikesell (eds.) *Readings in Cultural Geography*, Chicago: University of Chicago Press.

Census of Population (decennial): *Ireland* (1841–1911), London: Registrar General/HMSO; *Saorstát Éireann* (1926– 46), Dublin: Stationery Office; *Ireland* (1961–81), Dublin: Stationery Office. (Censuses in 1951 and 1956 did not cover language.)

Chadwick, H.M. (1945) *The Nationalities of Europe and the Growth of National Ideologies*, Cambridge: Cambridge University Press.
—— (1949) *Early Scotland: the Picts, the Scots and the Welsh of Southern Scotland*, Cambridge: Cambridge University Press.
Chubb, F. B. (1964) *Source Book of Irish Government*, Dublin: Institute of Public Administration.
CILAR: see Committee on Irish Language Attitudes Research.
Coakley, J. (1980) 'Self-government in Gaelic Ireland: the development of state language policy', *Europa Ethnica* 37, 3: 114–24.
Coimisiún na Gaeltachta, 1925: see Gaeltacht Commission.
Coimisiún um Athbheochan na Gaeilge, An, (1964) *An Tuarascáil Dheiridh* (Commission on the Restoration of the Irish Language, Final Report), Baile Átha Cliath: Oifig an tSoláthair. (Irish only.)
Cole, G. A. J. (1919) *Ireland the Outpost*, London: Oxford University Press.
Colum, P. (1959) *Arthur Griffith*, Dublin: Browne & Nolan.
Comber, P. (1960) 'The Revival', *An Múinteoir Náisiúnta* 5, 7: 23–4, 27.
Comhairle na Gaeilge (1971a) *Local Government and Development Institutions for the Gaeltacht*, Dublin: Stationery Office.
—— (1971b) *Submissions to the Higher Education Authority*, Dublin: Stationery Office.
—— (1971c) *Towards a Language Policy*, Dublin: Stationery Office.
—— (1972) *Implementing a Language Policy*, Dublin: Stationery Office.
—— (1974) *Irish in Education* (Report), Dublin: Stationery Office.
Comhairle nan Eilean (1982) *Bilingual Policy*, Stornoway: Comhairle nan Eilean (Western Isles Islands Council) (*sic*).
Comhaltas Uladh (1988a) *Irish in the Education System: an Assessment of the Government's Discussion Paper*, Belfast: Education Committee of Comhaltas Uladh.
—— (1988b) *Miscellaneous Working Papers and Memoranda* on Irish-medium education in Northern Ireland, with the case for wider provision, Belfast: Comhaltas Uladh. (Photocopied circulars.)
Comhchoiste um Oideachas sa Ghaeltacht, An: see Tuarascáil an Chomhchoiste um Oideachas sa Ghaeltacht.
Comhdháil Náisiúnta na Gaeilge (1953) *Memorandum for the Taoiseach: Board for the Gaeltacht*, Dublin: Comhdháil Náisiúnta na Gaeilge.
—— (1956) *Tuarascáil Chinnbliana* (Annual Report), Baile Átha Cliath: Comhdháil Náisiúnta na Gaeilge.
—— (1957) *Tuarascáil Chinnbliana*, Baile Átha Cliath: Comdhail Náisiúnta na Gaeilge.
—— (1964) *Tuarascáil Bhliantúil* (Annual Report), Baile Átha Cliath: Comhdháil Náisiúnta na Gaeilge. (Reports are in Irish only.)
Commins, P. (1988) 'Socioeconomic development and language maintenance in the Gaeltacht', *International Journal of the Sociology of Language* 70: 11–28.
Commission of the European Communities (1986) *Linguistic Minorities in Countries belonging to the European Community: Summary Report*, Luxembourg: Official Publications Office of the European Communities.

Commission on Higher Education 1960–67 (1967) *Presentation and Summary of Report*, Dublin: Stationery Office.
Commission on the Restoration of the Irish Language (1964) *Summary, in English, of the Final Report*, Dublin: Stationery Office.
Committee on Irish Language Attitudes Research ('CILAR', or 'CLAR') (1975), *Report*, Dublin: Stationery Office.
Congested Districts Board for Ireland (1891) *Base Line Reports, 1891*; in Library of Trinity College, Dublin. (Unpublished.)
—— (1898) *Seventh Report*, Dublin, HM Stationery Office.
—— (1909) *Eighteenth Report*, Dublin, HM Stationery Office.
—— (1912) *Twentieth Report*, Dublin, HM Stationery Office.
—— (1915) *Twenty-third Report*, Dublin: HM Stationery Office.
Connell, K. H. (1950) *The Population of Ireland, 1750–1845*, Oxford: Clarendon Press.
Connolly, J. (1910) *Labour in Irish History*, Dublin, Maunsel.
Connradh na Gaedhilge (n.d., c. 1963) *Meamram don Choimisiún um Athbheochan na Gaedhilge* (Memorandum to the Commission on the Restoration of the Irish Language), Baile Átha Cliath: Connradh na Gaedhilge. (Irish only.)
Conradh na Gaeilge (1978) *The Case of Ulster Irish on Ulster Radio and Television*, Report by a Study Group, Belfast: Conradh na Gaeilge.
Conroy, J. C. (1928) *A History of Railways In Ireland*, London: Longman.
Coogan, T. P. (1966) *Ireland since the Rising*, London: Pall Mall Press. (See especially chapter 9, 183–205, 'The Gaelic Movement'.)
Coote, Sir C. (1801a) *General View of the Agriculture and Manufactures of the King's County, with Observations on their Improvement, Drawn up in the Year 1801*, Dublin: Royal Dublin Society.
—— (1801b) *Statistical Survey of the County of Monaghan*, Dublin: Royal Dublin Society.
—— (1801c) *General View of the Agriculture and Manufactures of the Queen's County*, etc., Dublin: Royal Dublin Society.
—— (1802) *Statistical Survey of the County of Cavan, Drawn up in the Year 1801*, Dublin: Royal Dublin Society.
—— (1804) *Statistical Survey of the County of Armagh*, Dublin: Royal Dublin Society.
Corcora, D. Ó,: see Ó Corcora, D. (Corkery, D.).
Corkery, D. (1925) *The Hidden Ireland: a Study of Gaelic Munster in the Eighteenth Century*, Dublin: Gill (reprinted 1967).
—— (1948) *The Philosophy of the Gaelic League*, Dublin: Gaelic League.
—— (1954) *The Fortunes of the Irish Language*, Dublin: Fallon; new edn 1968, Cork: Mercier.
Cor na Gaidhlig (State of Gaelic) (1982) *Language, Community and Development: the Gaelic Situation*, Inverness: Highlands and Islands Development Board.
Coulter, H. (1862) *The West of Ireland: its Existing Conditions and Prospects*, Dublin: Hodges & Smith.
Coupland, Sir R. (1954) *Welsh and Scottish Nationalism: a Study*, London: Collins.

Cousens, S. H. (1960) 'The regional pattern of emigration during the Great
    Irish Famine 1846–51', *Transactions and Papers of the Institute of
    British Geographers* 28: 119–34.
—— (1961) 'Emigration and demographic change in Ireland 1851–61',
    Economic History Review, 2nd series, 14: 275–88.
—— (1963) 'Regional variations in population changes in Ireland,
    1881–91', *Transactions and Papers of the Institute of British
    Geographers* 33: 145–62.
Croft Dickinson, W. (1962) *A New History of Scotland*, vol. 1, London:
    Nelson.
Curtis, E. (1923) *A History of Medieval Ireland from 1086 to 1513*, London:
    Macmillan; enlarged edn 1938, Dublin: Talbot Press.
—— (1936) *A History of Ireland*, 6th edn 1950, London: Methuen.
Darby, J. (ed.) (1983) *Northern Ireland: the Background to the Conflict*,
    Belfast: Appletree.
Daunt, W. J. O'N. (1896) *A Life spent for Ireland: being Selections from the
    Journals of the late W. J. O'Neill Daunt*, London: Fisher Unwin.
Dauzat, A. (1948) *La Géographie linguistique*, Paris.
Davies, G. L. H. (ed.) (1984) *Irish Geography . . . 1934–1984*, Dublin:
    Geographical Society of Ireland.
Davis, T. O. (1914 edn) *Essays, Literary and Historical*, ed. D. J.
    O'Donoghue, Dundalk: Tempest.
Day, T. P. (1918) *Public Administration in the Highlands and Islands of
    Scotland*, London: University of London Press.
Demangeon, A. (1927) 'La situation linguistique et l'état économique de
    l'ouest irlandais', *Annales de Géographie* 36: 169–73.
—— (1929) 'La géographie des langues', *Annales de Géographie* 38:
    427–38.
Department of Education for Northern Ireland (1988) *Education in Northern
    Ireland: Proposals for Reform*, Belfast: Department of Education.
Department of Education Survey Team (1966) *Investment in Education:
    Report of the Survey Team appointed in October 1962*, Dublin:
    Stationery Office.
Devitt, S. M., Little, D. G., Ó Conchúir, S. P., and Singleton, D. M. (1982)
    Learning Irish with Anois is Arís, Dublin: Centre for Language and
    Communication Studies, Trinity College.
Devlin, B. (1972) 'The Gaelic League – a spent force?', in S. Ó Tuama (ed.)
    The Gaelic League Idea, Cork and Dublin: Mercier.
Dewar, D. (1812) *Observations on the Character, Customs and Superstitions
    of the Irish*, London: Gale & Curtis.
Dewar, M. W. (1958) *Why Orangeism?* Belfast: Grand Orange Lodge of
    Ireland.
Dillon, M. (ed.) (1954) *Early Irish Society*, Dublin: Cultural Relations
    Committee of Ireland, C. O. Lochlainn.
Dinneen, P. S. (1904) *Lectures on the Irish Language Movement*, etc., Dublin:
    Gaelic League.
—— (1927) Foclóir Gaedhilge agus Béarla: an Irish–English Dictionary,
    enlarged edn 1934, Dublin: Educational Company of Ireland, for Irish

Texts Society. (Essential for 'traditional' spelling.)

Donegal County Council (1967) *County Donegal Development Plan*, Letterkenny: Donegal County Council.

Dubourdieu, J. (1802) *Statistical Survey of the County of Down*, Dublin: Royal Dublin Society.

—— (1812) *Statistical Survey of the County of Antrim*, Dublin: Royal Dublin Society.

Duffy, Sir C. G. (1884) *Young Ireland: a Fragment of Irish History 1840–45*, Dublin. Reprinted in 2 vols. 1968, Shannon: Irish University Press.

—— (1898) *My Life in Two Hemispheres*, 2 vols., New York: Macmillan.

—— Sigerson, G., and Hyde, D. (1894) *The Revival of Irish Literature*, London: Fisher Unwin. Reprinted 1973, New York: Lemma. (Includes D. Hyde's 'The necessity for de-anglicizing Ireland'.)

Durkacz, V. E. (1983) *The Decline of the Celtic Languages: a Study of Linguistic and Cultural Conflict in Scotland, Wales and Ireland*, Edinburgh: Donald.

Dutton, H. (1808) *Statistical Survey of the County of Clare*, Dublin: Royal Dublin Society.

—— (1824) *Statistical Survey of the County of Galway*, Dublin: Royal Dublin Society.

Dwyer, D. J. (1963) 'Farming an Atlantic outpost: Clare Island, Co. Mayo', *Geography* 48: 255–67.

Dwyer, T. R. (1980) *Eamon de Valera*, Dublin: Gill & Macmillan.

Economic Development (1958) Dublin: Stationery Office.

Educational Development, White Paper on (1981) Dublin: Department of Education (Stationery Office).

Edwards, J. R. (1977) 'Report of the Committee on Irish Language Attitudes Research' (Review), *Language Problems and Language Planning* 1, 1: 54–9.

—— (1983) *The Irish Language: an Annotated Bibliography of Sociolinguistic Publications 1772–1982*, New York: Garland.

—— (1984a) 'Irish and English in Ireland', in P. Trudgill (ed.) *Language in the British Isles*, Cambridge: Cambridge University Press.

—— (1984b) 'Irish: planning and preservation', *Journal of Multilingual and Multicultural Development* 5, 3–4: 267–75.

—— (1984c) (ed.) *Linguistic Minorities, Policies and Pluralism*, London: Academic Press.

—— (1985) *Language, Society and Identity*, Oxford: Blackwell.

Edwards, R. D. (1947) 'The contribution of Young Ireland to the development of the Irish national idea', in S. Pender (ed.) *Féilscribhinn Tórna*, Cork: Cork University Press.

—— and Williams, T. D. (eds.) (1956) *The Great Famine: Studies in Irish History 1845–52*, Dublin: Browne & Nolan.

Egan, S. (1981) *Staidéar Treorach ar na Naíonraí* (Pilot Study of the Naíonraí), Baile Átha Cliath: An Chomhchoiste Réeamhscoilaíochta, Údarás na Gaeltachta (Pre-school Joint Committee, Údarás na Gaeltachta). (Irish only.)

Ellis, P. B., and Mac a'Ghobhainn, S. (1971) *The Problems of Language*

Revival, Inverness: Club Leabhar.

Emery, F.V. (1958) 'Irish geography in the seventeenth century', *Irish Geography* 3: 263–76.

Engels, F. (1844) *The Condition of the Working Class in England in 1844*, 1st English edn New York 1887; reprinted 1953 in K. Marx and F. Engels, *On Britain* (collected papers, etc.), Moscow: Foreign Languages Publishing House; London: Lawrence & Wishart.

European Communities, Commission of (1986) *Linguistic Minorities in Countries belonging to the European Community: Summary Report* (prepared by Istituto del Enciclopedia Italiana, Rome), Luxembourg: European Communities Commission.

Evans, E. Estyn (1942) *Irish Heritage: the Landscape, the People and their Work* 2nd edn 1951, Dundalk: Tempest.

—— (1951) *Mourne Country: Landscape and Life in South Down*, Dundalk: Dundalgan Press.

—— (1956) 'The ecology of peasant life in Western Europe', in W. L. Thomas (ed.) *Man's Role in Changing the Face of the Earth*, Chicago: University of Chicago Press.

—— (1957) *Irish Folk Ways*, London: Routledge.

—— Gresson, R. A. R., Semple, R. H., and Jones, E. (eds) (1952) *Belfast in its Regional Setting: a Scientific Survey*, Belfast: British Association.

Evans, W. S. H. (1977) 'The Irish-speaking Districts of Munster: a Study of the Economic and Social Geography of Relict Speech Areas', unpublished MA thesis, Postgraduate School of Modern Languages and European Studies, University of Bradford.

Fanning, R. (1983) *Independent Ireland*, Dublin: Helicon.

Farley, D. (1964) *Social Insurance and Social Assistance in Ireland*, Dublin: Institute of Public Administration.

Fels, E. (1927) *Der Wiederbelebung der irischen Sprache* (The distribution of the Irish language), Petermanns Mitteilungen 73: 37–41.

Fennell, D. (1958) *The Northern Catholic: an Inquiry*, Blackrock, Co. Dublin: Mount Salus Press.

—— (1973) *Sketches of the new Ireland*, Galway: Association for the Advancement of Self-government.

—— (1976) 'Léarscáil na Gaeltachta', *Amarach*, 21 Bealtaine: 2. (Map of the Gaeltacht, in Irish.)

—— (1977) 'Where it went wrong: the Irish Language Movement', *Planet*, February–March: 3–13.

—— (1980a) 'The last days of the Gaeltacht', *Irish Times*, 3 June.

—— (1980b) 'Why the Gaeltacht wasn't saved', *Irish Times*, 4 June.

—— (1981) 'Can a shrinking linguistic minority be saved? Lessons from the Irish experience', in E. Haugen, J. D. McLure, and D. Thomson (eds.) *Minority Languages Today*, Edinburgh: Edinburgh University Press.

—— (1983) *The State of the Nation: Ireland since the Sixties*, Swords, Co. Dublin: Ward River. (See especially chapter 5, 'A language of our own'.)

Fennell, R. (1961) 'The economic problems of western Ireland', *Studies* 50:

385–402.

Figgis, D. (1917) *The Gaelic State in the Past and Future*, Dublin: Maunsel.

Fishman, J. (ed.) (1968) *Readings in the Sociology of Language*, The Hague: Mouton.

FitzGerald, G. (1963) *State-sponsored Bodies*, Dublin: Institute of Public Administration.

—— (1984) 'Estimates for baronies of minimum level of Irish-speaking among successive decennial cohorts: 1771–1781 to 1861–1871', *Proceedings of the Royal Irish Academy* 84, C, 3: 117–55 and ten maps.

FitzGerald, W. (1925) 'The historical geography of early Ireland', *The Geographical Teacher*, supplement 1, London: Geographical Association.

Fitzpatrick, W. J. (ed.) (1888) *Correspondence of Daniel O'Connell, the Liberator*, 2 vols., London: Murray.

Fitzsimons, J. (1949) 'Official Presbyterian Irish language policy in the eighteenth and nineteenth centuries', *Irish Ecclesiastical Record*, 5th series, 72: 255–64.

Flannery, T. (1907) *For the Tongue of the Gael*, Dublin: Sealy Bryers.

Flatrès, P. (1957) *Géographie rurale de quatre contrées celtiques: Irlande, Galles, Cornwall et Man*, Rennes: Plihon.

Flower, R. (1944) *The Western Island or the Great Blasket*, Oxford: Clarendon Press.

—— (1947) The Irish Tradition, Oxford: Clarendon Press.

Foclóir Póca: English–Irish/Irish–English Dictionary (1986) (Pocket pronouncing dictionary; with associated cassette), Baile Átha Cliath: An Gúm/An Roinn Oideachais.

Foras Forbartha, An (1965) *Proceedings of the National Conference on Physical Planning*, Dublin: An Foras Forbartha.

—— (1966) Planning for Amenity and Tourism: Specimen Development Plan Manual 2–3 (County Donegal), Dublin: An Foras Forbartha.

Foras Talúntais, An (1966) *West Donegal Resource Survey*, 4 vols., Dublin: An Foras Talúntais.

Foster, C. R. (ed.) (1980) *Nations without a State: Ethnic Minorities in Western Europe*, New York: Praeger.

Foster, R. F. (1988) *Modern Ireland 1600–1972*, London: Allen Lane Penguin Press.

Fraser, R. (1801) *General View of the Agriculture and Mineralogy, Present State and Circumstances of the County of Wicklow*, Dublin: Royal Dublin Society.

—— (1807) *Statistical Survey. . . of Wexford*, Dublin: Royal Dublin Society.

Freeman, T. W. (1945) 'The agricultural regions and rural population of Ireland', *Irish Geography* (then Bulletin of the Geographical Society of Ireland) 1, 2: 21–30.

—— (1950) *Ireland: its Physical, Historical, Social and Economic Geography*, revised edn 1960, London: Methuen.

—— (1956) 'Galway: the key to west Connacht', *Irish Geography* 3, 4:

194–205.

—— (1957) *Pre-Famine Ireland: a Study in Historical Geography*, Manchester: Manchester University Press.

—— (1958) 'Inishbofin – an Atlantic Island', *Economic Geography* 34, 3: 202–9.

Fréine, S. de (1965) *The Great Silence*, Dublin: FNT (Foilseacháin Náisiúnta Teo).

Gaeilge don tSeirbhís Phoiblí (Irish in the public service) (n.d., c. 1967), Baile Átha Cliath: An Roinn Airgeadais/Oifig an tSoláthair (Department of Finance/Stationery Office). (Language manual.)

Gaelic League (1937) *You may Revive the Gaelic Language*, Dublin: Gaelic League.

Gaeltacht Commission 1925, Minutes of Evidence, issued daily, April to October 1925, Dublin: Stationery Office.

Gaeltacht Commission Report (1926), Dublin: Stationery Office.

Gaeltacht Department/Ministry (Roinn na Gaeltacht) (1956a) *Ministers and Secretaries (Amendment) Act, 1956*, Dublin: Stationery Office.

—— (1956b) *Gaeltacht (Transfer of Departmental Administration and Ministerial Functions) Order, 1956*, Dublin: Stationery Office.

—— (1956c) *Gaeltacht Areas Order, 1956*, Dublin: Stationery Office.

—— (1967) *Gaeltacht Areas Order, 1967*, Dublin: Stationery Office.

—— (1974) *Gaeltacht Areas Order, 1974*, Dublin: Stationery Office.

—— (1982) *Gaeltacht Areas Order, 1982*, Dublin: Stationery Office.

(Note that these Acts and Orders are issued under the authority of the Office of the Taoiseach but are usually associated with the department to which they mainly refer.)

Gaeltarra/SFADCO Working Group (1971) *Gníomh don Ghaeltacht: Action Programme for the Gaeltacht*, Galway: Gaeltarra Éireann.

Gallagher, F. (1957) *The Indivisible Island: the History of the Partition of Ireland*, London: Gollancz.

Garvin, T. (1981) *The Evolution of Irish Nationalist Politics*, Dublin: Gill & Macmillan.

Glór na nGael (1987) *Report of the Irish Language Survey in the Greater Ballymurphy Area of Belfast*, Belfast: West Belfast Committee of Glór na nGael.

Goblet, Y. M. (1930) *La Transformation de la géographie politique de l'Irlande au XVIIe siècle dans les cartes et essais de Sir William Petty*, 2 vols., Paris: Berger-Levrault.

Gorst, G. (1825) *A Narrative of an Excursion to Ireland*, London: Honourable Irish Society of London.

Gottmann, J. (ed.) (1980) *Centre and Periphery: Spatial Variations in Politics*, London: Sage.

Gough, J. (1817) *A Tour in Ireland in 1813 and 1814*, Dublin: Gough.

Grant, J. (1844) *Impressions of Ireland and the Irish*, 2 vols., London: Cunningham.

Gray, T. (1966) *The Irish Answer: an Anatomy of Modern Ireland*, London: Heinemann.

Greaves, C. D. (1961) *The Life and Times of James Connolly*, London:

Lawrence & Wishart.

Greene, D. (1966) *The Irish Language*, Dublin: Cultural Relations Committee of Ireland.

Gregor, D. B. (1980) *Celtic: a Comparative Study of the Six Celtic Languages . . . their History, Literature and Destiny*, Cambridge: Oleander.

Griffith, A. (1918) *Thomas Davis: the Thinker and Teacher*, Dublin: Gill.

Gunnemark, E., and Kenrick, D. (1986) *A Geolinguistic Handbook*, 1985 edn, Gothenburg: the authors.

Gwynn, S. (1923) *The History of Ireland*, Dublin: Talbot Press; London: Macmillan.

Hall, S. C. and A. M. (1853) *Handbooks for Ireland: the West and Connemara*, London: Virtue Hall & Virtue.

Handbook of the Ulster Question (1923) Dublin: North Eastern Boundary Bureau/Stationery Office.

Hanly, D. P. (1971) *Planning Report on the Galway Gaeltacht*, Dublin: An Foras Forbartha.

Hansen, M. L. (1940) *The Atlantic Migration 1607–1860*, Cambridge, Mass.: Harvard University Press.

Harris, J. (1983) 'Relationship between achievement in spoken Irish and demographic, administrative and teaching factors', *Irish Journal of Education* 17, 1: 5–34.

—— (1984) *Spoken Irish in Primary Schools: an Analysis of Achievement*, Dublin: Institiúid Teangeolaíochta Éireann.

—— (1988) 'Spoken Irish in the primary school system', *International Journal of the Sociology of Language*, 70: 69–88.

Harrison, M. (1976) 'The revival of Irish' *Secondary Teacher* 6, 1: 34–5.

Haugen, E., McClure, J. D., and Thomson, D. (eds.) (1981) *Minority Languages Today*, Edinburgh: Edinburgh University Press.

Haughton, J.P. (ed.) (1979) *Atlas of Ireland*, Dublin: Royal Irish Academy.

Hayes, R. (1938) 'The German colony in County Limerick', North Munster *Antiquarian Journal* 1: 45–53.

Hechter, M. (1975) *Internal Colonialism: the Celtic Fringe in British National Development 1536–1966*, London: Routledge.

Hederman, M. P., and Kearney, R. (eds.) (1982) *The Crane Bag Book of Irish Studies*, Dublin: Blackwater Press.

Hepburn, A. C. (1980) *The Conflict of Nationality in Modern Ireland*, London: Arnold.

Herries Davies, G. L. (ed.) (1984) *Irish Geography: the Geographical Society of Ireland Golden Jubilee 1934–1984*, Dublin: Geographical Society of Ireland.

Heslinga, M. W. (1962) *The Irish Border as a Cultural Divide: a Contribution to the Study of Regionalism in the British Isles*, Sociaal Geografische Studies Nr 6, Assen: University of Utrecht.

Hickey, D. J., and Doherty, J. E. (eds.) (1980) *A Dictionary of Irish History since 1800*, Dublin: Gill & Macmillan.

Higher Education, Commission on, 1960–67 (1967) *Presentation and Summary of Report*, Dublin: Stationery Office.

Hill, G. A., Lord (1845) *Facts from Gweedore, with Useful Hints to Donegal*

Tourists, Dublin. See 5th edn, 1887, London: Hatchard.

Hilliard, E. A. (1981) *Changes in the Usage of Irish among Gaeltacht Children at School Entry 1970–1980 and Associated Socio-demographic Factors*, Dublin: Institiúid Teangeolaíochta Éireann.

Hindley, R. (1950) 'Linguistic Distributions in North-east Wales: a Study in Geographical and Historical Evolution', unpublished BA dissertation, University of Leeds.

—— (1952) 'Linguistic Distributions in South-east Wales: a Study in Trends over the last Century', unpublished MA thesis, University of Leeds.

—— (1984) 'The decline of the Manx language: a study in linguistic geography', *Bradford Occasional Papers* (School of Modern Languages, University of Bradford) 6: 15–39.

—— (1989a) 'Defining the Gaeltacht – dilemmas in Irish language planning: summary', in N. Ó Gadhra (1989) *An Ghaeltacht (Oifigiúil) – agus 1992?* (The official Gaeltacht – and 1992?), Dumhach Trá/ Sandymount: Coiscéim.

—— (1989b) 'Defining the Gaeltacht – dilemmas in Irish language planning', in C. H. Williams (ed.) *Linguistic Minorities, Society and Territory*, Clevedon, Avon: Multilingual Matters.

Hogan, J. J. (1927) *The English Language in Ireland*, Dublin: Educational Company of Ireland.

Holmer, N. M. (1940) 'On some relics of the Irish dialect spoken in the Glens of Antrim', in *Universitets Aarskrift*, Uppsala: University of Uppsala.

—— (1942) *The Irish Language in Rathlin Island, Co. Antrim*, Dublin: Hodges Figgis.

—— (1962) 'The dialects of County Clare, Part 1', Royal Irish Academy Todd Lecture Series, 19, Dublin: Hodges Figgis.

Holmestad, E., and Lade, A.S. (eds.) (1969) *Lingual Minorities in Europe*, Oslo: Det Norske Samlaget.

Hooker, E. R. (1938) *Readjustment of Agricultural Tenures in Ireland*, Chapel Hill, N.C.: University of North Carolina Press.

Horner, A. S., Walsh, J.A., and Harrington, V. P. (1987) *Population in Ireland: Census Atlas*, Dublin: Department of Geography, University College.

Hughes, T. J. (1959) 'Landordism in the Mullet of Mayo', *Irish Geography* 4, 1: 16–34.

—— (1965) 'Society and settlement in nineteenth century Ireland', Irish Geography 5, 2: 79–96.

Hutchinson, J. (1987) *The Dynamics of Cultural Nationalism: the Gaelic Revival and the Creation of the Irish Nation State*, London: Allen & Unwin.

Hyde, D. (1899) *A Literary History of Ireland*, London: Fisher Unwin; reprinted 1967 with new introduction by B. Ó Cuív, London: Benn.

—— (1900) *A University Scandal*, Dublin: Eblana Press.

—— Also see Duffy, C. G., Sigerson, G., and Hyde, D.

Hymes, D. (ed.) (1964) *Language, Culture and Society*, New York: Harper.

Inglis, H. D. (1835) *A Tour throughout Ireland during the Spring, Summer and Autumn of 1834*, 2 vols., 3rd edn 1835, London: Whittaker.

Inter-departmental Committee on the Problems of Small Western Farms (1963) *Report*, Dublin: Stationery Office.

—— (1964) *Report on Pilot Area Development*, Dublin: Stationery Office.

Ireland: an Introduction to her History, Institutions, Resources and Culture (1950) Dublin: Department of External Affairs/Stationery Office.

Ireland: Gaeltacht Census of August 1925: see Gaeltacht Commission Report.

Irish Business (1981) 'Údarás na Gaeltachta – attracting lame ducks', 'Investigation', *Irish Business*, March: 2–9.

Irish Language Television Broadcasting: Working Group Report to the Ministers for the Gaeltacht and Communications (1987), Dublin: n.s.

Irish National Teachers' Organization (1941) *Report of the Committee of Inquiry into the Use of Irish as a Teaching Medium to Children whose Home Language is English*, Dublin: INTO.

—— (1947) *A Plan for Education*, Dublin: INTO.

Jackson, J. A. (1963) *The Irish in Britain*, London: Routledge.

Jackson, K. H. (1953a) *Language and History in early Britain*, Edinburgh: Edinburgh University Press.

—— (1953b) 'Common Gaelic: the evolution of the Goedelic languages', *Proceedings of the British Academy* 37: 71–97.

Jackson, T. A. (1947) *Ireland her Own*, London: Cobbett Press.

James, C. (1986) 'Indigenous non-English language communities in the United Kingdom', *Contact Bulletin* (of European Bureau for Lesser Used Languages) 3, 1 and 2: 1–4.

Johnson, J. H. (1957) 'The population of Londonderry during the Great Irish Famine', *Economic History Review*, 2nd series, 10, 2: 273–85.

—— (1961) 'The development of the rural settlement pattern of Ireland', *Geografiska Annaler* 43: 165–73.

—— (1963) 'Population changes in Ireland 1951–1961', *Geographical Journal* 129: 167–74.

—— (1967) 'Harvest migration from nineteenth century Ireland', *Transactions of the Institute of British Geographers* 41: 97–112.

Johnson, M. (1970) 'The co-operative movement in the Gaeltacht', *Irish Geography* 12: 68–81.

Johnston, E. M. (1963) *Great Britain and Ireland 1765–1800: a Study in Political Administration*, Edinburgh: Oliver & Boyd.

Joint Committee on the Irish Language in the House of the Oireachtas: see Tithe an Oireachtais, Joint Committee . . .

Jones, E. (1960a) *A Social Geography of Belfast*, London: Oxford University Press.

—— (1960b) 'Problems of Partition and segregation in Northern Ireland', *Journal of Conflict Resolution* 4: 96–105.

—— (1964) 'Cultural geography', in J. W. Watson and J. B. Sissons (eds.) *The British Isles: a Systematic Geography*, London: Nelson.

Jones, H. (1974) *Wales–Ireland: a TV Contrast,* Dublin: Conradh na Gaeilge.

Kallen, J. L. (1988), 'The English language in Ireland', *International Journal of the Sociology of Language* 70: 127–42.

Kane, Sir R. J. (1844) *The Industrial Resources of Ireland* ,2nd edn 1845, Dublin and London: Hodges & Smith.

Keane, M. J., Cawley, M., and Ó Cinnéide, M. (1983) 'Industrial development in Gaeltacht areas: the work of Údarás na Gaeltachta', *Cambria* 10, 1: 47–60.

Kearns, C. (1954) 'The revival of Irish – a case re-stated', *Irish Eccclesiastical Record* 81: 184–95.

Kearns, K. C. (1974a) 'Resuscitation of the Irish Gaeltacht', *Geographical Review* 64, 1: 82–110.

—— (1974b) 'Industrialization and regional development in Ireland, 1958–72', *American Journal of Economics and Sociology* 33: 299–316.

—— (1976) 'The Aran Islands: an imperilled Irish outpost', *Proceedings of the American Philosophical Society* 120: 421–38.

Kee, R.(1972) *The Green Flag: a History of Irish Nationalism*, London: Quartet.

Knight, P. (1836) *Erris in the Irish Highlands and the Atlantic Railway*, Dublin: Longman.

Knox, S. J. (1959) *Ireland's Debt to the Huguenots*, Dublin: APCK.

Kohl, J. G. (1844) *Ireland, Scotland, England*, London: Chapman & Hall. (Translated from German.)

Land Commission (1952) *Report of the Irish Land Commissioners for the Year from 1st April 1951 to 31st March 1952*, Dublin: Stationery Office. (With article on Gaeltacht colonies in Co. Meath.)

—— (1953) *Report of the Irish Land Commissioners for. . . 1st April 1952 to 31st March 1953*, Dublin: Stationery Office.

—— (1955) *Report of the Irish Land Commissioners for. . . 1st April 1954 to 31st March 1955*, Dublin: Stationery Office.

Latocnaye, B. de (1917) *Promenade d'un Francais dans l'Irlande, 1796–7*, trans. J. Stevenson (1917) as *A Frenchman's Walk through Ireland*, Dublin: Hodges Figgis.

Lee, J. J. (eds.) (1979) *Ireland 1945–1970*, Dublin: Gill & Macmillan.

Letters containing Information relative to the Antiquities of (each Irish county) *collected during the Progress of the Ordnance Survey* (1834–40, for the eastern counties). MSS, some typescript copies, Dublin: Royal Irish Academy. (The 'O'Donovan and O'Curry' letters.)

Letters from the Irish Highlands of Cunnemara: by a Family Party (1825), 2nd edn, London: Longman.

Lewis, S. (1837) *A Topographical Dictionary of Ireland*, 2 vols., London: Lewis; reprinted 1970, London: Kennikat Press.

Límistéirí Gaeltachta 1956, Dublin: Ordnance Survey. (Map, in Irish, of the Gaeltacht areas as defined in 1956.)

Little, D. G., Singleton, D. M., and Silvius, W. M. F. (1984) *Learning Second Languages in Ireland*, Dublin: Centre for Language and Communication Studies, Trinity College.

Lockwood, W. B. (1975) *Languages of the British Isles – Past and Present*, London: Deutsch.

Mac an Iomaire, P. (1983) 'Tionchar na Tionscailaíochta ar Ghaeilge Chonamara Theas' (The influence of industrialization on South Conamara Irish), *Teangeolas* 16: 9–18. (Irish only.)

Mac Aodha, B. S. (1969) *Galway Gaeltacht Survey*, Galway: Social Sciences Research Centre, University College.
—— (1972) 'Was this a social revolution?' in Ó Tuama, S. (ed.) *The Gaelic League Idea*, Cork: Mercier.
—— (1985–6) 'Aspects of the linguistic geography of Ireland in the early nineteenth century', Studia Celtica 20–1: 205–20.
Mac Cana, P. (1980) *Literature in Irish*, Dublin: Department of Foreign Affairs.
Macardle, D. (1937) *The Irish Republic*, London: Gollancz; 4th edn 1951, Dublin: Irish Press.
Mac Cárthaigh, M., and Ó Suilleabháin, D. (1962) *Meamram Telefís Éireann* (Memorandum on Irish television), Áth Cliath: Conradh na Gaeilge.
Mac Court, D. (1954) 'Traditions of rundale in and around the Sperrin Mountains', *Ulster Journal of Archaeology* 1953: 70–84.
MacDonagh, O., Hancock, W. K., Mandle, W. F., and Travers, P. (1983) *Irish Culture and Nationalism 1750–1950*, London: Macmillan.
MacDonald, P. I. (n.d., c. 1970) 'Tory Island: a North-west Donegal Survival', unpublished research report, Department of Civil Engineering, University of Leeds.
McDowell, R. B. (1944) *Irish Public Opinion 1750–1800*, London: Faber.
—— (1952) *Public Opinion and Government Policy in Ireland 1801–1846*, London: Faber.
—— (1957) *Social Life in Ireland 1800–1845*, Dublin: Ó Lochlainn.
—— (1964) *The Irish Administration, 1801–1914*, London: Routledge.
McElligott, T. J. (1966) *Education in Ireland*, Dublin: Institute of Public Administration.
MacEvoy, J. (1802) *Statistical Survey of the County of Tyrone, Drawn Up in the Years 1801 and 1802*, Dublin: Royal Dublin Society.
Mac Gearailt, S. (1986) 'Bilingualism in Education and Public Administration in Gwynedd, Wales', Tralee: Roinn na Gaeltachta/Department of the Gaeltacht. (Internal report on a study visit, May 1986.)
Mackey, W. F. (1977) *Irish Language Promotion: Potential and Constraints*, Occasional Paper 1, Institiúid Teangeolaíochta Éireann.
McKiernan, E. (1963) *The Will of a Nation: Ireland's Crisis*, St Paul, Minn.: Patrick Butler Foundation.
MacKinnon, K. (1985) *The Scottish Gaelic Speech-community – some Social Perspectives*, Business and Social Sciences Occasional Papers BSS 13, Hatfield: Hatfield Polytechnic.
Mac Lysaght, E. (1950 edn) *Irish Life in the Seventeenth Century*, Cork: Cork University Press.
—— (1973) *The Surnames of Ireland*, Dublin: Irish University Press.
MacManus, L. (1929) *White Light and Flame: Memories of the Irish Literary Revival and the Anglo-Irish War*, Dublin and Cork: Talbot Press.
MacManus, M. J. (1944) *Eamon de Valera*, 6th edn 1957, Dublin: Talbot Press.
Mac Mathúna, L., and Singleton, D. (eds.) (1982–3) *Language across Cultures*, Dublin: Irish Association for Applied Linguistics.
Macnamara, J. (1964) 'The Commission on Irish: psychological aspects',

Studies 53: 164–73.

—— (1966) *Bilingualism and Primary Education: a Study of Irish Experience*, Edinburgh: Edinburgh University Press.

—— (1967) 'The effects of instruction in a weaker language', *Journal of Social Issues* 23, 2: 121–35.

—— (1971) 'Successes and failures in the movement for the restoration of Irish', in J. Rubin and B. H. Jernudd (eds.) *Can Languages be Planned?* Honolulu: University Press of Hawaii.

—— (1977) 'The Irish language and nationalism', in M. P. Hederman and R. Kearney (eds.) *Crane Bag Book of Irish Studies*, Dublin: Blackwater Press.

MacParlan, J. (1802a) *Statistical Survey of the County of Donegal*, Dublin: Royal Dublin Society.

—— (1802b) *Statistical Survey of the County of Leitrim*, Dublin: Royal Dublin Society.

—— (1802c) *Statistical Survey of the County of Mayo*, Dublin: Royal Dublin Society.

—— (1802d) *Statistical Survey of the County of Sligo*, Dublin: Royal Dublin Society.

McQuige, J. (1818) *The Importance of Schools for Teaching the Native Irish Language*, London: Button Whittimore.

Macsween, A. (1983) *Western Isles Council Bilingual Policy*, Stornoway: Comhairle nan Eilean. (Miscellaneous internal papers on project implementation, including statistics of native speakers entering first-year secondary 1976–82).)

Mansergh, P. N. S. (1965) *The Irish Question, 1840–1921*, London: Allen & Unwin; 1st edn 1940, *Ireland in the Age of Revolution and Reform.*

Marchi, B. de, and Boileau, A.M. (eds.) (1982) *Boundaries and Minorities in Western Europe*, Milan: Angeli.

Martin, A. (1980) *Anglo-Irish Literature*, Dublin: Department of Foreign Affairs.

Marx, K., and Engels, F. (1953) *On Britain*, Collected works, Moscow: Foreign Languages Publishing House; London: Lawrence & Wishart, 1954.

Mason, W. S. (1814, 1816, 1819) *A Statistical Account or Parochial Survey of Ireland, drawn up from the Communications of the Clergy*, 3 vols., Dublin: Cumming.

Matsuoka, T. (n.d., *c.* 1982) 'The Irish language in the Galltacht areas', *Bulletin of the Faculty of Liberal Arts, Hosei University* (Japan) 45: 1–21. (Copy by courtesy of M. Ó Murchú.)

Meenan, J., and Webb, D. A. (eds.) (1957) *A View of Ireland: Twelve Essays on Different Aspects of Irish Life*, etc., Dublin: British Association.

Mellor, R. (1962–3) 'A minority problem in Germany', *Scottish Geographical Magazine* 78–9: 49–53. (The Sorbs.)

Mescal, J. (1957) *Religion in the Irish System of Education*, Dublin: Clonmore & Reynolds.

Micks, W. L. (1925) *An Account of the Constitution, Administration and Dissolution of the Congested Districts Board for Ireland from 1891 to*

1923, Dublin: Eason.

Minutes of Evidence on the State of Ireland, Sessional papers 1825, 9, London: HM Stationery Office.

Monypenny, W.F. (1913) *The Two Irish Nations: an Essay on Home Rule*, London: Murray.

Moody, T. W. (1945) *Thomas Davis, 1814–45*, Dublin: Trinity College Historical Society.

—— (ed.) (1977) *Nationality and the Pursuit of Irish Independence*, Belfast: Appletree.

—— and Beckett, J. C. (eds.) (1957) *Ulster since 1800: a Social Survey*, 2 vols., London: BBC.

—— and Martin, F. X. (eds.) (1967) *The Course of Irish History*, Cork: Mercier.

—— Martin, F. X., and Byrne, F. J. (eds.) (1976–86) *A New History of Ireland*, vols. 2, 3, 4, 8, 9, Oxford: Clarendon Press. (See especially B. Ó Cuív's chapters on Irish language and literature. Remaining vols. are still unpublished, April 1989.)

Mooney, C. (1944) 'The beginnings of the Irish Language Revival', *Irish Ecclesiastical Record*, 5th series, 64: 10–18.

Morgan, J. V. (1911) *A Study in Nationality*, London: Chapman & Hall.

Morrissey, P. J. (1958) *Working Conditions in Ireland and their Effect on Irish Emigration*, New York: Morrissey.

Morrissey, T. (1988) 'Saving the language: "the impatient revolutionary" ', *Studies* 77: 352–7.

Murphy. C. (1981) 'The crisis in Irish', *Irish Times*, 25–8 May (daily). (Four articles.)

Murphy, G. (1948) 'Irish in our schools, 1922–25', *Studies* 37: 421–8.

Murphy, J. A. (1975) *Ireland in the Twentieth Century*, Dublin: Gill & Macmillan.

Murphy, J.N. (1870) *Ireland Industrial, Political and Social*, London: Longman.

Nicholls, K. (1972) *Gaelic and Gaelicised Ireland in the later Middle Ages*, Dublin: Gill & Macmillan.

Northern Ireland Government (1956) *Why the Border must Be*, Belfast.

Norman, E. R. (1965) *The Catholic Church and Ireland in the Age of Rebellion, 1859–73*, London: Longman.

North East Boundary Bureau (1923) *Handbook of the Ulster Question*, Dublin: Stationery Office.

Ó Baoill, D. P. (ed.) (1986) *Lárchanúint don Ghaeilge* (Basic Irish Pronunciation), with associated illustrative cassette *Téip Léirithe*, Baile Átha Cliath: Institiúid Teangeolaíochta Eireann. (For learners. Explanation is in English.)

—— (1987) 'Cén chanúint í sin?' ('How do you say that?'), *Teangeolas* 23: 8–12. (On the need for standardized pronunciation in Irish.)

—— (1988) 'Language planning in Ireland: the standardization of Irish', *International Journal of the Sociology of Language* 70: 109–26.

O'Brien, D. C. C. (1960) *The Shaping of Modern Ireland*, London: Routledge.

—— (1972) *States of Ireland*, London: Hutchinson.

O'Brien, J. A. (1953) *The Vanishing Irish: the Enigma of the Modern World*, New York: McGraw-Hill.

O'Brien, T. (1987) 'Some developments in broadcasting provision for lesser used languages', *Contact Bulletin* 3, 3 and 4, 1: 7–11.

Ó Buachalla, S. (1984) 'Educational policy and the role of the Irish language from 1831 to 1981', *European Journal of Education* 19, 1: 75–92.

Ó Casaide, S. (1930) *The Irish Language in Belfast and County Down, A. D. 1601–1850*, Dublin: Gill.

O'Casey, S. (1963 edn) *Autobiographies,* 2 vols., London: Macmillan. First published as *I Knock at the Door* (1939), *Pictures in the Hallway* (1942), *Drums under the Windows* (1945), *Inishfallen, Fare thee Well* (1949), *Rose and Crown* (1952), and *Sunset and Evening Star* (1954).

Ó Catháin, S. (1973) 'The future of the Irish language', *Studies* 67: 303–22.

Ó Cathasaigh, S. (1943) 'Buailteachas in iarthar Chonamara' (Transhumance in west Conamara), *Béaloideas*: 159–60.

Ó Cinnéide, M. S. (1985) 'Community development courses in the Gaeltacht', *Community Education*: 78–83, AONTAS Report series, Dublin: AONTAS.

——— and Keane, M. (1987) 'The Industrialization of the Northwest Donegal Gaeltacht', paper given at 9th International Seminar on Marginal Regions, held in Skye and Lewis, July.

——— Keane, M., and Cawley, M. (1985) 'Industrialization and linguistic change among Gaelic-speaking communities in the west of Ireland', *Language Problems and Language Planning* 9, 1: 3–15.

Ó Coigligh, C. (1984) 'English words and expressions in the Irish of Inis Meáin and the use of English by the local community', in L. Mac Mathúna and D. Singleton (eds.) *Language across Cultures*, Dublin: Association for Applied Linguistics.

Ó Conaire, B. (Flann O'Brien) (1973), "An Béal Bocht" and other Irish matters', *Irish University Review* 3: 121–40. ('An Béal Bocht': 'the poor mouth', i.e. pleading poverty.)

Ó Conchúir, S. (1984) Muintearas na nOileán Preschool Component: Report submitted to Bernard van Leer Foundation and Údarás na Gaeltachta', Galway: unpublished but kindly made available.

Ó Conghaile, M. (ed.) (1986) *Gaeltacht Ráth Cairn: Léachtaí Comórtha* (Rathcarran Gaeltacht: collected papers), Beal an Daingin, Conamara: Raidió na Gaeltachta and Cló Iar-Chonnachta. (Irish only.)

O'Connell, T. J. (1968) *History of the Irish National Teachers' Organization, 1868–1968*, Dublin: INTO.

Ó Corcora, D. (1942) *What's this about the Gaelic League?*, Áth Cliath: Connradh na Gaedhilge. See also Corkery, D.

Ó Cuív, B. (1944) *The Irish of West Muskerry, Co. Cork*, Dublin: Dublin Institute for Advanced Studies.

——— (1951) *Irish Dialects and Irish-speaking Districts*, Dublin: Dublin Institute for Advanced Studies.

——— (1966) 'Education and language', in T. D. Williams (ed.) *The Irish Struggle 1916–26*, London: Routledge.

—— (ed.) (1969) *A View of the Irish Language*, Dublin: Stationery Office.
Ó Danachair, C. (1969) 'The Gaeltacht', in B. Ó Cuív (ed.) *A View of the Irish Language*, Dublin: Stationery Office.
O 'Doherty, E. F. (1958) 'Bilingual school policy', *Studies* 47: 259–68.
Ó Donaill, N. (1977) *Foclóir Gaeilge–Béarla* (Irish–English dictionary), Baile Átha Cliath: Oifig an tSoláthair. (The essential 'big' dictionary.)
O'Donnell, F. H. (1903) *The Ruin of Education in Ireland and the Irish Fanar*, 3rd edn, London: Nutt.
O'Donovan, J., and O'Curry, E. (1834–40 etc.) *Ordnance Survey Letters*: see under Ordnance Survey, and under Letters.
Ó Dubhda, P. (1943) *Maynooth and our National Language: some Startling Reports from the Gaeltacht*, Dundalk: the author.
O'Faolain, S. (1943) 'Gaelic: the truth', *The Bell* 5: 335–40.
—— (1947) *The Irish*, West Drayton: Penguin Books.
O'Farrell, P. N., and Crouchley, R. (1983) 'Industrial closure in Ireland 1973–81: analysis and implications', *Regional Studies* 17, 6: 411–27.
Ó Fiaich, T. (1969) 'The language and political history', in B. Ó Cuív (ed.) *A View of the Irish Language*, Dublin: Stationery Office.
—— (1972) 'The great Controversy', in S. Ó Tuama (ed.) *The Gaelic League Idea*.
—— and Patterson, V. (1970) 'Nordirland', in M. Straka (ed.) *Handbuch der europäischen Volksgruppen*, Ethnos 8, Vienna: Bramüuller.
O' Floinn, A. D. (1954) *The Integral Irish Tradition*, Dublin: Gill.
Ó Gadhra, N. (1978) 'Broadcasting in Ireland: problem or opportunity?', *Irish Broadcasting Review* 1: 33–4.
—— (1981) 'Language report: developments in 1980', *Éire–Ireland* 16, 1: 109–18.
—— (n.d., c. 1982) *Gaeltacht Mhaigh Eo*, Baile Átha Cliath: Clodhanna Teo. (Collected articles on the Mayo Gaeltachtaí. Irish only.)
Ó Glaisne, R. (1981) 'Irish and the Protestant tradition', *Crane Bag* 5: 33–44.
Ó Gliasáin, M. (1988) 'Bilingual secondary schools in Dublin 1960–1980', *International Journal of the Sociology of Language* 70: 89–108.
Ó hAdhmaill, F. (1985) *Report of a Survey on the Irish Language in West Belfast*, Coleraine: Department of Social Administration, University of Ulster.
Ó hAilín, T. (1969) 'Irish revival movements', in B. Ó Cuív (ed.) *A View of the Irish Language*, Dublin: Stationery Office.
O'Hegarty, P. (1952) *A History of Ireland under the Union 1801 to 1922*, London: Methuen.
O'Hegarty, P. S. (1924) *The Victory of Sinn Féin: How it Won it and How it Used it*, Dublin: Talbot Press.
Ó hEochaidh, S. (1943) 'Buailteachas i dTír Chonaill' (Transhumance in Donegal), *Bealoideas*: 130–58.
O'Mahoney, D. (1962) *The Irish Economy*, Cork: Cork University Press.
Ó Muircheartaigh, T. (1956) *An Dá Fhórsa* (The two forces), Áth Cliath: Connradh na Gaedhilge. (Irish only.)
Ó Muirithe, D. (ed.) (1977) *The English Language in Ireland*, Cork: Mercier.
Ó Muraíle, N. (1985) Mayo Places – their Names and Origins, Dublin: FNT.

Ó Murchadha, M. S. (1951) 'Gaedhilg Dhúthchaish Thír Eoghain' (Native Irish in Tyrone), *An tUltach* 27, 5: 1–3.

Ó Murchú, H, (1984) 'Interaction between Learner and Learning Environment: Issues. . . for Adult Learners of Irish', Research paper, Trinity College Dublin.

Ó Murchú, L. (1970) *Watch your Language*, Dublin: RTÉ.

Ó Murchú, M. (1970) *Language and Community*, Comhairle na Gaeilge Occasional Papers 1, Dublin: Stationery Office.

—— (1984a) 'Irish and English now', *Bulletin of the Department of Foreign Affairs* 1011: 11–13.

—— (1984b) 'An overview of bilingualism in Ireland', paper given to Highland Regional Council Conference on Bilingualism. (Typescript.)

—— (1985a) *The Irish Language*, Dublin: Department of Foreign Affairs and Bord na Gaeilge.

—— (1985b) 'Léamh na Gaeilge ar an raidió' (Reading Irish on the radio), *Teangeolas* 20: 18–21.

O'Neill, E. (1969) 'The lingual minority in Eire' and 'Problems of text-books in Eire', in E. Holmestad and A. J. Lade (eds.) *Lingual Minorities in Europe*, Oslo: Det Norske Samlaget.

Ó Nualláin, L. S. (1952) *Finances of Partition*, Dublin: Clonmore & Reynolds.

O'Rahilly, T. F. (1932) *Irish Dialects Past and Present, with Chapters on Scottish Gaelic and Manx*, Dublin: Browne & Nolan.

Ordnance Survey of Ireland MSS (1834–40), including the O'Donovan and O'Curry letters collected during the progress of the Ordnance Survey, and the unpublished parish memoirs. Some transcribed on to typescript. Dublin: Royal Irish Academy.

Ordú na Limistéirí Gaeltachta 1956 etc.: see Gaeltacht Department, as *Gaeltacht Areas Orders*.

Ó Riagáin, P. (ed.) (1971) *The Gaeltacht Studies* vol. 1, *Development Plan for the Gaeltacht*, Dublin: An Foras Forbartha.

—— (1978) 'Regional planning in Irish bilingual areas', *Cambria* 5, 2: 182–7.

—— (1987) 'Social class, education and Irish', *Teangeolas* 23: 13–14.

—— (ed.) (1988a) 'Language planning in Ireland', *International Journal of the Sociology of Language* 70: 3–142; single-subject issue.

—— (1988b) 'Public attitudes towards Irish in the schools: a note on recent surveys', *Teangeolas* 25: 19–21.

—— and Ó Gliasáin, M. (1979) *All-Irish Primary Schools in the Dublin Area: a Sociological and Spatial Analysis of the Impact of all-Irish Schools on Home and Social Use of Irish*, Dublin: Institiúid Teangeolaíochta Éireann.

—— and Ó Gliasáin, M. (eds.) (1984) *The Irish Language in the Republic of Ireland 1983: Preliminary Report of a National Survey*, Dublin: Institiúid Teangeolaíochta Éireann.

Orme, A. R. (1970) *Ireland*, World's Landscape series, London: Longman.

Ó Sé, L (1966) 'The Irish language revival: Achilles heel', *Éire–Ireland* 1, 1: 26–49.

Ó Snodaigh, P. (1973) *Hidden Ulster*, Dublin: Clodhanna Teo.

Ó Súileabháin, M. (1953 edn) *Twenty Years A-growing*, trans. M. L. Davies and G. Thomson, London: Oxford University Press. (1st edn in Irish, 1933, Baile Átha Cliath: Clólucht & Talbóidigh.)

O'Sullivan, D. (1940) *The Irish Free State and its Senate*, London: Faber.

Ó Tuama, S. (1964) *The Facts about Irish*, Dublin: ACP.

—— (ed.) (1972) *The Gaelic League Idea*, Cork and Dublin: Mercier.

Ó Tuathaigh, G. (1972) *Ireland before the Famine, 1798–1848*, Dublin: Gill & Macmillan.

—— (1979) 'Language, literature and culture in Ireland since the war', in J. J. Lee (ed.) *Ireland 1945–70*, Dublin: Gill & Macmillan.

Parker, A. J. (1972) '30,000 Gaeltacht Irishmen', *Geographical Magazine* 45, 2: 126–34.

Paul-Dubois, L. (1907) *L'Irlande contemporaine et la Question Irlandaise*, Paris; trans. as *Contemporary Ireland*, 1908, Dublin: Maunsel.

Paulin, T. (1985) 'A new look at the language question', in Field Day Theatre Company, *Ireland's Field Day*, London: Hutchinson.

Pearse, P. H. (1916) *The Murder Machine*, Dublin: Whelan; reprinted with other essays 1976, Cork: Mercier.

—— (1917) The Story of Success etc., ed. D. Ryan, Dublin: Maunsel.

Peillon, M. (1982) *Contemporary Irish Society: an Introduction*, Dublin: Gill & Macmillan. (See especially pp. 100–5, 'The paradox of Irish revival'.)

Pender, S. (ed.) (1947) *Féilscríbhinn Tórna: Tráchtaisí Léanta in Onóir don Ollamh Tadhg Ua Donnchadha* (Essays in honour of Professor Tadhg Ua Donnchadha), Cork: Cork University Press.

Petty, Sir W. (1927) *The Petty Papers: some Unpublished Writings*, 2 vols., ed. Marquis of Lansdowne, London: Constable.

Philbin, W. J. (1962) *The Irish in the new Europe*, Dublin: Gill.

Phillips, W. A. (ed.) (1933–4) *History of the Church of Ireland from Earliest Times to the Present Day*, 3 vols., London: Oxford University Press.

Piatt, D. S. (1933) *Dialect in East and Mid-Leinster: Gaelic Survivals*, Dublin: n.s.

Piers, Sir H. (1770) 'A chorographical description of the County of West-Meath, written AD 1682', in C. Vallancey, *Collectanea de Rebus Hibernicis*, 6 vols., 1770–84, Dublin: Ewing.

Plettner, H. J. (1979) *Geographical Aspects of Tourism in the Irish Republic*, Galway: Social Sciences Research Centre, University College Galway.

Pokorny, J. (1933) *A History of Ireland*, trans. S. D. King, London: Longman.

Pop, S. (1950) *La Dialectologie. Aperçu historique et méthodes d' enquêtes linguistiques*, 2 vols., Louvain: University of Louvain. (See pp. 925–55, 'Langues celtiques'.)

Power, P. C. (1949) 'The Gaelic Union: a nonagenarian retrospect', *Studies* 38: 413–18.

Praeger, R. L. (1937) *The Way that I went: an Irishman in Ireland*, Dublin: Hodges Figgis.

Prattis, J. I. (1983) 'Industrialisation and minority language loyalty – the example of Lewis', in J. C. Hansen, J. Naustdalslid, and J. Sewel (eds.) *Centre–Periphery Theory and Practice*, Proceedings of 6th

International Seminar on Marginal Regions, Sogndal, pp. 246–59. (Incomplete copy, no publisher stated.)

Prendergast, J. P. (1865) *The Cromwellian Settlement of Ireland*, 3rd edn 1922, Dublin: Mellifont.

Price, G. (1979) 'The present position and viability of minority languages', in A. E. Alcock, B. K. Taylor, and J. M. Welton (eds.) *The Future of Cultural Minorities*, London: Macmillan.

—— (1984a) *The Languages of Britain*, London: Arnold.

—— (1984b) 'Linguistic Censuses and Minority Languages', paper given at 7th World Congress of Applied Linguistics, Brussels.

Price, L. (1949) 'Place-name study as applied to history', *Journal of the Royal Society of Antiquaries of Ireland, Centenary Volume*: 26–38.

Pringle, D. G. (1985) *One Island, Two Nations? A Political Geographical Analysis of the National Conflict in Ireland*, Letchworth: Research Studies Press.

Pritchard, R. M. (1982) 'Modern language teaching in Northern Ireland', *Teangeolas* 14: 6–11.

Probert, B. (1978) *Beyond Orange and Green*, London: Academy Press.

Pryde, D. (1962) *A New History of Scotland*, London: Nelson.

Public Services Organisation Review Group 1966–1969 (1969) ('Devlin Report'), Dublin: Department of Finance/Stationery Office.

Quiggin, E. C. (1906) *A Dialect of Donegal, being the Speech of Meenawannia in . . . Glenties*, Cambridge: Cambridge University Press.

Radio Teilefís Éireann (1970) *Watch your Language*, Dublin: RTÉ.

Ravenstein, E. G. (1879) 'On the Celtic languages in the British Isles: a statistical survey', *Journal of the Royal Statistical Society* 42: 579–643.

Rawson, T. J. (1807) *Statistical Survey of the County of Kildare*, Dublin: Royal Dublin Society.

Rees, W. H. (1939) *Le Bilinguisme des pays celtiques*, Rennes: Simon.

Regan, C., and Breathnach, P. (1981) *State and Community: Rural Development Strategies in the Slieve League Peninsula, Co. Donegal*, Maynooth: Department of Geography, St Patrick's College.

Report from Select Committee on the new Plan for Education in Ireland, together with the Minutes of Evidence, (1837), 2 vols., London: HM Stationery Office.

Report of the Commissioners of Education, Ireland (1915), London: HM Stationery Office.

Report of the Department of Education 1932–33 (1934), Dublin: Stationery Office. (Article on the introduction of the *deontas*.)

Report of the Department of Education 1951–52 (1953), Dublin: Stationery Office.

Reports of the Commission on Emigration and other Population Problems, 1948–54 (1955), Dublin: Stationery Office.

Reports of the Irish Land Commissioners: see under Land Commission.

Restoration of the Irish Language, 'White Paper' (1965) Dublin: Stationery Office.

Restoration of the Irish Language, White Paper on, Progress Report for the

Period ended 31 March 1966 (1966) Dublin: Stationery Office.
Restoration of the Irish Language, White Paper on, Progress Report for the Period ended 31 March 1968 (1968), Dublin: Stationery Office.
Roberts, P. W. (1975) *Regional Planning in the Republic of Ireland: its Future Development. . .* , Liverpool: Department of Town and Country Planning, Liverpool Polytechnic.
Roinn na Gaeltachta: see Gaeltacht Department.
Rokkan, S., and Urwin, D. W. (eds.) (1982) *The Politics of Territorial Identity: Studies in European Regionalism*, London: Sage.
—— (1983) *Economy, Territory, Identity: Politics of West European Peripheries*, London: Sage.
Rubin, J., and Jernudd, B. H. (eds.) (1971) *Can Language be Planned?* Honolulu: University Press of Hawaii.
Rumpf, E., and Hepburn, A. C. (1976) *Nationalism and Socialism in Twentieth Century Ireland*, Liverpool: Liverpool University Press.
Ryan, D. (1939) *The Sword of Light: from the Four Masters to Douglas Hyde, 1636–1938*, London: Barker.
Salaman, R. N. (1943) *The Influence of the Potato on the Course of Irish History,* Dublin: Browne & Nolan.
—— (1949) *The History and Social Influence of the Potato*, Cambridge: Cambridge University Press.
Sampson, G.V. (1802) *Statistical Survey of the County of Londonderry*, Dublin: Royal Dublin Society.
Saorstát Éireann: Official Handbook (1932) Dublin: Stationery Office.
Savage, R. B. (1955) 'Ireland tomorrow', *Studies* 44: 1–4.
Savard, J. -G., and Vigneault, R. (1975) *Multilingual Political Systems: Problems and Solutions*, Québec: Presses de l'Université de Laval.
Savory , D. L. (1948) 'The Huguenot–Palatine settlements in the counties of Limerick, Kerry and Tipperary', *Proceedings of the Huguenot Society of London* 18: 1–23, 215–31.
Schiller, H. I. (1977) *New Modes of Cultural Domination*, Dublin: Conradh na Gaeilge.
Schrier, A. (1958) *Ireland and the American Emigration 1850–1900*, Minneapolis: University of Minnesota Press.
Scully, J. J. (1971) *Agriculture in the West of Ireland*, Dublin: Department of Agriculture and Fisheries/Stationery Office.
Second Programme for Economic Expansion (1963) Dublin: Stationery Office.
Seers, D., Schaffer, B., and Kiljunen, M. (eds.) (1979) *Underdeveloped Europe: Studies in Core–Periphery Relations*, Hassocks, Sussex: Harvester Press.
Senior, Nassau W. (1868) *Journals, Conversations and Essays relating to Ireland,* 2 vols., 2nd edn, London: Longman.
Shearman, H. (1949) *Ulster*, London: Hale.
Sheehy, M. (1955) *Divided we Stand: a Study of Partition*, London: Faber.
Sheridan, J. D. (1955) 'Irish writing today', *Studies* 45: 81–5.
Simms, J. G. (1956) *The Williamite Confiscation in Ireland 1690–1703*, London: Faber.
Sinn Féin (1979) *Éire Nua* (New Ireland)*: The Sinn Féin Policy: the Social,*

Economic and Political Dimension, Dublin: Sinn Féin.

Sjoestedt, M. -L. (1931) *Phonétique d'un parler irlandais de Kerry* (Dunquin), Paris: Leroux.

Sjoestedt-Jonval, M. -L. (1938) 'Les langues de culture en celtique', *Conférences de l'Institut de Linguistique de l'Université de Paris*, 6ᵉ année.

Smith, J. (ed.) (1961) *Gaelic-speaking Children in Highland Schools*, London: University of London Press.

Smyth, G. L. (1844–9) *Ireland, Historical and Statistical*, 3 vols., London: Whittaker.

Sölch, J. (1952) *Die Landschaften der Britischen Inseln*, Vienna: Springer.

Statesman's Year-book 1988–89 (and annually), (ed. J. Paxton), London: Macmillan.

Stephens, M. (ed.) (1973) *The Welsh Language Today*, Llandysul: Gomer.

—— (1976) *Linguistic Minorities in Western Europe*, Llandysul: Gomer.

Stephens, N., and Glascock, R. E. (eds.) (1970) *Irish Geographical Studies in Honour of E. Estyn Evans*, Belfast: Queen's University.

Stewart, A. T. Q. (1977) *The Narrow Ground: Aspects of Ulster, 1609–1969*, London: Faber.

Stokes, Whitley (1799) *Project for Re-establishing the Internal Peace and Tranquillity of Ireland*, Dublin: Moore.

—— (1806) *The Necessity of Publishing the Scriptures in Irish*, Dublin? (Cited by Anderson, 1828, 1846 edn; not in British Library or Library of Congress.)

Straka, M. (1970) *Handbuch der europäischen Volksgruppen*, Vienna: Braumüller. (Covers Northern Ireland only.)

Strauss, E. (1952) *Irish Nationalism and British Democracy*, London: Methuen.

Streib, G. F. (1974) 'The restoration of the Irish language: behavioural and symbolic aspects', *Ethnicity* 1: 73–89.

Sweeney, K. (1988) *The Irish Language in Northern Ireland, 1987: Preliminary Report of a Survey of Knowledge, Interest and Ability*, Policy, Planning and Research Unit Occasional Paper No. 17, Stormont: Department of Finance and Personnel.

Symes, D. G. (1965a) *The Population Resources of the Connemara Gaeltacht*, Department of Geography Miscellaneous Series 1, Hull: University of Hull.

—— (1965b) *The Population Resources of the Gaeltacht 2, Co. Donegal*, Department of Geography Miscellaneous Series 3, Hull: University of Hull.

Synge, J. M. (1907) *The Aran Islands*, Dublin: Maunsel.

Thackeray, W.M. (1843) *The Irish Sketch-book: by Mr. M. A. Titmarsh*, London: Chapman & Hall.

Thomas, C. (ed.) (1986) *Rural Landscapes and Communities: Essays presented to Desmond McCourt*, Blackrock: Irish Academic Press.

Thompson, R. (1802) *Statistical Survey of the County of Meath*, Dublin: Royal Dublin Society.

Thomson, D. S. (ed.) (1983) *The Companion to Gaelic Scotland*, Oxford,

321

Blackwell.

Tierney, M. (1927) 'The Revival of the Irish lanaguage', *Studies* 16: 1–10.
— (ed.) (1949) *Daniel O'Connell: Nine Centenary Essays*, Dublin: Browne & Nolan.

Tighe, W. (1802) *Statistical Observations relative to the County of Kilkenny, made in the Years 1800 and 1801*, Dublin: Royal Dublin Society.

Tithe an Oireachtais Joint Committee on the Irish Language (1985), *First Report on the Use of Irish in the Proceedings of the Dáil and Seanad*, Dublin: Tithe an Oireachtais/Stationery Office.
— (1986a) *Second Report on the Extension of the Use of Irish in the Proceedings of the Dáil and Seanad*, Dublin: Tithe an Oireachtais/Stationery Office.
— (1986b) *First Annual Report 1985/86*, Dublin: Tithe an Oireachtais/Stationery Office.

Tocqueville, A. C. H. M. C., Count de (1958 edn) *Journeys to England and Ireland*, trans. G. Lawrence and K. P. Mayer, ed. J. P. Mayer, London: Faber.

Todd, L. (1989) *The Language of Irish Literature*, London: Macmillan.

Tovey, H. (1977) 'The use of Irish in Gaeltacht areas: maintenance and erosion', *Teangeolas* 6: 15–20.
— (1978) *Language Policy and Socioeconomic Development in Ireland*, ITÉ Publication No. 13 (B), Dublin: Institiúid Teangeolaíochta Éireann.
— (1988) 'The state of the Irish language; the role of Bord na Gaeilge', *International Journal of the Sociology of Language* 70: 53–68.

Townsend, H. (1810) *Statistical Survey of the County of Cork*, Dublin: Royal Dublin Society.

Tracy, H. L. W. (1953) *Mind you, I've said Nothing: Forays in the Irish Republic*, London: White Lion.

Trench, W. S. (1868) *Realities of Irish Life*, London: Longman.

Trudgill, P. (ed.) (1984) *Language in the British Isles*, Cambridge: Cambridge University Press.

Tuarascáil an Chomhchoiste um Oideachas sa Ghaeltacht (1986) (Report of the Subcommittee on Education in the Gaeltacht), Baile Átha Cliath: Oifig an tSoláthair. (In Irish, with summary of recommendations in English.)

Údarás na Gaeltachta (1979) *Údarás na Gaeltachta Act 1979*, Dublin: Stationery Office.
— (1985–86) *Scéim Naíonraí Ghaeltachta 1984/1985: Modh Oibre* (The Gaeltacht Pre-school Playgroup Scheme 1984–1985: mode of operation). (Duplicated circular.)
— (1985a) *Údarás na Gaeltacht*a. General notes with particular reference to language support work; company grant agreements with reference to language conditions; form used to monitor language use in Gaeltacht companies; etc. (Duplicated information circulars.)
— (1985b) *The Irish Language in the Gaeltacht Company: Draft Plan*, with list of services available. (Duplicate circular.)
— (1986a) *Cúrsaí Gaeilge Leasmuigh den Údarás* (External Irish courses

of Údarás). List in Irish of all centres at which courses were held in 1986. (Duplicated.)

—— (1986b) *Liosta de na Naíonraí, Aibreán 1986* (List of all Naíonraí, April 1986). (Duplicated.)

—— (1986c) *Tuarascáil agus Cuntais 1985* (Report and accounts 1985), Na Forbacha, Gaillimh: Údarás na Gaeltachta.

—— (1986d) *Overview and Extracts from Accounts 1985,* Na Forbacha; Údarás na Gaeltachta. (English summary.)

—— (1987) *Ógchlubanna Chonamara 1986/87* (Conamara Irish-language youth clubs supported by Údarás). (Duplicated, with MS list for other Gaeltachtaí.)

Údarás na Gaeltachta (n.d. 1987) *An Pobal Beo: Scéim Forbartha agus Oid-eachais* ('The living people': development and education scheme), Na Forbacha: Údarás na Gaeltachta. (Community development for the Gaeltacht. Printed leaflet.)

'Údarás na Gaeltachta – attracting lame ducks' (1981) *Irish Business*, March: 2–9.

United Nations Department of Economic and Social Affairs (1955) *Economic Survey of Europe in 1954, including Studies of Regional Problems in European Countries*, Geneva: Economic Commission for Europe.

Ussher, A. (1950) *The Face and Mind of Ireland*, London: Gollancz.

Valéra, R. de (1949) 'Seán Ó Donnabháin agus a lucht cúnta' (John O'Donovan and his helpers: the early Irish Ordnance Survey), *Journal of the Royal Society of Antiquaries of Ireland, centenary volume*: 146–59.

Vendryes, J. (1940) 'La situation linguistique en Irlande', *Études Celtiques* 4: 177–9.

Wagner, H. (1958a) *Linguistic Atlas and Survey of Irish Dialects*, vol. 1, *Introduction*, Dublin: Dublin Institute for Advanced Studies.

—— (1958b) 'A linguistic atlas and survey of Irish dialects', *Lochlann: a Review of Celtic Studies*, 1: 9–48.

Wagner, P. L. (1958) 'Remarks on the geography of language', *Geographical Review* 48: 86–97.

—— and Mikesell, M. W. (eds.) (1962) *Readings in Cultural Geography*, Chicago: University of Chicago Press.

Wakefield, E. (1812) *An Account of Ireland, Statistical and Political*, 2 vols., London: Longman.

Wall, M. (1969) 'The decline of the Irish language', in B. Ó Cuív (ed.) *A View of the Irish Language*, Dublin: Stationery Office.

Walsh, F. (1980) 'The structure of neo-colonialism: the case of the Irish republic', *Antipode* 12, 1: 66–72.

Warburton, J., Whitelaw, J., and Walsh, R. (1818) *History of the City of Dublin*, 2 vols., London: Caddell & Davies.

Wardhaugh, R. (1987) *Languages in Competition*, Oxford: Blackwell.

Weinreich, U. (1968) *Languages in Contact: Findings and Problems*, The Hague: Mouton.

Weinstein, B. (1983) *The Civic Tongue: Political Consequences of Language Choice*, London: Longman.

Weld, I. (1832) *Statistical Survey of the County of Roscommon*, Dublin: Royal Dublin Society.

Williams, C. H. (1986) 'Political Expressions of Underdevelopment in the West European Periphery', paper given to Conference of the Rural Economy and Society Study Group and the Development Studies Association, Oxford, December.

—— (ed.) (1988a) *Language in Geographic Context*, Clevedon, Avon: Multilingual Matters.

—— (1988b) 'Language planning and regional development: lessons from the Irish Gaeltacht', in C. H. Williams, (ed.) *Language in Geographic Context*, Clevedon, Avon: Multilingual Matters.

—— (ed.) (1989) *Linguistic Minorities, Society and Territory*, Clevedon, Avon: Multilingual Matters.

Williams, T. D. (ed.) (1966) *The Irish Struggle 1916–1926*, London: Routledge.

Wilson, T. (ed.) *Ulster under Home Rule*, London: Oxford University Press.

Withers, C. W. J. (1984) *Gaelic in Scotland 1698–1981: the Geographical History of a Language*, Edinburgh: Donald.

Woodham-Smith, C. (1962) *The Great Hunger*, London: Hamish Hamilton.

Woodward, R. (1787) *The Present State of the Church of Ireland*, Dublin: Sleater; 7th edn 1787 (*sic*) London: Caddell.

Young, A. (1780) *A Tour in Ireland . . . in the Years 1776, 1777 and 1778, and Brought down to the End of 1779*, London: Caddell & Dodsley.

—— (1892) *Arthur Young's Tour in Ireland 1776–1779*, ed. A. W. Hutton, with bibliography by J. P. Anderson, 2 vols., London: Bell.

Index

Inis Oírr (Inisheer), Galway 104–5,
166, 272
Inis Oirthir (Inishsirrer), Donegal 180
Inis Tra Mhín (Inishtravin), Galway
98
Inishbarra (Inis Barr a'Chuain),
Galway 98
Inishbiggle (Inis Bigil), Mayo 85
Inisheer (Inis Oírr), Galway 104–5,
166, 271
Inishkeeragh (Inis Caorach), Donegal
180
Inishmaan (Inis Meáin), Galway 105,
107, 271
Inishmor (Inish Mór), Galway 104–5,
107, 270
Inishsirrer (Inis Oirthir), Donegal
180
Inishtravin (Inis Tra Mhín), Galway
98
Iniskea (Inis Gé), Mayo 83
Inny Valley (Gleann na hUíne), Kerry
115
internal colonialism 218–20
Inverin (Indreabhán), Galway 99, 171
Iorras (Erris), Mayo 17, 29, 80, 82–3,
168
Ireland, integration with English
speaking world 190–4; size of 192
Irish language, aids to survival of
29–30, 36–9, 41–2, 163–78;
attitudes towards 146–8, 155–6,
159, 177–8, 179, 208–15, 252;
before 1800 3–12; books and
journals 167, 173, 185–7, 204–5;
broadcasting 156, 171, 173–4, 181,
185–7, 208; causes of decline
179–220; characteristics of 60,
218–20; death of 248–54; Donegal
(Ulster) Irish 63, 70; Dublin Irish
41–2, 60–1, 205; employment
requirement 167—8; 'fanatics'
210–13; and high-technology
industry 101; and national identity
163–4, 211; nationalist rallying
point 149, 157; nineteenth century
13–20; not territorially based
143–4; official language 37, 242;

outside Gaeltacht 194–5; pre-
school playgroups *see naíonraí*; in
schools *see deontas*, schools; a
sensitive issue 214–15; social class
and social norms 144–5, 175–7;
transmission within family 143,
215–6; twentieth century 21–42;
writers in 185
Irish National Teachers' Organization
(INTO) 23, 37–8
Irish speakers, age-grouped 26–7,
34–5; basic community of 145,
248; in census returns 14–15, 17,
19–20, 21, 23, 27, 35, 46–8, 250,
252, 287–94
Irish-speaking scheme (Scéim
Labhairt na Gaeilge) 48–62
Irish-speaking town (An Baile
Gaelach) 144
island evacuation 68–9
The Islands (Na hOileáin), Galway
97–8
Israel 190, 243–6
Italian 242
Italy 237
Iveragh (Uibh Ráthach), Kerry
115–17, 272–3

James, C. 158
James VI and I 225
Joyce's Country (Dúiche
Sheoigheach) 86–91, 187, 268–9

Kells (Ceanannas Mór), Meath
129–30
Kenrick, D. 232, 245
Kerry 14, 108–17, 187, 249, 271–3
Kilcar (Cill Charthaigh), Donegal 78,
267
Kildare 4, 26
Kilkieran (Cill Chairáin), Galway
93–4, 252
Killeany (Cill Éinne), Galway 104
Killeenleeha (An Chillín Liath), Kerry
115, 273
Killitiane (Coill an tSiáin), Mayo, 89,
268
Kilmaine, Mayo 17